Contents

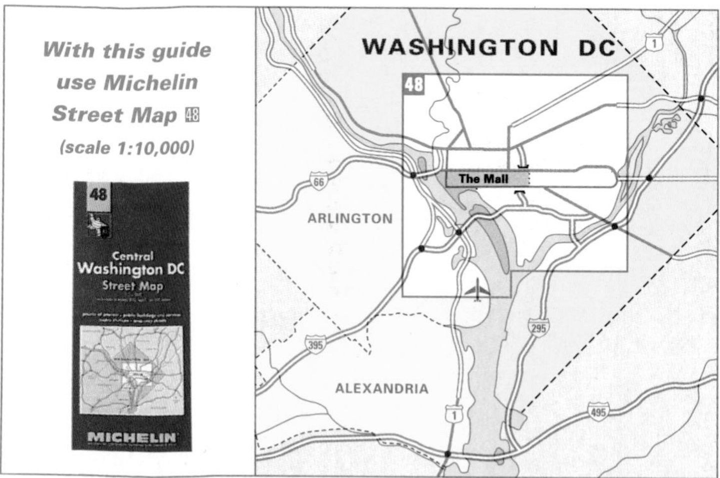

Addresses, telephone numbers, opening hours, and prices given in this guide are accurate at the time of publication. We apologize for any inconveniences resulting from outdated information, and we welcome corrections and suggestions that may assist us in preparing the next edition. Send us your comments:

Michelin Travel Publications, PO Box 19001, Greenville SC 29602-9001.

STAR-RATED SIGHTS IN WASHINGTON AND ARLINGTON

Consult the index (p 183) for the page reference of sight descriptions.

★★★

1 The Capitol
2 The Memorials
- Jefferson Memorial
- Lincoln Memorial
- Vietnam Veterans Memorial
- Washington Monument

2 National Air and Space Museum
2 National Gallery of Art
3 White House

★★

1 Library of Congress
1 Supreme Court
2 Arthur M. Sackler Gallery
2 Freer Gallery of Art
2 Hirshhorn Museum and Sculpture Garden
2 National Archives
2 National Museum of African Art
2 National Museum of American History
2 National Museum of Natural History
2 US Holocaust Memorial Museum
3 Corcoran Gallery of Art
4 National Portrait Gallery
5 Diplomatic Reception Rooms
5 John F. Kennedy Center for the Performing Arts
6 Dumbarton Oaks
7 Arlington National Cemetery
8 The Phillips Collection

Additional Sights
- Hillwood Museum
- Washington Cathedral

★

1 Folger Shakespeare Library
1 National Postal Museum
1 Union Station
2 Bureau of Engraving and Printing
2 Smithsonian Quadrangle
3 Daughters of the American Revolution (DAR)
3 Decatur House
3 Old Executive Office Building
3 Renwick Gallery
4 Federal Bureau of Investigation (FBI)
4 Ford's Theatre and Petersen House
4 National Museum of American Art
4 National Museum of Women in the Arts
5 The Octagon
6 C & O Canal and Towpath
6 Cox Row
6 N Street
6 Smith Row
6 Tudor Place
7 Arlington House
7 Marine Corps War Memorial
8 Society of the Cincinnati
9 Textile Museum
10 Frederick Douglass National Historic Site

Additional Sights
- National Geographic Society Explorers Hall
- National Zoological Park

EXCURSIONS *(see map p 145)*

★★★ Mount Vernon ★★ Alexandria ★ Gunston Hall ★ Woodlawn Plantation

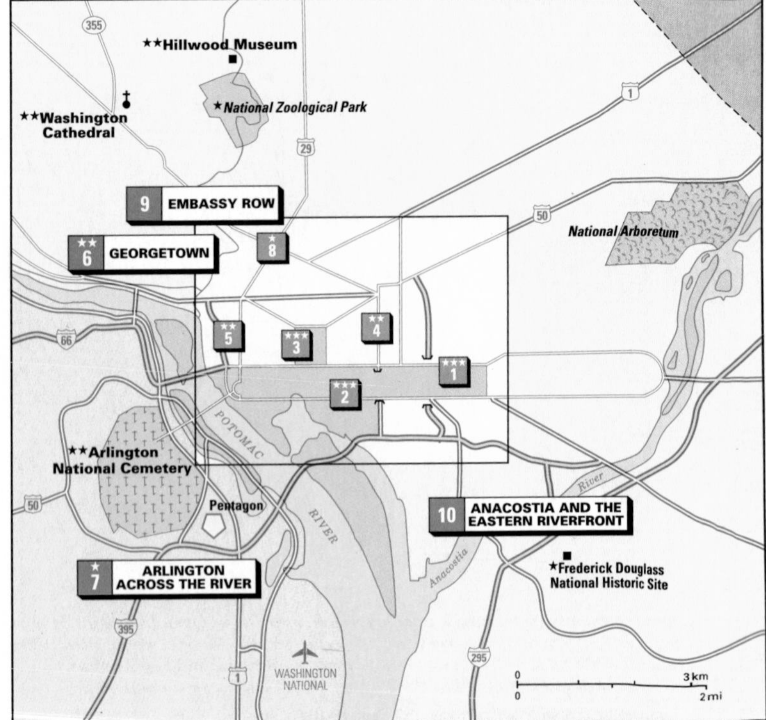

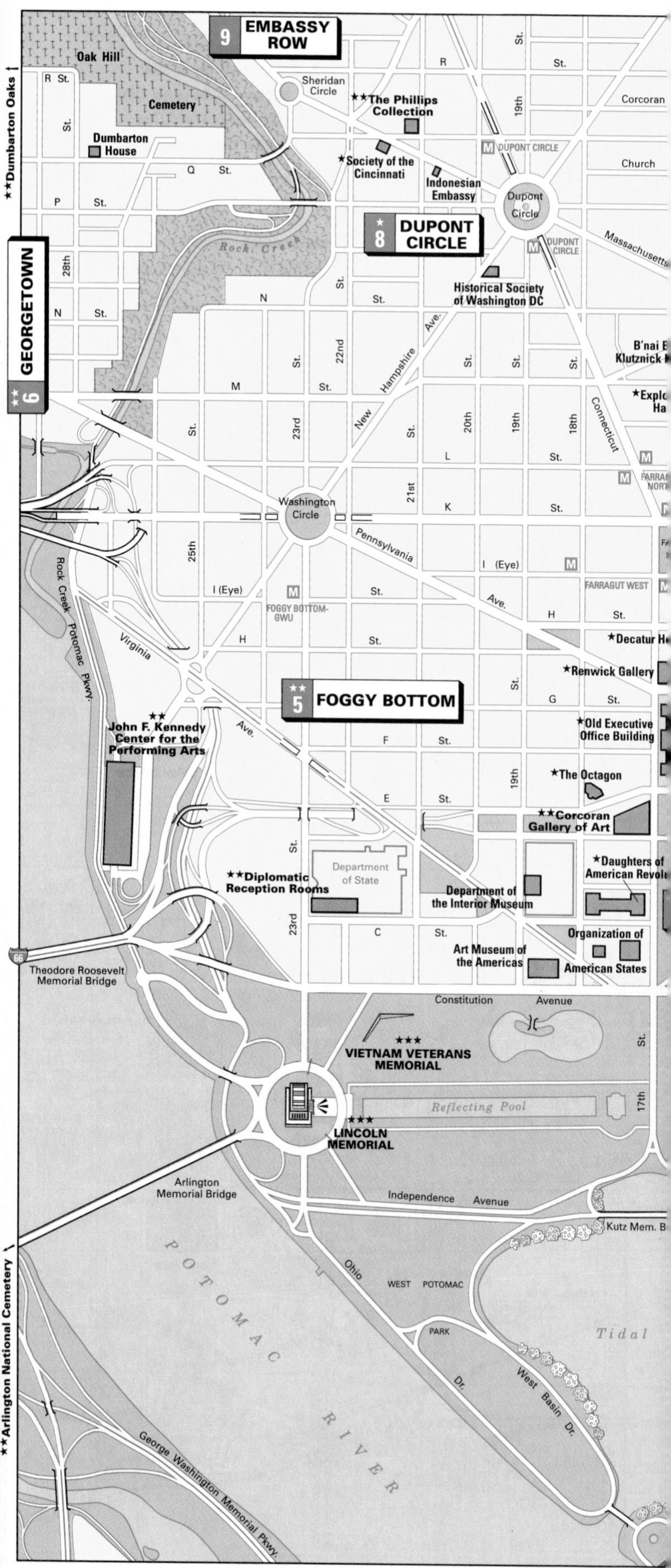
9 EMBASSY ROW
8 DUPONT CIRCLE
6 GEORGETOWN
5 FOGGY BOTTOM
★★Dumbarton Oaks
★★Arlington National Cemetery
Oak Hill Cemetery
Dumbarton House
Sheridan Circle
★★The Phillips Collection
★Society of the Cincinnati
Indonesian Embassy
Dupont Circle
DUPONT CIRCLE
Historical Society of Washington DC
Rock Creek
Washington Circle
FOGGY BOTTOM-GWU
FARRAGUT WEST
★Decatur H
★Renwick Gallery
★Old Executive Office Building
★The Octagon
★★Corcoran Gallery of Art
★Daughters of American Revolu
Organization of American States
Art Museum of the Americas
Department of the Interior Museum
Department of State
★★Diplomatic Reception Rooms
★★ John F. Kennedy Center for the Performing Arts
Rock Creek Potomac Pkwy.
Theodore Roosevelt Memorial Bridge
★★★ VIETNAM VETERANS MEMORIAL
★★★ LINCOLN MEMORIAL
Reflecting Pool
Constitution Avenue
Independence Avenue
Arlington Memorial Bridge
Kutz Mem. B
WEST POTOMAC PARK
Ohio Dr.
West Basin Dr.
POTOMAC RIVER
Tidal
George Washington Memorial Pkwy.
Pennsylvania Ave.
Virginia Ave.
New Hampshire Ave.
Connecticut
Massachusetts
Corcoran
Church
B'nai B Klutznick
★Explo Ha

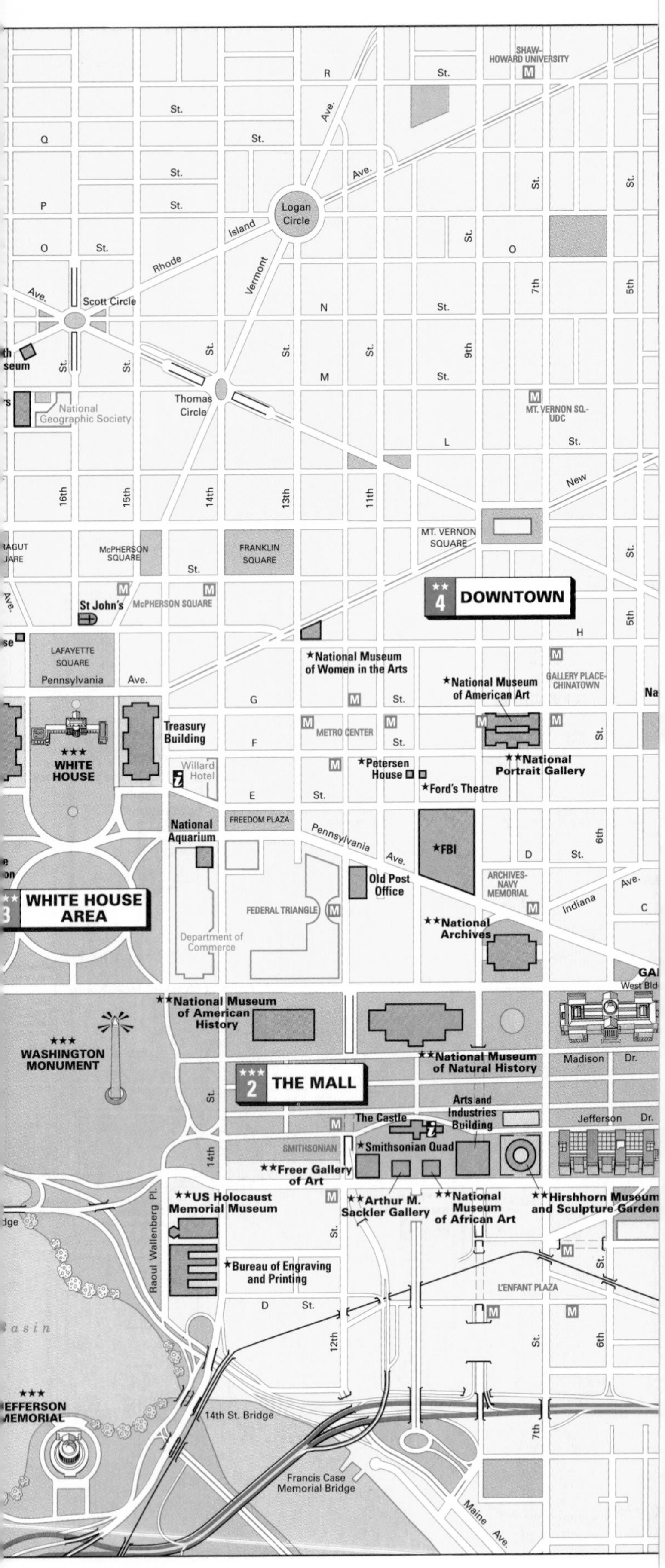

SHAW-HOWARD UNIVERSITY
Logan Circle
Scott Circle
Thomas Circle
National Geographic Society
MT. VERNON SQ.-UDC
MT. VERNON SQUARE
McPHERSON SQUARE
FRANKLIN SQUARE
4 DOWNTOWN
St John's
McPHERSON SQUARE
LAFAYETTE SQUARE
★National Museum of Women in the Arts
★National Museum of American Art
GALLERY PLACE-CHINATOWN
METRO CENTER
★★★ WHITE HOUSE
Treasury Building
Willard Hotel
★Petersen House
★Ford's Theatre
★★National Portrait Gallery
FREEDOM PLAZA
National Aquarium
★FBI
Old Post Office
ARCHIVES-NAVY MEMORIAL
3 WHITE HOUSE AREA
FEDERAL TRIANGLE
Department of Commerce
★★National Archives
★★National Museum of American History
★★★ WASHINGTON MONUMENT
★★National Museum of Natural History
2 THE MALL
The Castle
Arts and Industries Building
SMITHSONIAN
★Smithsonian Quad
★★Freer Gallery of Art
★★US Holocaust Memorial Museum
★★Arthur M. Sackler Gallery
★★National Museum of African Art
★★Hirshhorn Museum and Sculpture Garden
★Bureau of Engraving and Printing
Raoul Wallenberg Pl.
L'ENFANT PLAZA
★★★ JEFFERSON MEMORIAL
14th St. Bridge
Francis Case Memorial Bridge
Madison Dr.
Jefferson Dr.
Pennsylvania Ave.
Rhode Island Ave.
Vermont Ave.
New York Ave.
Indiana Ave.
Maine Ave.

TWO- AND FOUR-DAY ITINERARIES

Planning Tips – The fast-paced itineraries described below and shown on the fold-out map to the left are designed for visitors pressed for time and are best suited to the period from April to September, when daylight is more plentiful. To avoid long lines at the White House, Capitol, and FBI, it is best to reserve those tours in advance *(see p 162)*. Advance tickets for the Holocaust Museum are strongly advised *(p 67)*.
Tourmobile shuttle buses run daily (except December 25) from 9am to 6:30pm (9:30am–4:30pm from Labor Day to mid-June). Tickets are valid all day for unlimited reboarding at any of the stops indicated with a blue and white sign *(for prices and further information see p 169)*.

Eating – On-site eating facilities are indicated in the individual sight description in this guide by the symbol ✗. In warm seasons, snacks are available from kiosks around the Mall or from street vendors along Independence Avenue. Picknicking is permitted in various locations on the Mall. The commercial complexes in Union Station and the Old Post Office (Pennsylvania Avenue and 12th Street NW) house a multitude of eateries for all tastes and budgets.
The upscale establishments on the K Street–Connecticut Avenue corridors offer formal dining, while the large waterfront restaurants on Maine Avenue SW specialize in seafood. Many Chinese and Vietnamese eateries are located in **Chinatown** and Arlington, while the vibrant **Adams Morgan** neighborhood in the vicinity of Columbia Road and 18th Street NW, known mainly for its Hispanic and Ethiopian cuisine, today hosts a wide variety of ethnic restaurants. Historic **Georgetown** and **Alexandria**, each with a large concentration of restaurants, offer a full range of dining experiences.

TWO-DAY ITINERARY

First Day — *Itinerary in red* 1⟹

Morning The Capitol★★★ *(p 30)*, Supreme Court★★ *(p 35)*, Library of Congress★★ *(p 37)*.
Lunch Supreme Court or National Air and Space Museum.
Afternoon National Air and Space Museum★★★ *(p 43)*, National Gallery of Art★★★ *(p 48)*.
Evening and Dinner Kennedy Center★★ *(p 100—for reservations see p 171)*.

Second Day — *Itinerary in purple* 2⟹ *(with Tourmobile; see above)*

Morning White House★★★ *(p 76)*, National Museum of American History★★ *(p 59)*.
Lunch National Museum of American History.
Afternoon US Holocaust Memorial Museum★★ *(p 67)*, Jefferson Memorial★★★ *(p 71)*, Lincoln Memorial★★★ *(p 72)*, Vietnam Veterans Memorial★★★ *(p 73)*; Arlington National Cemetery★★ *(p 114—open until 7pm Apr–Sept)*.
Evening City lights. Begin at the observation room of the Washington Monument★★★ *(p 70—open until midnight mid-Apr–Labor Day)*, then tour by car the other illuminated sights shown on the map.

FOUR-DAY ITINERARY

Third Day — *Itinerary in green* 3⟹

(For the first two days, follow the itinerary described above.)
Morning National Museum of Natural History★★ *(p 56)*, Arthur M. Sackler Gallery★★ *(p 65)* or Freer Gallery of Art★★ *(p 66)*, National Museum of African Art★★ *(p 64)* or Hirshhorn Museum and Sculpture Garden★★ *(p 62)*.
Lunch On the Mall *(see* **Eating** *above)*.
Afternoon National Archives★★ *(p 55)*; FBI★ *(p 95)*, Ford's Theatre and Petersen House★ *(p 94)*, National Portrait Gallery★★ *(p 90)*. *Return to Pennsylvania Ave. and take any no. 30s bus to Georgetown.*
Late-Afternoon/ Evening and Dinner Georgetown Walking Tour *(p 107)* and dinner in Georgetown.

Fourth Day — *See map p 145*

Morning Mount Vernon★★★ *(p 152)*, Woodlawn Plantation★ *(p 155)*.
Lunch Mount Vernon.
Afternoon/ Evening and Dinner Gunston Hall★ *(p 156)*, Alexandria Walking Tour: Old Town★★ *(p 147)* and dinner in Alexandria.

The following sights are listed for the benefit of visitors who have additional time in the area or for those who might wish to substitute certain sights on the suggested itineraries to suit their specific interests: Washington Cathedral★★ *(p 137)*, The Phillips Collection★★ *(p 124)*, Corcoran Gallery of Art★★ *(p 80)*, Diplomatic Reception Rooms★★ *(p 101—advance reservation required)*, Hillwood Museum★★ *(p 139—advance reservation required)*, Bureau of Engraving and Printing★ *(p 68—long entry lines in season)*.

©Charles Shoffner 1993

Introduction

Conceived as a national showplace, Washington DC embodies the spirit of American idealism in its neoclassical monuments, its grand museums, and its sweeping vistas. As the seat of Government, the capital city is remarkably accessible, opening the doors of Congress, the White House, and several other Federal institutions to hosts of visitors who come to witness democracy in progress.

Though long considered a cultural backwater, the capital has gradually shed that image to emerge as a truly international city, with a world-class performing arts complex, fine restaurants and shops, and a mixed population of foreign nationals. Gracious in appearance, steeped in national history, and rich in cultural offerings, Washington DC is unique among American cities.

THE DISTRICT OF COLUMBIA

Location and Climate – Washington DC lies approximately in the middle of the eastern seaboard of the US, about 90 miles inland from the Atlantic Ocean. Situated on the northern banks of the Potomac River, the city rises from low bottomland along the riverfront to a series of hills in the north. At its highest elevation in the Northwest quadrant of the city, it is 390ft above sea level. Rock Creek, a tributary of the Potomac, follows a shallow, wooded valley extending through the north-south heart of the city. Located at 39° north latitude and 77° west longitude, the city has a temperately continental climate. Winds are generally from the west, and humidity is often high because of proximity to the ocean and the Chesapeake Bay, 25 miles east of the city. The Potomac River in the vicinity of Washington has an average channel depth of roughly 14ft, making it unnavigable for large cargo-carrying vessels.

Size and Population – Shaped like a truncated diamond ten miles on each side, the city is carved out of Maryland and separated from Virginia by the Potomac. It covers 67sq miles and is divided into four quadrants: **Northwest** (NW), **Northeast** (NE), **Southeast** (SE), and **Southwest** (SW). The longest distance from its southern to its northern tip is 12 miles. The total population numbers about 607,000, making Washington the 19th largest city in the US. Its racial mix is roughly 70 percent black and 30 percent white. In the Northeast, Southeast, and Southwest quadrants, blacks predominate; the Northwest quadrant is largely white. The neighborhood known as Adams Morgan, concentrated mainly in the area of Columbia Road and 18th Street NW, is the hub of Washington's Hispanic community, which comprises about two percent of the population. Recent years have seen an influx of East Asians into Washington and its metropolitan area.

The District Government – After a century of congressional rule, Washington was given the federally mandated authority to govern itself under the Home Rule Act of 1973. The city government now comprises an elected mayor and a 13-member legislative council, a board of education, and a series of advisory neighborhood commissions. Though the city functions somewhat independently of the Federal legislature, Congress retains veto power over bills passed by the District council. In addition, many agencies and commissions exercise oversight jurisdiction in District matters. The National Capital Planning Commission, a 12-member body appointed by the President and the mayor, reviews city development plans, while the Commission of Fine Arts oversees the design of buildings, parks, and monuments. The Pennsylvania Avenue Development Corporation, a public-private partnership, has jurisdiction over planning in the lower portion of the avenue. Congress itself sets height restrictions on all District buildings, and the President's Office of Management and Budget establishes limits for the city budget.

George Washington
1789-1797

John Adams
1797-1801

Thomas Jefferson
1801-1809

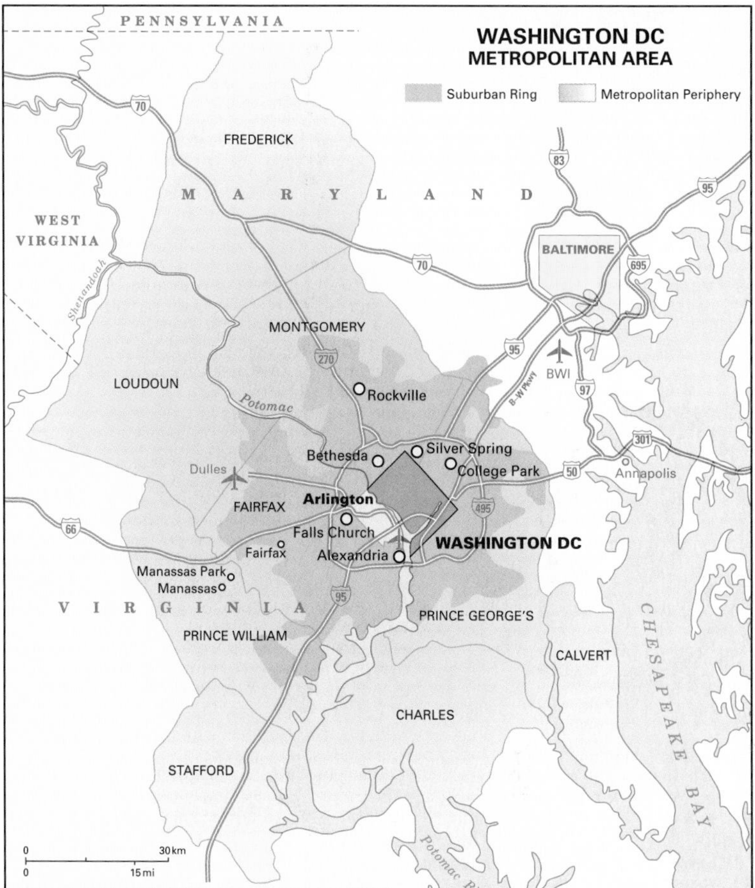

WASHINGTON DC METROPOLITAN AREA

Suburban Ring | Metropolitan Periphery

Boundaries of the metropolitan area and its counties as defined by the Office of Management and Budget (30 June 1990)

Historically, suffrage has been a matter of concern to the citizens of Washington. In 1964, they were allowed to vote in the presidential election for the first time. As part of the 1973 Home Rule Act, they were also allowed to elect one delegate to the House of Representatives. The delegate serves a two-year term and, as of 1994, is allowed to vote on the floor of Congress. In recent years, there has been a movement in support of statehood for the District, championed by such political veterans as Sen Edward Kennedy and Rev Jesse Jackson. In November 1993, a bill proposing DC statehood was defeated by Congress, however.

The Metropolitan Area – The Washington DC metropolitan area comprises ten counties and the District of Columbia itself. Five of the counties (Charles, Calvert, Frederick, Montgomery, and Prince George's) are in Maryland; the other five (Arlington, Fairfax, Loudoun, Prince William and Stafford) are in Virginia. The total metropolitan area encompasses 3,957sq miles. With a population of 3,924,000, it ranks eighth among the nation's 284 metropolitan areas. Between 1980 and 1990, the area's population increased by nearly 21 percent.

Continued growth has drawn many of the outlying towns and villages into a steadily expanding ring of suburban settlements. The municipalities bordering the Capital Beltway (Interstate 495), which encircles the District at a distance of approximately 12 miles from the center, tend to be suburban "bedroom" communities closely attached to Washington culturally and economically. As the suburban reach of Washington extends farther into the metropolitan hinterland, even the more distant, traditionally more rural, counties and the independent cities of Virginia, such as Fairfax, Manassas, and Manassas Park, are slowly developing as commuter communities as well.

James Madison
1809-1817

James Monroe
1817-1825

John Quincy Adams
1825-1829

THE FEDERAL GOVERNMENT

Under the system of checks and balances established by the US Constitution, the Federal Government is composed of three branches: the Legislative (both houses of Congress), the Executive (the President and the Executive office), and the Judicial (the Supreme Court and all other Federal courts).The WHITE HOUSE, seat of the Executive branch, is situated within a mile of Capitol Hill, where the CAPITOL, home of Congress, and the SUPREME COURT building are located. Each of these branches fulfills specific functions and duties of its own, as well as overseeing and keeping in check the powers exercised by the other two branches.

The Legislative Branch – Conceived by the Founding Fathers as a bicameral system of government, the Congress comprises two bodies: the Senate and the House of Representatives. Jointly, they are responsible for drafting and passing laws; for handling matters of national finance, such as setting and collecting taxes and coining money; for ensuring, in conjunction with the President, the defense of the nation; for regulating commerce; and for admitting new states to the Union. Within these broadly defined powers, each house has separate duties, as described below.

A specific Congress serves for two years (the 103nd Congress convenes from 1994-1995), beginning new sessions each year in late January, and generally recessing in August and again in the fall.

The **Senate** is composed of 100 senators, two for each of the 50 states in the Union. Senators are elected to six-year terms by popular vote, in accordance with the 17th Amendment, which was added to the Constitution in 1913 (originally, the Constitution specified that senators be elected by state legislatures).

Senate terms are staggered in such a way that no more than one-third of the Senate seats are renewed each year. The Vice President is the official presiding officer of the Senate, but in his absence, senators elect a president *pro tempore* from among their ranks.

The Senate's specific duties include approving presidential appointments; ratifying foreign treaties by a two-thirds majority (a power now little used); and trying a President who has been impeached by the House. (Andrew Johnson, who took office after the assassination of Abraham Lincoln, is the only US President to stand trial before the Senate. Johnson was acquitted by one vote in 1868.)

The **House** is composed of 435 representatives (often referred to as Congressmen and Congresswomen), with the number of representatives per state based on population. As of 1994, California had the greatest number of representatives (52). The US territories of Guam, the Virgin Islands, and the District of Columbia are represented by non-voting delegates to the House.

Members of the House serve two-year terms, and their presiding officer is the speaker of the House, elected anew with each Congress. Under the Constitution, the House is responsible for originating all bills relating to taxes; impeaching, that is charging a President with criminal actions; and determining the outcome of a presidential election if there is no clear electoral majority.

Historically, Congress has been dominated by two opposing political parties, whose names and policies have changed over time. Today, the major parties are Democratic and Republican, though nothing prevents "independents" or members of smaller parties from running for office.

In both houses, the dominant party elects a **majority leader** and his deputy, the **majority whip**. The minority party, likewise, elects its own minority leader and whip. If the majority party in one or both houses of Congress is different from the party of the President, legislation may bog down, as Congress votes against supported initiatives or the President vetoes congressional acts.

In both chambers, much of the work of formulating and drafting new laws is done within the standing committees *(see* How a Bill Becomes Law *p 15)*. There are 22 such committees in the House and 16 in the Senate. Normally, each member of Congress serves on two committees.

During your stay in Washington, witness the Federal Government at work. View a session of Congress or a committee session (see p 34).

Andrew Jackson
1829-1837

Martin Van Buren
1837-1841

William Henry Harrison
1841

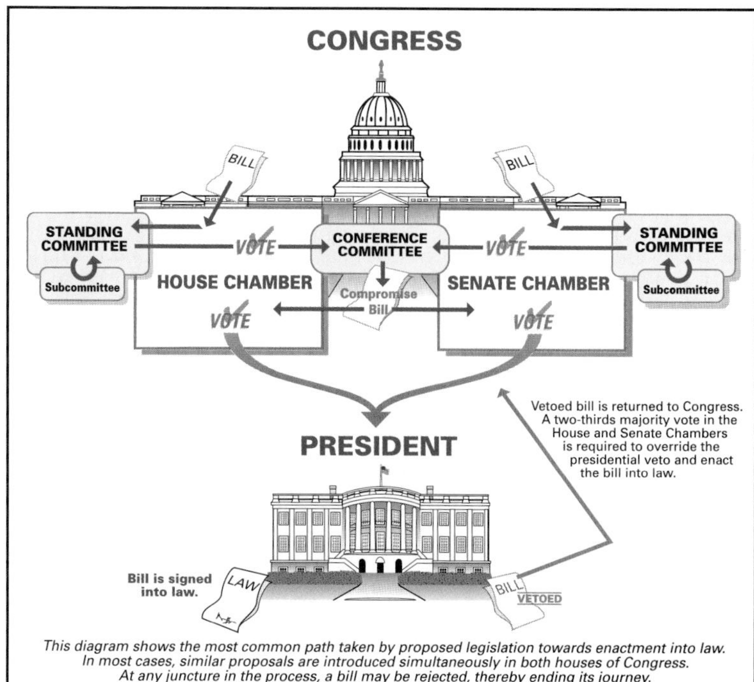

This diagram shows the most common path taken by proposed legislation towards enactment into law. In most cases, similar proposals are introduced simultaneously in both houses of Congress. At any juncture in the process, a bill may be rejected, thereby ending its journey.

How a Bill Becomes Law – Any interested person or group, whether within or outside the political system, may draft a bill and seek the support of a US senator or representative to introduce it for congressional consideration. Of the many bills proposed annually, only a handful are enacted into laws. Throughout the legislative process described below, a corps of lobbyists is generally operating behind the scenes to persuade legislators to protect the interests of their clients.

Each bill begins its journey when it is introduced on the floor of either the House or the Senate chambers; in many cases a similar proposal is introduced simultaneously in both houses. The chamber's parliamentarian then assigns it to an appropriate **standing committee** for consideration, and if deemed worthwhile, the proposal is normally referred to a **subcommittee** for further study. The subcommittee holds hearings, in which it elicits the opinions of experts and interested parties. Such hearings, especially in the House, are generally open to the public. The subcommittee must then "mark up" the bill, or rework the language and intent of various sections in light of the conclusions drawn from hearings. The marked-up bill then passes back to the full standing committee, which after further study either rejects the bill or "reports" it, that is, recommends its passage to the chamber. In the House, reported bills are then submitted to the Rules Committee before returning to the chamber. In the Senate, the leadership determines the course of action on each piece of legislation.

Having received committee approval, the bill is placed on the chamber's calendar, and at the scheduled time, it is debated, amended and put to a vote. At this point, a bill that has been introduced in only one chamber is sent to the other chamber, where the legislative process begins anew. If the bill has been introduced simultaneously in the Senate and the House, and passed by both, the two versions are then referred to a **conference committee**, composed of members from both chambers who meet to resolve differences in wording and intent. Their compromise version is then sent back to both House and Senate, which separately vote on the identical version of the bill. After passage in both houses, the approved legislation next proceeds to the President, who may sign it into law or exercise **veto** by returning the bill to Congress unsigned, with a statement of his objections. Congress may override a presidential veto with a two-thirds majority vote in both chambers. The President has a third option: if he wishes to register his disapproval without actually vetoing, he may simply retain the unsigned bill, and after ten days, it automatically becomes law, provided Congress is in session. If Congress is adjourned at that time, the President's failure to sign constitutes a "pocket veto," and the bill dies.

John Tyler
1841-1845

James K. Polk
1845-1849

Zachary Taylor
1849-1850

The Executive Branch – The President and Vice President are the only elected officials of the branch's 3.5 million employees (including armed forces personnel). Presidential elections are held every four years, and a President may now serve a maximum of two four-year terms in office, as stipulated by the 22nd Amendment (1951) to the Constitution.

The Constitution also requires that a presidential candidate be at least 35 years old; be born in the US, and live in the US 14 years prior to running for office. Presidential candidates choose their running mates at the commencement of campaigns. In the event of the President's resignation, impeachment, or death, the Vice President assumes the presidency.

The President serves as Commander-in-Chief of the Armed Forces, with ultimate control over the defense of the nation. However, as required by the War Powers Act of 1975, he must petition Congress before making a declaration of war. In addition, the President serves as the nation's Chief Executive. As such he appoints all ambassadors, ministers, consuls, and persons serving in cabinet-level positions, and approves the appointments of many policy-making personnel within the Executive branch. Whenever a vacancy occurs on the Supreme Court or among other judges on the Federal bench, the President makes a new appointment (which is subject to congressional approval). Through such appointments, the President exerts an influence that lasts far beyond his own tenure in office. The President may also grant pardons and reprieves to those convicted of committing crimes against the US Government. Finally, the President, through his veto power, is instrumental in the law-making process *(see* How a Bill Becomes Law *p 15)*.

US Constitution

J. Feingersh/Uniphoto

The Executive branch comprises the President's personal staff—called the **Executive Office of the President**—and the employees of all 14 **cabinet departments** (Departments of State, Treasury, Defense, Justice, Interior, Agriculture, Commerce, Labor, Health and Human Services, Education, Transportation, Housing and Urban Development, Energy and Veteran Affairs). The "secretary," or head, of each cabinet department, advises the President on setting national policy.

The Executive Office of the President includes a number of independent agencies (such as the Central Intelligence Agency, the National Security Agency, and the National Aeronautics and Space Administration) and Federal regulatory agencies (such as the Federal Trade Commission, and the Securities and Exchange Commission). A powerful component within the Executive Office is the **Office of Management and Budget**, which prepares the President's annual Federal budget, works with Congress on legislative objectives, and acts as an organizational overseer for the entire Executive branch.

The Judicial Branch – *See also p 36.* The smallest of the three branches, the Judiciary interprets the law of the land. It is composed of a three-level hierarchy: **Federal district courts** (numbering 94), **US courts of appeals** (13), and the **US Supreme Court**. Judges at all three levels are appointed for life to the Federal bench by the President and must be confirmed by the Senate.

Federal cases may be civil or criminal in nature. For a civil case to be heard in Federal court, it must involve one of the following criteria:

1) a Federal statute
2) a constitutional issue
3) plaintiffs from different states
4) a sum in excess of $50,000.

Criminal cases must concern a violation of Federal law.

Normally, Federal cases are first filed and tried on the district level, though they may begin in special Federal courts, such as the US Claims Court or the Tax Court. Once a decision has been handed down in district court, a dissatisfied party who feels that the district wrongly applied the law may file an appeal with the US Court of Appeals serving his district.

The final court of review, the SUPREME COURT, is made up of eight associate justices and a chief justice. This body hears only about two percent of the petitions it receives annually, focusing attention on cases that call into question the constitutionality of existing laws. Decisions handed down by the Supreme Court set the legal precedents for all other courts of the land.

Millard Fillmore
1850-1853

Franklin Pierce
1853-1857

James Buchanan
1857-1861

HOW WASHINGTON WORKS

Washington's principal industry has always been government. The Federal presence in the metropolitan area dominates the economy, directly through the civil service bureaucracy and indirectly through government-related businesses. Politics and government also help determine the social climate of the capital city. With only five percent of its work force involved in manufacturing, Washington looks and functions like a white-collar town.

Federal Government – Some 359,000 people living in the metropolitan area are on the Federal payroll. They range from presidential aides to park rangers, from custodians to museum curators. Most permanent government positions are within the purview of the Office of Personnel and Management, an independent agency of the Executive branch. However higher level departmental and agency jobs are generally held by presidential appointment, and new appointees are customarily brought in with each change of administration.

Daily, hordes of employees commute from the surrounding suburbs to work in the government offices scattered throughout the city. Some 40 percent of the city's land is Federally owned property. After hours, whole corridors of the city where government buildings are concentrated (particularly in Foggy Bottom) are virtually deserted.

Social life in the capital city tends to be conducted at private gatherings, where the nation's leaders, foreign diplomats, and prominent figures in the business world informally share political and economic ideas that ultimately influence the direction of Government. The national and international elite may meet in private homes, at embassy receptions, in reception rooms on Capitol Hill, and in such private clubs as the COSMOS CLUB, SLUGRAVE CLUB, and Metropolitan Club.

Government-related Sector – In order to be near the Federal nerve center, hundreds of national and international organizations have offices in Washington. The PENTAGON, wellspring of the military-industrial complex, fosters innumerable defense contracting companies throughout the metropolitan area.

Since the 1970s, a number of research and development complexes have been built around the Capital Beltway. Like all government-related businesses, their fortunes are very much dependent on the political climate and the congressional appropriation of Federal resources.

Numbering as high as 10,000 according to some estimates, Washington-based **lobbyists** maintain a strong presence in political and social affairs. Representing special interest groups, political action organizations (PACs), professional and trade associations, and foreign countries and businesses, lobbyists work to persuade legislators to support laws helpful to their clients' interests. The term *lobbyist* derives from the last century, when such influence-peddlers would haunt the lobbies of public buildings where politicians congregated. Today, far from buttonholing Congressmen on the run, lobbyists conduct their business at fine restaurants and well-orchestrated social gatherings.

Also exerting a powerful influence on the city's sociopolitical fabric is the **fourth estate**. Washington's formidable press corps is comprised of correspondents from national and regional newspapers, many of whom maintain Washington offices in the National Press Building *(14th and F Sts. NW)*. In addition, *USA Today, National Geographic, International Wildlife,* and other major publications have their headquarters in the capital. Dominated by *The Washington Post,* one of the country's most influential newspapers, the press has become a major player in shaping public opinion. The *Post's* involvement in uncovering and reporting the Nixon-Watergate debacle in the mid-1970s broke new ground in investigative reporting. Today, print journalists and television reporters have become celebrities in their own right, and members of Washington's power elite.

Tourism – Attracted by the capital's renowned monuments and museums and by the numerous conventions held in the area, nearly 20 million visitors come to Washington each year, making tourism the city's second largest industry. Over $2.5 billion dollars in annual revenue goes to the hotels, restaurants, and other service-related businesses that cater to visitors. Traditionally a place of pilgrimage for Americans, in recent years the capital has begun to draw more and more foreign tourists.

The International Element – Once a rather provincial town with only a small contingent of foreigners, Washington has become, in recent decades, a cosmopolitan city. Over 150 foreign missions maintain embassies and consulates here, and such international organizations as the World Bank, International Monetary Fund, and ORGANIZATION OF AMERICAN STATES are based in the city.

The influx of Asian, Middle Eastern, and African immigrants that began in the late 1970s has given the city a distinctly international flavor. Washington's shops, restaurants, and festivals now reflect this urbane mix of cultures.

Abraham Lincoln
1861-1865

Andrew Johnson
1865-1869

Ulysses S. Grant
1869-1877

DC TIME LINE

The Colonial Period

1608 Capt John Smith sails up the Potomac.
1662 The first land patent on the future site of the District is granted.
1749 **Alexandria** is laid out.
1751 **Georgetown** is established.
1763 The **French and Indian War** ends, affirming British supremacy in eastern North America.
1775-83 The **American Revolution**.
1776 Members of the Continental Congress meeting in Philadelphia sign the **Declaration of Independence**.
1783 Britain recognizes the independence of the 13 colonies.
1788 Maryland cedes territory on the north shore of the Potomac for the establishment of a new Federal City.
1789 The **US Constitution** is ratified. New York is designated capital. George Washington is elected first US President.
1790 The nation's capital is moved to Philadelphia. Congress passes the **Residence Act**, giving Washington the power to choose the site for the new capital and ten years in which to create a Federal City.

Building a Capital

1791 President Washington selects a site along the Potomac for the Federal District and authorizes **Pierre Charles L'Enfant** to draft city plans. Congress appoints three commissioners, who name the 10sq mile diamond-shaped area the Territory of Columbia (subsequently known as the District of Columbia), and the capital, the City of Washington.
1792 L'Enfant is dismissed by President Washington. The cornerstone is laid for the WHITE HOUSE.
1793 The cornerstone is laid for the CAPITOL.
1800 President Adams is the first occupant of the White House. Congress convenes for the first time in Washington in the unfinished Capitol building.
1802 Under congressional jurisdiction, the City of Washington is chartered. The first District government buildings are erected. City population: 3,000.
1808 Construction begins on the Washington Canal along current-day Constitution Avenue.
1812 **War of 1812**. The US declares war on Britain.
1814 The British invade Washington and burn the Capitol, White House, and other public buildings. Washington banks offer $500,000 in loans to help rebuild the city and to quell a movement to abandon the capital.
1815 President Madison signs the Treaty of Ghent, ending the War of 1812.

A Century of Growth

1824 City-wide celebrations take place on the occasion of the second visit of the **Marquis de Lafayette**, America's Revolutionary ally.
1832 A severe cholera epidemic sweeps the city.
1835 Baltimore and Ohio Railroad reaches the District, initiating the eventual decline of canal traffic through Georgetown and Washington City.
1838 Construction of the TREASURY and PATENT OFFICE BUILDINGS gets underway.
1846 Congress establishes the **Smithsonian Institution**. District territory south of the Potomac is retroceded to Virginia, reducing the District by one-third of its original size.
1850 Chesapeake & Ohio Canal is completed.
1857 The CASTLE, the Smithsonian's first building, opens on the Mall.
1861 Beginning of the **Civil War**. Many public buildings in the District become hospitals and barracks for Union soldiers. A network of forts is erected around the city's southern perimeter.
1862 Congress grants compensatory emancipation of all slaves in the District.
1863 President Lincoln issues the **Emancipation Proclamation**.
1864 Confederate Gen Jubal Early is repulsed at nearby Fort Stevens, saving the capital from capture by the South.
1865 End of the Civil War. Gen Robert E. Lee surrenders to Gen Ulysses S. Grant at Appomattox. President Lincoln is assassinated five days later while attending a performance at FORD'S THEATRE.

Rutherford B. Hayes
1877-1881

James A. Garfield
1881

Chester A. Arthur
1881-1885

1867 DC citizens are granted suffrage.
Howard University, the capital's first black university, is chartered by Congress.
1871 The city's first art museum, the CORCORAN GALLERY OF ART, opens on Pennsylvania Ave. DC population (over 130,000) has doubled since the beginning of the decade due largely to the influx of former slaves.
Georgetown is incorporated with Washington.
1871-74 An act of Congress establishes a brief period of territorial government for the District. **Alexander "Boss" Shepherd** begins a major citywide public works project that results in a much beautified but near-bankrupt city.
1880s Establishment of streetcar lines leads to the growth of outlying areas.
1884 Completion of the WASHINGTON MONUMENT, begun in 1848.
1897 The first LIBRARY OF CONGRESS building opens.

The "City Beautiful"

1900 Washington celebrates its centennial.
1901 The **McMillan Commission** *(see p 23)* is established to beautify the capital.
1908 UNION STATION is completed.
1914 The LINCOLN MEMORIAL is begun in the reclaimed **West Potomac Park**.
1917 US enters **World War I**. Washington experiences a wartime boom. Rows of temporary war buildings or "tempos" are erected around the Mall.
1918 Armistice ends WWI. DC population has risen to nearly 440,000.
1926 The National Capital Parks and Planning Commission is established. The Public Buildings Act leads to the construction of many Federal edifices.
1931-32 Hunger Marchers demonstrate in Washington.
1941 US enters **World War II**. DC experiences another wartime boom.
The NATIONAL GALLERY OF ART opens on the Mall.
1945 World War II ends in victory for the US and Allied Forces.
1950-53 Korean War. DC population peaks at 800,000.
1961 **John F. Kennedy** is inaugurated 34th US President and appoints a committee to study the rejuvenation of Pennsylvania Avenue. Congress ratifies the 23rd Amendment to the Constitution, giving District residents the right to vote in presidential elections.
1963 **Martin Luther King, Jr** leads 200,000 in the March on Washington for Jobs and Freedom. King delivers his "I have a dream" speech from the Lincoln Memorial. President Kennedy is assassinated in Dallas and buried in ARLINGTON NATIONAL CEMETERY.
Late 60s Racial riots in the capital. Various areas of the city are looted and burned.
Early 70s Anti-war demonstrations are staged on the Mall. District residents are allowed to elect one non-voting delegate to the House of Representatives.

Toward the 21C

1971 JOHN F. KENNEDY CENTER FOR THE PERFORMING ARTS opens.
1973 Congress passes the **Home Rule Act**, establishing self-government for DC. US troops are withdrawn from Vietnam.
1974 President Nixon resigns in the wake of the Watergate scandal.
1976 US Bicentennial celebrations. **Metrorail**, the city's first subway system, begins operations. Cooperative Use Act is passed, allowing commercial activities in Federal buildings, and encouraging restoration of historic governmental structures.
1979 Farmers' Tractorcade invades Washington; protesters camp on the Mall.
1982 The Washington Convention Center opens, spurring Downtown development.
1984 The renovated OLD POST OFFICE opens, heralding the rebirth of Pennsylvania Ave. Pope John Paul II delivers a Mass on the Mall.
1987 Opening of the SMITHSONIAN QUADRANGLE.
1990 Completion of the WASHINGTON CATHEDRAL, begun In 1907.
1991 Bicentennial of L'Enfant's plan of Washington.
1993 Opening of the US HOLOCAUST MEMORIAL MUSEUM and the Smithsonian Institution's NATIONAL POSTAL MUSEUM.
Dedication of the Vietnam Women's Memorial.
Bill proposing DC statehood is defeated in Congress.
Mid-90s Construction of colossal office building to complete the Federal Triangle complex.
2000 Opening of the Museum of the American Indian on the Mall.

Grover Cleveland
1885-1889, 1893-1897

Benjamin Harrison
1889-1893

William McKinley
1897-1901

200 YEARS OF GROWTH

Selecting a Site – After the Revolutionary War, the delegates of the newly formed government expressed interest in designating a Federal District to be the seat of power for the new country. A number of existing cities, including New York and Philadelphia, vied to be selected, offering money and land as incentives. Rivalry between the northern and southern states concerning the site of the new capital was resolved through a political compromise: in exchange for agreeing to locate the city in the "southern" precinct, the northern states would be relieved of the heavy debts they had incurred during the Revolution.

L'Enfant Plan for the Federal City
Adapted from Thackara & Vallance plan, 1792. Silhouette redrawn from a work in the collection of the Diplomatic Reception Rooms, Department of State

In July 1790, Congress passed the Residence Act empowering President Washington to select a site for the new Federal district. Ultimately, Washington designated a tract on the Potomac River in the vicinity of Georgetown, though he left its exact boundaries and size undefined. Washington was well-acquainted with this area, as his own plantation MOUNT VERNON was 16 miles down the Potomac, and he believed that the site had great commercial potential as a port if it were linked by canal to the productive lands of the western frontier. In order to facilitate its development, Washington convinced major landholders in the area to give portions of their land to the new capital.

L'Enfant's "City of Magnificent Distances" – In 1789, even before Congress voted to create a Federal District, the Frenchman Maj **Pierre Charles L'Enfant** (1754-1825) expressed to President Washington his eagerness to draw up the plans for the new capital. Trained at the Royal Academy of Painting and Sculpture in Paris, L'Enfant arrived in the US in 1777 at the age of 22 and fought under General Washington in the American Revolution. After the war, L'Enfant established himself in American social circles and enjoyed a fine reputation as a designer and architect, particularly for his work in remodeling Federal Hall in New York City. Impressed with L'Enfant's ideas, and realizing that there were few trained engineers from which to choose, Washington eventually appointed him to design the city and its public buildings.

Theodore Roosevelt
1901-1909

William H. Taft
1909-1913

Woodrow Wilson
1913-1921

Following his appointment by Washington, L'Enfant traveled to Georgetown, arriving in March 1791. He had in hand a city layout sketched by Thomas Jefferson, who, along with Washington, was instrumental in the early development of the Federal City. L'Enfant immediately began reconnoitering the area, which at that time had been settled by several landowners and contained three settlements: the well-established GEORGETOWN, and the fledgling towns of Carrollsburg (adjacent to present-day FORT LESLEY J. MCNAIR) and Hamburg (now the site of the State Department Building in Foggy Bottom). One of L'Enfant's first decisions was to situate the future "Congress house" on Jenkins Hill, which had a commanding view of the Potomac River. Along this western axis, L'Enfant planned a 400ft wide "Grand Avenue" (now the Mall) to be lined by foreign ministries and cultural institutions. The avenue would culminate in an equestrian statue of George Washington, connected on a north-south axis with the "President's house." This mansion in turn would be linked back to the Capitol via a mile-long commercial corridor (present-day Pennsylvania Avenue). Tiber Creek, a tributary of the Potomac situated south of this projected corridor, would be harnessed into a city canal that would run along the northern side of the Grand Avenue, turning south at the foot of Jenkins Hill before emptying into the Eastern branch. The watercourse was to be decorative as well as functional, punctuated by reflecting pools, a cascade, and fountains.

L'Enfant laid out the remainder of the city in a grid pattern of streets intersected by broad diagonal avenues at "round-points" intended to serve as the focus of neighborhood areas. In emphasizing monumental buildings, grand perspectives, gracious circles, wide avenues, and expansive views, the Frenchman was influenced by the baroque notions of urban planning then prevalent in Europe. L'Enfant's widely dispersed, multi-centered city, which later earned the sobriquet "the City of Magnificent Distances," anticipated a population of approximately 800,000 people and extended north to the present Florida Avenue escarpment, encompassing an estimated 6,000 acres.

Dreams and Realities – Once Washington had approved the expanded city plan, L'Enfant directed his energies toward implementing his grand scheme. Refusing to divert his attention to practicalities, L' Enfant was seen as uncooperative and peremptory by the city surveyor **Andrew Ellicott**, by Jefferson, and by the three city commissioners appointed by Washington to oversee the capital's development.

In September 1791, the commissioners named the new diamond-shaped Federal District the "Territory of Columbia" (the current designation, "District of Columbia," came into use in the 19C). Ten miles long on each side, the territory encompassed the County of Alexandria on the Virginia shore of the Potomac and portions of Maryland on the northern shore. The commissioners named the capital itself the City of Washington and stipulated that its street grid be designated by numbers and letters.

To generate revenue for public works and buildings, the commissioners held an auction of lots in October 1791, but only 35 parcels in the as-yet-undeveloped city were sold. Before long, a series of conflicts arose between L'Enfant and the commissioners, and finally in February 1792, unable to defend the designer's recalcitrance any longer, Washington dismissed him. Gathering up most of his plans and drawings, L'Enfant left the town he had conceptualized. Thirty-three years later the talented Frenchman died penniless and forgotten in nearby Maryland, having never received just compensation and recognition during his lifetime. (In 1909, L'Enfant's remains were transferred to ARLINGTON NATIONAL CEMETERY—*see p 117.* The L'Enfant plan of 1791, restored in 1991, is now in the custody of the LIBRARY OF CONGRESS.)

Andrew Ellicott took over where L'Enfant left off, reconstructing the Frenchman's original plan from preparatory sketches. Ellicott recruited the gifted, self-taught mathematician Benjamin Banneker, a free black, to assist with the surveying, and proceeded to lay out streets and avenues. On instructions from Jefferson and Washington, Ellicot named the latter after states of the Union.

During the same period, competitions were held to design the President's House and a home for Congress, but even after architects were chosen, work proceeded slowly because the lot sales needed to finance construction continued to lag. A syndicate of private financiers was formed in the late 1790s to act as a real-estate development company for Washington, but the syndicate's bankruptcy in 1797 curtailed further growth. In addition to the lack of an economic and revenue base, the city suffered from a critical shortage of stone masons and other skilled laborers.

"City of Magnificent Intentions" – When Congress and President Adams relocated from Philadelphia to Washington in November 1800, they found the skeleton of the nascent city etched into the wilderness. Both the CAPITOL and WHITE HOUSE were incomplete; Pennsylvania Avenue was a rutted, marshy thoroughfare; and the town was bereft of finesse or comfort. In August 1814, the fledging capital suffered a major setback when the British invaded the town and set fire to the CAPITOL, WHITE HOUSE, and other public buildings.

Warren G. Harding
1921-1923

Calvin Coolidge
1923-1929

Herbert Hoover
1929-1933

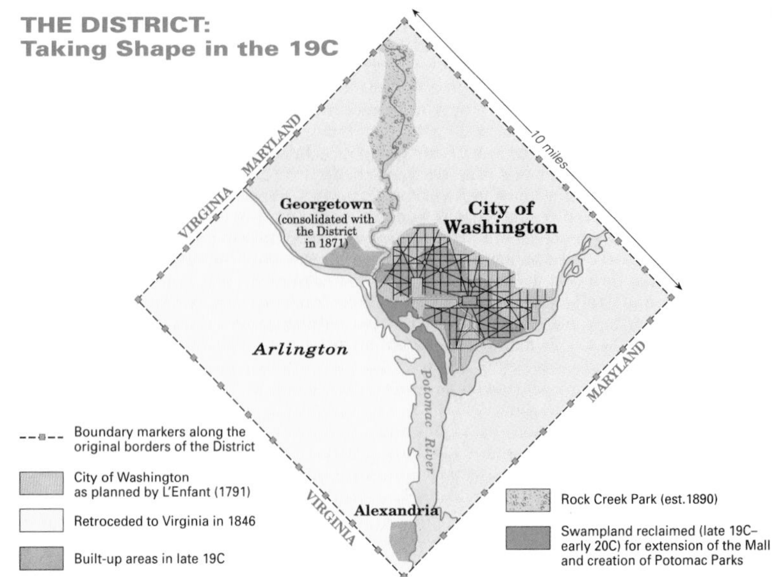

After the war, a contingent of Federal officials, despairing that the town would ever become a capital, lobbied to desert Washington and move the Federal Government to a more established city. A group of local entrepreneurs put up their own funds as loans for rebuilding, thereby successfully persuading the lawmakers to remain in Washington. Congress appropriated additional monies to repair the damaged CAPITOL and Executive Mansion, and development continued as before, slowly but a little more surely.

In 1815, the Washington Canal opened along Pennsylvania Avenue. Unfortunately, the canal provided neither the decorative element intended by L'Enfant nor the commercial boon that had been hoped for by George Washington and others.

In 1835, the Baltimore and Ohio Railroad reached Washington, at once signaling the age of rail transport and the doom of the canal trade so necessary to the prosperity of Alexandria and Georgetown. Alexandrians, feeling they had suffered economically and politically by their integration into the Federal district, petitioned for retrocession to Virginia. Their petition was granted in 1846.

While visiting the inchoate capital in the 1840s, the British novelist Charles Dickens noted wryly, "It is sometimes called the City of Magnificent Distances but it might with greater propriety be termed the City of Magnificent Intentions...spacious avenues that begin in nothing and lead nowhere; streets mile long that only want houses, roads and inhabitants; public meetings that need but a public to be complete; and ornaments of great thoroughfares, which only lack great thoroughfares to ornament...."

In spite of numerous setbacks, by the mid-19C Washington was on its way to becoming a city, and its prevailing neoclassical flavor had been established, thanks to such monumental structures as the Old City Hall, the TREASURY BUILDING, and the OLD PATENT OFFICE BUILDING. Impressive Federal-style residences were also scattered throughout the burgeoning city. Washington had newspapers, theaters, and, if not a rich, at least a respectable, cultural life.

in 1850, President Millard Fillmore commissioned **Andrew Jackson Downing** to devise a major landscape plan for Washington's central quarters, particularly Lafayette Square and the present-day Mall. Although Downing's plans were never funded, they were an early and instrumental effort to unify the green spaces of the "monumental city." In 1855, the newly created Smithsonian Institution opened its brick CASTLE on the Mall.

During the Civil War, development in Washington came to a halt as the city turned its attention to national and local defense. A ring of forts was built along the Potomac, and several of the city's grand public structures became hospitals for the Union wounded.

The brief period of territorial government that began in 1871 was dominated by **Alexander "Boss" Shepherd**, the driving force behind a citywide public works program that developed such outlying areas as Dupont Circle; altered street levels to improve drainage; paved over the old, unsanitary canal; and planted thousands of trees. Shepherd's grand plan also bankrupted the city, which, as always, relied on Federal cof-

Franklin D. Roosevelt
1933-1945

Harry S. Truman
1945-1953

Dwight D. Eisenhower
1953-1961

fers for subsidy. A disgruntled Congress revoked territorial government and returned the city to district status in 1874. 1n 1871, Washington was significantly enlarged by the incorporation of Georgetown. As the century drew to a close, railroad, streetcar, and trolley lines led to the growth in nearby Virginia and Maryland of suburban communities that were linked economically and culturally to the city.

Courtesy WMATA

Metro Station

The "City Beautiful" – In 1901, the US Senate appointed the four-member **McMillan Commission** to recommend an overall building and landscape plan for the Mall area, which was then an unsightly hodgepodge. The commission's report, inspired by L'Enfant's original plan, established an 800ft greensward for the Mall and extended it west and south along the reclaimed Potomac flats, where the grand monuments to Lincoln and Jefferson were subsequently positioned.

To oversee all future planning for and building in the capital, a Commission of Fine Arts was created in 1910. In the same year, the Height of Buildings Act stipulated that no structures exceed 15 stories, thus ensuring that Washington would remain a horizontal and spacious city. Another law, the Public Buildings Act of 1926, resulted in the construction of a number of the city's monumental Classical Revival buildings, including those on Federal Triangle and the structures housing the NATIONAL ARCHIVES and the SUPREME COURT.

During the first half of the 20C, Washington's population increased from 278,000 to 800,000. The two world wars and the 1930s Works Progress Administration attracted an influx of workers to the city and its suburbs. To meet the administrative needs of the war efforts, a number of temporary buildings were constructed in the Mall area. In the post-war decades, Washington became a decentralized city with a decaying central core and an ever-increasing dependence on the automobile. While a system of expressways was built around the periphery of the District, traffic remained a critical problem. To alleviate congestion, a subway system, the **Metrorail**, began operations in 1976 and since has continually expanded its intercity and suburban service *(see map p 191)*. The system's efficiency and elegant—albeit stark—design by architect Harry Weese has won national acclaim.

The Contemporary City – In the 1960s and 70s, tax laws favored the demolition of the city's old structures, and many charming architectural features were removed forever from the cityscape. At the same time, however, an awareness of historic preservation was burgeoning. The Kennedy administration (1961-1963) began efforts to rejuvenate and restore historic Pennsylvania Avenue. In 1978, the city passed the Historic Landmark and Historic District Protection Act, which set guidelines for the designation and protection of historic structures and districts. By the 1980s, the growing awareness of Washington's architectural heritage was reflected in commercial, as well as public, endeavors. Old buildings were renovated rather than demolished, new buildings were designed to interface with traditional architecture, and the resuscitation of Washington's historic Downtown was well underway.

In addition to this architectural awareness, increasing focus was placed on developing and maintaining the parks and green spaces for which the city is famous. During her tenure as First Lady, **Mrs Lyndon Johnson** was instrumental in a city beautification process that led to the landscaping of park areas and public squares. Throughout the late 1960s and 70s, the National Capital Planning Commission instituted long-range plans that strove to achieve an integrated look for the city and its natural areas. About 7,000 acres of the District currently are devoted to public parkland, administered and maintained by the National Park Service.

Development in the city is now closely monitored by a number of local and Federal commissions and agencies, who combine their efforts to ensure that the capital retains its reputation as "the City Beautiful."

John F. Kennedy
1961-1963

Lyndon B. Johnson
1963-1969

Richard M. Nixon
1969-1974

ARCHITECTURE

From its inception, Washington has attracted the talents of nationally prominent architects, whose skills and vision are reflected in the city's many historic buildings. Because of the dominance of the neoclassical style within the city and strict building codes that set a 15-story height limit, modern Washington never developed as a center of innovative, high-rise architecture. Designed as a showcase for the new democracy, it remains in appearance a city of government featuring massive-columned buildings adorned with allegorical themes that recall the democratic and aesthetic ideals of ancient Greece and Rome. The District inventory of historic sites currently lists some 465 individual buildings, parks, and other sights, as well as two dozen historic districts.

From photo by Photri

The Octagon

18C – Washington preserves few vestiges from the 18C, since the city's foundation dates back to the 1790s. During the colonial period, the **Georgian** style, so named because it was popular in England under Kings George I-IV (1714-1830), predominated in the design of brick and stone plantations and manor houses in nearby Virginia and Maryland. Existing examples of this style, which is typified by porticoes, cornices, quoins (prominent corner masonry), and hipped roofs, include CARLYLE HOUSE, and GUNSTON HALL in Virginia.

In Georgetown, the simple OLD STONE HOUSE is one of the few extant buildings that reflect colonial vernacular architecture prior to the Revolution. Following Independence, the influence of the successful English architects, the **Adam Brothers**, was seen in the work of colonial designers who adapted the Adam style to an American idiom that became known as **Federal** architecture. This style relies on symmetry and decorative elegance, often integrating such adornments as delicate columns, rosettes, urns, and swags. The circular and oval-shaped rooms that characterize this style were used to great effect in THE OCTAGON and TUDOR PLACE, both private residences designed by **Dr William Thornton** (1759-1828), the first architect of the CAPITOL. Many of the late-18C and early-19C row houses in Georgetown and Old Town Alexandria also exemplify the Federal style.

19C – In America as in Europe, the 19C gave rise to an eclectic mix of revival styles. In Washington, however, the prevailing taste for neoclassical style frequently led to criticism of buildings that broke with this tradition. Some fine 19C structures that did not adhere to classical principles, such as the OLD POST OFFICE, the OLD EXECUTIVE OFFICE BUILDING and the PENSION BUILDING, were little appreciated, neglected, and even threatened with demolition.

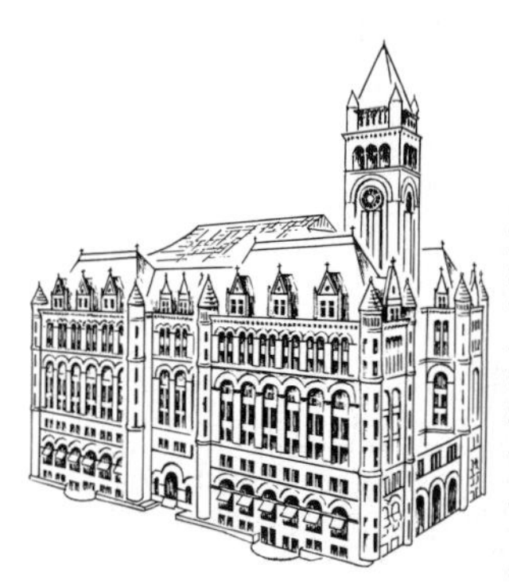
From photo by M. Mackenzie/Uniphoto

Old Post Office

The **Greek Revival** style, modeled on the Doric temple, gained prominence in the 1800s under the talented hands of **Benjamin H. Latrobe** (1764-1820), who modified the original WHITE HOUSE design and was responsible for many small architectural gems, such as DECATUR HOUSE and ST JOHN'S CHURCH. Another proponent of this style, **Robert Mills** (1781-1855) created the TREASURY BUILDING, the OLD PATENT OFFICE BUILDING, and the original design of the WASHINGTON MONUMENT.

By mid-century, a few architects began experimenting with the **Romanesque Revival** style, as exemplified in the turrets and battlemented cornices of the Smithsonian CASTLE, designed by **James Renwick** (1818-1895). In the 1870s and 80s, Henry Hobson Richardson (1838-1886) modified this approach into the popular **Richardsonian Romanesque.** Distinctive for its massive stone constructions that feature arched windows, doorways, and turrets, this style can be found in the OLD POST OFFICE and in private residences in the Northwest quadrant, such as the HEURICH MANSION.

The **Italianate**, a simpler residential style, can be seen in several of the 19C brick row houses in Georgetown, the Dupont Circle area, and Foggy Bottom. One of many versions of what is popularly called Victorian architecture, the Italianate employs overhanging cornices, decorative brackets, bow windows, and porches.

Gerald R. Ford
1974-1977

Jimmy Carter
1977-1981

Ronald Reagan
1981-1989

The **Second Empire** style, a mid-19C French innovation, first made its appearance in America in the early 1860s, with the building that now houses the RENWICK GALLERY. Named after its architect, James Renwick, this building features the characteristic Second Empire mansard roof—a dual-pitched roof pierced with dormer windows on the steep lower slope. During the Grant Administration (1869-1877), the style became so prevalent that it was known as the General Grant style. The massive OLD EXECUTIVE OFFICE BUILDING is one of the nation's finest examples of the style.

At the turn of the century, the exuberant **Beaux-Arts** style dominated the new buildings of Washington. Developed in France's famous Ecole des Beaux-Arts, where many prominent American architects studied, this style was typified by a monumentality that reflected the optimistic spirit of the nation in the late 19C and early 20C. Its eclecticism combines classical elements with elaborate detailing, as is seen in such public buildings as the LIBRARY OF CONGRESS and UNION STATION, by Daniel H. Burnham, one of the leading advocates of the Beaux-Arts. In residential architecture, Waddy B. Wood and Jules Henri de Sibour *(see pp 120 and 127)* designed a number of the palatial homes along Embassy Row in the Beaux-Arts manner.

From photo by Photri

Library of Congress

20C – In the 1920s, Beaux-Arts enthusiasm gradually became restrained, evolving into the more formal **Classical Revival** architecture that again dominated Washington from the 1920s through World War II. The Federal Triangle complex, built in the 1930s, includes seven buildings designed in the Classical Revival style by seven different architects, one of whom was **John Russell Pope** (1874-1937). The most prolific proponent of this style, Pope is responsible for such grand public buildings as the NATIONAL GALLERY OF ART, the NATIONAL ARCHIVES, the Scottish Rite House of the Temple (1733 16th St. at S St. NW), and the JEFFERSON MEMORIAL. Sweeping staircases, domes, pedimented porticoes, and unadorned surfaces are hallmarks of Pope's edifices.

National Archives

Post-World War II modernism has had little impact on Washington architecture. Rather than producing innovative architectural design, the 1950s-1970s saw the loss of many fine 19C structures, as undistinguished box-like office buildings proliferated throughout the city. It was during this uninspired period that the KENNEDY CENTER and the new NATIONAL GEOGRAPHIC SOCIETY building, both by Edward Durrell Stone, were erected.

Washington does, however, possess a few exceptional examples of modern architecture: Dulles International Airport (1962, Eero Saarinen), the Martin Luther King Memorial Library (1972, Mies van der Rohe), and the East Building of the National Gallery of Art (1978, I. M. Pei).

In recent years, post-Modernist currents have resurrected the use of columns, arches and other embellishments that had been banished during the austere modernist period. Washington Harbour, designed by Arthur Cotton Moore, embodies the extravagances of the 1980s, while a more restrained and academic approach can be seen in new structures along the historic Pennsylvania Avenue corridor, where classical elements are used in an attempt to integrate new architecture with the existing building stock. The Market Square complex (between 6th and 7th Sts.) by Hartman-Cox, exemplifies this trend. A decidedly post-Modern influence is apparent in the architecture of the US Holocaust Memorial Museum (James Freed), which opened in 1993 *(p 67)*.

Presidential Portraits © White House Historical Assoc.; photos by National Geographic Society except A. Lincoln (Edimedia), J.F. Kennedy (painting by E. Lumanian/J.F. Kennedy Library), G. Bush (UPI/Bettmann), B. Clinton (Office of the President-Elect).

George Bush
1989-1993

Bill Clinton
1993-

CULTURAL SCENE

Traditionally considered a cultural backwater, Washington has emerged in recent decades as a vital center for the performing arts, thereby taking its place among the nation's leading cultural hubs.

Museums – Founded in 1846 through a bequest to the US from an English scientist named James Smithson, the **Smithsonian Institution** now comprises the largest complex of museums in the world. Of its 14 existing museums and galleries, eight are located on the Mall. (Although loosely affiliated with the Smithsonian, the NATIONAL GALLERY OF ART is an independent institution.) The Smithsonian's NATIONAL ZOOLOGICAL PARK and five of its six other museums are also located in Washington.
The collections of the Smithsonian number more than 140 million objects, including cultural and scientific artifacts and artworks ranging from the prehistoric to the contemporary. In addition to its exhibit functions, the institution operates six major research facilities supporting work in the arts and sciences. It also sponsors public lectures, concerts, classes, festivals, and travel agendas.

SMITHSONIAN INSTITUTION

Mall museums

Arthur M. Sackler Gallery
Arts and Industries Building
Freer Gallery of Art
Hirshhorn Museum and Sculpture Garden
National Air and Space Museum
National Museum of African Art
National Museum of American History
National Museum of Natural History
National Museum of the American Indian *(opening in 2000)*

Off the Mall

Anacostia Museum
National Museum of American Art
National Portrait Gallery
National Postal Museum
National Zoological Park
Renwick Gallery

New York City

Cooper-Hewitt *(see Michelin Green Guide to New York City)*

In addition to the Smithsonian attractions, the capital boasts several fine privately owned museums created through the generosity of prominent Washington collectors. Foremost among these institutions are the CORCORAN GALLERY OF ART, THE PHILLIPS COLLECTION, HILLWOOD, and DUMBARTON OAKS. The area has preserved many historic house museums *(see p 28)* that offer glimpses into the capital's illustrious past. The Federal City also abounds in exemplary public buildings, many of which are open to the public. A visit to such sights as the CAPITOL, SUPREME COURT, FBI, or the BUREAU OF ENGRAVING AND PRINTING can provide a unique learning experience in the workings of the US Government.
Throughout the year, the area's cultural and educational institutions—both public and private—sponsor an impressive schedule of (usually free) exhibits, lectures, and concerts catering to a wide range of tastes and interests.

Performing Arts – *For addresses, telephone numbers and other practical information, see p 171.* With the opening of the JOHN F. KENNEDY CENTER FOR THE PERFORMING ARTS in 1971, Washington finally began to attract an increasing number of world-class performers. Housing four theaters and the resident National Symphony Orchestra, the center offers drama, concerts, and dance performances. Its affiliate, the National Theatre, established on Pennsylvania Avenue in 1835, focuses on plays and musicals. A number of private theaters, including the well-respected Arena Stage complex, offer traditional and experimental productions.
The National Park Service maintains two theaters: historic FORD'S THEATRE located Downtown and the highly acclaimed Wolf Trap Farm for the Performing Arts, an outdoor summer theater in the nearby Virginia suburbs, which features world-renowned dance troupes and musicians.
In addition, the city benefits from an exceptional number of free summer concerts given by US military bands at various locations in the city *(see p 172)*.

FURTHER READING

Above Washington by Robert Cameron *(Cameron and Co., San Francisco, 1989).*

AIA Guide to Washington DC *(Johns Hopkins University Press, Baltimore MD, 1994).*

Buildings of the District of Columbia by Pamela Scott and Antoinette J. Lee *(Oxford University Press, New York, 1993).*

Going Places with Children in Washington DC *(Green Acres School, Washington DC, 1989).*

The United States Capitol *(Stewart, Tabori & Chang, New York, 1993).*

The White House: The History of an American Idea by William Seale *(AIA Press, Washington DC, 1992).*

Washington, Then and Now by Charles S. Kelley *(Dover Publications, New York, 1984).*

Sights

Photri

WHERE TO FIND IT

Locations of Washington's popular artifacts, treasures, and collections:

Archie Bunker's chair	National Museum of American History *(p 59)*
Athenaeum portrait of George Washington by Gilbert Stuart	National Portrait Gallery *(p 91)*
Charters of Freedom	National Archives *(p 55)*
Derringer used to assassinate Abraham Lincoln	Lincoln Museum at Ford's Theatre *(p 94)*
Enola Gay	National Air and Space Museum (Paul E. Garber Facility—*p 47)*
Fabergé Imperial Easter Eggs	Hillwood Museum *(p 139)*
First Ladies' gowns	National Museum of American History *(p 61)*
Giant Panda	National Zoological Park *(p 140)*
Ginevra de' Benci by Leonardo da Vinci	National Gallery of Art *(p 49)*
Gutenberg Bible	Library of Congress *(p 37)*
Hope Diamond	National Museum of Natural History *(p 58)*
IMAX films *(To Fly!, The Dream is Alive)*	National Air and Space Museum (Langley Theater—*p 45)*
Japanese cherry trees	Tidal Basin *(p 70)*
Kennedy graves	Arlington National Cemetery *(p 115)*
Kitty Hawk 1903 Flyer	National Air and Space Museum *(p 45)*
The Luncheon of the Boating Party by Renoir	The Phillips Collection *(p 124)*
Niagara by Frederick Edwin Church	Corcoran Gallery of Art *(p 81)*
Spirit of St Louis	National of Air and Space Museum *(p 45)*
Star-Spangled Banner	National Museum of American History *(p 61)*
George Washington's tomb	Mount Vernon *(p 154)*
Watergate tapes	National Archives (College Park MD facility—*p 56)*

American Decorative Arts	Carlyle House *(p 147)* Daughters of the American Revolution *(p 83)* Diplomatic Reception Rooms *(p 101)* Dumbarton House *(p 111)* Gunston Hall *(p 156)* White House *(p 76)*
Pre-Columbian Art	Dumbarton Oaks *(p 110)* Textile Museum *(p 130)*
Byzantine Art	Dumbarton Oaks *(p 109)*
Russian Decorative Arts	Hillwood Museum *(p 139)*
20C Art	Art Museum of the Americas *(p 86)* Corcoran Gallery of Art *(p 80)* Hirshhorn Museum and Sculpture Garden *(p 62)* National Gallery of Art (East Building) *(p 54)* National Museum of American Art *(p 93)* The Phillips Collection *(p 124)* Washington Project for the Arts *(p 89)*
House Museums	Arlington House *(p 116)* Boyhood Home of Robert E. Lee *(p 149)* Carlyle House *(p 147)* Decatur House *(p 83)* Dumbarton House *(p 111)* Frederick Douglass National Historic Site *(p 134)* Gunston Hall *(p 156)* Hillwood Museum *(p 139)* Historical Society of Washington DC *(p 122)* Lee-Fendall House *(p 150)* Mount Vernon *(p 152)* The Octagon *(p 102)* Society of the Cincinnati *(p 123)* Tudor Place *(p 110)* Woodlawn Plantation *(p 155)*
Gardens	Dumbarton Oaks *(p 110)* Gunston Hall *(p 156)* Hillwood *(p 140)* Kenilworth Aquatic Gardens *(p 142)* National Arboretum *(p 142)* Woodlawn Plantation *(p 155)*

1

★★★

Capitol Hill

The city's high eastern ground, bearing the popular designation Capitol Hill, is crowned by massive stone buildings serving the legislative and judicial branches of the Federal Government. Beyond them stretch the Hill's residential streets, neighborhoods of 19C row houses that reflect a true cross section of Washington's population.

Seat of Government – In 1791 when L'Enfant chose this hilltop, then known as Jenkins Hill, on which to site the future home of the Congress, he expected the city's residential core to develop on its east flank. In order to stimulate growth in that area, George Washington himself constructed two town houses on North Capitol Street, while several wealthy individuals began their own mansions in the vicinity. In his design for the CAPITOL, William Thornton positioned the main facade on the building's east side, presumably in anticipation of the area's development. The establishment of the NAVY YARD and the **Marine Barracks** *(8th and I Sts. SE)* in the early years of the 19C provided employment in the vicinity of the Hill and encouraged the growth of neighborhoods extending from the Capitol southeast to the river.

In 1814, the British invaded the area and burned the Capitol, but the Hill quickly recovered. In the decades following the War of 1812, it grew steadily as a residential area, though never to the degree L'Enfant had expected. Opened in 1870 at the 200 block of 7th Street SE, **Eastern Market** extended the reaches of Capitol Hill eastward. As the 19C drew to a close, the Hill became a middle-class enclave of pleasant brick row houses and neighborhood churches.

Federal Building Boom – At the turn of the century, the grandiose Beaux-Arts edifice housing the LIBRARY OF CONGRESS, now known as the Thomas Jefferson Building, was erected across from the Capitol. Several years later, two other colossal Beaux-Arts structures—UNION STATION and the CITY POST OFFICE, both designed by Daniel H. Burnham—were built at the northern foot of Capitol Hill. In the 1930s, a flurry of construction resulted in the FOLGER SHAKESPEARE LIBRARY, the John Adams Annex of the Library of Congress, and the SUPREME COURT building, all in the immediate vicinity of the Capitol. Meanwhile, Congress was steadily adding new buildings to the Hill. The Senate erected three office buildings to the northeast of the Capitol: the **Russell Building** (1909, designed by Carrère and Hastings), the **Dirksen Building** (1958), and the **Hart Building**. Similarly, the House erected three buildings on the south side: the **Cannon Building** (1908, Carrère and Hastings), the **Longworth Building** (1933), and the **Rayburn Building** (1965). In 1980, the Library of Congress added a third building, the James Madison Memorial Building, to its complex.

Revitalized Neighborhood – The social composition of Capitol Hill's residential streets has fluctuated throughout the 20C. In mid-century, its middle-class population gradually moved to suburban Maryland and Virginia. Meanwhile, low-income families began to occupy the old, often run-down row houses. At the same time, the streets between the Capitol and Lincoln Park underwent renovation and restoration as well-paid professionals bought up the 19C homes here. Since the 1970s, the Hill's residents have gained notoriety as civic activists capable of effectively preventing development that would alter the residential character of this area. Today, Eastern Market, reputedly the city's only surviving market, has become the nucleus for a pleasant commercial area of small shops and restaurants. Independence Avenue, another commercial corridor, serves the Capitol legislators and their staffs, while renovated Union Station, still the city's major rail terminal, now houses shops, restaurants, and a cinema complex.

★★★ THE CAPITOL

Michelin map 48 K11 *time: 1 1/2 hours*

1st St. between Independence and Constitution Aves. M *Capitol South or Union Station. Open daily 9am–3:45pm; closed Jan 1, Thanksgiving Day and Dec 25. Free admission. Guided tours (25min) daily every 15min; Congressional visits also available—**see p 162.* ☎*225-6827.*

Extending along the eastern end of the Mall, the labyrinthine Capitol building, with its cast-iron dome topped by the statue of Freedom, is the city's most prominent landmark. This massive symbol of democracy in progress has housed the US Congress since 1800.

HISTORICAL NOTES

Early Construction – When L'Enfant chose Jenkins Hill as the site for the Capitol in 1791, the Frenchman characterized it as "a pedestal waiting for a monument." L'Enfant himself was called upon to design the Capitol and other public buildings, but was dismissed in 1792 before realizing a single project. President Washington and Secretary of State Jefferson elicited architectural plans for the Capitol by holding a public competition, but the entries proved so uninspiring that **Dr William Thornton**, a respected amateur architect, was allowed to submit a drawing five months late. His entry called for a stone structure of classical proportions with a low-domed central section modeled after the Pantheon in Rome *(see illustration below)*. The design met with immediate approval, winning Thornton $500 and a city lot.

Library of Congress

Thornton's design for the Capitol

On September 18, 1793, Washington presided over the laying of the cornerstone in a ceremonial Masonic service that would be repeated in the building of future additions to the Capitol. A lack of skilled workers, tools, and supplies in the then virtually nonexistent city hampered construction, as did a lack of funds. The revenue from the sale of city lots in the new capital was expected to finance building costs, but few people were attracted by the high prices and rudimentary conditions. By 1800, however, Congress was able to leave the temporary capital of Philadelphia and move to the nascent Federal City. On November 22, 1800, President John Adams addressed the first joint session of Congress in the completed north wing (the original Senate wing) of the new Capitol.

Professional rivalry among the various architects working on the Capitol (including James Hoban, designer of the White House) led to Thornton's resignation. In 1803, British architect **Benjamin Henry Latrobe** was appointed Surveyor of Public Buildings, and by 1807, he had succeeded in completing the south wing (the original House wing). The two wings were linked by a wooden walkway crossing the present site of the Rotunda. Latrobe's first House chamber featured a half-domed coffered ceiling. With the south wing completed, Latrobe began renovating and improving the north wing and submitted revised plans for the Capitol exterior, which included a colonnaded central section.

Conflagration – The War of 1812 saw the only enemy attack on the Capitol. In August 1814, the British set fire to it, gutting the interior. A providential downpour prevented total ruin, but when Congress returned in the fall, many members advocated abandoning the building and the city and finding a new home for the Federal Government. To discourage desertion, a group of private citizens had a temporary brick structure erected for Congress on the site where the Supreme Court now stands.

From 1815 to 1817, Latrobe worked at restoring the Capitol's interior, and in the process he added low domes over the building's two original wings and redesigned the House chamber (now Statuary Hall) into the semicircular shape it has retained to this day. Among the decorative elements that attest to Latrobe's inventiveness are the tobacco fronds and ears of corn that top the columns lining the House chamber. Though the building's grace was much admired, the echoes produced in the cavernous space led one representative to quip that it was "handsome and fit for anything but the use intended." Red draperies were hung behind the gallery to help muffle sounds. (The chamber is depicted in Samuel Morse's *Old House of Representatives,* on view in the CORCORAN GALLERY.)

When Latrobe resigned because of a clash with the Commissioner of Public Buildings, Boston architect **Charles Bulfinch** took over, and Congress was able to again meet in the Capitol in December 1819. Bulfinch served as the official Architect of the Capitol until 1829. During his tenure, he completed the building more or less according to Thornton's original plans, substituting a lofty copper-sheathed wooden dome for the hemispherical stone vault designed by Thornton.

The Civil War Years – During the early 19C, the legislature, keeping pace with the nation it represented, grew rapidly. By 1850, it comprised 62 Senators and 232 Representatives. Spurred on by Sen Jefferson Davis, who later became President of the Confederacy, Congress appropriated $100,000 for two new wings to house the cramped Senate and House. Once again a contest was held, but no clear winner emerged. Rather, composite design based on several entries was favored, and one of the contestants, **Thomas U. Walter** from Philadelphia, was asked to draw up plans. Thomas Crawford was commissioned to design the statue topping the new dome. Crawford's 19 1/2ft bronze **Freedom** was outfitted with flowing robes and the liberty cap of a freed Roman slave. When Southerner Jefferson Davis objected to the implications of her headdress, Crawford changed it to the present feathered, eagle's-head helmet.

With civil strife in the air, construction began. When war finally did come, Congress was not in session, and the War Department quartered troops in the Capitol for several months. Soldiers called it the "Big Tent," and Army bakers built enormous ovens in the basement committee rooms, producing enough bread to feed troops bivouacked around the city. A year later, the Capitol served briefly as a hospital for the wounded.

Throughout the war, construction on the Capitol proceeded, as "a sign," President Lincoln declared, "that we intend the Union shall go on." Walter's enlarged dome, designed to replace the now disproportionately small dome built by Bulfinch, was made of cast iron and weighed almost nine million pounds. By 1863, the dome, considered a marvel of 19C engineering, was ready to receive Crawford's crowning statue. The two new wings were finally completed in 1867.

Expansion – The nation's foremost landscape architect, **Frederick Law Olmsted**, was appointed in 1874 to lay out the grounds. His addition of the broad plaza on the east and the marble stairway and terraces on the west facilitated the creation of much-needed office space on the lower levels of the building. Olmsted's landscaping reflects his propensity for natural sweeps of lawn and trees.

For the next 75 years, interior changes such as electrification (1897), fireproofing, and improved plumbing continued. Under Elliott Wood's term as Architect of the Capitol (1902-1923), a fourth floor was added, and the Latrobe domes in the two original wings were rebuilt in fireproof cast iron.

By the late 1950s, Congress had again outgrown the Capitol. To provide more space, the central section of the east facade was extended 32 1/2ft, as shown on the drawing below. The new marble front was designed as an exact copy of the original sandstone facade so as not to alter the essential appearance of this national landmark (the columns of the original facade are conserved at the NATIONAL ARBORETUM).

CONSTRUCTION OF THE CAPITOL

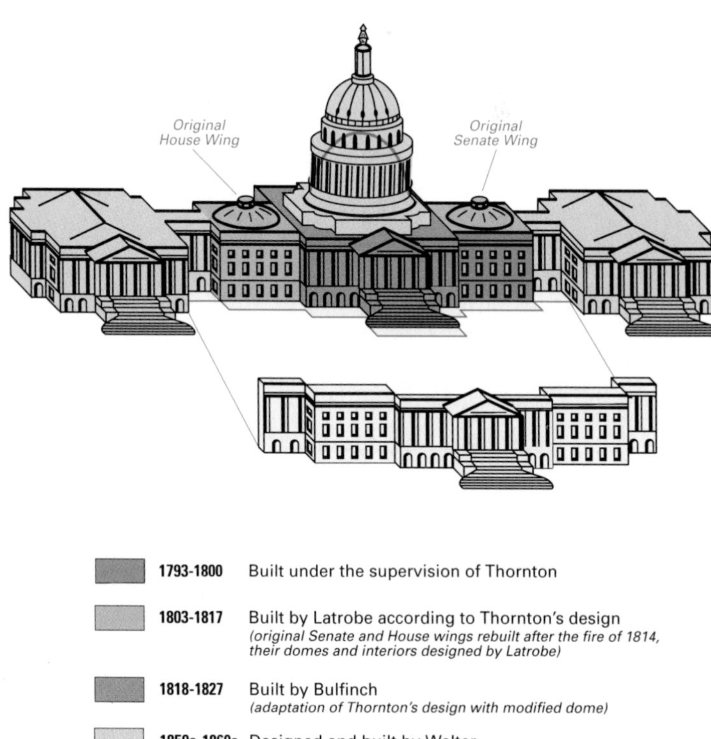

1793-1800 Built under the supervision of Thornton

1803-1817 Built by Latrobe according to Thornton's design
(original Senate and House wings rebuilt after the fire of 1814, their domes and interiors designed by Latrobe)

1818-1827 Built by Bulfinch
(adaptation of Thornton's design with modified dome)

1850s-1860s Designed and built by Walter

1958-1962 East Front extension

THE CAPITOL

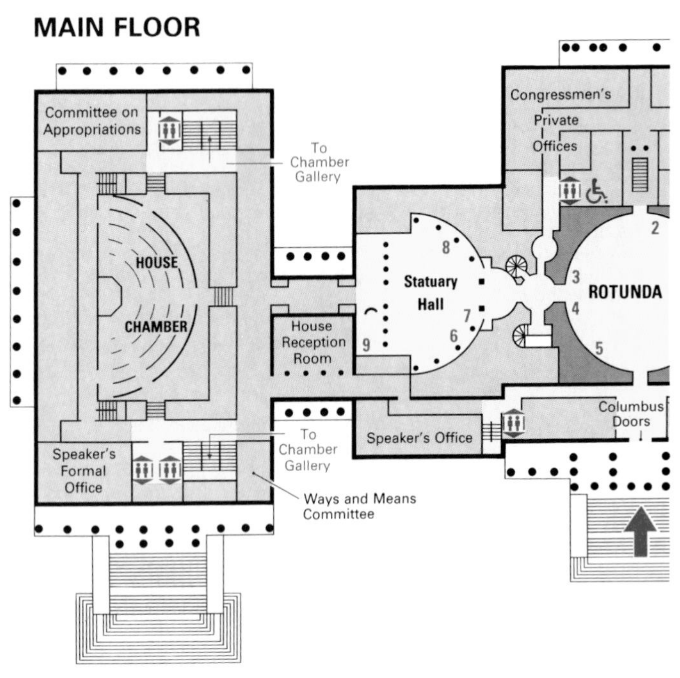

Not open to the public

THE

GROUND FLOOR

House Appointments Desk

Hall of Columns

Hall of Capitols

Small House Rotunda

Crypt

10

11

Capitol

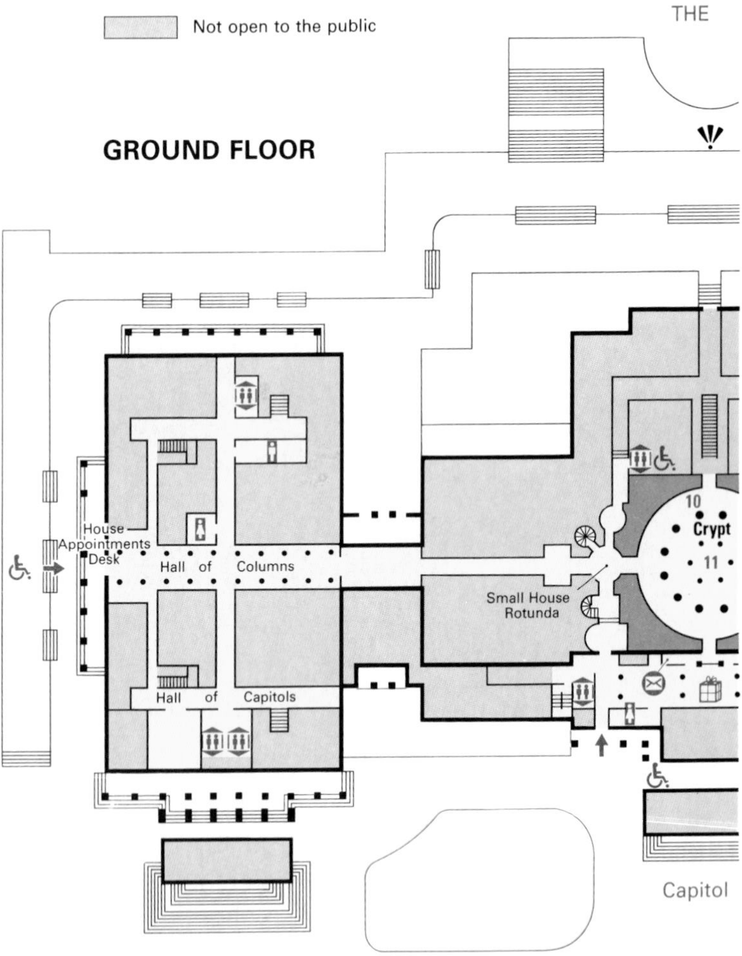

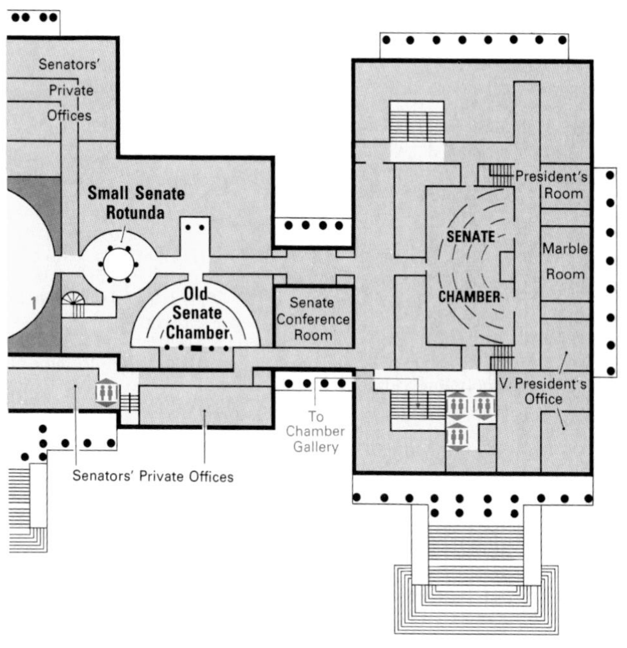

Senators' Private Offices
Small Senate Rotunda
1
Old Senate Chamber
Senate Conference Room
SENATE CHAMBER
President's Room
Marble Room
V. President's Office
To Chamber Gallery
Senators' Private Offices

MALL
0
50 m
100 ft
N
Special Services
Small Senate Rotunda
Old Supreme Court Chamber
Senate Appointments Desk
Brumidi Corridors
To Chamber Gallery
Plaza

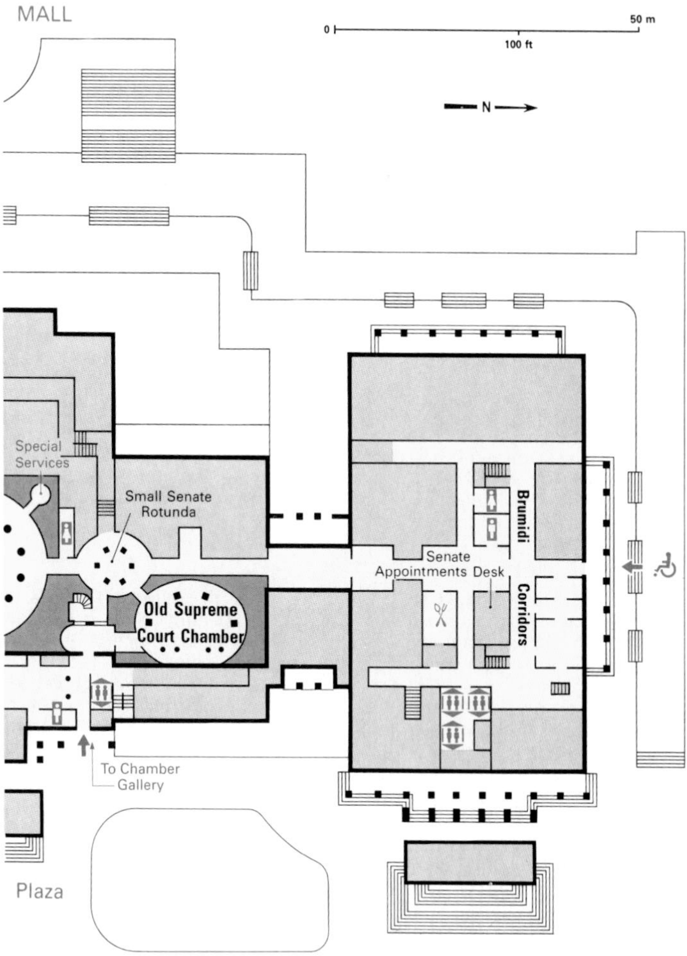

VISIT

The general public is allowed free access to all of the areas described below. Only the Rotunda, Statuary Hall, crypt, and the current chambers of the Senate and House, when the bodies are not in session, are included on guided tours of the Capitol.

Main Floor

The Rotunda – The ornate Capitol **dome**★★—180ft high and 95ft across—soars above rich artwork relating to the history of the country. The allegorical fresco in the eye of the dome, entitled the *Apotheosis of Washington,* was painted by Italian-born **Constantino Brumidi**, who had done restoration work in the Vatican. Brumidi worked on the Capitol from 1855 to 1880 and executed so many of its frescoes that he is often referred to as its "Michelangelo."

The *grisaille* frieze circling the base of the dome (total length of frieze: 300ft) records over 400 years of American history from the landing of Columbus to the birth of aviation. Brumidi began the fresco series when he was 72, but completed only six panels before an accidental fall on the scaffolding eventually led to his death. Filippo Costaggini carried on the work, but when he left in 1889, a 31ft gap remained in the frieze. Not until 1953 was the work completed by the American artist Allyn Cox.

On the east side of the Rotunda, the eight-paneled, ten-ton bronze **Columbus doors** depict in high relief scenes from Christopher Columbus' life. Of the eight large paintings around the room, the four on the east side show early events in American history, such as the *Embarkation of the Pilgrims at Delft Haven, Holland* by Robert Weir, dated 1843 (**1**).

The four paintings on the west side, all by John Trumbull, portray important moments of the Revolution, including the *Surrender of Cornwallis at Yorktown* (early 19C) (**2**). Statues of Americans leaders from Washington (**3**) and Jefferson (**4**) to Martin Luther King, Jr (**5**) encircle the room. During the Capitol's long history, such popular national figures as Abraham Lincoln and John F. Kennedy have lain in state here.

Statuary Hall – This elegant semi-circular, half-domed space was restored for the 1976 Bicentennial to its architectural appearance (unfurnished) of 1857 when it functioned as the House Chamber. A Congressional act of 1864 allowed each state to place statues of two of its distinguished citizens in the Capitol. Until the 1930s, these statues were all displayed in Statuary Hall. However, their combined weight was considered dangerous, so some now stand in other Capitol corridors. Notable among the 38 still in the room are the statues of Robert E. Lee of Virginia (**6**), 19C social reformer Frances Willard of Illinois (**7**), 18C missionary pioneer Father Junipero Serra of California (**8**), and King Kamehameha of Hawaii (**9**).

The room's unusual acoustics considerably amplify words spoken within.

Old Senate Chamber – Also restored for the Bicentennial, this room has the general appearance and many of the furnishings it did during the period the Senate occupied it (1810-1814, 1819-1859). Note the gilt shield and eagle over the Vice President's desk and the porthole portrait of George Washington (1823, Rembrandt Peale). From 1860 to 1935, the chamber housed the Supreme Court.

Visiting the Offices of Your Senator or Representative – Offices are located in six buildings accessible from the Capitol via the basement-level subway: Russell, Dirksen and Hart Bldgs (Senate); Cannon, Longworth and Rayburn Bldgs (House)—*see* Michelin map 48 J 11-K 11. For assistance in locating offices ☎ 224-3121 or inquire at the Senate and House Appointment Desks *(ground floor)*. For an appointment with your senator or representative, write in advance *(see p 162)*.

Viewing a Session of Congress *(3rd floor galleries)* – Passes to view a House or Senate session must be obtained at the office of your senator or representative *(see above)*. Certain committee sessions are also open to the public. Consult *The Washington Post* or ☎ 224-3121 for recess schedule and the day's agenda. Foreign visitors apply to the Senate and House Appointment Desks *(ground floor)*.

Ground Floor

Forty Doric columns ring the low-ceilinged **crypt** directly below the Rotunda. It was originally planned to enshrine the body of George Washington in a vault below the crypt, but his descendants preferred that MOUNT VERNON preserve his remains *(see p 154)*. The crypt features displays on the history of the Capitol. The compelling sculpture of Lincoln's head (**10**) was done by Gutzon Borglum, who carved Mount Rushmore. Borglum intended the statue to show in Lincoln's face "all the complexity of his great nature." He left off the statue's left ear as a symbol of Lincoln's unfinished life. A compass stone embedded in the floor (**11**) marks the zero point from which the city's four quadrants emanate.

Continue to the Senate wing.

Old Supreme Court Chamber – An intimate and gracious chamber with red carpeting and green-topped desks, this room housed the Court from 1810 to 1860, except during the period of reconstruction after the War of 1812. Note the many original 19C furnishings and the room's vaulting, designed by Latrobe. Here, the Marshall court *(see p 35)* heard many of the cases that would profoundly influence the development of the young nation.

Brumidi Corridors – The arched ceilings and walls of these two intersecting corridors are embellished with Brumidi's classically inspired murals depicting nature, famous Americans, and historical scenes. Interspersed among the murals are works of later painters, such as Allyn Cox's mural of the 1969 moon landing. Minton floor tiles further enhance the decorative scheme of the corridors.

Return to the crypt and continue to the House wing.

A number of the state statues originally destined for Statuary Hall now stand among the tobacco-leafed pillars of the **Hall of Columns**. Paralleling this hall is the **Hall of Capitols**, which is decorated with murals by Allyn Cox depicting historic events as well as realistic scenes of everyday life.

Third Floor (Gallery Level)

House and Senate Chambers – *See Viewing a Session of Congress p 34.* The East Stairway in the House wing *(not open to the pubic when the House is in session)* leads to the third-floor visitors' gallery for the House Chamber. The *Scene of the Signing of the Constitution of the United States* (1940) by Howard Chandler Christy hangs on the second-floor landing. The **House Chamber**, a richly appointed room, is dominated by a broad podium faced by the seats of the 435 members of the House (Democrats are placed to the right of the presiding speaker of the House, Republicans to the left). Beside the podium hangs a full-length portrait of *George Washington* (1834) by John Vanderlyn and to the right, a portrait of Washington's Revolutionary compatriot, *General Lafayette* (1824) by Ary Scheffer. Medallions of historic lawgivers hang on the gallery walls.

A third-floor hallway extends along the east face of the Capitol to the Senate wing. Round windows and the stone of the building's original facade (prior to the late 1950s extension) are visible along the interior wall of this hall.

The **Senate Chamber** is more soberly appointed than the House Chamber. The only works of art on display are the busts of early Vice Presidents that occupy the niches on the gallery level. When the Senate is in session, the Vice President (in his absence, the *president pro-tempore*) flanked by the secretary of the Senate, the sergeant at arms and various clerks, presides from behind the veined marble podium. The 100 senators are seated at dark mahogany desks (Democrats right side, Republicans left side). Note on the second-floor landing of the East Stairway in the Senate wing W. H. Powell's monumental painting *Battle of Lake Erie* (1873).

Upon leaving the Capitol, stroll around the broad **west terrace**, where you can admire a sweeping **view**★★ across the Mall to the Washington Monument.

If Washington should ever grow to be a great city, the outlook from the Capitol will be unsurpassed in the world. Now at sunset I seem to look westward far into the heart of the Continent from this commanding position.

Ralph Waldo Emerson, 1843

★★ SUPREME COURT

Michelin map 48 K12 — *time: 3/4 hour*

1st and E. Capitol Sts. NE. M *Capitol South or Union Station. Open Mon–Fri 9am–4:30pm; closed Sat, Sun and holidays. Free admission. When the Court is not in session, lectures on the Supreme Court are held in the Courtroom on the half-hour 9:30am–3:30pm.* ♿ ✕ ☎*479-3211.*

Positioned directly across the street from the Capitol, this white marble monument to the supremacy of law houses the highest court in the land. Within its walls, the third branch of Government exercises its mandate to protect and interpret the spirit of the US Constitution.

Historical Notes – Article III of the US Constitution, ratified in 1788, called for a "supreme Court" of the land, to act as a final arbiter of law and as a counterbalance to the other two branches of Government (executive and legislative). The first US Supreme Court convened in 1790 at the Royal Exchange Building in the temporary capital of New York. During the first three years, the Court, as a body, had little work. However, the individual justices were kept busy riding circuits as they were required to do until 1891, hearing cases in their districts. Because of the difficulty of travel at the end of the 18C, many justices served only a few years.

One of the earliest judicial precedents was set in 1793 when President Washington asked the Court to advise him on questions of international law. Under its first Chief Justice, John Jay, it declined, explaining that in view of the Constitution's requirement of separation of powers, the judicial branch had no place advising the executive branch.

To jurists, the fourth Chief Justice, **John Marshall**, is the "Great Chief Justice." Appointed by President Adams in 1801, Marshall served until his death in 1835. During his long tenure, he firmly established the fledgling Court as supreme authority over the law of the land. Among the many important cases the Marshall court ruled on, *Marbury v. Madison* (1803) set a critical precedent. In this case, the Supreme Court affirmed its power to declare an act of Congress unconstitutional. Other important decisions reached under Marshall, in such cases as *McCulloch v. Maryland, Cohens v. Virginia,* and *Gibbons v. Ogden*, reaffirmed the power of the Union and its authority over state laws.

A Body of Controversy – "We are very quiet here, but it is the quiet of a storm center," explained Justice Oliver Wendell Holmes, Jr, who served from 1902 to 1932. Throughout its history, the Court has been involved in controversy, sometimes settling it, at other times kindling it. In 1857, the Court handed down perhaps its most infamous decision, when, under Chief Justice Taney, it heard the case of a slave named Dred Scott. The Court's ruling that Congress had no authority to limit the expansion of slavery helped bring on the Civil War and badly damaged public respect for the Court.

A Home of its Own – In its early years, the Court had no regular meeting place, convening in various public buildings in New York, then Philadelphia. In 1800, it moved to the new Federal City and occupied different rooms in the CAPITOL, including the room now known as the Old Supreme Court Chamber *(p 34)*. After the British burned the Capitol in 1814, the Court was forced to meet in a number of temporary locations, including a private home and a tavern. When the Capitol was sufficiently repaired, the Court returned to the Old Supreme Court Chamber, which it occupied from 1819 to 1860. It then moved upstairs to the Old Senate Chamber, which remained its home for the following 75 years.

William Howard Taft (1921-1930), the tenth Chief Justice and the only US President to serve on the Court, convinced Congress in 1928 to allocate funds for a building to house the Court. In October 1935, the present edifice was completed at a cost of $9,650,000, but to mixed reviews from the justices. Justice Harland Fiske Stone called the new structure "almost bombastically pretentious...wholly inappropriate for a quiet group of old boys such as the Supreme Court."

A few of the precedent-setting cases heard in the Courtroom of the current building include *Brown v. Board of Education,* which established school integration nationwide; *Engel v. Vitale,* outlawing school prayer; and cases involving the constitutionality of abortion.

The Court at Work – Woodrow Wilson called the Supreme Court "a kind of Constitutional Convention in continuous session." As the highest court in the country, it is the court of last appeal. The chief justice and associate justices are appointed by the President, with Senate approval, as vacancies occur. Only voluntary retirement or resignation, death, or congressional impeachment can remove a sitting justice. Through his appointees to the Supreme Court, a US President continues to exercise influence long after his term has ended.

Congress, not the Constitution, sets the number of justices on the Court. In the Court's first century, that number changed six times. Now, based on the Judiciary Act of 1869, it is set at nine justices *(see list below)*.

The Court's term begins on the first Monday in October. From October through April, the Court hears oral arguments on cases it has consented to review. Of the over 6,000 requests for review it receives annually, the Court hears from 120 to 150 cases. It generally sits two weeks a month, Monday to Wednesday *(10am to 3pm)* with a lunch recess *(noon-1pm)*. Most case arguments are limited to one hour, with 30 minutes allotted to each side. The remainder of the week, the justices review arguments heard and consider requests for future reviews. In May and June, the Court convenes on Mondays *(10am)* to deliver its opinions on the cases argued in that term.

Sessions are open to the public on a first-come, first-served basis. Consult The Washington Post *for the daily schedule of Court hearings. For further information ☎479-3030.*

Visit – An oval plaza fronts the cross-shaped building of gleaming white marble, designed by Cass Gilbert. Flanking a broad staircase that leads up to a colonnade of 32 Corinthian columns are two massive allegorical figures. Sculpted by James Fraser, they represent *The Contemplation of Justice (left)* and *The Authority of Law (right)*. Carved under the bas-relief in the pediment are the words "Equal Justice Under Law."

A wide columned hall, adorned with a coffered 44ft-high ceiling and busts of chief justices, leads from the entrance to the **Courtroom**. Here the justices sit on a raised bench positioned in front of four of the 24 massive veined columns that ring the 82ft by 91ft chamber. The justices' places are ordered by their seniority, with the chief justice taking the center position.

Visitors may descend to the ground floor, which features changing exhibits on the history and function of the Court. Dominating the main hall on this level is a massive **statue of John Marshall**, depicting him in a relaxed seated pose that suggests his renowned affability and lack of pretense. *A film on the history and work of the Court is shown continuously in the theater at the end of the hall to the right of the Marshall statue.*

The Supreme Court Justices

The nominating President and the year in which the judicial oath was taken are shown in parentheses.

Chief Justice William H. Rehnquist
(Associate Justice: Nixon 1972, Chief Justice: Reagan, 1986)

Associate Justices

Harry A. Blackmun (Nixon, 1970; retiring 1994)
John Paul Stevens (Ford, 1975)
Sandra Day O'Connor (Reagan, 1981)
Antonin Scalia (Reagan, 1986)
Anthony M. Kennedy (Reagan, 1988)
David H. Souter (Bush, 1990)
Clarence Thomas (Bush, 1991)
Ruth Bader Ginsburg (Clinton, 1993)

★★ LIBRARY OF CONGRESS

Michelin map 48 K12 *time: 1 1/2 hours*

1st St. and Independence Ave. SE. M *Capitol South or Union Station. The Library of Congress functions as a reference library and may be used by any individual 18 years or older pursuing research. The general public is welcome to visit the complex. The main facilities are open to the public Tue, Fri, Sat and Sun 8:30am–6pm (9:30pm rest of week); closed Jan 1 and Dec 25. An orientation video (20min) is shown on the half hour on the ground floor of the Madison Building. Guided tours (45min) are given weekdays; times may vary because of continuing renovation.* ♿ ✗. *For tour information* ☎ *707-5458.*
For current visitor information and assistance in using the research facilities, consult the touch-screen information terminals located in the lobby of the Madison Building. General information ☎ *707-8000; research information* ☎ *707-6500.*
In view of the extensive renovation program in progress, parts of the complex may be closed to the public.

A renowned Beaux-Arts landmark, the original Library of Congress is reputedly Washington's most richly ornamented building. The largest library in existence, it retains in its varied and ever-growing collections some 28 million books, as well as a myriad of historical and artistic treasures.

HISTORICAL NOTES

Congress' Library – In 1800, while still convening in Philadelphia, Congress appropriated $5,000 for the establishment of a library for its own use. Originally, the library was housed in the Capitol for the convenience of the legislators. When the library's 3,000 volumes were destroyed in the Capitol fire of 1814, Thomas Jefferson offered his extensive personal library to Congress, which purchased the 6,487 volumes for $23,950. The collection was shipped in ten horse-drawn wagons from Monticello, Jefferson's Virginia estate, to the Capitol. Unfortunately, another fire in 1851 destroyed two-thirds of the existing library collection. Congress immediately appropriated funds to replenish the holdings and to build a new multi-tiered library area along the west side of the Capitol.

A Library for the People – Though intended to serve only members of Congress and Supreme Court justices, the library was gradually opened to other governmental and diplomatic officials. In 1864, **Ainsworth Rand Spofford** was appointed Librarian of Congress and began a process that changed the library into a public institution. In order to amass a more extensive collection, Spofford lobbied Congress to amend existing legislation so that the copyright for books, musical scores, maps, and charts would be granted by the Library of Congress rather than the Department of Interior. This procedure ensured that newly published materials would find their way into the library's holdings, a practice that continues to this day. The collection increased rapidly under Spofford, and all available space in the Capitol was quickly filled.
In 1873, Congress approved a separate building for the library. In 1886, ground was broken but the work progressed slowly, causing Congress to dismiss the building's principal architects **John Smithmeyer** and **Paul Pelz**. They were replaced by Thomas Casey, the Chief of Army Engineers, and a civilian engineer, Bernard Green. Along with Casey's son Edward, Green planned the interior artwork and commissioned a small army of American artists to execute the ambitious decorative scheme, which blended mosaics, murals, marblework, and sculptures. The library opened in 1897, under budget (total cost: $6.5 million) and ahead of schedule; it has functioned as the "national library of the United States" ever since.

A Growing Concern – In 1939, the library expanded to a second structure, the **John Adams Building** *(located on 2nd St. SE, behind the main building)*, noteworthy for its Art Deco ornamentation. At that time, the original building was designated the Thomas Jefferson Building. A third facility, the austere marble **James Madison Memorial Building** *(Independence Ave., between 1st and 2nd Sts. SE)*, was opened in 1980. With more than twice the floor space of either of the two older library structures, the Madison Building now features the visitor information desk and a number of exhibits based on materials from the library's special collections. The main exhibit area, the Madison Memorial Hall *(left side of lobby)*, is dominated by a seated statue of James Madison, the fourth US President.
The library offers a regular series of concerts by its resident string quartet, the **Juiliard Quartet**. It also features public lectures and poetry readings, as well as showings of old films in its Pickford Theater. *For schedules, consult the touch screen at the information desk in the Madison Building. Concert information* ☎ *707-5503.*

Holdings – The Library of Congress retains some 101 million items, which fill the equivalent of 575 miles of shelves. These possessions include more than 41 million manuscripts, 4 million maps and atlases, and 8 million musical items, such as scores, instruments, and correspondence among musicians. The library is acquiring new holdings at the rate of 10 items per minute. Foremost among the valuable works of art owned by the Library of Congress are two mid-15C masterpieces: the manuscript Giant Bible of Mainz, and a Gutenberg Bible. American artifacts include Jefferson's first version of the Declaration of Independence and President Lincoln's handwritten drafts of the Emancipation Proclamation and the Gettysburg Address. The library's renowned music division contains a noted collection of Stradivarius violins and original manuscripts by Brahms, Liszt, Beethoven, and other composers. *Rare documents are generally conserved under special storage conditions and only occasionally displayed in the library's temporary exhibits.*

THE THOMAS JEFFERSON BUILDING

Exterior – This Beaux-Arts showplace occupies a full block across from the Capitol on 1st Street SE. At street level, the exuberant **Neptune Fountain** by Roland Hinton Perry depicts the sea god and his cavorting entourage.
The building's central section is vaulted by a massive green copper dome surmounted by a lantern that supports the symbolic "torch of learning" *(step back from the facade across 1st St. to view).* The intricate entrance stairway, replete with side flights, ornamented stone balustrades, and candelabras, provides a ceremonial access to the edifice. The granite facade, which resembles the 19C Paris Opera House, features a second-story portico of paired Corinthian columns and massive quoins, or corner stones. Busts depicting famous men of letters are framed in the oculi, or round openings, that punctuate the portico *(see illustration p 25).*

G. Cralle/Image Bank
The Main Reading Room

★★ **Interior** – Murals, sculptures, detailed mosaics, marble columns and floors, and vaulted corridors make the 2-story **Great Hall** one of the most impressive spaces in the city. The hall's vestibule is especially noteworthy for the gold leaf adorning its ceiling, while blue and amber stained-glass skylights punctuate the vaulting of the hall proper. A grand staircase sculpted with elaborate bas-relief cherubs leads to the second-story colonnade, where a visitors' gallery overlooks the Main Reading Room.
Occupying the vast rotunda under the library dome (height: 160ft from floor to lantern), the **Main Reading Room** is ringed by colossal Corinthian columns and arched windows, embellished with stained-glass state seals and eagles. In the lantern of the coffered dome is an allegorical mural entitled *Human Understanding.* The eight 11ft stone statues between the arches symbolize such subjects as commerce, law, poetry, and science. Sixteen bronze statues along the balustrade of the galleries represent pivotal figures in the development of civilization.

★ FOLGER SHAKESPEARE LIBRARY

Michelin map 48 K12 *time: 1/2 hour*

201 E. Capitol St. SE. M Capitol South or Union Station. Open Mon–Sat 10am–4pm; closed Sun and Federal holidays. Free admission. Guided tour (30min) 11am. ♿ ☎544-7077.

The world's largest collection of Shakespeare's works is conserved behind this Art Deco exterior. Renowned as a research institution, the Folger also encourages a larger public appreciation of the traditions of Elizabethan England and the Renaissance through its program of exhibits, concerts, readings, and theater performances.

The Folger Bequest – The son of a Martha's Vineyard schoolmaster, Henry Clay Folger became a lifetime devotee of Shakespeare while attending Amherst College. There, in 1879, inspired by a lecture given by the aging Ralph Waldo Emerson, Folger bought a volume of Shakespeare's complete works.
Ten years later, he made his first serious Shakespeare acquisition: a 1685 Fourth Folio edition purchased at an auction for $107.50. At the time, his finances were such that he was forced to request 30 days to raise the money. Through the years, however, his fortunes steadily increased, and he eventually became chairman of the board of the Standard Oil Company of New York.
His wife and co-collector, Emily Jordan, was a schoolteacher and student of literature. She was particularly interested in acquiring different copies of the 1623 First Folio, the first collected edition of Shakespeare's plays, for the sake of scholarly comparison.

In the 1920s, the Folgers, who lived in New York state, began searching in both England and America for a site to establish a research library. They ultimately chose this nation's capital, and in 1930, the cornerstone was laid. Folger himself did not live to see the 1932 opening of the building that housed the 75,000 books, manuscripts, prints, and engravings he and his wife had collected. Mrs Folger continued to be active with the library until her death in 1936. The ashes of both are interred in the library, which today is administered by the trustees of Amherst College.

The Library's Holdings – *Research facilities are not open to the general public.* The Folger now owns some 275,000 books and manuscripts relating to the Renaissance period in England and other European countries. About a third of its holdings are considered rare, the most valuable being the only known copy of Shakespeare's early play, *Titus Andronicus.* It was discovered in a cottage in Sweden and purchased for $10,000 by the Folgers in 1905.
The library holds 79 of the 240 first editions of the collected works of Shakespeare that are known to exist (Japan's Meisei University, the next largest owner of first editions, owns only eight). The library also owns theatrical memorabilia—playbills, costumes, promptbooks, etc.—from 18C and 19C Shakespearean productions.

Title page of 1623 First Folio

Folger Shakespeare Library

The Building – Paul Cret incorporated classical elements in this simple Art Deco marble facade, winning numerous accolades from fellow architects for the "traditional modernism" of his design. Nine long rectangular windows covered in a geometrical grillwork are offset by bas-relief underpanels depicting scenes from Shakespeare's plays. Chiseled into the facade, above the windows, are quotes about the bard and above the two entrances, the masks of Tragedy and Comedy. Along the Second Street side of the building is a free-standing marble statue of the character Puck from *A Midsummer Night's Dream,* inscribed with his famous quote "Lord, what fools these mortals be."

Interior – The 190ft-long **Great Hall**, with oak paneling and a barrel-vaulted ceiling reminiscent of a Tudor gallery, features a changing series of exhibits based on the books, manuscripts, and memorabilia in the library's collection.
The east end of the building houses a reproduction of an **Elizabethan theatre**, its stage flanked by wooden columns. The Folger Consort, a resident chamber music ensemble, holds scheduled performances in the theater and in the Great Hall. The library also sponsors a rich program of poetry and fiction readings.
Outside, the small Elizabethan Garden features a knot garden and plants well known in Shakespeare's day *(by guided tour only, Apr–Oct, the third Sat of the month at 10 and 11am).*

★ UNION STATION

Michelin map 48 H12 — *time: 1/2 hour*

40 Massachusetts Ave. NE. M *Union Station. Public areas open daily 24 hours.* P ♿ ✗ ☎*371-9441.*

When the first trains pulled into this monumental granite terminal in 1907, it was the largest train station in the world, measuring 760ft by 344ft, and an embodiment of the oft-quoted premise of its architect, **Daniel H. Burnham** (1846-1912), "make no little plans." Burnham designed the station with the colossal columns, arches, and statues that characterize the Beaux-Arts style, of which he was a leading proponent. For half a century Union Station served as the city's main point of arrival, greeting soldiers, presidents, government representatives, and royalty, as well as a steady flow of tourists.
With the demise of rail travel in the 1950s and 60s, the station steadily deteriorated. A renovation done in the 1970s met with much criticism, and an entirely new revamping was begun in 1986. The large-scale restoration project, which returned the station to its original splendor, was completed in 1988 at a cost of $160 million. In addition to being the main railway terminal for the metropolitan area, the station also houses scores of shops, eateries, and a cinema complex.

The Building – A fountained plaza featuring a statue of Columbus and the Freedom Bell (a replica of the Liberty Bell) fronts the station, whose triple-arched, colonnaded entrance is modeled after Rome's Arch of Constantine. Another ancient Roman monument, the Baths of Diocletian, served as the inspiration for the station's cavernous **main hall**. A vaulted ceiling with gilded octagonal coffers soars 96ft, and 36 statues of Roman legionnaires look down from the second-story balcony rimming the hall.

★ NATIONAL POSTAL MUSEUM

Michelin map 48 H11 *time: 1 hour*

Massachusetts Ave and 1st St. NE. M Union Station. Open daily 10am–5:30pm; closed Dec 25. Free admission. Guided tours (1 hour) available. ♿ ☎357-2991.

Occupying part of the ground floor of the stately Beaux-Arts **City Post Office Building** next to Union Station, the Smithsonian's newest museum houses the world's largest philatelic collection and chronicles America's mail service from colonial times to the present.

A gift of Confederate postage stamps initiated the Smithsonian's philatelic collection in 1886. By 1908, the growing assemblage was housed on the Mall in the ARTS AND INDUSTRIES BUILDING and in 1964, was transferred to the NATIONAL MUSEUM OF AMERICAN HISTORY. The landmark City Post Office Building (1914, Daniel Burnham), was chosen as the site for a new museum, which was established in 1990 by the joint efforts of the US Postal Service and the Smithsonian. It opened in 1993 after extensive renovation to the building, which also houses a large postal facility and other government offices. At present, the museum comprises a research library, a theater, and a discovery center, as well as its six galleries, a stamp shop, and a museum shop.

Visit – The 16-million item collection includes historic postal artifacts, personal letters, photographs, and transport vehicles, in addition to rare stamps and premiere covers. Only a fraction of the collection is on display.

The lobby of the building, with its 40ft-high coffered ceiling, Ionic columns, and marble floors, provides a grand passageway to the exhibit area *(located on the lower level)*, which is entered through a polished bronze and stainless steel **escalator arcade**. Three vintage mail planes, suspended from the ceiling, dominate the 90ft glass **atrium** gallery, where a walk-through railroad car with mail sorting bins, a Concord-style mail coach, and a 1931 Model A Ford are also on view. The highlight in the **Stamps and Stories** gallery is the vault of philatelic rarities, such as the first prepaid stamps (1840) called "Penny Blues." Other galleries showcase a variety of postal memorabilia and mail-related novelties. A number of interactive videos, including an electronic souvenir postcard kiosk, invite visitor participation.

CAPITAL CHILDREN'S MUSEUM

Michelin map 48 G12 *time: 1 1/2 hours*

800 3rd St. NE. M Union Station. Open daily 10am–5pm; closed Jan 1, Easter Sunday, Thanksgiving Day and Dec 25. Admission: $6; children under 2 and seniors free. Guided tours (90min) 10am, 11:30am and 1pm (1-day advance reservation required). ♿ ✗ ☎543-8600.

This privately funded learning playground conceived for children between the ages of 2 and 12 features "hands on" exhibits that integrate the arts, sciences, humanities, and technology.

The whimsical **Sculpture Garden**, situated at the museum's entrance, is inhabited by fantastic human and animal figures crafted out of tiles, rocks, broken bracelets, and other scrap material by the Indian folk artist Nek Chand.

Inside, the flavor of Mexico is re-created in the International Hall *(2nd floor)*, where activities include preparing tortillas and petting a goat. The communications exhibit *(2nd and 3rd floors)*, which traces the history of transmitting information, features drums, a printing press, telephones, and a radio and television station. The Future Center *(3rd floor)* introduces young people to the world of computers. Special exhibits and workshops are scheduled throughout the year.

SEWALL-BELMONT HOUSE

Michelin map 48 J12 *time: 1/2 hour*

144 Constitution Ave. NE. M Union Station or Capitol South. Open Tue–Fri 10am–3pm, Sat, Sun and holidays noon–4pm; closed Jan 1, Thanksgiving Day and Dec 25. Free admission. Guided tours (20min) available. ☎546-3989.

Reputedly one of the oldest buildings on Capitol Hill, this gracious house was erected in 1800 by Robert Sewall around a pre-existing structure thought to date back to the late 17C. The residence remained in the Sewall family for 123 years and served as one of Washington's first social centers. Among its noted tenants was Albert Gallatin, Secretary of the Treasury under Presidents Jefferson and Madison. According to certain sources, Gallatin worked out the financial arrangements for the Louisiana Purchase on the premises. Over the years, the house has undergone major exterior and interior alteration.

In 1929, the building was purchased by the **National Woman's Party**, which has maintained its headquarters there ever since. Designated a National Historic Site, the building commemorates the women's movement with portraits and busts of the Suffragists, who fought for passage of the 19th Amendment (1920) granting women the right to vote.

2
★★★
The Mall

A sweeping greensward linking the nation's most revered monuments and museums, the Mall serves as the cultural heart of the capital and a political forum for the nation. Its imposing buildings and broad vistas underscore Washington's reputation as the "City Beautiful."

"A Vast Esplanade" – The city's designer, Pierre Charles L'Enfant, envisioned the Mall as a grand avenue extending from Jenkins Hill to the current site of the Washington Monument. L'Enfant's configuration of the Mall was in part determined by the courses of Tiber Creek and the Potomac, which at that time ran along present-day Constitution Avenue, 17th Street, and Maine Avenue. Until the mid-19C, little development took place here. Then in 1848, ground was broken for the WASHINGTON MONUMENT and a year later, for the Smithsonian CASTLE, paving the way for a growing institutional presence on the Mall. In 1850, Andrew Jackson Downing was commissioned to produce a landscape proposal for the Mall. Though his plan for intricate paths and gardens was not realized, his attempt at a cohesive design for the area influenced future plans.

After a severe flood in 1881, Congress appropriated funds for draining the Potomac flats south and west of the Mall and for dredging the Washington Channel. By the turn of the century, 621 acres had been reclaimed for the creation of Potomac Park, mandated by Congress "for the recreation and pleasure of the people." The Tidal Basin has been formed to ensure a flow of fresh water through the Washington Channel.

Early 20C Development – By 1900, the original Mall area was a labyrinth of then-fashionable walks and drives bordering the Smithsonian Castle, the National Museum (now the ARTS AND INDUSTRIES BUILDING), and several other governmental structures. A railroad station stood on the present site of the National Gallery of Art. The McMillan Commission *(see p 23)*, appointed in 1900 to assess the future development of the city, called for transforming the Mall into a broad tree-lined promenade.

Though the commission was unable to implement all of its improvements, it did succeed in negotiating the removal of the railroad facilities to the newly proposed UNION STATION. It also managed to protect the future 800ft-wide Mall greensward from encroachment by further construction, and it extended the boundaries of the Mall west by siting the planned memorial to Lincoln on the reclaimed flats of West Potomac Park. In 1917, to accommodate wartime exigencies, rows of barracks-like wooden structures known as "tempos" were constructed on and around the Mall. Although these temporary buildings were left standing until after World War II, the beautification of the Mall proceeded. In 1923, the Smithsonian opened the FREER GALLERY OF ART on the south side of the Mall, and then in 1941, the NATIONAL GALLERY OF ART rose on north side of the Mall, near the new NATIONAL ARCHIVES. The southwestern axis of the general Mall area was extended in the late 1930s when the JEFFERSON MEMORIAL was built on the shores of the Tidal Basin.

A Dream Realized – Following the war, gardens, monuments, and museums gradually replaced the unsightly tempos. Since the mid-1960s, the Smithsonian has added five new museums, and the National Gallery of Art has constructed its widely acclaimed East Building. West Potomac Park has been further developed, and in 1982, "the Wall" an eloquent monument to Vietnam veterans, was erected. Plans are currently underway for a new Smithsonian attraction, the National Museum of the American Indian. Opening in 2000, it will occupy the land east of the National Air and Space Museum, the last building site on the Mall.

Traditionally a rallying point for political demonstrations, the Mall also hosts major national events such as the 1979 visit of Pope John Paul II and the annual Independence Day celebration on the Fourth of July.

THE EAST MALL (1st-15th Streets)

The mile-long, tree-lined esplanade extending from the foot of Capitol Hill to 15th Street contains one of the world's densest concentrations of museums. The dominating presence here is the Smithsonian Institution, which operates eight important museums on the Mall proper. The independently administered NATIONAL GALLERY OF ART, comprising two structures, dominates the northeast corner of the Mall. Just off the Mall are such governmental institutions as the NATIONAL ARCHIVES, the BUREAU OF ENGRAVING AND PRINTING, and the US BOTANIC GARDEN. The eastern end of the Mall is anchored by the Capitol Reflecting Pool, overlooked by an equestrian statue of President Grant that commemorates his leadership of Union troops in the Civil War. On the south side of the Reflecting Pool is a memorial to President Garfield, and on the north an allegorical memorial to Peace.

Helpful Hints on the Mall – All museums and attractions on the Mall are free of charge. Smithsonian sights are open daily (closed Dec 25) from 10am–5:30pm. Street parking is allowed from 10am–10pm, with a 3-hour limit per car; spaces tend to be filled immediately after 10am, especially during the peak tourist seasons. Several Metro stations serve the Mall and make a visit here free of time restraints. The Tourmobile *(p 169)* also loops through the entire Mall area, including West Potomac Park, allowing visitors to get on and off at various sights. Due to the general proximity of the Mall museums to one another, touring the area on foot is recommended.

The Smithsonian Information Center *(p 43)* in the Castle building should be the first stop, as it is designed to help visitors plan their time on the Mall and elsewhere in the city. Cafes and cafeterias are located in many of the museums (indicated by the ✗ symbol in the sight descriptions that follow). Lines can be very long, so eating an early or late lunch is suggested. Street vendors along Independence Avenue also sell hot dogs, soft drinks, and snacks. On the Mall, there are a number of pleasant spots to enjoy a picnic lunch.

In late June and early July, the Smithsonian holds its annual Festival of American Folklife. From June through August, concerts are presented by military bands and other musical groups several times weekly in the Sylvan Theatre, an outdoor stage situated to the south of the Washington Monument *(see Calendar of Events p 160)*.

THE CASTLE Smithsonian Institution Building

Michelin map 48 K8 — *time: 1/2 hour*

Jefferson Dr. at 10th St. SW. M Smithsonian. Open daily 9am–5:30pm; closed Dec 25. Free admission. ♿ ✗ ☎357-2700.

The turreted red sandstone "castle" on the Mall has become the symbol of the **Smithsonian Institution**, the nation's preeminent museum and research complex. The building functions as a visitor information center providing orientation to the Smithsonian's many museums and to other Washington sights.

The Gift of an Englishman – The Smithsonian Institution is the brainchild of an Englishman who never visited America, **James Smithson** (1765-1829), an enlightened thinker and prominent Oxford scientist. As the illegitimate son of Elizabeth Macie and Hugh Smithson, the first duke of Northumberland, James Smithson spent the first 34 years of his life as James Macie. Eventually the British Crown granted his petition to bear the Smithson name.

Presumably due to the complications of his own lineage, Smithson wished to acknowledge blood ties before all else, and consequently left his wealth to his only surviving relative, a nephew. When the nephew died in 1835 without descendants, the remaining money went, as Smithson's will had stipulated, "to the United States of America, to found at Washington, under the name of the Smithsonian Institution, an Establishment for the increase and diffusion of knowledge among men." In making this generous bequest, James Smithson had prophesied, "My name shall live in the memory of men, when the titles of the Northumberlands...are extinct and forgotten."

A National Institution – In considering Smithson's unexpected bequest, some members of Congress opposed it, declaring it "beneath the dignity of the United States to receive presents of this kind." Thanks primarily to the efforts of John Quincy Adams, Congress finally passed a bill establishing the Smithsonian Institution in 1846, thereby ending years of heated debate. The bill called for the formation of a board of regents that would include the Chief Justice of the Supreme Court, the Vice President, members of both houses of Congress, and private citizens. Smithson's assets were converted into 105 bags of gold sovereigns, worth at the time roughly $515,000.

In 1846, Congress appointed the respected American physicist Joseph Henry as the Smithsonian's first secretary. During his controversial 32-year tenure, Henry resolutely insisted on focusing the Institution's role on scientific research rather than on museum development.

It was Henry's assistant secretary and successor, the biologist Spencer Fullerton Baird, who developed the Smithsonian as a Federal institution of public exhibitions. Over the decades, the Institution has grown through the generosity of major benefactors as well as the general public. Today, it is the largest museum network in the world, with an annual budget, from both trusts and Federal appropriations, of more than $445,000,000. Its 14 museums, of which eight are located on the Mall *(see list p 26)*, have total holdings of some 140,000,000 artifacts, works of art, and specimens. Exhibits range from Lindbergh's plane, the *Spirit of St Louis,* and Picasso paintings to a living coral reef and include such popular Americana as Archie Bunker's chair and the ruby slippers Judy Garland wore in the *Wizard of Oz.* The Smithsonian also administers the NATIONAL ZOOLOGICAL PARK.

Renwick's "Castle" – The Smithsonian's first building, a leading example of Romanesque Revival architecture, was designed by **James Renwick** in the late 1840s and completed in 1855. Inspired by 12C Norman architecture, the asymmetrical building is topped with nine towers that soar above a battlemented cornice. When it was first completed, the Castle housed research and administrative facilities, living quarters for scientists and Smithsonian personnel, and exhibit space.
In 1989, a renovation of the building's interior restored the **Great Hall**, with its flanking columned arches, to its original appearance. The Castle's state-of-the-art **information center** features a series of interactive touch screens and wall maps, as well as three-dimensional maps and an orientation film to help the visitor locate Washington attractions.
The Castle also houses administrative offices, in addition to the Woodrow Wilson International Center for Scholars, and a crypt containing the body of James Smithson, which was moved here in 1904. The **Children's Room**, refurbished with Victorian wicker furnishings, contains the original turn-of-the-century ceiling mural depicting a vine-covered arbor.

★★★ NATIONAL AIR AND SPACE MUSEUM

Michelin map 48 K9 *time: 1/2 day*

Independence Ave. at 6th St. SW. M *L'Enfant Plaza. Open daily 10am–5:30pm (extended hours in spring and summer); closed Dec 25. Free admission. Guided tours (1 1/4 hours) available.* ♿ ✗ ☎*357-2700.*

From Icarus' ill-fated flight to the far-flung space missions of recent decades, humans have attempted to conquer earth's relentless pull. This fascinating museum, commemorating man's aeronautical and astronautical achievements, welcomes more than eight million visitors annually, making it Washington's most popular museum.

The Smithsonian in the Vanguard of Flight – The Smithsonian's interest in flight dates back to the early days of the Institution. In 1861, the Smithsonian's first secretary, Joseph Henry, gave encouragement to Thaddeus Lowe in his balloon experiments, resulting in President Lincoln's decision to use balloons in the Civil War. Fifteen years later, a group of kites brought from China for the Philadelphia Centennial Exposition was given to the Smithsonian, and became the cornerstone of the National Aeronautical collection that evolved into the present National Air and Space Museum.
The appointment in 1887 of **Samuel Pierpont Langley** (1834-1906) as the third secretary of the Smithsonian was a key factor in the development of flight in the US. Though largely self-educated, Langley gained renown as an astronomer, inventor, writer, and eminent researcher by the time he joined the Smithsonian. In May 1896, his *Aerodrome No. 5* proved that sustained mechanical flight with a device heavier than air was feasible. Although criticized during his lifetime for a series of unsuccessful flight projects, Langley prepared the way for manned flight and what he forecast as "the great universal highway overhead." The results of Langley's lifetime research in the field of aeronautics are recorded in his influential work, *The Langley Memoir on Mechanical Flight* (1911).
In the 20C, the idea for a museum dedicated to the history of flight evolved from the concern that the aircraft used by the US Air Force in World War II would be relegated to the scrap heap. With congressional support, a conservation program was conceived, and in 1946, the National Air Museum was established by law "to memorialize the national development of aviation...." In 1966, the museum's scope was enlarged to include space flight.

The Building – Designed by the St Louis-based architect Gyo Obata, the building, which took four years to complete, opened in July 1976, as a part of the nation's bicentennial celebration. The unadorned structure, measuring 635ft by 225ft and nearly 83ft in height, comprises four massive rectangles connected by three glass "hyphens." The building is faced with Tennessee marble similar to that used on the NATIONAL GALLERY OF ART across the Mall. This spacious building contains 23 galleries, a theater, a planetarium, and a library. A glass annex housing a large dining facility was added to the building's east end in the late 1980s.

The Collections – The museum possesses hundreds of aircraft and space artifacts, including manned vehicles, rockets, launching devices, space probes, and satellites. As the museum has title to all flown US manned spacecraft, its holdings constitute by far the most comprehensive collection of its kind in the country. Major hanging exhibits, like the planes, are permanent, while other galleries are likely to change every two to three years. Smaller exhibits are added more frequently.
Authenticity is the keynote of the whole museum; all of the aircraft displayed are genuine, as are most of the spacecraft, except in those cases where it was impossible to recover the original object. In such instances, actual backup craft have been placed on exhibit.

A FLIGHT CHRONOLOGY

Air and spacecraft in the museum's collections appear in **bold.**

Beginnings

early16C	Leonardo da Vinci studies bird flight and draws plans for flying devices—precursors of the airplane, helicopter, and parachute.
1783	First manned balloon flight by the Montgolfier brothers in Paris.
1793	G. Washington witnesses the first US balloon flight in Philadelphia.
1861-65	Observation balloons are used in the Civil War.
1891-96	Otto Lilienthal makes 2,000 glides in weight-controlled monoplanes.
1896	The first successful engine-driven craft flight by Langley's Aerodrome No. 5 in Washington DC.

20C Innovations

1903	In Kitty Hawk, North Carolina, the Wright brothers successfully perform the first manned motorized flight in their **1903 Flyer**.
1909	Louis Bleriot crosses the English Channel in 36 minutes, flying a **Type XI monoplane**.
c.1910	Glenn H. Curtiss develops the first seaplanes, which are subsequently used by the US Navy.
1911	G.P. Rodgers makes the first coast-to-coast flight aboard the **Wright EX "Vin Fiz."**
1918	Scheduled airmail service begins with a route between New York City and Washington DC via Philadelphia.
1920	Beginning of regular passenger flights in Europe.
1923	The first nonstop coast-to-coast flight in the Dutch-built **Fokker T-2**.
1924	First round-the-world flight by two US Army **Douglas World Cruisers**.
1926	The first liquid propellant rocket is developed.
1927	Charles Lindbergh makes the first solo nonstop crossing of the Atlantic in the **Spirit of St Louis**, covering 3,610 miles in 33 1/2 hours.
1932	Amelia Earhart is the first woman to make a solo nonstop transatlantic flight.
1944	The Germans begin launching the **V-2**, the world's first long-range ballistic missile.
1947	Air Force pilot Chuck Yeager flies the **Bell X-I Glamorous Glennis** faster than the speed of sound.

Into the Space Age

1957	The Soviets launch **Sputnik 1**, the first artificial satellite.
1958	The Boeing 707, the first US jet, begins commercial service. Creation of the National Aeronautics and Space Administration (NASA)
1962	In **Friendship 7**, John Glenn is the first American to orbit the earth.
1965	Edward White traveling aboard **Gemini 4** capsule is the first American to walk in space.
1969	Astronauts fly **Apollo 11** to the moon and walk on its surface.
1970	Beginning of regular commercial service of the supersonic Concorde.
1973-74	The manned space missions of the **Skylab** orbital workshop conduct experiments and gather valuable data. Pioneer 10 is the first spacecraft to reach Jupiter.
1977	**Voyager 1** and 2 are launched to photograph the outer planets.
1979	Voyager 1 and 2 reach Jupiter.
1981	Voyager 2 reaches Saturn. Space shuttle Columbia is launched.
1986	Voyager 2 reaches Uranus.
1989	Galileo space probe is launched toward Jupiter.
1990	Magellan space probe begins mapping the surface of Venus. **Hubble Space Telescope** is launched into orbit.
1991	First close-up views of an asteroid obtained by Galileo probe.
1993	The longest Space Shuttle mission (14 days) is completed.

The Wright Brothers – A helicopter toy given as a present to young Wilbur (1867-1912) and Orville (1871-1948) Wright in 1878 sparked a passion for flight that remained with the brothers throughout their lives. As adults, the self-taught engineers were among many in the US and abroad dedicated to making manned flight a reality. Drawing heavily from the experiences of Otto Lilienthal and other predecessors, they developed the *1903 Flyer,* an aircraft controlled by "wing warping," or changing the shapes of the wing tips to deflect the air.

On December 17, 1903 in Kitty Hawk, North Carolina, their efforts succeeded. The longest of their four flights that day was 852ft in 59 seconds, after which a sudden gust of wind smashed the craft. There was little publicity about the Wright's breakthrough until 1905, but they patented their discovery and went on to build an airplane factory in Dayton, Ohio.

Museums on the Mall are open daily (except December 25) from 10am to 5:30pm (extended hours in spring and summer). Admission is free.

VISIT

First Floor

The spacious lobby is adorned with two spectacular murals. On the west wall, **Earthflight Environment** (A) by Eric Sloan depicts an ever-changing sky. On the east wall, Robert McCall painted **The Space Mural—A Cosmic View** (B) which represents his vision of the universe past, present, and future.

Before beginning your visit of the museum, go to the **Langley Theater** box office (C) to reserve a seat for one or several of the popular **films★** (including two classics: *The Dream is Alive* and *To Fly!*) that are shown on a rotating basis throughout the day *(admission: $3.25, seniors and children $2. Recorded information on films and screening times ☎357-1686).* The theater's IMAX projection system and five-story screen create the illusion of being airborne.

The three vast glass halls on the 1st floor contain several suspended artifacts (air and spacecraft), many of which are best viewed from the 2nd floor.

Milestones of Flight – In the large hall that occupies the central part of the building, several epoch-making airplanes and spacecraft are displayed. Among the highlights are the Wright Brothers' 1903 Flyer (2), Charles Lindbergh's *Spirit of St Louis* (3), Chuck Yeager's *Bell X-1 Glamorous Glennis* (4), John Glenn's *Friendship 7* (5) and *Apollo 11* (6). The exhibit also features a replica of the Soviet satellite *Sputnik* (7), a surprisingly small (22.8in) polished sphere with four rod-shaped antennae. Visitors can touch a 4-billion-year-old basalt moon rock (8) retrieved by the crew of *Apollo 17* in 1972.

Air Transportation – The key stages of air transport are illustrated by the colorful aircraft filling this hall. The sporty Pitcairn Mailwing (9) was designed specifically for short mail routes in the eastern US. The Ford Tri-Motor (10) was the airlines' favorite workhorse until the mid-40s. The DC-3 (11) is still in use as a passenger transporter. The Boeing 247 (12) is the first of the familiar series whose later models, the Stratoliners, could fly above turbulence on long flights.

The gallery devoted to **Vertical Flight** houses a fine collection of autogiros, helicopters, and other special craft. The **Golden Age of Flight** highlights the history of aviation between the two world wars. The Curtiss P-40E (13), a well-known World War II air-fighter plane, and an aerobatic Grumman Gulfhawk II (14) are hanging above the adjacent gallery, which features rotating exhibits of recently restored aircraft. In **Jet Aviation,** the mural (D) spanning the length of the wall depicts 27 planes, from the Heinkel HE (1939) to the Concorde (1971) and the Airbus Industry A300B (1972). Opposite the mural, there are three jet fighters: a Messerschmitt Me262 (15), a Lockheed XP-80 (16), and an FH-I Phantom (17). **Early Flight** displays craft in a facsimile of a 1913 indoor aeronautical exhibition. Among other planes located in this gallery are a glider (1894) designed by Lilienthal, the Wright 1909 Military Flyer (18), which was the world's first military airplane, and a Bleriot Type XI monoplane (19).

Cross the entrance hall to the east wing.

The development of flight research aircraft is chronicled in **Flight Testing**. The development of aerial photography and its practical applications are presented in **Looking at Earth.** A Lockheed U-2 is on display, along with interactive touch screens that show a Landsat view of each of the 50 states.

Space Hall – Large rockets, guided missiles, and manned spacecraft are featured in this exhibit. On display are a model of the Columbia Space Shuttle (20) as well as the *Apollo-Soyuz* spacecraft (21) used for a joint docking-in-space experiment with the Russians in 1975. Visitors can walk through the Skylab Orbital Workshop (22) *(accessible from the 2nd floor).*

Washington, DC Convention & Visitors Assoc.

Air Transportation Hall

Rocketry and Space Flight displays historic rockets, engines for missiles and spacecraft, some exotic rocket engines, and a variety of space suits. The east end is occupied by **Lunar Exploration Vehicles**. Although the Apollo Lunar Module (**23**) was never sent into space, it was nevertheless used for ground testing. In the **Stars** gallery, it is possible to view the tools of astronomy from age-old artifacts to modern space telescopes.

Second Floor

Pioneers of Flight – This open gallery houses planes that made historic flights. Among the artifacts displayed is Galbraith Perry Rodgers' Wright EX *Vin Fiz* (**24**), named after a grape drink his sponsor was making at the time. This plane was the first to succeed in a coast-to-coast flight, albeit with many stops and repairs. Rodgers crossed the continent from September 17 to November 5, 1911, covering 4,321 miles in 82 hours with an average speed of 52 mph. The *Fokker T-2* (**25**), built in the Netherlands and modified in the US, was the first to fly nonstop coast-to-coast. On May 2-3, 1923, this plane, manned with two pilots, flew almost 27 hours at an average speed of 92 mph. The biplane Douglas World Cruiser *Chicago* (**26**), and its companion craft *New Orleans* (owned by the Santa Monica Museum of Flying), were the first airplanes to go around the world, logging 27,553 miles in 175 days from April 6 to September 28, 1924. **Amelia Earhart** (1898-1937), the legendary aviator who lost her life in the South Pacific while attempting a round-the-world flight, set two world records with her bright red Lockheed Vega 5B (**27**) in 1932. In May of that year, Earhart became the first woman to fly alone nonstop across the Atlantic, covering a total of 2,026 miles, in less than 15 hours. Three months later (August 24-25), she flew solo the 2,448 miles between Los Angeles and Newark in 19 hours.

SECOND FLOOR

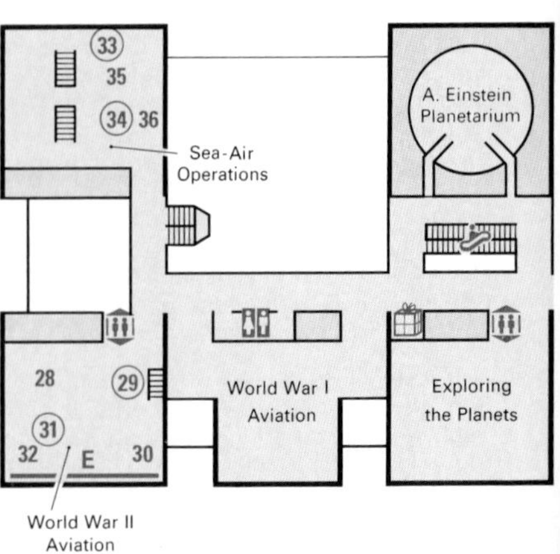

FIRST FLOOR

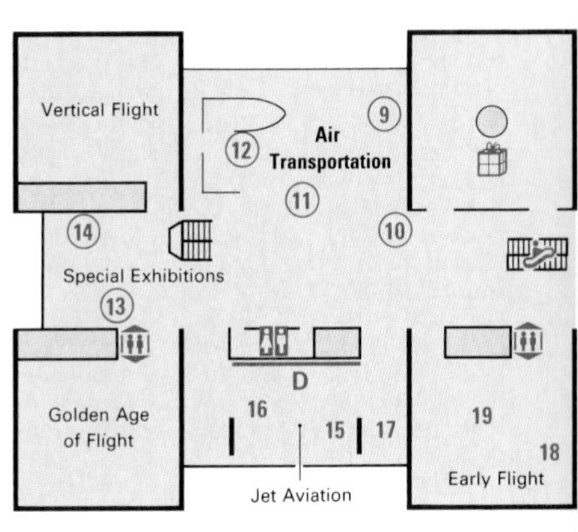

The **Albert Einstein Planetarium** features regularly scheduled shows and special presentations during which the heavens are simulated on a 70ft overhead dome, and discoveries of past centuries are re-created. *(Open daily 10:50am–4:50pm. Admission: $3.25, seniors and children $2. Recorded information ☎357-1686.)*

A replica of the *Voyager 1* probe is the main attraction of **Exploring the Planets**, which presents an introduction to the solar system. Some of the airplanes that determined the fate of nations can be viewed in **World War II Aviation**. Displays here include a Messerschmitt Bf 109 (**28**) a Mitsubishi Zero (**29**), a Supermarine Spitfire (**30**), a Macchi 202 (**31**), and a North American P-51 D Mustang (**32**). The mural (**E**) was executed by Keith Ferris in 1976. **Sea-Air Operations** is a reproduction of a carrier hangar deck, and features some of the most important fighters of World War II including the Boeing F4B-4 (**33**), the Douglas SBD-6 Dauntless divebomber (**34**), the Douglas A-4C Skyhawk (**35**), and the Grumman FM-1 Wildcat (**36**).

Return to the Pioneers of Flight gallery and continue to the east side.

The story of US manned space flight programs from Project Mercury to *Apollo 17* is retold in **Apollo to the Moon**. Lunar samples are displayed along with a variety of space suits and lunar surface equipment such as a prototype of *Apollo 15*'s Lunar Rover. The rotating exhibit entitled **Flight in the Arts** features artists' interpretations of themes related to flight. **Beyond the Limits: Flight Enters the Computer Age** is devoted to the increasing use of computers in aerospace technology, highlighting their importance in such areas as air testing, aerodynamics, manufacturing, and simulation. The exhibit features interactive displays and the Cray Serial 14 computer used from 1978 to 1986 at the National Center for Atmospheric Research.

NATIONAL AIR AND SPACE MUSEUM

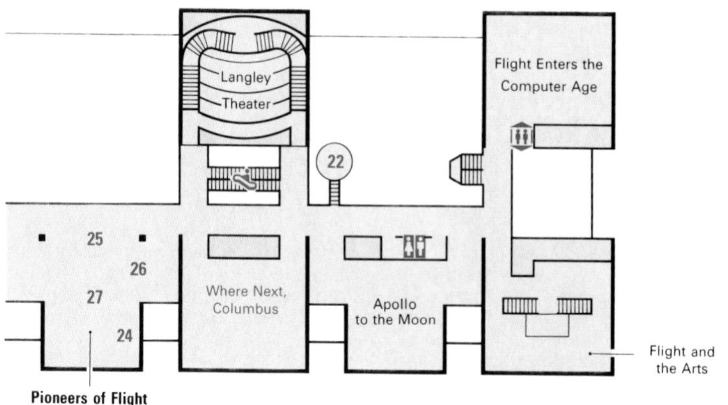

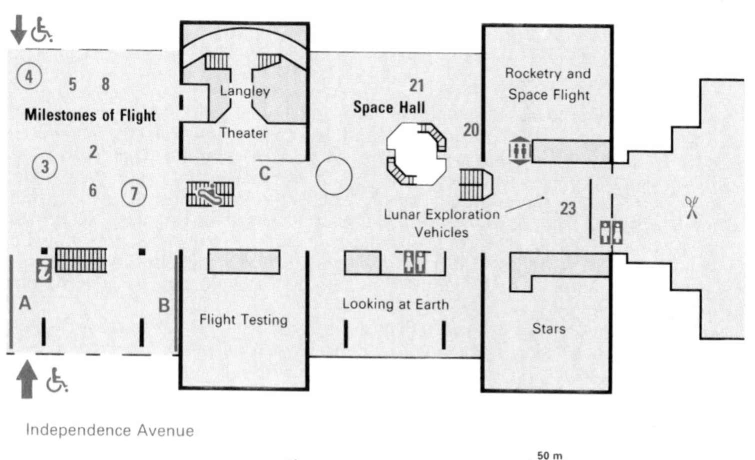

PAUL E. GARBER PRESERVATION, RESTORATION AND STORAGE FACILITY *map p 165* (BZ)

3904 Old Silver Hill Rd., Suitland, Maryland. Seven miles from the Mall. From Downtown drive southeast on Pennsylvania Ave. One mile past I-295 turn right on Branch Ave. and continue until reaching Iverson Mall. Turn left on Silver Hill Rd. and left on Old Silver Hill Rd. Visit by guided tour (3 hours) only Mon–Fri 10am, Sat and Sun 10am, 1pm (2-week advance reservation required); closed Dec 25. Free admission. P ♿ ☎*357-2700.*

Paul Garber joined the museum in 1920 and was a motivating force for over 70 years. It was his idea to send a cable to Charles Lindbergh in Paris before the pilot landed in that city, asking him to donate the *Spirit of St Louis* to the nation's aircraft collection. Lindbergh agreed, and the following year the historic aircraft entered the Smithsonian's collection. Garber's artful machinations finally brought the Wright Brothers' *1903 Flyer* to the Smithsonian in 1948, from the London Science Museum, where it had been on display for 20 years.

The facility has been used as a storage and restoration center since the 1950s, but today, it also serves as a "no frills" **museum** where visitors can see skilled craftsmen at work as well as the many of the holdings not on view at the National Air and Space Museum on the Mall. Among the over 150 artifacts on display are a MiG-15, the Soviet jet fighter used in the Korean War; a Curtiss JN-4D Jenny, the World War I trainer made famous by barnstormers in the postwar period; a Hawker Hurricane IIC, a World War II British fighter of the kind used in the Battle of Britain; and a J-2 engine, one of the powerplants for the Saturn launch vehicles. Also conserved here is the **Enola Gay**, the Boeing B-29 SuperFortress that dropped the world's first nuclear bomb on Hiroshima on August 6, 1945.

The P symbol indicates that on-site parking (generally free) is available.

★★★ NATIONAL GALLERY OF ART

Michelin map 48 J9-J10 *time: 4 hours*

Madison Dr. between 3rd and 7th Sts. NW. M *Archives. Open Mon–Sat 10am–5pm, Sun 11am–6pm; closed Jan 1, Dec 25. Free admission.* ♿ ✕ ☎ *737-4215.*

One of the world's preeminent museums, the National Gallery houses an outstanding collection of masterpieces that trace the development of Western art from the Middle Ages to the present. The original West Building concentrates primarily on European works from the 13C through the early 20C. Its contemporary counterpart, the East Building, highlights the works of modern artists.

HISTORICAL NOTES

One Man's Dream – The financier, industrialist, and statesman **Andrew Mellon** (1855-1937) was the impetus behind the National Gallery of Art. Mellon began collecting art in the 1870s, traveling to Europe with his friend Henry Clay Frick, benefactor of the famed Frick Collection *(see Michelin Green Guide to New York City)*, for the purpose of acquiring 17C and 18C paintings. In the late 1920s, while serving as secretary of the treasury, Mellon conceived of endowing a National Gallery of Art. From that time until his death in 1937, he became one of the world's foremost collectors of art. His intent was to amass masterpieces that would show the development of Western art, from the 13C through the 19C. Among his acquisitions were 21 works from the Hermitage Gallery in Leningrad. They included paintings by such masters as Raphael, Titian, Velazquez, and Rembrandt.
In 1937, Congress granted a charter to the new National Gallery of Art and pledged funds to support it. The stately building erected on the Mall was a gift from Mellon to the American people. Further, Mellon left the museum an endowment, 141 paintings, and a collection of fine 15 to 16C Italian sculpture. The National Gallery's original building (today known as the West Building) opened to the public in March 1941.

Other Benefactors – Following Mellon's lead, other major American collectors have contributed to the gallery. Many of these collectors were active early in the 20C, when outstanding works of art were more readily available in the marketplace. Consequently, they were able to assemble private collections rich in the works of Old Masters and Impressionists. Joseph Widener gave the renowned Widener family collection of painting, sculpture, and decorative arts to the National Gallery in the 1930s. Samuel Kress, a self-made business magnate, already had plans drawn up for a museum in New York City to house his superb Italian paintings and sculptures when he was persuaded in 1939 to donate his collection to the uncompleted National Gallery.
Works by French Impressionists and post-Impressionists were donated by financier Chester Dale; Lessing J. Rosenwald left the gallery 25,000 prints and drawings; and Col and Mrs Edgar Garbisch gave a collection of American primitives. More than 150 donors have contributed works of art to the National Gallery's holdings.

A New Building – In only 30 years, the expanding collections had outgrown the gallery's more than 100,000sq ft of floor space in the original building. Mellon's son Paul, along with various Mellon family foundations, funded construction of a second building on the Mall just east of the original one. The $95,000,000 East Building opened in 1978. Devoted to 20C works, it has established the National Gallery's reputation as a vital center for the presentation and appreciation of modern art.

The Collections – The gallery's collections include an estimated 2,827 paintings, 1,956 pieces of sculpture, 556 pieces of decorative art, and over 47,000 works on paper. Roughly 50 percent of these holdings are on display at one time. The Italian works constitute one of the finest collections of its kind in the world. The gallery's *Ginevra de' Benci* represents the only painting by Leonardo da Vinci in the Western Hemisphere. Though Federal funds support museum operations and maintenance, the National Gallery functions as an independent institution, all of its acquisitions being made through private means.

WEST BUILDING *time: 3 hours*

Main entrance on the Mall between 7th and 4th Sts. NW.

The capital's leading proponent of Classical Revival architecture, John Russell Pope, designed this formidable domed structure. The West Building's appeal derives from the five shades of glowing pink Tennessee marble incorporated in its facade. Windowless and sober, the exterior is adorned only by simple portals and pilasters. Ionic porticos highlight the north and south sides. The 785ft-long edifice ranks as one of the world's largest marble structures.

Collection highlights are indicated in green.

Main Floor

Flanking the entrance hall are an information center *(left)* and the **Founders' Room** *(right)*, a lounge hung with portraits of major benefactors. The hall leads to the **rotunda**, where green-black Tuscan marble columns surround a fountain whose centerpiece is a statue of Mercury. The broad sculpture halls of the building's two wings extend from the rotunda past the galleries, culminating in garden courts. The **East Sculpture Hall** features marble statuary, while works in bronze are displayed in the **West Sculpture Hall**.

Florentine and Central Italian Renaissance – *Galleries 1-15, and 20.* Representing the evolution of Western painting from 1200 to 1350, this section begins with the stylized Byzantine iconography that developed in Constantinople, capital of the Eastern Roman Empire and cradle of the Orthodox faith. The **icons**, or devotional images, are painted in egg tempera on wooden panels and enhanced with gold leaf. The Byzantine tradition transplanted in Italy gave rise to a more natural style. The Sienese school, whose most influential master was Duccio di Buoninsegna (1255-1318), is particularly well-represented in the collection. In the late 13C, Florentine artists, notably Giotto (c.1266-c.1337), developed a realistic rendering of space that ushered in the Italian Renaissance. Gradually, strict iconography was replaced with more sensual paintings depicting Biblical allegories, and secular portraiture. In the Quattrocento (15C), Florentine artists like Fra Filippo Lippi, and Botticelli looked to classical antiquity for its scientific notions of anatomy and perspective. The High Renaissance of the early 16C, the Cinquecento, attained an unparalleled level of delicacy and grace, enhanced by the manipulation of light and shadow as expressed in the art of such masters as Leonardo da Vinci (1452-1519) and Raphael (1483-1520) *(gallery 20).*

The Alba Madonna by Raphael
National Gallery of Art

Madonna and Child	Giotto	c.1320-1330
Adoration of the Magi	Fra Angelico and Fra Filippo Lippi	c.1445
Giuliano de' Medici	Botticelli	c.1478
Ginevra de' Benci	Leonardo da Vinci	c.1474
The Small Cowper Madonna	Raphael	c.1505
The Alba Madonna	Raphael	c.1510

Italian Sculpture and Furniture – *Galleries 9, 11, and 14.* The marble, bronze, wood, porphyry, and painted terra-cotta sculpture (13-16C) displayed here closely follows the evolution in Italian painting: the earlier pieces depict religious themes, while in later works, portrait busts, particularly of prominent Florentines, begin to appear. Among the furnishings exhibited are elaborately carved chests or *cassoni* (16C).

Lorenzo de' Medici	Andrea del Verrocchio	c.1478

Venetian and Northern Italian Renaissance – *Galleries 16-28.* The Renaissance that began in 15C Florence spread to northern Italy, in part through the works of Andrea Mantegna (1431-1506). His bold lines and sense of perspective influenced artists in Ferrara and Venice. Another very different innovation in Venetian art of the 15C came from Giorgione (c.1478-1510), whose delicate use of color gave this period its characteristic style. Giorgione's teacher, Giovanni Bellini (c.1427-1516), preferred the three-quarter portrait to the traditional Renaissance profile, thus allowing more expression of emotion and character. The 16C is dominated by the prolific master Titian (c.1490-1576), whose outstanding talent was sought after by the leading European rulers of the day. Tintoretto (1518-1594) carried innovations of his predecessors further with his own impressionistic, emotionally charged paintings. The allegorical representation of religious figures and classical gods and goddesses against a pastoral setting became the predominant subject of Northern Italian art, sensuality and color its hallmarks.

The Adoration of the Shepherds	Giorgione	c.1505-1510
The Feast of the Gods	Giovanni Bellini and Titian	1514
Venus and Adonis	Titian	c.1560
Doge Andrea Gritti	Titian	c.1546-1548

17-18C Italian Painting – *Galleries 29-33.* Marked by the creative vision of Annibale Carracci (1560-1609), 17C Bologna was the birthplace of the exuberant art of the Baroque, which had its greatest flowering in papal Rome. In the next century, Giovanni Battista Tiepolo (1696-1770) refined the Baroque's expansiveness into a

NATIONAL GALLERY OF ART

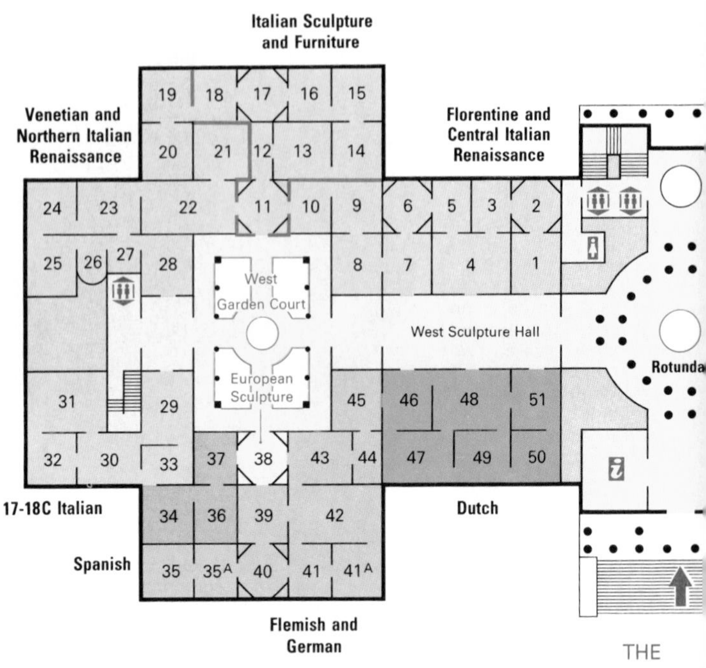

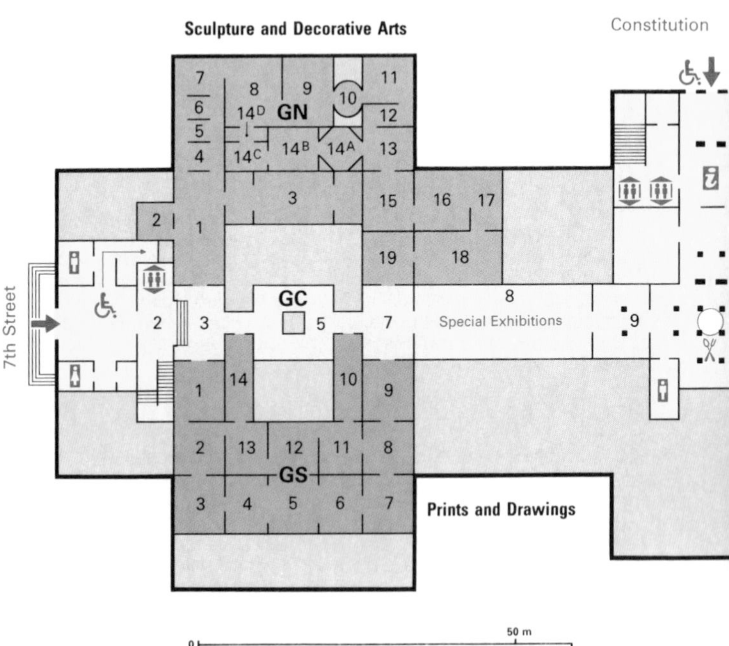

lighter and more decorative style. Tiepolo's frescoes adorned ceilings throughout Europe, but his genius marked the end of Italian dominance in art. Thereafter, the main innovations in art came from new centers in northern Europe. Also popular in 18C Italy were detailed cityscapes and architectural representations, such as those of Canaletto and Panini, which reflected fashionable interests in the Grand Tour of Italian antiquities. Featured in gallery 32 are works by French artists Nicholas Poussin *(p 52)* and Claude Lorrain *(p 52)*, both of whom lived and painted in Rome.

River Landscape	Annibale Carracci	c.1590
Scene from Ancient History	Tiepolo	c.1749
The Porta Portello, Padua	Canaletto	c.1741
Holy Family on the Steps	Poussin	1648

West Building

MAIN FLOOR

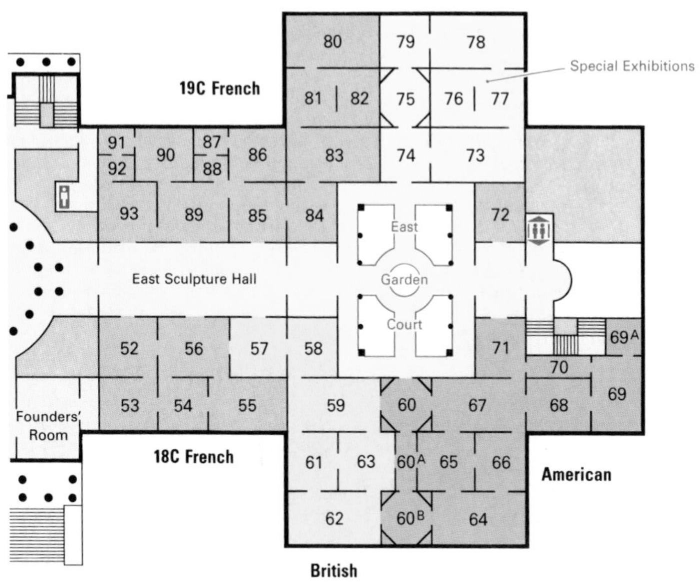

GROUND FLOOR

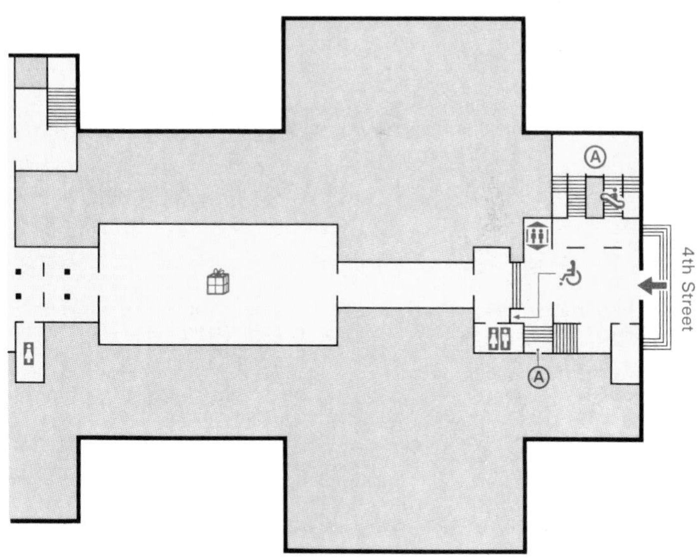

Ⓐ to Concourse East Building,

Spanish Painting – *Galleries 34-37, and 52.* Restraint characterizes the work of most Spanish artists during the 16C, with the notable exception of El Greco (c.1541-1614). Born on the island of Crete and trained in Venice, El Greco is nonetheless considered a Spanish artist, whose elongated shapes and religious fervor distinguish his unique style.

The preeminent 17C Spanish artist Diego Velázquez (1599-1660) obtained in his later works "impressionistic" effects of color and light that foreshadow 19C stylistic trends. A court painter, Velázquez was renowned for his portraits of the Spanish royal family.

In the 18C, Francisco de Goya (1746-1828) *(gallery 52)* was Madrid's most fashionable portraitist. His early works reflect the light-hearted rococo spirit of the period, while his more probing later portraits anticipate the psychological expressionism of the 20C.

Laocoön	El Greco	c.1610
The Needlewoman	Velázquez	c.1640
Two Women at a Window	Murillo	c.1655
Teresa Louise de Sureda	Goya	c.1803

Gallery 38 is devoted to European sculpture from the 14C and 15C.

Flemish and German Painting – *Galleries 35-41A.* During the 15C, Flanders, in what is now part of Belgium, was a leading artistic center, thanks largely to Jan van Eyck (c.1390-1441). A technical virtuoso, van Eyck mastered the representation of interior space, and, more importantly, is credited with having revolutionized painting by employing oil, as opposed to tempera, as the medium. This innovation, which allowed more subtlety in brushwork, attracted artists from throughout Europe to Flanders, among them Hans Memling, whose delicate and serene paintings enjoyed great popularity. Another Flemish master, Rogier van der Weyden (c.1400-1464), achieved a virtuosity of brushstroke that influenced generations.
Albrecht Dürer (1471-1528), the preeminent German artist of the late 15C and early 16C, has been called the "Leonardo of the North." Renowned throughout Europe, Dürer was recognized as a master printmaker as well as an outstanding painter. Dürer's contemporary Matthias Grünewald the Elder (c.1475-1528) was a matchless interpreter of religious intensity, while Lucas Cranach (1472-1553) was renowned for both his religious works and his portraits.

Portrait of a Lady	van der Weyden	c.1460
Portrait of a Clergyman	Dürer	1516
The Small Crucifixion	Grünewald	c.1511
"Diane de Poitiers"	François Clouet	c.1571

Dutch Painting – *Galleries 42-51.* The robust vitality of Peter Paul Rubens (1577-1640) dominates the 17C Flemish Baroque. An artist of great versatility, Rubens enjoyed international renown for his allegories and portraits. His student Anthony van Dyck (1539-1641) became one of Europe's most celebrated portrait painters.
Among the numerous painters of the varied styles and genres developed in 17C Holland, Rembrandt van Rijn (1606-1669) stands out as the abiding genius of this time. His mastery of chiaroscuro—the subtle play of light and shadow—influenced art for two centuries. *The Mill,* considered one of Rembrandt's finest landscapes, profoundly affected the work of 19C British artists such as J. W. M. Turner *(gallery 57)* and Sir Joshua Reynolds *(gallery 59).* Rembrandt's deeply psychological approach to portraiture takes the inventiveness of a slightly earlier Dutch artist, Frans Hals (c.1580-1666), a step farther. Employing lively brushwork, Hals had broken with the staid portraiture of the past to show his sitters with striking informality. Jan Vermeer (1632-1675), another Dutch genius, used light and space in such a way that his scenes of the upper middle classes are infused with an ethereal quality. The numerous still lifes, landscapes, and genre paintings that were produced by Dutch artists in the 17C often had allegorical meaning underlying their apparent realism.

Daniel in the Lions' Den	Rubens	c.1615
Willem Coymans	Frans Hals	1645
Self-Portrait	Rembrandt	1659
The Mill	Rembrandt	c.1650
Woman Holding a Balance	Vermeer	c.1664

18C French Painting – *Galleries 53-56.* During the reign of Louis XIV, the French Academy controlled all aspects of cultural life, and traditions of classicism prevailed in art. The most noted proponent of classicism, Nicolas Poussin (1594-1665) *(gallery 32),* worked much of his life in Italy, yet strongly influenced French art. His works depict harmoniously composed subjects set against an Arcadian backdrop. Claude Lorrain (1600-82) *(gallery 32)* shared Poussin's love of landscape but gave it a nostalgic interpretation. The Le Nain brothers concentrated on realistic genre paintings. By the early 18C, Paris had become the cultural hub of Europe, and the French rococo style was the fashion. This florid style is best exemplified in the work of Antoine Watteau (1684-1721), who created whimsically poetic images that emphasized color and depicted the sophisticated manners of 18C French society. Later, Boucher (1703-1770) introduced new sensuous pastoral reveries, while Boucher's student Jean-Honore Fragonard (1732-1806) focused on French subjects, representing them in quick, colorful brushstrokes. Traditional classicism persisted, however, in the works of Jacques-Louis David (1748-1825) and Auguste-Dominique Ingres (1780-1867).

Italian Comedians	Watteau	c.1720
A Young Girl Reading	Fragonard	c.1776
Madame Bergeret	Boucher	1746

19C French Painting – *Galleries 72, 80-93.* In the early 19C, the French Academy sanctioned the classicism of David and Ingres, but artists such as Delacroix (1798-1863) and Corot (1796-1875) rebelled against such conventions, painting romantic landscapes in their own idiom. Gustave Courbet (1819-1877), Honore Daumier (1808-1879), and Edouard Manet (1832-1883) discarded romanticism in favor of an unsentimental realism that depicted everyday scenes. A group of young painters inspired by Manet's example broke from the state-sponsored Salon exhibitions in 1874 to show their works independently. Known as the **Impressionists** because of their unprecedented exploration of atmospheric light and color in natural landscapes and figure painting, the group was informally led by Claude Monet (1840-1926) and Auguste Renoir (1841-1919). Edgar Degas (1834-1917) and Henri de Toulouse-Lautrec (1864-1901) depicted contemporary Parisian nightlife. Gauguin (1848-1903), Cézanne (1839-1906), and Van Gogh (1853-1890) each developed a highly personal style that was little appreciated in their own time but had a profound effect on the development of modern art.

Agostina	Corot	c.1866
Gare Saint-Lazare	Manet	1873
Woman with a Parasol–Madame Monet and Her Son	Monet	1875
A Girl with a Watering Can	Renoir	1876
La Mousmé	Van Gogh	1888
Quadrille at the Moulin Rouge	Toulouse-Lautrec	1892
Fatata te Miti (By the Sea)	Gauguin	1892
The Boating Party	Mary Cassatt	1893-94
The Artist's Father	Cézanne	1866
Four Dancers	Degas	c.1899

British Painting – *Galleries 57-61.* British painting first achieved a distinctive voice in the mid-18C with William Hogarth (1697-1764), whose works depicted the London middle classes. Later in the century, Thomas Gainsborough (1727-1788) created his softly romantic portraits of English nobility, while his rival Sir Joshua Reynolds (1723-1792) adopted the formal grandeur of the Baroque in his portraiture.
In landscape painting, the works of J.M.W. Turner (1775-1851), executed in swirls of colored light, are dramatically charged. The landscapes of his contemporary John Constable (1776-1837) are executed with scientific realism but convey a pastoral tranquillity. Both artists influenced the work of the French Impressionists.

Lady Caroline Howard	Sir Joshua Reynolds	1778
Miss Juliana Willoughby	George Romney	1781-83
Mrs Richard Brinsley Sheridan	Gainsborough	1785-87
Wivenhoe Park, Essex	Constable	1816
Keelmen Heaving in Coals by Moonlight	Turner	1835
A Scene from The Beggar's Opera	Hogarth	1728-29

American Painting – *Galleries 59-71.* Like British painting of the 18C and early 19C, American art focuses on portraiture in the grand manner. Eminent artists of this period include Benjamin West, Thomas Sully, Charles Wilson Peale, John Singleton Copley, and Gilbert Stuart, sometimes called the "court portraitist to the young Republic" because of his many paintings of early leaders.
By the mid-19C, landscape painting emerged as the dominant force in American art, with painters such as Thomas Cole and Frederic Church (1826-1900) depicting the awe-inspiring natural wonders of the New World. Highly personal expression, as evidenced in the works of Winslow Homer (1836-1910) and the mystical paintings of Albert Pinkham Ryder (1847-1917), followed later in the century. European influence and particularly Impressionism are seen in the works of James McNeill Whistler and John Singer Sargent, all of whom lived and studied abroad.

The Skater	Gilbert Stuart	1782
Rubens Peale with a Geranium	Rembrandt Peale	1801
Breezing Up	Winslow Homer	1876
The White Girl	James McNeill Whistler	1862
Siegfried and the Rhine Maidens	Albert Pinkham Ryder	1888-91
Both Members of This Club	George Bellows	1909
Repose	John Singer Sargent	1911
Autumn–On the Hudson River	Jasper Francis Cropsey	1860

Galleries 73-79 are devoted to special exhibitions.

Ground Floor

Sculpture and Decorative Arts – *Galleries GN1-GN19.* The decorative arts featured here include 15C and 16C Flemish and 18C French tapestries, as well as Italian Renaissance and 18C French rococo furnishings (GN1, GN14 A-D). Small ecclesiastical artworks—relic chests, enamels, and stained glass—of the Middle Ages and Renaissance are displayed in gallery GN2. Gallery GN3 houses a fine collection of K'ang-Hsi and Ch'ien Lung Chinese porcelain (17-19C).
Galleries GN11-12 contain small sculpture and medals dating from the 16C to the early 18C. The works of two 18C French sculptors, Clodion and Houdon, are featured in gallery GN13, while galleries GN15-19 are devoted to sculpture from the 19C to the mid-20C, including the works of Degas, Rodin, and Maillol. GC5 houses marble busts and statuary from the 17C to 19C.

Prints and Drawings – Galleries GS1-14 are devoted to changing exhibits from the museum's permanent collection of prints and drawings, containing works dating from the 13C to the present. Frequent loan exhibits of graphic arts from around the world are also shown here. Galleries GN20-20A feature rotating exhibits from the **Armand Hammer collection** of drawings, which spans five centuries and includes the works of Leonardo da Vinci, Michelangelo, Dürer, Manet, Degas, and Cézanne.

To reach the East Building, exit on 4th St. and cross the plaza, or take the underground concourse.

EAST BUILDING *time: 1 hour*

The **plaza**, which fronts the East Building and links it visually to the West Building, is dominated by seven glass tetrahedrons, four-sided shapes repeated often in the architecture of the East Building. The tetrahedrons also serve as skylights for the underground concourse connecting the buildings, while the plaza fountain flows down a *chadar,* or waterslide, that is visible in the concourse as well. The gallery's buffet, cafe, and a bookstore are situated in the concourse.

Generally considered Washington's most impressive example of modern architecture, the massive marble **building★★** by **I. M. Pei** stresses line and angle over adornment. Pei's task was threefold: to design a structure that would showcase modern art, that would harmonize with the West Building, and that would be monumental enough to anchor the northwest corner of the Mall. Given a trapezoidal lot formed by the intersections of Constitution and Pennsylvania Avenues, Pei chose a trapezoid formed of two distinct triangles. The northwest isosceles triangle houses gallery space; the southeast right triangle contains administrative and research facilities. Polygonal towers top the points of the triangles; each tower rises 108ft high, one foot less than the height of the West Building. The structure's marble facing came from the same Tennessee quarry as that of the West Building.

20C Art – The gallery's stated goal is to "present the great European and American movements and masters of the century rather than to speculate on new trends." Represented in its collection are the works of such 20C artists as Wassily Kandinsky, Henri Matisse, Constantin Brancusi, Pablo Picasso, Georgia O'Keeffe, Max Ernst, Joan Miró, Henry Moore, Alberto Giacometti, Mark Rothko, and Arshile Gorky.

Washington, DC Convention & Visitors Assoc.

The East Building

Visit – *The East Building's fluid interior space is easily adapted to changing exhibits. In addition to housing rotating exhibits of art from the permanent collection, the gallery features major traveling exhibits from all artistic periods.* The angular lines of the building's exterior are offset by the rounded bronze form of Henry Moore's monumental *Knife Edge Mirror Two Piece,* situated outside the main entrance. From the low-ceilinged lobby, the building soars into a skylit **atrium**, dominated by an immense red, blue, and black **mobile** (untitled) by Alexander Calder, specially commissioned for this space. Another commissioned work, a sculpture entitled *Ledge Piece,* by Anthony Caro, is displayed over the door to the administrative wing *(located near the escalator).* Two small ground-floor galleries feature rotating exhibits of smaller works, including prints and drawings, and French paintings from the collection of Ailsa Mellon Bruce.

Additional exhibit spaces are situated on the mezzanine level, the upper level, the intimate **tower gallery**, and the underground concourse galleries.

We welcome your assistance in the never-ending task of updating texts and maps in this guide. Send us your comments and suggestions:

Editorial Department
Michelin Travel Publications
PO Box 19001
Greenville, SC 29602-9001

★★ NATIONAL ARCHIVES

Michelin map 48 J9 *time: 1/2 hour*

Constitution Ave. between 7th and 9th Sts. NW. M Archives or Federal Triangle. Open daily Apr 1–Labor Day 10am–9pm, the rest of the year 10am–5:30pm; closed Dec 25. Free admission. Guided tours (90min) of the rotunda and research facilities daily at 10:15am and 1:15pm (3-week advance reservation recommended). ♿ ☎501-5205 for reservations.

This imposing Classical Revival "temple" just off the Mall holds the nation's documentary treasures, including the Declaration of Independence, the Constitution, and the Bill of Rights.

A Strongbox for the Nation – Completed in 1937, the Archives answered a pressing need for a central repository of official and historical records. Before this institution's establishment, each department of the Federal Government stored its own archival material. Important documents were frequently lost or damaged due to haphazard treatment. In 1921, a fire destroyed all of the 1890 census records. That loss, coupled with the Public Building Act of 1926, finally precipitated plans to build a fireproof Federal archives. Today, the National Archives and Records Administration, as it is officially designated, safeguards 5 billion paper documents, 9 million aerial photographs, 6 million still photographs, and 300,000 video, film and sound recordings. The collection includes such varied items as letters from private individuals to US Presidents, Commodore Matthew Perry's journals from his historic 19C mission to Japan, the Civil War photographs of Mathew Brady, and the photo albums of Hitler's mistress, Eva Braun.

Exterior – The massive rectangular limestone building, designed by John Russell Pope to engender a sense of awe, occupies an entire city block. Corinthian colonnades embellish its four facades, and elaborate bas-relief pediments top the entrance porticos on the north and south sides of the building.

The Rotunda – *Enter from Constitution Ave.* A sweeping staircase leads visitors up to the entrance of the National Archives' rotunda. Popularly known as the Shrine, the cavernous 75ft-high, half-domed space, with its coffered ceiling, inspires reverence. Its centerpiece is an altar-like marble dais where the **Charters of Freedom★★★** are permanently enshrined. On view are the **Declaration of Independence**, two pages of the **Constitution** (preamble page and signature page), and the **Bill of Rights**. Sealed in helium-filled cases that are covered with a green ultra-violet filter, the fragile parchments are lowered each night into a vault 20ft below the rotunda.

Two 34ft-long murals, painted in the 1930s by Barry Faulkner, adorn the walls on either side of the dais. The left mural, *the Declaration of Independence*, is Faulkner's fictitious depiction of Thomas Jefferson presenting a draft of the Declaration to John Hancock, while the Continental Congress looks on. *The Constitution,* on the right, shows, again in an imagined scene, James Madison offering the final document to George Washington at the Constitutional Convention. Displayed in a separate case is a 1297 version of England's **Magna Carta**, on indefinite loan to the National Archives from the Texas billionaire Ross Perot. A circular gallery *(access from the rotunda)* features changing exhibits from the Archives' permanent collection.

S. Brown/National Archives

The Charters of Freedom

Research Facilities – *Pennsylvania Ave. entrance. Open Mon–Fri 8:45am–10pm, Sat 9am–5pm; closed Sun and Federal holidays. Free admission. Photo ID required to enter facility. Children under 16 must be accompanied by an adult. ♿ ☎501-5400.* The National Archives functions as a major source of historical material for researchers from the US and abroad. The ornately paneled **Central Research Room** on the second floor serves visitors engaged in scholarly research. Among the holdings are the papers of the Continental Congress, court and congressional records, historic correspondence, and records of Federal agencies deemed to be of "enduring value."

As of 1978, certain presidential papers were declared Federal property and came under archival jurisdiction. Most are housed in separate presidential libraries administered by the Archives. The **Microfilm Research Room**, located on the fourth floor, serves persons engaged in genealogical research. It contains such materials as census, military service and pension records, and ship passenger arrival lists. A film, pamphlets, and staff offer instruction on how to trace family histories. The **Nixon Watergate tapes**, kept in an archives facility in College Park, Maryland, are accessible to the public *(shuttle buses to the facility leave from the Archives daily on the hour from 9am–4pm).*

★★ NATIONAL MUSEUM OF NATURAL HISTORY

Michelin map 48 J8-K8 *time: 2 hours*

Constitution Ave. at 10th St. NW Ⓜ *Smithsonian. Open daily 10am–5:30pm (extended hours in spring and summer); closed Dec 25. Free admission. Guided tours (20min) available Sept–Jun, daily 10:30am and 1:30pm. ♿ ✗ ☎357-2700.*

Possessing a multifarious collection of plants, animals, fossils, rocks, and artifacts of human cultures, this museum and research center aims to give both visitor and scientist a better understanding of our universe and its innumerable life forms.

The Building – Soon after the completion of the ARTS AND INDUSTRIES BUILDING (1881), designed to complement the CASTLE and to house the exhibits from the 1876 Centennial Exposition, the need arose for additional space to accommodate the rapidly expanding Smithsonian collections. In 1903, Congress authorized the construction of the Smithsonian's third building, today known as the National Museum of Natural History. Designed by Hornblower and Marshall in the Classical Revival style, the original four-story granite structure faced with a seven-column entrance portico was completed in 1911. Its octagonal rotunda is 80ft in diameter and rises to a height of 124 1/2ft. With the addition of the six-story east and west wings in 1963 and 1965, the building now covers over 16.5 acres, including 300,000sq ft of exhibition space. Today, the building conserves more than 118 million specimens and provides laboratory facilities for geologists, zoologists, botanists, anthropologists, and paleontologists.

VISIT

Flanking the stairs to the Madison Drive entrance of the building are twin pedestals displaying samples of banded iron ore (2.25 billion years old) and petrified wood (over 200 million years old).

Planning an Itinerary – To select an itinerary best suited to your interests and schedule, start your visit in the first-floor rotunda where a series of colored banners mark the major exhibit areas. The rotunda is dominated by a 13ft 2in **African bush elephant**, which weighed eight tons at its death in 1955 at the age of 50.

Smithsonian Institution, National Museum of Natural History

African bush elephant in the rotunda

First Floor

Mammals – A trail of window cases and dioramas offers the visitor an overview of the mammal class in all its diversity. Along with more familiar animals, the exhibit includes specimens of such exotic creatures as the jaguar, kinkajou, jerboa, tapir, wallaby, Chinese civet, and dik-dik. Several dioramas illustrate habitats and survival mechanisms, such as food gathering, migration, and defense strategies, that either led these mammals to their present stage of development or caused them to perish.

NATIONAL MUSEUM OF NATURAL HISTORY

SECOND FLOOR

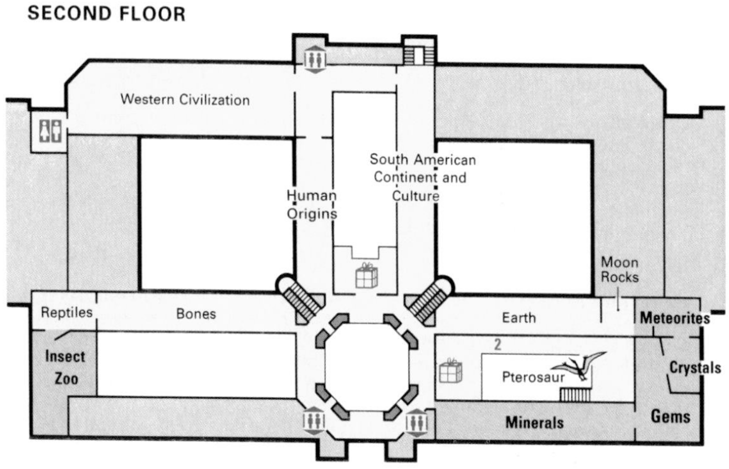

FIRST FLOOR

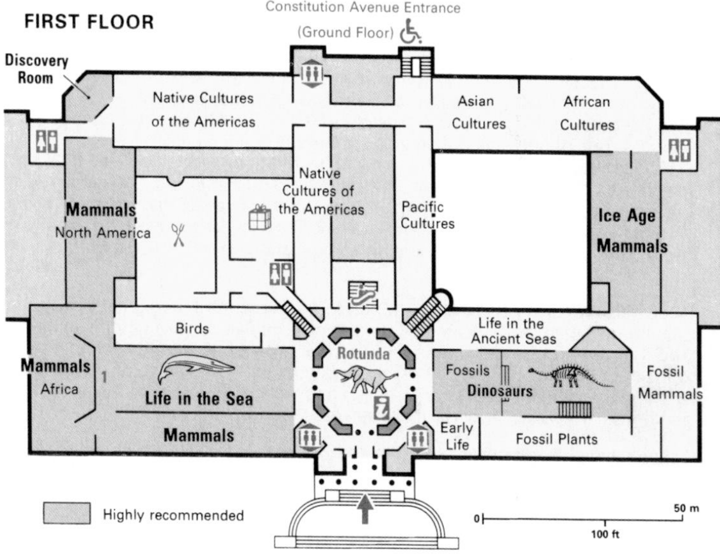

Life in the Sea – *Parts of this hall may be closed for renovation.* The walrus is a member of the Pinniped family whose movie biography is shown under its platform (1). The plastic life-size model of a 135-ton **blue whale**, billed as the "largest animal that has ever lived," is 92ft long. Although able to hold a ton of food in its stomach at one time, the whale has no teeth and must subsist on tiny organisms such as plankton and krill, which will pass unchewed through its small throat. Also on view here is a living **coral reef**★, one of the few conserved in a museum.

The Discovery Room – *Mon–Fri noon–2:30pm; Sat and Sun 10:30am–3:30pm. Capacity: 40 persons.* This hands-on educational exhibit offers visitors the opportunity to touch and examine various objects and artifacts (e.g., fossils, minerals, animals, both living and preserved) that are representative of those found in the museum.

Cultural Regions Exhibits – The dioramas and murals in **Native Cultures of the Americas** depict the indigenous inhabitants of North and South America, from Point Barrow, Alaska to Cape Horn. The displays are grouped according to geographical and cultural regions, and include a fine collection of North American Indian art objects. In the nearby halls are the exhibits devoted to **African** *(exhibit may be closed for renovation)*, **Asian, and Pacific Cultures.** Here, aspects of sociology, spirituality, heritage, and livelihood are displayed through dioramas that incorporate objects from the museum's collection. The cultural disparity of Africa's 50-plus nations is apparent from the diverse ritual objects, weapons, tools, utensils, and items of clothing on view. A 14ft calcite stone disk from Micronesia—an island group in the Pacific—may be one of the largest coins ever used. Examples of calligraphy illustrate the Chinese writing system, which is a unifying factor among the multitude of spoken languages and dialects in the nation's 21 provinces.

Ice Age Mammals – *Parts of this exhibit may be undergoing renovation.* A brief presentation of glacial history precedes this impressive display of fossilized mammal skeletons from the Pleistocene epoch, also known as the Ice Age. The woolly mammoth and the mastodon are both "cousins" of the elephant. The saber-toothed cat was recovered from Los Angeles' La Brea tar pits, where it met its sticky end along with more than one million other animals. Fossilized reptiles can be seen in **Life in the Ancient Seas**, which contains a life-size model of an ancient reef.

Dinosaurs – A 90ft **Diplodocus skeleton** towers over those of its companions; these creatures became extinct about 65 million years ago. Suspended above the enormous room is a life-size model of a **pterosaur**. With its 40ft wingspan, it was much bigger than any bird that ever lived. A large, razor-toothed **shark jaw** (2) yawns above the ramp to the second-floor balconies; a 40ft silhouette on the adjacent wall illustrates the size of the actual prehistoric animal.

Second Floor

Gems and Minerals – *As this exhibit is scheduled to undergo renovation, some of the objects described may be temporarily relocated or removed from display. Consult the information desk in the rotunda.* Thirteen large mineral samples provide a colorful introduction to the mineral exhibit; they are followed by cases of interesting specimens in many shapes, colors, and consistencies. Smithsonite, or zinc carbonate, was first identified by James Smithson, founder of the institution that bears his name. The state of California donated the large piece of neptunite resembling snow peppered with black crystals, as well as gold flakes from the Eureka mine. Minerals on view are grouped in families of increasing chemical complexity, while the last four windows contain samples arranged by their places of origin.

The museum's most popular attraction is the fabulous **Gem collection**★★★. As visitors enter the exhibit, a flawless 12 7/8in Burma **quartz ball** draws immediate attention. A headlight-size **golden topaz** from Brazil is the largest cut gemstone in the world at 22,892.5 carats. **Diamonds** on view show a remarkable range of sizes and colors, from the 253.7-carat **Oppenheimer Diamond**, which is uncut and unpolished, to the 2.9-carat pink beauty from Tanzania. An extremely rare red diamond of 5.03 carats is one of only five publicly documented.

The legendary **Hope Diamond**, the largest blue diamond in the world at 45.5 carats, is celebrated for its exquisite color and clarity. Next to it are the 330-carat **Star of Asia** sapphire from Sri Lanka and the 138.7-carat **Rosser Reeves Ruby**. A display of **Jewelry Fit for a Queen** includes a flawless emerald necklace of 15C Spanish origin, and a diadem studded with 950 diamonds given by Napoleon to Empress Marie-Louise at their wedding in 1810.

Moon Rocks and Meteorites – Moon rocks have contributed greatly to our understanding of the solar system and its origins. The five samples in this exhibit were brought to earth by astronauts on four different Apollo flights *(Apollo 14-17)* and constitute the world's largest public display of lunar rocks. Also on view are pieces of more than 150 meteorites, including a fragment of the 4.6 billion-year-old Allende meteorite, the oldest mineral specimen ever found.

Insect Zoo – The arthropod group comprises 90 percent of animal life on earth. Many of the living and preserved insects in this exhibit exemplify the adaptations that have enabled arthropods to survive for 475 million years. Most are contained in low-set cases, enabling children to see natural habitats as well as physical details. Video monitors installed on a re-created 18ft African termite mound show a colony of the tiny builders at work. A bustling ant farm forms a complete, small-scale society, and a buzzing beehive is equipped with an exit tube to the outdoors, allowing inhabitants to forage for food. *Tarantula feedings: Mon–Fri at 10:30am, 11:30am and 1:30pm; Sat, Sun and holidays at 11:30am, 12:30pm and 1:30pm.*

Other Exhibits – A series of dioramas in the exhibit of **South American Continent and Culture** show the effects of diverse climactic conditions on the development of South American cultures. The remainder of the exhibit space is devoted to dioramas illustrating aspects of Western civilization and prehistoric North America.

Sights described in this guide are rated:

★★★ ***Highly recommended***
★★ ***Recommended***
★ ***Interesting***

★★ NATIONAL MUSEUM OF AMERICAN HISTORY

Michelin map 48 J8-K8 *time: 3 hours*

Constitution Ave. between 12th and 14th Sts. NW. Ⓜ Federal Triangle or Smithsonian. Open daily 10am–5:30pm (extended hours in spring and summer); closed Dec 25. Free admission. Guided tours (1 hour) available. ♿ ✗ ☎357-2700.

The repository for such popular national icons as the Star-Spangled Banner, the Model T Ford, and the First Ladies' gowns, this unique museum captures the essence of America by presenting the objects and the ideas that have figured prominently in the nation's material and social development.

The Collection – Now totaling some 16 million objects (including stamps and coins), the museum's collection traces its origins to 1858 when the models from the US Patent Office were transferred to the Smithsonian Institution. Beginning in 1881, selections from this collection—known as the Museum of History and Technology—were exhibited in the ARTS AND INDUSTRIES BUILDING. To provide adequate space for the rapidly expanding collection of diverse artifacts illustrating America's scientific cultural, political, and technological achievements, the current marble structure was opened in 1964. Renamed the National Museum of American History in 1980, this institution has in recent years committed itself to presenting issue-oriented exhibits that explore key events and social phenomena in American culture.

Before beginning your visit of the museum, take a few minutes to view the attractions that are found on the museum's grounds. *Infinity* (1967), the stainless steel abstract sculpture located outside the Mall entrance is the work of the American artist Jose de Rivera. On the west side of the building stands a 19C **bandstand**, transported from its original site in Jacksonville, Illinois. This wooden structure with ornamental fretwork is the setting for band concerts and a good place to take a break during your visit to the Mall. **The Gwenfritz**, the 40ft wrought-iron stabile positioned near the corner of 14th Street and Constitution Avenue, was designed by the noted sculptor Alexander Calder.

Enter the museum from Constitution Ave.

VISIT

In view of the long-term renovation program undertaken by the museum, certain sections may be closed to the public for several months at a time, and specific objects or collections may be exhibited in locations other than those indicated. Information regarding new installations and the location of such popular artifacts as Archie Bunker's chair and Dorothy's ruby slippers can be obtained at the information desk near the entrance.

First Floor

The authentic **post office-general store** situated near the entrance was constructed in Headsville, West Virginia and transferred to the museum in 1971. Visitors can buy stamps and mail letters that will be cancelled with a special museum postmark.

A **Material World**, the exhibit occupying the central gallery, explores the evolution of the materials used to produce everyday objects and their impact on American lifestyles over the last two centuries. The enlightening exhibit comprises numerous artifacts ranging from a 19C handcrafted wooden washing machine to Tupperware to an industrially designed aluminum and steel bicycle of recent vintage. On prominent display is the *Swamp Rat XXX* (1), a dragster whose remarkable aerodynamic qualities are attributed to the combination of synthetics and alloys used in its design.

East Wing – The galleries in this wing illustrate the extent to which agriculture, transportation, and power machinery made the "good life" possible in America. Resting on a section of an iron bridge from the Philadelphia and Reading Railroad, the **John Bull** (1831) is the nation's oldest operable steam locomotive. This type of locomotive replaced the likes of the buckboard, the Concord coach, and the river boat, all of which were too slow and too labor-intensive to satisfy the demands put upon them. The 280-ton Pacific-type locomotive 1401 in the **Railroad Hall** was used by the Southern Railway between 1926 and 1951 when the age of steam came to its close. The **American Maritime Enterprise** offers a look at new forms of motive power such as steam- and later gasoline-operated vessels that navigated lakes, rivers, and canals to move people and products from farm to market. The 1913 Model T Ford (2) displayed in **Road Transportation**, along with the subsequent rapid growth of the automobile industry, inevitably sent the horse-drawn wagon into retirement. The 15 million Model T cars built between 1908 and 1927 set the American way of life into perpetual motion.

Farm implements on display reflect the importance of **Agriculture** throughout the nation's development. Around the turn of the 20C, the wooden plow, the cradle scythe, and the 20-mule team Holt combine gave way to the internal combustion tractors, which led to dramatic transformations in rural America. The advent of **"Old Red"** (3), the International Harvester mechanical cotton picker, marked the end of the labor-intensive cotton industry and improved the lot of the average farmer by paving the way for modern large-scale farming.

Engines of Change: The American Industrial Revolution, 1790-1860 gives an overview of not only the machines but also the work habits and ideas that provided the impetus for the change from manual to industrial labor.

The adjacent exhibit, **Electricity**, gives prominent coverage to Thomas Edison's inventions (his 1879 light bulb is on display), and presents the new motors and engines that sparked the industrialization process.

THIRD FLOOR

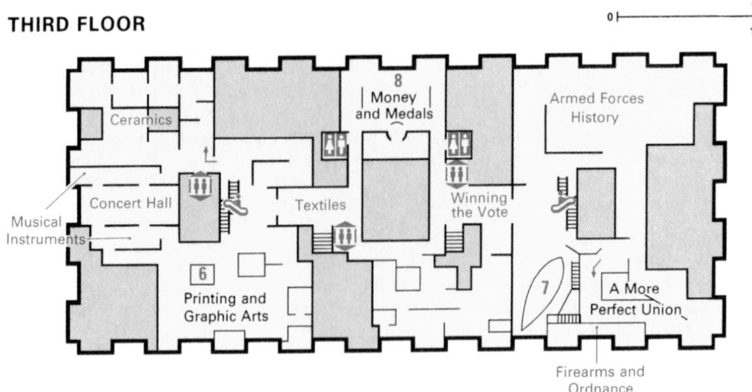

NATIONAL MUSEUM OF AMERICAN HISTORY

SECOND FLOOR

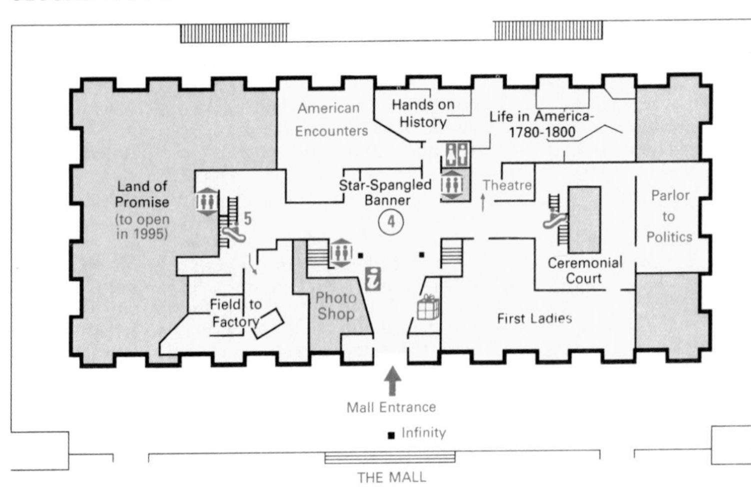

FIRST FLOOR

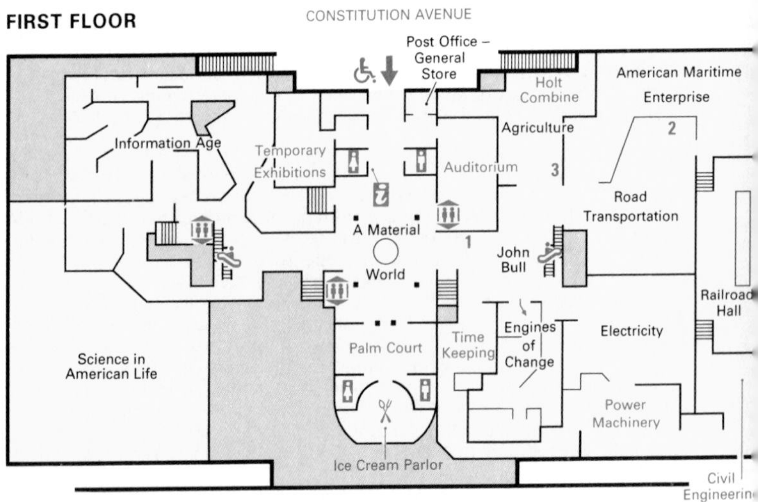

West Wing – **Science in American Life** highlights the country's scientific history from 1876 to the present. On display are over 1,000 instruments and appliances, many of which reflect science's expanded influence on society. Some 25 interactive videos and a hands-on science center complete the exhibit.

The Information Age explores the history of information transfer and its effects on American economy and society. Telegraphs dating from the 1840s, Alexander Graham Bell's induction telephone (1876), and one of Thomas Edison's early bulbs (1883) can be seen here. The exhibit also traces the rapid development of computers, and emphasizes the impact of these technologies, which expand the horizon while shrinking the world.

Second Floor

Portions of this floor may be undergoing renovation.

In 1851, French physicist Jean-Bernard-Leon Foucault suspended a pendulum from the ceiling of the Pantheon in Paris to demonstrate the rotation of the earth. The **pendulum** (4) displayed in the Mall entrance area is a 240lb hollow brass bob hanging by a cable from the fourth floor. It swings slowly back and forth, toppling one at a time the red markers arranged on a wheel over the inlaid compass rose that is visible on the first floor. Mounted on the wall behind the pendulum is the **Star-Spangled Banner★**, the enormous flag (originally 30ft by 42ft) that was "still there" the morning of September 14, 1814, after an intensive British bombardment of Fort McHenry in Baltimore during the War of 1812. In British custody during the attack, Francis Scott Key saw this flag still waving through the haze of battle. He penned the words of the poem that was later set to music and became the National Anthem of the United States of America. *(The flag's protective cover is lowered briefly on the half hour, beginning at 10:30am.)*

National Museum of American History

The Star-Spangled Banner

East Wing – The **Ceremonial Court** at the center of the east wing replicates White House interiors as they appeared in the early 20C. Some authentic White House and presidential artifacts from different administrations have been incorporated in the period rooms. The popular exhibit entitled **First Ladies: Political Role and Public Image** profiles the lives of the White House hostesses and features ball gowns worn by them. Everyday **Life in America, 1780-1800** presents characteristic features of life in rural and urban communities in the early days of the new Republic. Its sections illustrate the wide disparity among the lifestyles of a Virginia planter, a black slave, a Seneca Indian, and a Philadelphia artisan.

West Wing – Horatio Greenough's majestic **sculpture** (5) of George Washington stands at the entrance to this wing. Commissioned by Congress in 1832, the sculpture quickly became an object of derision after its installation in the Capitol Rotunda in 1841. When the floor beneath it began to sink, the piece was moved to the Capitol gardens. The sculpture was presented to the Smithsonian in 1908. **Field to Factory** is a dramatic chronicle of the African-American migration from the rural South to the industrialized North between 1915 and 1940, and its impact on American cities.

Third Floor

This floor has something for everyone: ceramics, coins, musical instruments, and military memorabilia. **Printing and Graphic Arts** presents the history and technology of printing and printmaking. Examples of works by both Old Masters and modern photographers provide a history of etching, woodcut, lithography, silkscreen, and photoengraving. A noteworthy collection of presses and four period print shops are on display, including the early 19C shop with the 1720 Press (6) on which journeyman Benjamin Franklin may have worked in London.

The massive gunboat **Philadelphia** (7) is the oldest existing American gunboat. It sank while under the command of Benedict Arnold in 1776, the same year it was built. **A More Perfect Union** presents a case study of the American constitutional process by chronicling the Japanese-American experience during World War II. The artifacts, photographs, and personal accounts attest to the US Government's violation of the Constitutional rights of some 120,000 American citizens of Japanese ancestry. A series of cases illustrating the history of money highlights the **Money and Medals** exhibit. The cases contain ancient coins (7C BC) from Asia Minor and some 15-16C Japanese gold and silver coins that were a gift to President Grant. In the Gold Room (8), do not miss the 20-dollar high relief gold coin (1907), which was designed by Augustus Saint-Gaudens at the request of President Theodore Roosevelt. Only 11,000 were minted before the design was changed to low relief.

★★ HIRSHHORN MUSEUM AND SCULPTURE GARDEN

Michelin map 48 K9 *time: 1 1/2 hours*

Independence Ave. at 7th St. SW. M L'Enfant Plaza or Smithsonian. Open daily 10am–5:30pm (hours may be extended in spring and summer); closed Dec 25. Free admission. Museum guided tours (1 hour) available Mon–Sat at 10:30am, noon, 1:30, 2:30pm; Sun at 12:30pm. Sculpture garden tours May and Oct daily 12:15pm. ♿ ✗ (outdoors, summer only) ☎357-2700.

An unmistakable architectural statement on the Mall, this cylindrical building houses one of the finest collections of modern art in the country. Its sculpture holdings, ranging from the realistic to the monumental and abstract, make up the world's most comprehensive collection of 20C works in that medium.

The Benefactor – Born in Latvia on the eastern coast of the Baltic Sea, **Joseph Hirshhorn** (1899-1981) immigrated to Brooklyn with his widowed mother and ten siblings when he was a boy of six. At age 13, he left school to help support his family. At 18, he was a broker on Wall Street, and he eventually became a wealthy financier and uranium magnate.

Hirshhorn traced his first interest in art to a series of paintings by Salon masters he saw reproduced in an insurance calendar. His early collecting followed in that vein, but by the late 1930s, his tastes had turned to the works of French Impressionists and post-Impressionists. That interest also passed, as he increasingly focused his collecting on contemporary American and European painting and on modern sculpture from throughout the world.

In 1962, with the first major public exhibition of his art treasures at the Solomon R. Guggenheim Museum in New York, his collection drew international attention. Representatives from several foreign countries approached Hirshhorn, offering to establish museums for the collection in their respective countries. However, in the mid-1960s, President Johnson and Smithsonian Secretary S. Dillon Ripley convinced Hirshhorn to donate his collection to the Smithsonian. In 1966, Congress established the Hirshhorn Museum and Sculpture Garden, to which the benefactor contributed more than 6,000 works. He continued to be an avid collector until his death in 1981. At that time, he bequeathed another 6,000 works to the museum. The core collection is continually being expanded by an active acquisition program.

A "Doughnut" on the Mall – Almost every new addition to the Mall has met with a certain degree of controversy, but the so-called "doughnut" by architect **Gordon Bunshaft** incited harsh criticism, since it was the first unabashedly modern building erected on the prestigious national showplace. Dillon Ripley said of Bunshaft's design, "If it were not controversial in almost every way, it would hardly qualify as a place to house contemporary art." Elevated on four piers, the drum-shaped, unadorned concrete building wraps around a fountained plaza that extends beneath the raised building, serving almost as a first floor. Gallery windows along the interior circumference overlook the plaza.

VISIT

The Hirshhorn's collection comprises some 5,000 paintings, 3,000 pieces of sculpture and mixed media, and 4,500 works on paper. Roughly 5 percent of the collection is on view at any one time.

Paintings – The paintings in the collection are organized chronologically, beginning with early 20C American works on the third floor. Among the artists featured here are such renowned painters as George Bellows and George Luks, adherents of the Ash Can school; and prominent 20C artists Edward Hopper, Marsden Hartley, Max Weber, Stuart Davis, and Georgia O'Keeffe, among others. The third-floor galleries devoted to European and American modernism feature paintings and three-dimensional works by Constantin Brancusi, Alberto Giacometti, Jean Arp, Joan Miró, Isamu Noguchi, Jean Dubuffet, Francis Bacon, noted Abstract Expressionists (Willem de Kooning, Mark Rothko, Franz Kline), and others.

L. Stalsworth/Hirshhorn Museum

The Hirshhorn Sculpture Garden

Also on this floor is a gallery entitled **Directions**, devoted to rotating exhibits that highlight the work of emerging contemporary artists.
The second-floor galleries are reserved for major special exhibits and a variety of small, changing exhibits of art from the permanent collection.
Contemporary art is housed on the underground level. Featured are works by proponents of Pop Art (Jasper Johns, Robert Rauschenberg, Andy Warhol, and others), and representative works of more recent tendencies by artists such as Christo, Antoni Tàpies, and Anish Kapoor.

Sculpture Ambulatories – On the second and third floors, continuous galleries following the interior circumference of the building feature small sculptural works. The display begins on the second floor with such 19C European artists as Aristide Maillol, Auguste Rodin, Degas, and Renoir. The Hirshhorn's collection of sculptures by **Henri Matisse** is particularly rich.
The third-floor ambulatory is devoted to 20C sculpture by such masters as Pablo Picasso, Alberto Giacometti, and Alexander Archipenko. The Hirshhorn possesses one of the country's most extensive collections of **Henry Moore** (1898-1986) sculptures, with some 60 sculptures and 20 works on paper representing the entire career of the celebrated British sculptor.

Outdoor Sculpture – The **plaza** on which the building stands is a showplace for monumental contemporary sculpture, including the works of Alexander Calder, Claes Oldenburg, David Smith, and Lucio Fontana.
Smaller figurative works are featured in the sunken and walled **Sculpture Garden** *(across Jefferson Drive)*. Prominent among these are the works of **Auguste Rodin** and Aristide Maillol. Also on display are sculptures by Gaston Lachaise and Henry Moore, as well as two series of rare relief plaques, one by Matisse *(Backs)* and the other by Thomas Eakins *(Battle of Trenton)*.

★ SMITHSONIAN QUADRANGLE

Michelin map 48 K8

Independence Ave. between 9th and 12th Sts. SW. M *Smithsonian or L'Enfant Plaza.*

Topped by a street-level garden, this handsome underground complex occupies a prime site in the shadow of the venerable Castle building. Opened in September 1987, the Quadrangle comprises two Smithsonian museums—the NATIONAL MUSEUM OF AFRICAN ART and the ARTHUR M. SACKLER GALLERY—and an education center, the S. Dillon Ripley Center.

Historical Notes – The Smithsonian Quadrangle is the brainchild of S. Dillon Ripley, Secretary of the Smithsonian from 1964 to 1984. During his tenure, the noted collector Dr Arthur M. Sackler pledged a significant portion of his Asian and Near Eastern artifacts to the Smithsonian, but the Institution lacked a suitable space for its display. Ripley also faced the problem of finding a larger facility for the Museum of African Art that had outgrown its cramped quarters in a row of Capitol Hill town houses. Appreciating the Institution's need to enlarge its focus to international fields of research and to house the two art collections, Ripley spearheaded a major development program for an "international center of advanced study." Ripley's project neatly addressed these needs while bringing a more international flavor to the cultural offerings on the Mall. In October 1982, Congress appropriated $36.5 million (approximately half of the total cost) for the project. In the following year, construction of the complex began on the quadrangular site bordered by the CASTLE, the FREER GALLERY, the ARTS AND INDUSTRIES BUILDING, and Independence Avenue.

The Enid A. Haupt Garden – *Open Memorial Day–Sept daily 7am–8pm (rest of year 5:45pm); closed Dec 25.* This 4.2-acre garden, named after its New York benefactor, is a peaceful, contemplative haven replete with antique benches, urn planters, walkways, and 19C-style lampposts. The centerpiece of the garden is the ornamental parterre, adorned in the 19C fashion with changing seasonal plantings. The iron and red sandstone gate opening onto Independence Avenue is based on designs by James Renwick, architect of the Castle.
On either side of the gate stand the attractive entrance pavilions that lead to the two underground museums. Though similarly proportioned, these structures are adorned with motifs intended to create a visual link with the surrounding landmarks: the pyramided roof and diamond shapes of the Sackler pavilion echo the lines of the Arts and Industries Building, while the domes and rounded arches of the Museum of African Art pavilion complement the exterior of the Freer Gallery.
Behind the Sackler Gallery entrance pavilion is an intimate garden with a circle-in-square fountain based on the Temple of Heaven in Beijing and two 9ft pink granite "moongates." Adjacent to the Museum of African Art pavilion is a series of fountains and canals terminating in a water wall or *chadar*, inspired by the Alhambra gardens in Granada, Spain.

Concourse – *3rd underground level; accessible through the street-level kiosk situated between the Freer Gallery and the Castle.* Visitors enter the glass-enclosed kiosk and descend one floor down a circular staircase, accompanied by streams of light from above. An escalator ride completes the descent to the third level, known as the S. Dillon Ripley Center, where passage through a gallery ends on a skylit "street" complete with trees and "shops" (actually classrooms and offices). A *trompe l'oeil* mural by Richard Haas dominates the eastern wall. This broad airy concourse housing an exhibit gallery, classrooms, workshops, and offices is the focal point of the Smithsonian's international activities.

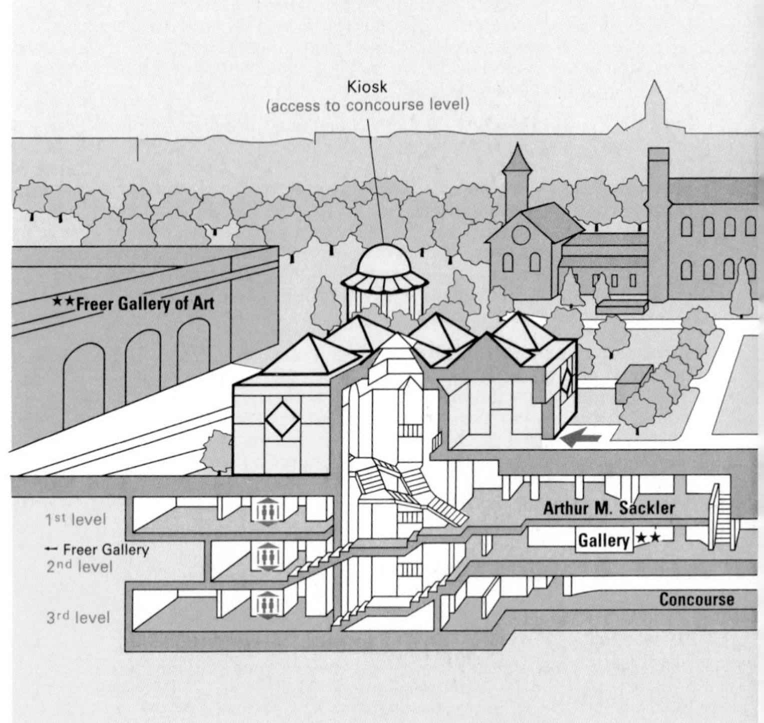

Museums – *See descriptions below.* The showpieces of the Smithsonian Quadrangle complex are the NATIONAL MUSEUM OF AFRICAN ART and the ARTHUR M. SACKLER GALLERY. The two museums, which are administered separately, each feature approximately 20,000sq ft of exhibit space situated principally on the first and second underground levels.

Upon entering the naturally lit entrance pavilions, from which the descent to the museums begins, the visitor can appreciate the fine building materials, the elegant detailing, and the fluid interior space, all of which greatly enhance the display of the exquisite objects within.

★★ NATIONAL MUSEUM OF AFRICAN ART

Michelin map 48 K9 *time: 1 hour*

The Smithsonian Quadrangle at 950 Independence Ave. SW. M Smithsonian. Open daily 10am–5:30pm; closed Dec 25. Free admission. Guided tours (1 hour) available. ♿ ☎357-4600.

Originally located in a row of Capitol Hill town houses, the National Museum of African Art today occupies more spacious quarters in the underground Smithsonian Quadrangle complex.

Devoted to the research, acquisition, and display of traditional African arts, especially those of the sub-Saharan regions, the museum possesses a permanent collection of over 7,000 pieces in bronze, copper, wood, ivory, and fiber, which are exhibited on a rotating basis. Only a small selection of this expanding collection is exhibited at any particular time. The sculptures, utilitarian objects, architectural elements, decorative arts, and textiles on display are organized by regions, thereby emphasizing the importance of geography on selection of materials, as well as form and style.

To complement the museum's permanent collection, temporary exhibits of African art are arranged from private and public collections in the US and abroad.

Notes on African Art – Given the pervasive role of religion in African culture, most objects created for utilitarian, economic, aesthetic, or ritual purposes bear religious significance. Unlike most cultures throughout the world, which keep written documents, many African cultures rely on sculptured works and other artifacts to preserve values and beliefs from generation to generation. These objects are generally infused with symbolic meanings. An enlarged head, for example, is a symbol of power and wisdom.

Collection Highlights – The museum's collection of **Royal Benin Art** from the historic West African kingdom of Benin (present-day Nigeria) includes several cast-copper alloy sculptures on permanent display. The ceremonial figures, heads,

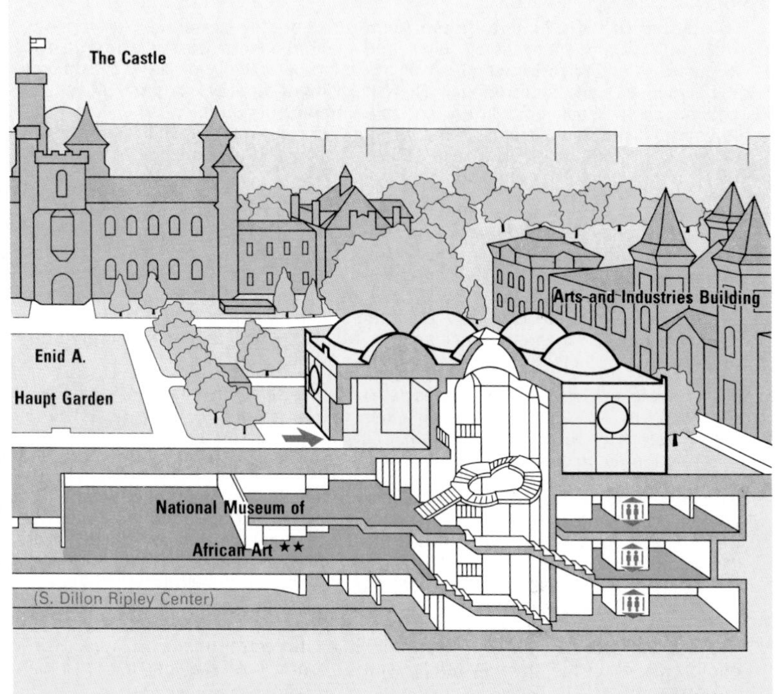

Adapted from illustration by Johnstone Quinan—Washington Post

pendants, and plaques were created between the 15C and 19C and reveal the elaborate rituals and ornate regalia of the Benin oba (king) and his entourage. Note especially the statue of an oba (17C); his regalia symbolizes his role as a divine ruler. A 16-17C carved ivory spoon, produced specifically for export, illustrates foreign influences on the style of Benin art.

Objects on display illustrate the tremendous variety of shapes, proportions, and designs present in African sculpture. Given the vastness of Africa and the continent's more than 900 distinct cultural groups, it is difficult to imagine a more complete and representative collection of African wood sculpture. Among the fine pieces that may be on display are initiation masks, woman-and-child figures created as icons of human perfection and fertility, and reliquary guardian figures.

The permanent collection also includes a number of **ritual objects** that are believed to be conduits of communication with spirits. Medicinal figurines, arranged in a Chokwe fiber divination basket, play a significant role in the healing process. Finally sculpted Sherbo Bullom stone figures, like those owned by the museum, are still used by the Mende people of the Guinea Coast to assure a good harvest. An Igala shrine figure was part of an altar created as an intermediary space between the spiritual and physical worlds.

★★ ARTHUR M. SACKLER GALLERY

Michelin map 48 K8 — *time: 1 hour*

The Smithsonian Quadrangle at 1050 Independence Ave. SW. M *Smithsonian. Open daily 10am–5:30pm; closed Dec 25. Free admission. Guided tours (1 hour) available. ♿ ☎357-2700.*

The Sackler Gallery is dedicated to the study and exhibition of the arts of Asia from the Neolithic period to the present. The major strengths of the expanding collection are Chinese jades and bronzes, ancient Near Eastern gold and silverwork, and a collection of 11-19C Islamic manuscripts. Selections from the permanent collection are complemented by international loan exhibits offering a comprehensive study of the breadth and beauty of Asian art and culture.

An underground gallery links the Sackler to the adjacent FREER GALLERY, with which it is associated.

The Inaugural Gift – The core of the museum's holdings was donated by **Dr Arthur M. Sackler** (1913-1987), the New York psychiatrist, medical researcher, and publisher, who donated 1,000 objects from his personal collection to the Smithsonian Institution in 1982. Sackler began acquiring Asian art in the 1950s to supplement his already extensive collection of Western art. The avid collector was the principal benefactor of Harvard University's Arthur M. Sackler Museum, and he contributed generously to the Eastern Art holdings of the Metropolitan Museum of Art *(see Michelin Green Guide to New York City)*. Since its inception, the Gallery has sought to expand the core collection donated by Sackler.

Highlights of the Chinese Collections – Ancient Chinese culture placed particular importance on tradition: laws and customs were passed through the generations and ancestor worship was a common practice, which explains in part the presence of ancestor figures in the decoration of ritual bronzes and jades. The economy was largely agricultural, and the attributes of nature became a powerful force in ancient Chinese religion. Clouds, rain, wind, and stars appear frequently as symbolic ornamentation on vessels and objects, which the Chinese used to deflect evil spirits and invoke protection of particular deities.

Jade Collection – The mountains of the Chinese provinces contained rich veins of nephrite jade, a gemstone so prized by the Chinese that they associate it with the five cardinal virtues of charity, modesty, courage, justice, and wisdom. The Sackler's jade collection of more than 450 carved objects dates from 3000 BC. Artifacts from the Neolithic period (c.4000-3000 BC) include axe blades produced in most cases as ceremonial burial objects. The jades of the Shang dynasty (1700 BC) were ornamental and used for ceremonial functions. Many of the Shang images and forms reappear in art of later periods.

Chinese Bronzes – The gallery's bronzes date from the Shang through the Han dynasties (1650 BC-AD 220). While their exact use is unknown, these objects are extensively inscribed, providing a wealth of information about this period, which has long remained obscure to researchers.

Ancient Near Eastern Gold and Silver – The civilizations that developed in ancient Iran, Anatolia (present-day Turkey), and the region around the Caucasus Mountains are credited with introducing the use of metals as early as 7000 BC. Over the following millennia, the craftsmen of these regions produced exquisite objects in copper, silver, gold, and lead employing a wide range of metallurgical techniques. Many of the gold and silver vessels and ornaments in the Sackler collection are gilded or inlaid with niello (an enamel-like alloy) and date from 3000 BC to the 8C AD. These objects, which were used principally for ceremonial occasions, offer glimpses of often sumptuous court life of the nations that developed in the Tigris-Euphrates valley.

Vever Collection – In 1986, the Sackler Gallery acquired the exquisite collection of Near Eastern and Indian manuscripts assembled in the early 20C by French jeweler and art connoisseur, Henri Vever. The nearly 500 works, dating from the 11C to 19C, constitute one of the world's finest collections of Islamic manuscripts, miniatures, and calligraphy.

★★ FREER GALLERY OF ART

Michelin map 48 K8 *time: 1 hour*

Jefferson Dr. at 12th St. SW. Ⓜ *Smithsonian. Open daily 10am–5:30pm; closed Dec 25. Free admission. Guided tours (1 hour) available.* ♿ ☎357-2700.

The Smithsonian's first museum on the Mall devoted exclusively to art, the Freer Gallery possesses an outstanding Asian collection, and one of the world's largest collections of works by James McNeill Whistler (1834-1903).

The Connoisseur – A successful railroad car manufacturer, Charles L. Freer (1854-1919) became, like Arthur Sackler *(p 65)*, a keen collector of Asian art. From his first purchase in 1887 of a Japanese fan, he gradually amassed some 9,000 objects, many of which were acquired during his trips to Japan, India, and China. In that same year, he bought several Whistler prints, his initial acquisition of works by the artist who would become his good friend. Retiring at age 45, Freer became a full-time collector and world traveler, expanding both his Asian and American holdings. In 1904, he revealed plans to bequeath a significant portion of his collections to the Smithsonian Institution, and to finance construction of a building to house the art. At his death, his bequest totaled some 9,000 works. Today, the museum's Asian properties have grown to over 27,000 works (Freer stipulated that his American collection not be expanded).

The Building – After the announcement of his proposed gift, Freer embarked on a search for a suitable building design, visiting American and European museums to gather ideas as to gallery size, ventilation, and lighting. In 1912, he hired New York architect Charles A. Platt, who employed neoclassical symmetry in the marble and granite Renaissance-style structure, built, as Freer had specified, around a central courtyard. The building's two entrances on Jefferson Drive and Independence Avenue are distinguished by triple arches. The arch motif is repeated in the bronze-framed Palladian windows and glass doors surrounding the 60sq ft fountained courtyard, which is faced with white Tennessee marble. The stone balustrade of the exterior parapet appears again above the courtyard's arches.

The museum was officially opened in 1923. After extensive renovation, begun in 1988, the museum reopened in 1993 with 19 galleries on the first level, and study rooms, an auditorium, conference room, and gallery shop on the lower levels. An underground exhibition gallery permits passage between the Freer and the SACKLER galleries.

The Asian Collection – Highlights of the Chinese holdings *(galleries 10, 11, 13-16)* include ornamental implements of the emperors of the Ming (1368-1644) and Qing (1644-1911) dynasties, 15C blue-and-white porcelain bowls from the imperial workshop in Jingdezhen in southeast China, and bronzes, jades, and lacquerware from the Ancient Chinese collection, which dates from 5000 BC to 1C AD. Traditional Japanese painting and calligraphy *(galleries 5-8)* can be seen on 15-19C folding screens or *byobu*, and hanging scrolls (ink and color on silk or paper); late 16-19C porcelain pieces and lacquered wooden boxes; and stone and earthenware tea bowls 13-17C. Korean ceramics from 10-14C, Indian 16-19C court paintings, and Islamic manuscripts are showcased in separate galleries *(9, 18, 19)*.

The American Collection – Galleries 1 to 4 house paintings by prominent American artists. Note Whistler's *Caprice in Purple and Gold: The Golden Screen* (1864) and John Singer Sargent's *Breakfast in the Loggia* (1910) mounted at the galleries' entrance. Gallery 1 presents Whistler's *Notes*, miniature oils depicting Chelsea shops and English landscapes c. 1882, and *Nocturnes*, dramatic paintings of the Thames River at night, inspired by Japanese prints. Full of light and grace are "The Six Projects" of the late 1860s—varied compositions of figures against the backdrop of the sea. Oil portraits and landscapes by Abbott Thayer, Thomas Dewing's paintings of women in fields, and Dwight Tryon's large oil and pastel landscapes adorn the other galleries.
Permanently installed in Gallery 12 is **The Peacock Room★**, Whistler's only extant interior design (1876-1877). Asked by English shipping tycoon Frederick Leyland to redecorate portions of his 20ft by 32ft London dining room, the artist began what evolved into a major (ostensibly unauthorized) overhaul. The result was a highly original, gilded setting for Leyland's blue and white Chinese porcelain collection. Intricate paintings of golden peacocks and peacock motifs embellish the walls, shutters, and ceiling. Dominating the mantel is Whistler's painting, *The Princess from the Land of Porcelain*, which Leyland had purchased. In the mural *(south wall)* depicting two fighting peacocks, the artist immortalized his dispute with Leyland over payment for his interior work. Freer purchased the room in 1904 from a London art dealer; prior to the museum's opening, the room was transferred from his Detroit home to the premises. The porcelain pieces on view are similar to those in Leyland's collection, and were acquired for the room's 1993 restoration.

★★ US HOLOCAUST MEMORIAL MUSEUM

Michelin map 48 K7 — *time: 2 1/2 hours*

South of Independence Ave. between 14th St. and Raoul Wallenberg Pl. SW. Ⓜ*Smithsonian. Open daily 10am–5:30pm (box office 9am). Free admission, but timed tickets, available at the box office, may be required for the permanent exhibit; advance tickets obtainable from Ticketmaster (432-7328; outside of DC 800-551-7328) carry a service charge.* ♿ ☎*488-0400.*
In lieu of the permanent exhibit, a special exhibit entitled "Daniel's Story: Remember the Children" *is available for young visitors.*

A deeply moving, wholly absorbing history lesson awaits visitors to this large museum/research complex, conceived "to commemorate the dead and to educate the living." Occupying nearly 2 acres of land adjacent to the BUREAU OF ENGRAVING AND PRINTING, just off the Mall, the striking edifice houses a compelling permanent exhibit that focuses on the Nazi extermination of millions of Jews and other victims during World War II.
In 1980, Congress chartered the United States Holocaust Memorial Council—the museum's governing body—and the Federal Government donated a museum site just south of the Washington Monument. Soon thereafter, the council began extensive fund-raising and international artifacts-collection efforts. In 1986, the New York firm of I.M. Pei & Partners was chosen, with James Freed as principal architect, to design an appropriate structure. Construction commenced on the $90 million building project in the spring of 1989, and the museum formally opened in April 1993.

An Unconventional Building – Given the museum's highly charged subject matter, the challenge to design a suitable structure, able to match its powerful message with dignity and sensitivity, was immense. The main 5-story brick and limestone building is a post-Modern "penitentiary," with its series of "watch" towers lining the north and south walls. The exposed metal beams, railings, and metal-framed glass doors of the building's 7,500sq ft glass-roofed central atrium, the **Hall of Witness**, amplify the feeling of imprisonment. The contrasting hexagonal, 6,000sq ft beige limestone annex *(located on the west side)* houses, on the second-floor, the 60ft high **Hall of Remembrance**, an unadorned, natural light-filled space provided for quiet contemplation and commemorative ceremonies. Four nonrepresentational works by prominent artists were commissioned for the museum: wall art by Ellsworth Kelly and Sol LeWitt graces transition rooms between the floors of the permanent exhibit, Richard Serra's steel monolith anchors the atrium's lower staircase, and Joel Shapiro's monumental sculpture fronts the west entrance. The 250,000sq ft complex also contains an auditorium, a theater, museum shop, education center, and learning center as well as temporary exhibit space.

Visit – *The permanent exhibit covers three floors. Visitors board an elevator for the ride to the 4th floor, and then walk their way down to the 2nd floor.*
Before entering the elevator, visitors are given a keepsake photo identification card containing the background and fate of a Holocaust victim. In the darkened surroundings of the fourth floor, visitors are confronted with photographs, archival

films, and artifacts in the exhibit entitled "Nazi Assault 1933-1939." Informative panels begin the tragic story of the calculated deprivation of the property, human rights, dignity, and eventually the lives of nearly six million European Jews, and some five million others, including three million Soviet POWs, as well as Slavs (Czechs, Poles and Russians), Gypsies, communists, homosexuals, Jehovah's Witnesses, and the handicapped. The exhibit is augmented by documentaries, newspaper headlines, vintage newsreels, documents, letters, and architectural casts. Two small theaters offer continuous showings of a film on antisemitism *(14min)* and on the Nazi regime's rise to power *(13min)*. Ghetto and concentration camp life is evoked on the third floor in "Final Solution: 1940-1944." Personal articles, food bowls, and work implements are interspersed with an actual railcar, which visitors can walk through, and a scale model of a gas chamber. Especially sensitive topics are presented discretely, for optional viewing, by way of sunken video monitors surrounded by chest-high walls. In "Voices of Auschwitz," visitors can listen, via headsets, in a glass-paneled sitting area to survivors' stories. In "Aftermath 1945 to the Present" on the final floor of the permanent exhibit, the valor and success of various rescue and resistance efforts are hailed. Here, resistance fighters' weapons and hundreds of photos of rescuers, prison martyrs, and survivors are on view, as are photos of "death" marches, and film footage recording the liberating armies' arrival at the camps, and the Nuremburg trials. A display is devoted to **Raoul Wallenberg**, the Swedish diplomat stationed in Budapest, who led the War Refuge Board's mission to save Hungarian Jews. Near the exit, a small, open theater presents recent filmed interviews with Holocaust survivors.

★ BUREAU OF ENGRAVING AND PRINTING

Michelin map 48 L7 *time: 1/2 hour*

14th and C Sts. SW. M Smithsonian. Open Mon–Fri 9am–2pm (visitor center 8:30am–3:30pm); closed Federal holidays and between Christmas and New Year's Day. Free admission, but same-day tickets, available from the kiosk on the bureau's west side (R. Wallenberg Pl.), are required the weeks before and after Easter and the Fri before Memorial Day through the Fri before Labor Day. It is advisable to pick up tickets before 11:30am during peak season. Congressional visits available—see p 162. ♿ ☎874-3188.

This nondescript 20C building at the foot of the 14th Street Bridge calls itself, justifiably, "the nation's money factory." Here, the paper currency, postage stamps, and many of the official documents issued by the US Government are produced.

Historical Notes – The most widely circulated currency during the colonial period was the Spanish *peso de 8 reales*, or "piece of eight." During the Revolution, hoarding of reales and other coins led to a shortage and consequently to the Continental Congress' issuing of its own currency. Backed by no reserves, this currency gave rise to the expression "not worth a Continental." Under the Articles of Confederation enacted after the war, the dollar was adopted as the unit of currency, but no paper money was issued until 1862. Then, "demand notes," intended in part to help finance the Civil War, resulted in the establishment of the Bureau of Engraving and Printing.

Functioning as an arm of the Treasury Department, the bureau initially consisted of four women and two men, who, working in the basement of the TREASURY BUILDING, sealed and separated notes printed by private companies. After a year, the bureau began printing some notes on its own, and by 1877, was responsible for all currency printing. The green ink chosen for one side of these bills, because of its resistance to physical and chemical change, earned the notes the name "greenbacks."

The bureau's expanding operations warranted more space, and in 1879, it moved into its own building at the corner of Independence Avenue and 14th Street. Known as the Auditor's Building, the brick structure, crowned by a slim tower, is now part of the Department of Agriculture. In 1914, the bureau moved to its current building, slightly south on 14th Street, and in 1938, the annex building was constructed across 14th Street. Engraving facilities are now housed in the annex *(not open to the public)*. The total floor space of bureau operations encompasses 27 acres. In addition to bills and postal stamps, these facilities also produce Executive and Treasury seals, official engravings of Presidents and governmental buildings, presidential invitations, and military certificates.

Some Hard Currency Facts – The Bureau of Engraving and Printing annually produces 8 million notes, worth $100 billion, and 30 billion postage stamps, making it the largest such producer in the world. Its presses run nonstop, and $200 million dollars in paper currency is continually in process at these facilities. About 95 percent of the bills are intended as replacement for worn-out currency already in circulation. A dollar bill, for example, has a life span of 18 months, while a $100 note lasts approximately 9 years. The Federal Reserve Board regulates the number of bills to be printed and their denominations. Typically, half the bureau's production is devoted to manufacturing $1 bills, 20 percent to $20, 12 percent each to $5 and $10 bills, and 2 percent each to $50 and $100 notes. The $100 bill is the largest denomination produced since 1947. The cost to manufacture each bill is 4 cents.

Visit – The entrance hall contains displays and a film on the history of currency and US paper money production. The remainder of the self-guided tour leads past three processing rooms. In the first room, bills are printed by a process called intaglio printing, in which impressions are made by pressing inked engravers' plates into the currency fabric, a blend of 75 percent linen and 25 percent cotton. Each fabric sheet holds 32 bills.

In the second area, sheets are trimmed and examined for imperfections. Any defective sheets, called "muts"—an abbreviation of mutilated—are shredded. However, 99.9 percent of the printed bills are without defect. The third processing room is devoted to printing just the Treasury seals and serial numbers on bills. After this final printing, the bills are cut, stacked, and banded in preparation for their dispersal to the 12 different Federal Reserve banks throughout the country. The tour ends in an exhibit hall displaying stamps, bills, and historical materials.

ARTS AND INDUSTRIES BUILDING

Michelin map 48 K9 *time: 1/2 hour*

Jefferson Dr. at 9th St. SW M *Smithsonian or L'Enfant Plaza. Open daily 10am–5:30pm; closed Dec 25. Free admission. ♿ ☎357-2700.*

The First National Museum – In 1876, the US celebrated its centennial by hosting the nation's first world's fair, known as the International Exhibition, in Philadelphia. When it ended, 60 freight cars full of centennial exhibits were shipped to the Smithsonian. As the institution's only building at that time, the CASTLE was unable to accommodate these acquisitions. Congress authorized the construction of a national museum, now called the Arts and Industries Building, on the Mall. Adolph Cluss designed the elaborate brick and Ohio sandstone structure with four turreted wings radiating from a fountained, skylit rotunda. A sculptural trio entitled *Columbia Protecting Science and Industry* by Casper Buberl ornaments the gable above the main entrance. Completed in 1881, the museum was the setting for President Garfield's inaugural ball.

A Monument to Victoriana – A restoration undertaken for the 1976 bicentennial celebration returned the building to its former glory and reinstated exhibits from the Philadelphia Centennial, which celebrated the coming of the industrial age.
The north hall now displays late 19C consumer goods, such as furniture, clocks, books, and hardware. The west hall is devoted to turbines, steam engines, drills, and other large machinery. In the east hall are exhibits representing the resources and products of various states and foreign countries, including such eclectic items as Oriental cloisonné, Viennese bentwood rockers, Swiss watches, and an American locomotive. The south hall houses a new Experimental Gallery devoted to exploring innovative exhibition techniques.

US BOTANIC GARDEN

Michelin map 48 K11 *time: 1/2 hour*

1st St. SW. Mall entrance on Maryland Ave. M *Federal Center. Open daily 9am–5pm. Free admission. ♿ ☎225-7099.*

Situated at the foot of Capitol Hill, this lush conservatory provides a pleasant respite from the bustle of the Mall.

The Nation's Greenhouse – This federally owned institution was chartered by Congress in 1818. The first greenhouse was established in 1842 to conserve the collection of exotic specimens brought from the South Seas by a US team of explorers. Originally located on the premises of the PATENT OFFICE BUILDING, the collection was transferred to the Mall in 1850. The present conservatory, begun in 1931, features a skillful blend of two building types traditionally used for storing and displaying plants: the 19C iron-and-glass greenhouse and the stone orangerie of French palace gardens, with its characteristic full-length arched windows. The facility provides some 40,000sq ft for the display of the national collections.
The entrance hall, the setting for resplendent seasonal floral exhibits, leads into a large glass pavilion with towering subtropical plants. The two smaller pavilions flanking this central space house exotic plants: flowering orchids; coffee, chocolate, and banyan trees; and a collection of cycad trees similar to those existing on earth 200 million years ago.
The park situated across Independence Avenue blooms with myriad seasonal flowering plants that provide a colorful setting for the cast-iron **Bartholdi Fountain**, executed by Frédéric-Auguste Bartholdi (1834-1904), sculptor of the Statue of Liberty.

Cross-references to sights described in this guide are indicated in SMALL CAPITALS.
Consult the index (p 183) for the appropriate page number.

★★★ THE MEMORIALS West Mall

Michelin map 48 K4-M7 *time: 3 hours*

The portion of the Mall west of 15th St. is the setting for the nation's most venerated monuments. Offset by the graceful **Tidal Basin**, and the Potomac River, the landscaping in this area lends both grandeur and contemplative beauty to the memorials to Presidents Washington, Jefferson, and Lincoln. Skillfully positioned at major focal points of the city's monumental axes, these three memorials command striking vistas that further enhance their tremendous emotional impact. The centerpiece of West Potomac Park is the impressive **Reflecting Pool**, which stretches 350ft beyond the east facade of the Lincoln Memorial. Created in the 1970s, **Constitution Gardens**, with its 45 acres of landscaped grounds surrounding a pleasant pond, borders the pool to the north. The small island in the pond provides a placid setting for the semicircular memorial to the Signers of the Declaration of Independence, which was dedicated in 1984. Discreetly positioned in the northwest corner of Constitution Gardens is "the Wall," a simple, but revered black granite monument to America's fallen and missing Vietnam soldiers. A classically inspired memorial (1924) to DC veterans graces the green expanse on the south side of the Reflecting Pool.

Encircling the Tidal Basin are the city's famous **Japanese cherry trees**★★ *(generally in bloom late March or early April),* which originated as a gift from the mayor of Tokyo to Washington DC in 1912. In 1958, the Japanese presented the city with two additional gifts: a 17C granite lantern to commemorate Commodore Perry's voyage to Japan (1853-54) and a stone pagoda. Both objects now stand among the cherry trees on the west bank of the Tidal Basin.

East Potomac Park, the peninsula projecting southeast from the Tidal Basin, is also bordered by cherry trees. The park is devoted to general recreational uses.

WASHINGTON MONUMENT *time: 1/2 hour*

The Mall at 15th St. M Smithsonian. Open mid-Apr–Labor Day daily 8am–midnight; the rest of the year 9am–5pm; closed Dec 25. Free admission. From mid-Apr–Labor Day, we strongly recommend visiting the monument at night; entry lines are generally shorter and the view of the lighted city is spectacular. ☎ *426-6840.*

The capital's most conspicuous landmark, this austere white marble obelisk rises from a knoll in the middle of the Mall. Though it took nearly four decades to complete, the monument, ringed by US flags, now stands as a symbol of both the man and the city whose name it bears.

Father of the Nation – Soldier, statesman, and leader, George Washington began his long service to this country while in his early 20s, distinguishing himself as a commander during the French and Indian War in the 1750s. Following the war, Washington served as a loyal British member of the Virginia House of Burgesses in Williamsburg. However, as tension over British taxation grew among the colonists, Washington himself became increasingly disenchanted with the mother country. Along with other discontented colonists, he served as one of seven Virginia delegates to the 1774 Continental Congress in Philadelphia. A year later, at the second Continental Congress, he was elected unanimously to head the Continental Army. For eight years, Washington spearheaded the fight against Britain, frequently keeping the war effort alive through the strength of his own convictions. In addition to battling the superior forces of the British, Washington had to contend with his own poorly trained, often unenthusiastic troops, as well as with the vicissitudes of a Congress frequently reluctant to provide the necessary funds or moral support. After countless setbacks and lost battles, the Continentals, thanks to Washington's military brilliance and the help of French allies, won a decisive victory against Lord Cornwallis' troops on October 19, 1781, at Yorktown, Virginia.

For six years, from 1783 to 1789, Washington enjoyed a respite from public life at his plantation, MOUNT VERNON, near Alexandria, Virginia. But, in 1787, when growing anarchy and lack of centralized government threatened the new confederation of states, he presided over the Constitutional Congress in Philadelphia. Washington, judicious and nonpartisan, served as a stabilizing force that allowed the contentious delegates to arrive at a mutually acceptable constitution for the young Republic. Two years later, in 1789, the new electoral college unanimously voted Washington the first President of the nation. On April 30, 1789, he took the oath of office on the steps of Federal Hall in New York. Faced with defining what the presidency meant, Washington proceeded cautiously. He managed to keep the young country out of European wars, to establish Federal authority over that of individual states, and presidential authority over issues of foreign policy. He tried, though unsuccessfully, to discourage the adoption of a partisan political system, and he set a standard of ceremonial decorum for his office. He also approved and began construction of the new Federal city that would bear his name. After eight years and two terms as President, he refused a third and in 1797, retired for a final time to Mount Vernon.

A Monument to the Man – In 1783, the Continental Congress passed a resolution to erect an equestrian statue honoring the hero of the Revolution. Washington approved L'Enfant's plan to position the statue at the center of the Mall, where the east-west axis, originating at the Capitol, intersected the north-south axis aligned with the White House. Lack of funds delayed the project for decades. Finally, in 1833, a group of prominent citizens formed the Washington National Monument Society. In a public drive to raise funds, the society solicited each American for one dollar. Having raised $28,000 by 1836, the group held a contest to choose a design for the monument. The well-respected architect **Robert Mills** won with his concept of a "grand circular colonnaded building...from which springs an obelisk shaft." The cornerstone was laid in 1848, though not at the site originally intended by L'Enfant, as that proved too marshy to bear the weight. Instead, the site was moved 360ft east and 120ft south to higher ground. Mills' design was also altered to become, as one congressman put it, "a simple shaft...free from anything tinsel or tawdry."

Progress was slow due to insufficient funding. To speed construction, the Monument Society invited states, citizens, and even foreign countries to contribute embellished memorial stone blocks for the interior. During the Civil War, work ceased, leaving the monument a truncated 150ft shaft that languished in unsightly neglect until 1876. Then, the Monument Society ceded the shaft and grounds to the Federal Government. Stone from the same Maryland quarry was used for the later work, but it was extracted from a different stratum, causing a change in shading still clearly visible about a third of the way up the structure.

Dedicated on February 21, 1885, the monument opened to the public in 1888. During the past century, some 75 million people have visited it.

Visit – An elevator makes a 70-second ascent from the ground to the observation room at the summit of the monument. Eight small windows, two on each side of the pyramidal apex of the obelisk, afford the best **panorama★★★** available of the capital city. The south-facing windows overlook the Tidal Basin and the Jefferson Memorial; the western view highlights the Reflecting Pool and the Lincoln Memorial; the north faces the Ellipse and the White House, and the east overlooks the long stretch of Mall ending in the Capitol. Photographs above the windows reproduce the views and identify major landmarks.

Visitors exit one level below the observation room. On the one-hour "Down the Steps" tour *(Sat and Sun at 10am and 2pm)*, guides explain some of the 193 embellished memorial stones given as gifts by individuals, groups, and foreign governments.

JEFFERSON MEMORIAL *time: 1/2 hour*

South bank of Tidal Basin. M Smithsonian. Open daily 8am–midnight; closed Dec 25. Free admission. Guided tours (15min) available on request. P ♿ ☎426-6821.

In a peaceful shaded spot on the south shore of the Tidal Basin, the nation's third President is commemorated with a 20C adaptation of the ancient Roman Pantheon. Inscribed on its marble walls are Jefferson's own writings concerning the role of government in safeguarding human liberties.

The Man – Statesman, philosopher, architect, musician, inventor, planter, and President, Thomas Jefferson was one of the country's greatest geniuses. He brought his talents to bear on many aspects of the new nation, helping to formulate its system of government, assisting in the planning of its capital city, and developing such fundamental principles as public education and religious freedom. In 1962, President Kennedy paid Jefferson a lasting homage when he greeted a group of Nobel prize winners by saying that they were "the most extraordinary collection of talent, of human knowledge, that has ever gathered together at the White House—with the possible exception of when Thomas Jefferson dined alone."

Early Years – Born into a well-respected Virginia family, Jefferson spent his boyhood on the edge of what was then the western frontier, in Albemarle County. His father, Peter, was a civil engineer and prominent local figure, serving as a justice of the peace, a colonel of the local militia, and a member of the House of Burgesses. As a student at the College of William and Mary, in Williamsburg, Virginia, young Tom turned his prodigious intellect to the study of the natural sciences, the arts, and especially law, which he believed shaped the social and political conditions of man. While at college, he also became acquainted with a number of Virginians who would become Revolutionary leaders.

W. Clark/National Park Service

Jefferson Memorial

After studying law for five years with the famous Virginia jurist, George Wythe, Jefferson practiced on his own for another seven years. In 1769, he was elected a member of the House of Burgesses and, while serving, participated in the colonists' protests against British taxation. In 1774, he was elected to the first Continental Congress in Philadelphia. A year later, at the second Continental Congress, he was appointed to a five-man committee charged with drafting a statement to the British Crown that justified the colonists' stand on independence. Noted for his eloquent writings, Jefferson was encouraged by his fellow committee members to draft the document himself. On July 4, 1776, his Declaration of Independence was signed by the Continental Congress.

Serving the New Nation – In 1790, President Washington appointed Jefferson as the first Secretary of State. Jefferson's architectural interests and talents were invaluable during the period. Along with Washington, he was a major force behind implementing plans for the new Federal City. It was also at this time that he became embroiled in his historic conflict with Secretary of Treasury Alexander Hamilton. Their strident opposition to one another's views on the extents of state vs. Federal powers under the Constitution led to the formation of a two-party political system. From 1797 to 1801, Jefferson served as Vice President under John Adams before becoming the third President. Jefferson was the first US President to be inaugurated in Washington. During his two terms in office (1801-1809), the US negotiated the Louisiana Purchase, buying from France the lands west of the Mississippi for $27,267,622. The accession of this vast territory greatly strengthened the young country's position internationally and led to westward expansion.

The Final Years – Jefferson retired to his beloved Monticello outside Charlottesville, Virginia, the domed plantation house he had designed in his elegant and sober brand of neoclassicism. Here, he pursued his long-cherished dream of founding an institution of public education. Jefferson personally conceived both the architecture and educational approach for the nearby University of Virginia in Charlottesville, which opened in 1825. On July 4, 1826, Thomas Jefferson died at Monticello.

A Controversial Monument – In 1934, Congress enacted a resolution authorizing this memorial, which became the last in the city's triumvirate of presidential monuments along with those honoring Lincoln and Washington. From the beginning, the project was beset by controversy. **John Russell Pope**, the designer of numerous Federal buildings in the capital city, planned the structure as an adaptation of the Pantheon in Rome, in deference to Jefferson's love of classical architecture. Critics alternately charged that a more contemporary architectural plan be used or that a utilitarian building, such as a national auditorium or stadium, be built rather than a monument. Ultimately, Pope's design, though scaled down to half its initial size, was constructed.

The first site chosen for the memorial, 450ft north of its present location, also met with public protests. It would have required reshaping the Tidal Basin and destroying many of the site's cherry trees given as a gift by the mayor of Tokyo in 1912. The current site lies on an axis with the White House, thus creating a monumental north-south perspective consistent with the spirit of L'Enfant's original plan for the city *(see p 20)*.

Visit – *Enter on the Tidal Basin side.* The wide paved plaza in front of the monument along the Tidal Basin offers a sweeping **view** of the capital's famous cherry trees, which bloom profusely around late March and early April. Stairs lead from the plaza to the monument's entrance portico, which supports a sculpted marble pediment depicting Jefferson surrounded by the four other members of the committee chosen to draft the Declaration of Independence (from left to right: Benjamin Franklin, John Adams, Jefferson, Roger Sherman, and Robert Livingston).

Encircled by an Ionic colonnade, the open-air interior of the monument is dominated by a 19ft bronze **statue** of Jefferson by Rudulph Evans. Standing on a 6ft pedestal, the likeness of a middle-aged Jefferson, in knee breeches and a fur-collared coat, clutches a rolled parchment containing the Declaration of Independence. The four wall panels surrounding the statue are inscribed with Jefferson's writings, including portions of the Declaration of Independence, admonitions against slavery, and statements promulgating religious freedom and flexibility in government.

LINCOLN MEMORIAL *time: 1/2 hour*

The Mall at 23rd St. NW. M Foggy Bottom. Open daily 8am–midnight; closed Dec 25. Free admission. Guided tours (15min) available on request. P ♿ ☎426-6895.

From this stately memorial, the famous marble likeness of a seated, brooding Lincoln stares across the Reflecting Pool to the Washington Monument, and to the Capitol beyond. On the southwest side of the monument, Arlington Memorial Bridge serves as a symbolical link between Lincoln and the South's great hero, Robert E. Lee, whose home, Arlington House, overlooks the monument from the Virginia bluffs. Along the same axis is positioned the eternal flame marking the Arlington gravesite of J.F. Kennedy, the popular 20C President *(the flame is visible from the rear of the memorial).*

Preserver of the Union – Born in Kentucky in 1809 to a poor farming family, Abraham Lincoln was a self-educated, self-made man who became this country's 16th President and perhaps its most admired political hero. He is remembered by an affectionate public as Honest Abe, the down-home, commonsensical statesman; as the Great Emancipator, who ultimately freed the country of slavery; and as the President who fought a protracted civil war in order to keep the nation intact. Catapulted from state politics to the presidency, Lincoln was faced with a nation in turmoil even before he took the oath of office in March 1861. South Carolina, knowing Lincoln to be an opponent of slavery, seceded from the Union after he was elected. Six other southern states quickly followed suit. The month after his inauguration, Confederate and Union troops exchanged fire at Fort Sumter. For the next four years, Lincoln waged a war to bring the southern states back into the Union.

In 1863, he issued his renowned **Emancipation Proclamation**, decreeing that slaves in the Confederate states would thereafter be free. Though this was more a symbolic gesture than a real reversal of slavery nationwide, it helped set the stage for the eventual passage in 1865 of the 13th Amendment to the Constitution, which did in fact abolish slavery.

In 1865, while Lincoln was serving his second term, Lee surrendered to Ulysses S. Grant at Appomattox, Virginia. With the long war over, Lincoln began plans for the reconstruction of the South, but his plans were never realized. On April 14, 1865, he was shot at FORD'S THEATRE by the actor John Wilkes Booth. The following day, at age 56, the President died of his wounds.

An Anchor for the Mall – A congressional commission was established after Lincoln's death to plan a monument in his memory. For years, various proposals were made concerning the monument's design and location. In 1902, the McMillan Commission *(p 23)*, with the backing of the Commission of Fine Arts, endorsed a memorial at the western end of the recently extended Mall, but not until 1912 were these plans implemented.

The monument's designer, Henry Bacon, inspired by Greek architecture, produced his version of a Doric temple, reminiscent of the Parthenon in Athens. Unlike the builders of antiquity, however, Bacon positioned the main entrance on the long side of the structure, overlooking the Mall. Work began on the memorial in 1914; it was dedicated in 1922.

A National Forum – Over the years, this monument epitomizing Lincoln's ideals has served on many occasions as the forum for public protests and demonstrations. In 1963, Martin Luther King Jr addressed a crowd of 200,000 gathered here with his famous "I have a dream..." oratory. The acclaimed black opera singer Marian Anderson gave a historic outdoor concert here in 1939, after being refused permission to perform at the DAR'S Constitution Hall *(p 83)*. During the Vietnam War, President Richard Nixon paid an unofficial late-night visit to the protesters gathered here.

W. Clark/National Park Service

Abraham Lincoln

Exterior – Reproduced on copper pennies and five-dollar bills, the facade of this building is easily identifiable. Thirty-six Doric columns form a continuous colonnade ringing the edifice and symbolize the states in the Union at the time of Lincoln's death. The names of the 36 states are inscribed in the entablature above the columns. The parapet crowning the structure is adorned with a frieze sculpted with bas-relief swags and bearing the names of the 48 states that existed at the time the monument was completed.

Interior – Ascending a long flight of marble stairs, the visitor is gradually exposed to Lincoln's craggy aspect. **Daniel Chester French** collaborated with Bacon to create a statue of Lincoln that would harmonize with the architecture. French's powerful and massive marble **statue★★★**, 20ft high, depicts a contemplative Lincoln and captures the force of the man himself. Lincoln's own words adorn the memorial. The right wall is inscribed with his second inaugural address and a mural by Jules Guerin, allegorically portraying the freeing of slaves. The Gettysburg Address (1863), the celebrated oratory that begins with the oft-quoted words, "Four score and seven years ago...," is chiseled into the left wall and topped by a similar Guerin mural showing the unity of the North and South.

The monument steps afford a grand **view★★** of the Mall extending the length of the Reflecting Pool to the Washington Monument.

VIETNAM VETERANS MEMORIAL *time: 1/2 hour*

Constitution Gardens at Constitution Ave. and 22nd St. NW. Ⓜ Smithsonian. Open daily 8am–midnight; closed Dec 25. Free admission. Guided tours (15min) available on request. 🅿 ♿ ☎634-1568.

Though it was conceived in controversy, this long solemn black wall has become one of the nation's most cherished and moving memorials. Tucked away in the sylvan setting of Constitution Gardens, it bears the names of all those killed or missing in the Vietnam War.

"Serenity, Without Conflict" – The impetus for this monument came from a small group of Vietnam veterans living in the capital. Troubled by the public's indifference toward those Americans who served in the Southeast Asian conflict, they formed the Vietnam Veterans Memorial Fund in 1979, soliciting congressional support and contributions from individuals and corporate donors. In July 1980, President Jimmy Carter signed a joint congressional resolution authorizing the placement of the monument on a 2-acre plot in Constitution Gardens just northeast of the Lincoln Memorial.

The fund then held a national design competition for the memorial and appointed an eight-member jury of architectural and landscape professionals to judge the entries. The following criteria had to be met: that the memorial be reflective and contemplative, that it harmonize with its site, that it bear the names of the dead and missing, and that it make no political statement about the Vietnam War. The competition attracted 1,421 entries. The winning design, characterized by one juror as "a simple solution of serenity, without conflict," was submitted by **Maya Ying Lin**, a 21-year-old architectural student at Yale University. Lin's wall was conceived as a symbol of healing. As she explained, "Take a knife and cut open the earth, and with time the grass would heal it."

Begun in March 1982, the Wall was completed by the following November. Its abstract simplicity aroused some controversy, and in an attempt to quell the dissatisfaction, a realistic sculpture by Frederick Hart was added nearby in 1984. The life-size work, portraying three young soldiers of different ethnic origins, is intended to commemorate all US military men who served in the conflict. However, the Wall quickly became accepted as the moving shrine it was intended to be, a place where family and friends could touch the names of loved ones lost in battle.

In 1989, President Bush authorized the construction of a memorial to the more than 265,000 women who served in the US Armed Forces in Vietnam. A grove of trees just south of the Wall is the site of the **Vietnam Women's Memorial**. Dedicated in 1993, it features a bronze statue (1992, Glenna Goodacre), nearly 7ft high, depicting three military women tending a wounded male soldier.

The Wall – Inset in a low hill, the memorial is actually two triangular walls that join at a 125°angle, with their ends pointing toward the WASHINGTON MONUMENT and the LINCOLN MEMORIAL. Composed of granite from Bangalore, India, they are intended to reflect the surroundings in their polished surface. The memorial extends 493 1/2ft in length and rises to a height of 10ft at its apex. The names of the more than 58,000 men and women incised in the Wall are arranged chronologically, beginning with the first casualty in 1959 and ending with the last in 1975. Those who died in the war are indicated by a diamond; those missing or imprisoned are denoted by a cross. *Directories specifying the memorial panels on which names appear are located at the approaches to the Wall.*

Vietnam Veterans Memorial

A. Rippy/Image Bank

3

★★★

White House Area

Inspired by the stately presence of the Executive Mansion, this area maintains a decorous gentility, with manicured parks, elegant row houses, and grandly conceived public structures.

Lafayette Square – In L'Enfant's plan, the "President's house" was to be surrounded by an 80-acre park. However, Jefferson felt that this was too large an area to be held only for presidential enjoyment, and he ordered Pennsylvania Avenue extended in front of the still incomplete WHITE HOUSE in the early 19C. The 7-acre plot to the north of it thus became a public park known as President's Square.
Around 1815, ST JOHN'S CHURCH took its place on the north side of the park and three years later, the square's first private home, DECATUR HOUSE, was built on the northwest corner. Before long some of the nation's most prominent citizens took up residence in dignified homes facing the square. In 1824, the park was renamed Lafayette Square to honor America's French ally in the Revolution, the Marquis de Lafayette, then on a triumphal second visit to America. That same year, another celebrated historic house, **Blair House**, was erected within view of the White House on Pennsylvania Avenue *(no. 1651)*. Restored in 1988, the house *(not open to the public)* serves as an official guest house for foreign dignitaries.
In the early 1850s, an equestrian statue of Andrew Jackson was placed in the center of the park. The installation led to the later erection of four statues to foreign heroes who aided in the American Revolution: Lafayette (1891, southeast corner); Jean Baptiste Rochambeau (1902, southwest corner); Friedrich von Steuben (1910, northwest corner); and Thaddeus Kosciuszko (1910, northeast corner). During the Civil War, troops were quartered on the square, and following the war, the first major landscaping of the park was carried out in keeping with an 1850s design prepared by Andrew Jackson Downing *(see p 22)*.
Today, many of the remaining Federal row houses bordering Lafayette Square serve as offices. While most of the square itself is a tranquil park, its Pennsylvania Avenue side is frequented by demonstrators protesting White House policies.

Grandiose Buildings – Though work began on the White House in 1792, the building evolved gradually and has been continually enlarged. On its east side is the stately TREASURY BUILDING, which was erected between 1836 and 1869. To the west of the White House is the colossal OLD EXECUTIVE OFFICE BUILDING, completed in 1881.
In the early 20C, the 17th Street corridor south of the White House witnessed the construction of several dignified buildings including the CORCORAN GALLERY OF ART, the headquarters for the American Red Cross, the DAUGHTERS OF THE AMERICAN REVOLUTION complex and the ORGANIZATION OF AMERICAN STATES.

From "White Lot" to Ellipse – South of the White House, the open expanse of ground now called the **Ellipse** was once marshy lowland. During the Civil War, military livestock were enclosed here behind a whitewashed fence that, by tradition, gave rise to the designation "white lot." In the late 19C, the area was reclaimed. At the corner of Constitution Avenue and 17th Street, a stone **lock keeper's house** still stands as a reminder of the Washington Canal *(p 22)*. Across the avenue, on either side of the Ellipse, are a pair of gatehouses, designed by Charles Bulfinch, which once stood on the Capitol grounds.
For decades, the Ellipse expanse served as a recreational area. Then in the mid-20C, it became a ceremonial grounds for the White House. On its north side is the **Zero Milestone**, from which all distances in the Federal City are computed. Also on this side is the **National Christmas Tree**, a blue spruce planted during the administration of President Jimmy Carter.

★★★ WHITE HOUSE

Michelin map 48 H7 — *time: 3/4 hour*

1600 Pennsylvania Ave. NW. M McPherson Square or Metro Center. Open Tue–Sat 10am–noon; closed Sun, Mon and some holidays. Free admission. Due to the large number of visitors in peak season, tickets are required from mid-Mar–mid-Sept. Free tickets are issued at the booth located on the Ellipse on a first-come, first-served basis from 8am until the day's supply is distributed. At the time indicated on your ticket, proceed to the designated tour formation area near the booth.
From mid-Sept–mid-Mar, visitors may go directly to the line that forms at the Southeast Gate on East Executive Ave. Congressional visits (p 162) are available. As the White House may close without advance notice to accommodate official functions, we recommend calling the evening before and the morning of your visit for current tour information ♿ ☎456-7041.

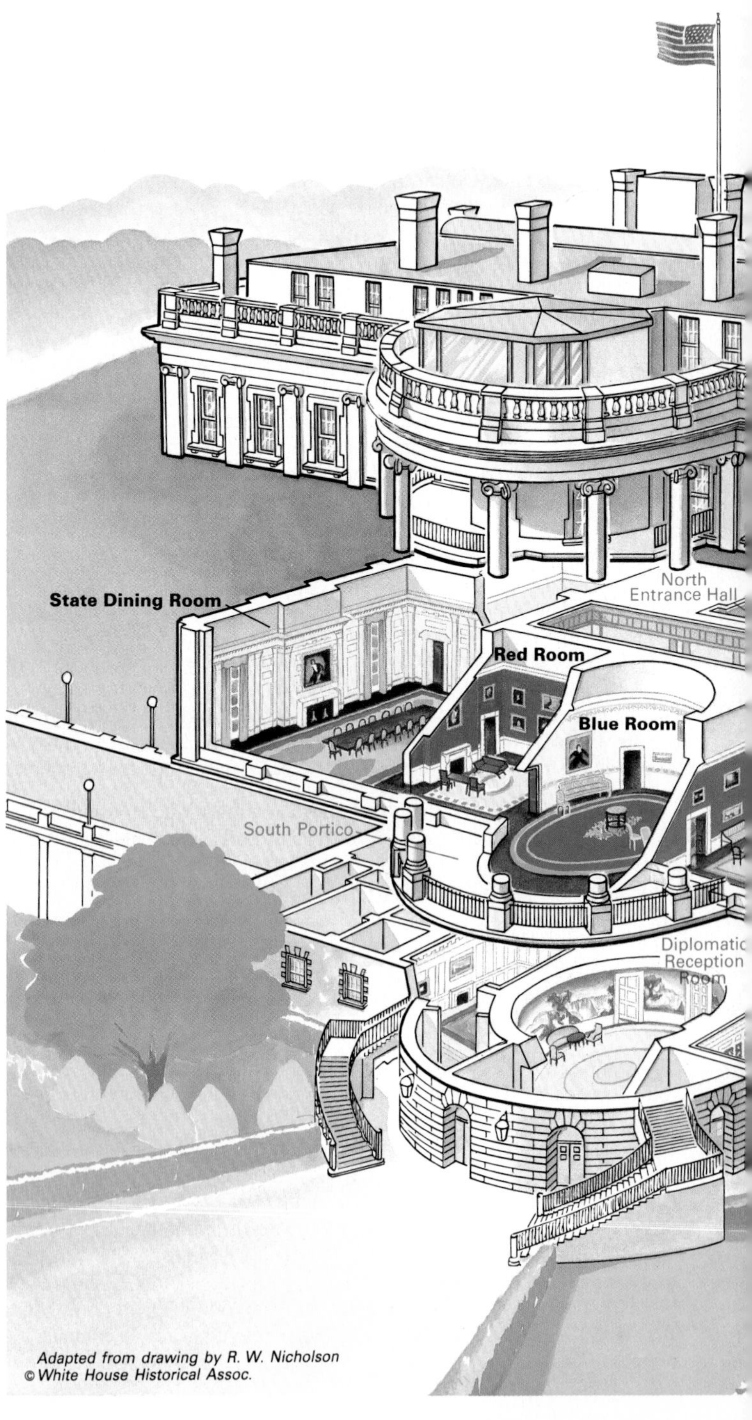

Adapted from drawing by R. W. Nicholson
© White House Historical Assoc.

Special events – The White House organizes a series of public annual events, all of which traditionally attract immense crowds. An **Easter Egg Roll** and Egg Hunt, customarily held the Monday after Easter on the White House's south lawn, are open to children three to six years of age. Activities for older children are held on the Ellipse at the same time. Spring and fall **garden tours** are held twice a year on designated Saturdays and Sundays in April and October. **Christmas candlelight tours** take place on three evenings in late December. As these events are free of charge and do not require tickets or reservations, entry lines are often very long. For further information ☎ 456-2200.

For almost two centuries, the White House has been the home of America's First Families. More than just an official residence, the stately structure has become a universally recognized symbol of the US presidency. Today, its public rooms house an exemplary collection of Americana, both furnishings and historic memorabilia, reflecting the tastes of the nation's leaders.

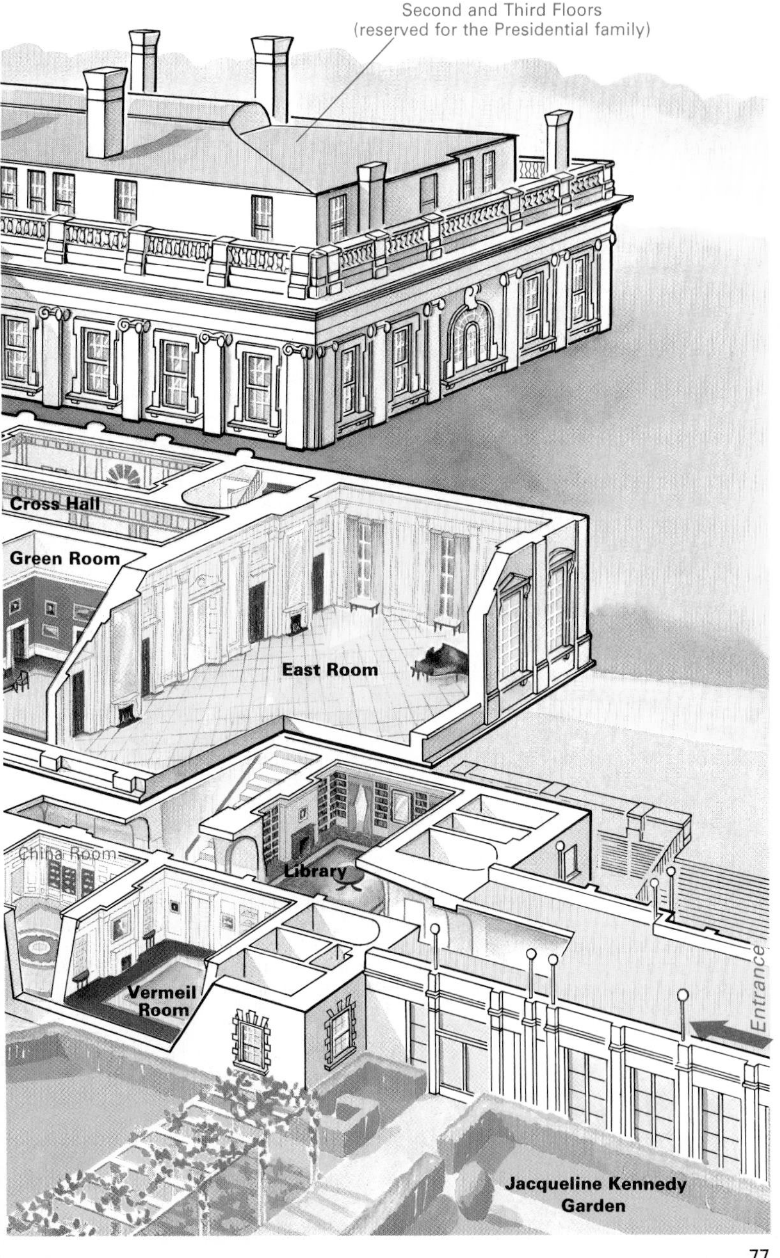

HISTORICAL NOTES

The President's Palace – L'Enfant had envisioned the "President's house" as a grand palatial structure, five times its current size, but after the Frenchman's acrimonious departure in 1792 *(see p 21)*, the city commissioners announced a public design competition for the official residence. Among the drawings submitted was an anonymous entry executed by Secretary of State Jefferson, who, as a self-taught architect, was involved in the planning of the new Federal City. The $500 prize went to **James Hoban**, a young Irish builder. His plan called for a 3-story stone structure reminiscent of a Georgian manor, with a hipped roof surrounded by a balustrade. The main facade featured a columned portico with an eagle carved in the pediment. Jefferson considered the proposed size "big enough for two emperors, one Pope and the grand Lama."

The cornerstone was laid on October 13, 1792, but due to a serious lack of skilled labor, particularly stonemasons, and a shortage of public funds, the work proceeded slowly. The three city commissioners, faced with financial exigencies, approached President Washington with a plan to reduce the mansion's dimensions. In October 1793, Washington compromised by agreeing to delete the third floor, and Hoban redrew plans for a 2-story building.

First Occupants – The structure was not completed during Washington's presidency; while serving his two terms in office, the first President lived in private homes in New York and Philadelphia, both of which served as temporary capitals while the new Federal City was being built. The house was complete enough for the second President, John Adams (1797-1801), to move in a few months prior to the end of his term. In November 1800, Adams became the first President to occupy the mansion. Though conditions in the still incomplete house were drafty and unpleasant, Adams nonetheless left a lasting benediction on it. After his first night there, he wrote, "May none but honest and wise men ever rule under this roof!"

The mansion's first long-term resident, Thomas Jefferson (1801-1809), turned his architectural attentions to the design of the White House, as the whitewashed sandstone building had come to be known. Collaborating with his Surveyor of Public Buildings, **Benjamin H. Latrobe**, Jefferson designed colonnaded wings on the east and west sides to house domestic and office spaces. Latrobe also replaced the mansion's heavy slate and mortar roof with a lighter one of steel.

Conflagration and Reconstruction – James Madison's stay in the Executive Mansion (1809-1817) was marked by disaster. In August 1814, during the War of 1812, the British entered the city and set fire to several public buildings, among them the White House. Thanks to the forethought of Mrs Dolley Madison, many important documents, as well as a Gilbert Stuart portrait of George Washington that now hangs in the East Room, were saved from destruction. Had a summer rain not put out the fire, the mansion would probably have burned to the ground.

The city commissioners called on James Hoban to salvage the mansion he had initially begun. Finding that many of the stone walls were seriously weakened, Hoban had them demolished and began rebuilding. In 1818, President Monroe was able to occupy the house. During the Monroe administration, the south portico was added, and the elaborate French Empire pieces that remain at the core of the White House's historic furnishings were acquired.

Throughout the 19C, architectural changes and redecorating occurred as funds were available. In order to customize the house to his own taste, a new President frequently resorted to raising funds by selling old furnishings at public auction. Congressional appropriations for the upkeep and refurbishing of the chief executive's home were generally dependent on the political and economic climate. During the popular administration of Andrew Jackson (1829-1837), for example, bountiful funds allowed for the purchase of new china and glassware, the installation of indoor plumbing, and the completion of the north portico. In other administrations, however, furnishings became seriously dilapidated.

During James Polk's tenure (1845-1849), gas lights were added and long-term interior transformations were initiated. Chester A. Arthur undertook a major refurnishing of the mansion in 1882. According to contemporary reports, he had 24 wagonloads of old furniture carted away for public auction. He then called on the celebrated New York designer, Louis C. Tiffany, to redecorate the interior. Electricity was installed in the White House in 1891.

20C – In 1902, vast changes were again wrought on the mansion by Theodore Roosevelt (1901-1909), who entrusted the prominent architectural firm, McKim, Mead and White, with large-scale renovation. The extensive greenhouses that had flanked the west and south sides of the house for decades were demolished. The west wing was added and an expansive carriage porch built on the east. The interior, whose old plumbing, wiring, heating, and flooring were in dangerous disrepair, was revamped and modernized. The Roosevelt renovation began the process of restoring the White House to its original appearance—a process that has been continued by succeeding Presidents. In 1942, while Franklin D. Roosevelt was in residence, the current east wing was built. Under Roosevelt's successor, Harry S. Truman (1945-1953), another major structural renovation was undertaken to shore up and replace the weakened flooring, walls, and foundations. The second-story balcony was added to the south portico during the Truman presidency.

During her stay in the White House (1961-1963), Jacqueline Kennedy began a campaign to acquire items of historic and artistic interest. Following her precedent, in 1964, President Johnson established the Committee for the Preservation of the White House, which provided for a permanent curator. The curatorial staff today continues to expand and document the White House collection.

TOUR

The White House is set off by 18 acres of flower gardens, lawns, and trees *(grounds not included on tour)*. A balustraded roofline, Ionic pilasters, and windows with alternating rounded and triangular pediments adorn the rectangular facade of the main structure. The columned and balconied south portico extends out in an expansive bay overlooking the sweep of the south lawn and the Ellipse beyond. The colonnade of the north portico facing Pennsylvania Avenue and Lafayette Park supports an unadorned pediment. Elaborate carvings grace the area above the fanlight of the double entrance doors. Pavilions connect the 1-story east and west wings to the main mansion.

The west wing *(not open to the public)* houses the Cabinet Room, several staff and reception rooms, and the President's Oval Office, which opens onto the Rose Garden. In the central mansion, the ground floor and first-floor rooms function as formal state reception areas, while the First Family's private living quarters are located on the second and third floors.

Ground Floor – *Visitors first enter a security building on East Executive Ave.* In the paneled entrance hall of the east wing, as elsewhere in the mansion, portraits of First Ladies and Presidents adorn the walls. A glassed colonnade overlooking the intimate **Jacqueline Kennedy Garden** displays exhibit panels explaining the history of the White House .

Just beyond the White House book sales area is an elegant vaulted marble corridor. Portraits of recent First Ladies also hang here, and a large Sheraton breakfront holds an assortment of presidential porcelains. The **library**, which opens off the right side of the hall, is decorated in late Federal style and contains some 2,700 volumes. The **Vermeil Room**, situated directly across the hall, is so named for its collection of French and English gilded silver, or vermeil, dating from the 17C to the early 20C.

The China Room and Diplomatic Reception Room, situated on the ground floor, are included on congressional visits only *(see p 162)*.

First Floor – The vast and ornate **East Room**, the setting for White House concerts, dances, and official ceremonies, contains elaborate plaster ceiling decorations and entablatures, fluted pilasters, Bohemian cut-glass chandeliers and four marble mantels. Because it is used for a variety of purposes, the gold and white room is sparsely furnished. The legendary 1797 **portrait of George Washington** that Dolley Madison saved hangs in this room. The small drawing room off the East Room is known as the **Green Room**, owing to the color scheme it has retained since the days of President John Quincy Adams (1825-1829). An intricately patterned Turkish Hereke carpet complements the room's green watered-silk wall coverings and the tones of the upholstered Sheraton-style chairs and settees, many from the early 19C workshop of Duncan Phyfe. Over the mantel is a portrait of Benjamin Franklin by David Martin. On the dropleaf sofa table is the silverplated coffee urn that John Adams considered one of his "most prized possessions."

Note the folding Honduran mahogany doors that form a paneling in the alcoves between rooms.

The French Empire furnishings in the elliptical **Blue Room** include seven of the original Bellange gilded armchairs ordered from Paris by James Monroe (1817-1825). The gilded wood chandelier and Carrara marble mantel contain classical motifs mirrored in the wallpaper frieze that forms a border around the wainscoting and entablature. Portraits of the first Presidents to live in the house are among the paintings hanging in this reception room. The three long casement windows afford a striking view of the WASHINGTON MONUMENT and the JEFFERSON MEMORIAL beyond. From this standpoint, the visitor can easily discern the extent to which the Washington Monument is positioned off the axis that links the White House with the Jefferson Memorial *(for explanation see p 71)*. The small parlor known as the **Red Room** also contains French Empire-style furnishings prevalent from 1810 to 1830, including gilded chairs upholstered in red and gold damask. Displayed on the wall between the windows is a bust of Martin van Buren (1837-1841) by Hiram Powers. Above the fireplace hangs a painting depicting van Buren's daughter-in-law and official hostess, Angelica. Note that the bust is featured in the painting. Other paintings in this room are an 1804 portrait of Dolley Madison by Gilbert Stuart and Albert Bierstadt's *The Rocky Mountains* (1870).

The Red Room

© White House Historical Assoc.; photo by National Geographic Society

In the gold and white **State Dining Room**, the neoclassical pilaster, wall paneling, and ceiling molding are modeled on decor found in late 18C English estates. Gold upholstered Queen Anne-style chairs surround the long mahogany dining table, which holds the gilded plateau from a service ordered by James Monroe.
Over the mantel is the Lincoln portrait executed by G. P. A. Healy in 1869. Marble-topped side tables with gilded eagle pedestals rim the room. When prepared for a state dinner, this room can seat 140 people.
Marble columns separate the long **Cross Hall** from the North Entrance Hall, both of which are hung with portraits of recent Presidents. The carpeted marble staircase, connecting the state rooms to the First Family's private quarters, is frequently used by the President and First Lady to make ceremonial entrances.

The tour exits through the north portico.

Tonight took a long look at the President's house. The white portico—the palace-like, tall, round columns, spotless as snow—the walls also—tender and soft moonlight, flooding the pale marble, and making peculiar faint languishing shades, not shadows—everywhere a soft transparent, hazy, thin, blue moon-lace, hanging in the air—the brilliant and extra-plentiful cluster of gas, on and around the facade, columns, portico, etc.,—everything so white, so marbly pure and dazzling, yet soft—the White House of future poems, and of dreams and dramas, there in the soft and copious moon—the gorgeous front, in the trees, under the lustrous flooding moon, full of reality, full of illusion—the forms of the trees, leafless, silent, in trunk and myriad angles of branches under the stars and sky—the White House of the land, and of beauty and night....

Walt Whitman, *Specimen Days (24 February 1863)*, 1882

★★ CORCORAN GALLERY OF ART

Michelin map 48 H6-J6 *time: 1 hour*

17th St. and New York Ave. NW. Ⓜ Farragut West or Farragut North. Open Wed–Mon 10am–5pm (9pm Thu), hours may vary on holidays; closed Tue and Jan 1, Dec 25. Suggested contribution: $3, students and seniors $1, children under 12 free. Guided tours (30min) 12:30pm (and 7:30pm Thu). ♿ ✕ ☎638-1439.

In a city now dominated by Federal museums, the Corcoran Gallery of Art can claim to be the capital's oldest institution and its most venerable private gallery. Although it houses a fine collection of European art, the Corcoran is primarily renowned as a showcase for American art.

The Benefactor – A self-made man, self-educated connoisseur, and respected philanthropist, **William Wilson Corcoran** (1798-1888) began constructing a museum to house his private collection in 1859. That original building, now called the RENWICK GALLERY, was almost complete when Corcoran halted the project in 1861. As a Southern sympathizer, Corcoran found himself unwelcome in wartime Washington, and he left for Europe in 1862. He returned in 1865, his patriotism still in question, and resumed his museum project, in part to prove his goodwill toward the nation. In 1870, he formed a board of trustees to govern the new museum, which was to be used "for the purpose of encouraging American genius." Corcoran generously donated his personal collection, the building and grounds, and a $900,000 endowment.
One of the nation's first major galleries of art, the Corcoran opened in 1874. From the outset, it enjoyed great popularity, both with the public and with American artists, who considered it a great honor to be exhibited there. In order to further the cause of the arts in America, Corcoran made another endowment of $100,000 in 1879 for an art school, to function as an adjunct to the museum.

The "New" Corcoran – William Corcoran died in 1888 and so never saw the elegant Beaux-Arts building that now bears his name. In 1897, this new, larger Corcoran opened several blocks south of the old building, which was no longer big enough for its school and its expanded, 700-work collection.
The building's architect, Ernest Flagg, faced with a trapezoidal plot, designed the new museum with a semicircular amphitheater at the lot's acute angle, where 17th Street and New York Avenue intersect. The facade of white Georgia marble is set off by a green copper roof, ornate grillwork, and a frieze inscribed with the names of 11 great artists, among them Dürer, Raphael, and Rembrandt. Above the entrance is W. W. Corcoran's motto: "Dedicated to Art." The prominent 20C architect Frank Lloyd Wright considered the Corcoran "the best designed building in Washington."
In 1925, Sen William Andrew Clark of Montana bequeathed to the Corcoran his noted European collection of works by such masters as Rembrandt, Turner, Corot, and Degas. The **Clark Bequest** also includes tapestries, rugs, and stained glass, as well as an 18C French salon. A gift of $700,000 from Clark's family went to build a wing to house his bequest. This addition, off the southwest end of the original building, was designed by Charles A. Platt, architect for the Freer Gallery *(p 66)*. In 1937, Edward and Mary Walker donated their collection, which includes the paintings of such pivotal French Impressionists as Renoir, Pissarro, and Monet.

VISIT

The Corcoran Gallery has over 11,000 objects in its permanent collection. Since it can display only a small portion of these at any one time, its exhibits change frequently, as does the specific location of pieces of art within the museum.

First Floor – Just beyond the entrance to the museum are a pair of 2-story atriums. The pillared, skylit galleries display 19C marble portrait busts by American neo-classic sculptors, notably Hiram Powers.

One of the Corcoran's most well-known works, Powers' famous nude sculpture the **Greek Slave** (1846), scandalized Victorian audiences when it was first shown in the old Corcoran Gallery (now the RENWICK GALLERY).

Gallery 1, a small space opening onto the south atrium, is devoted to rotating exhibits featuring the works of contemporary American artists. A series of connected galleries *(5-8)* off the far end of the south atrium display 19C European landscape and genre paintings, predominantly from the Clark collection. An exception is **The Veiled Nun**, an enigmatic marble bust by Giuseppe Croff, which was purchased by Corcoran himself.

The **Salon Doré** *(gallery 9)* was bequeathed to the Corcoran by Senator Clark, who had the room and its furnishings transplanted from an 18C Parisian mansion to his own New York residence. The salon, richly appointed with gilded woodwork moldings and paneling, is considered one of the finest examples of late French rococo interiors in this country.

The long, L-shaped gallery adjacent to the Salon Doré is normally devoted to contemporary photography and works on paper.

The rotunda gallery, visible from the atrium hall and connected to it by a marble stairway, showcases the *Hope Venus*, a replica of a work executed by the 19C Italian sculptor Canova. The sculpture was commissioned by Thomas Hope, a descendant of the owner of the famous Hope Diamond. Paintings from the museum's permanent collection are also exhibited here.

Second floor – The four main galleries flanking the atrium chronicle American art from the colonial period to the early 20C. The far left gallery features art from the early days of the Republic, including such historical paintings as Rembrandt Peale's *Washington Before Yorktown* (1824-25), a heroic depiction of the general on horseback, and *The Old House of Representatives* (1822) by Samuel F. B. Morse, inventor of the Morse code. The latter realistically portrays the original House chamber and each of the 80-some members of the 17th Congress.

Corcoran Gallery of Art

Niagara by Frederic Edwin Church

The middle gallery is devoted to mid-19C landscapes, most prominently the works of such Hudson River school painters as Thomas Cole, Frederic Edwin Church, and Albert Bierstadt. Notable works displayed here include Church's **Niagara** (1857), considered America's most popular 19C landscape rendering, and Bierstadt's *Mount Corcoran* (1875-77), a painting that created controversy because the artist named it after a nonexistent American peak, in order to curry favor with Corcoran. The work of late 19C and early 20C masters are displayed in the third gallery, including Thomas Eakins' compelling genre painting **The Pathetic Song**. John Singer Sargent's painting of **Madame Edouard Pailleron** (1879) was instrumental in establishing his reputation as a portraitist in Paris in the 1880s. A different kind of portrait, *Susan on a Balcony Holding a Dog,* characterizes Mary Cassatt's artistic style of juxtaposing well-defined figures against an impressionistic background. Winslow Homer's *A Light on the Sea* (1897) echoes the artist's theme of mankind's precarious flirtation with the forces of nature.

The two galleries off the south end of the atrium normally display 20C art from the museum's impressive and constantly growing collection. Prominent in its holdings are the works of John Sloan and Robert Henri, reflecting the **Ash Can school** of early 20C realism, and the large canvases of such Abstract Expressionists as Hans Hofmann, Mark Rothko, and Helen Frankenthaler. Andy Warhol and other Pop artists are also represented in the collection.

The remainder of the second-floor galleries feature temporary and traveling exhibits, and new museum acquisitions typifying the most current movements in American art.

★ RENWICK GALLERY

Michelin map 48 H6 *time: 3/4 hour*

Pennsylvania Ave. and 17th St. NW. M *Farragut West or Farragut North. Open daily 10am–5:30pm; closed Dec 25. Free admission. Guided tours (1 hour) daily 10am–1pm (2-week advance reservation required).* ♿ ☎*357-2700.*

The earliest major example of the Second Empire style in America and an embodiment of Victorian tastes, this ornate brick building adds a touch of quiet elegance to the bustling intersection of Pennsylvania Avenue and 17th Street. Inside, its galleries highlight the best works of contemporary and traditional American craftsmanship.

The City's First Art Museum – In 1858, the wealthy financier William Wilson Corcoran *(see p 80)* commissioned one of the period's most influential architects, **James Renwick**, to design a building to house his private art collection. Impressed by the innovative contemporary architecture he had seen on a recent visit to Paris, Corcoran requested that Renwick adopt the fashionable Second Empire style. Renwick's use of that style influenced architectural tastes in America and was copied in many of the public buildings constructed in the later Grant administration, such as the OLD EXECUTIVE OFFICE BUILDING, situated across the street.

In 1874, after a hiatus brought on by the Civil War, the Corcoran Gallery of Art, as the building was then called, opened as Washington's first art museum. Exhibiting the paintings and sculpture given it by its founder, the museum also displayed, in Victorian fashion, plaster copies of classical sculpture in its statuary hall. Because of the nude and seminude nature of these works, separate visiting hours were maintained for men and women.

The Corcoran School of Art had its inception here in 1879. By 1897, the collection and school had outgrown the original building and were moved down 17th Street to the building they occupy today *(see p 80)*.

Sold to the Government for $300,000, the old building was used by the US Court of Claims until 1964, the year in which demolition was proposed. The successful campaign to preserve the threatened landmark was championed by the Kennedy and Johnson administrations. Renamed the Renwick Gallery, it became part of the Smithsonian Institution in 1965. To return the building to its original appearance, restoration architects used old drawings and the photographs of Mathew Brady. The refurbished Renwick opened as a department of the NATIONAL MUSEUM OF AMERICAN ART in 1972.

Exterior – The brick facade is embellished with sandstone pilasters, vermiculated quoins, garlands, and window trim. Filigreed ironwork caps the ridges of the building's distinctive mansard roof. On the long western facade, niches hold statues of Rubens and Murillo, replicas of two of the original 11 statues of artists that once adorned the facades. With American flair, the capitals of the two pilasters flanking the entrance feature sculpted tobacco fronds and ears of corn. Above the entrance bay is a medallion profile of Corcoran, inscribed with his monogram and motto: "Dedicated to Art."

National Museum of American Art

Portal Gates by Albert Paley

Victorian Rooms – A red-carpeted staircase leads from the entryway to the second-floor **Grand Salon**. Decorated in the style of a Victorian picture gallery, the 90ft-long room is furnished with red velvet "poufs"—circular settees—and brocade sofas and chairs. Paintings, hung in tiers, cover its raspberry walls from the wainscoting to the ceiling molding. Dominating the north wall is a portrait of William Wilson Corcoran (1870, William Oliver Stone). The only other painting in the room from Corcoran's original collection is Edwin Abbey's *Trial of Queen Katherine*. The other works—19C landscapes, portraits, and genre paintings—are part of the permanent collection of the NATIONAL MUSEUM OF AMERICAN ART.

The **Octagon Room**, a smaller Victorian gallery *(directly opposite the Grand Salon)*, was initially designed to showcase Hiram Powers' daring nude sculpture *The Greek Slave* (1846), now in the CORCORAN GALLERY. Today, a 5ft vase made in a Berlin porcelain factory in the late 19C occupies the center of the room, surrounded by a blue pouf. Two female portraits by the popular 19C painter George Peter Alexander Healy hang on the walls.

American Crafts – The remainder of the museum is devoted to outstanding works by American crafts people. The rotating exhibit, "American Crafts: The Nation's Collection," located in the galleries on both sides of the Octagon Room, features selected pieces from the Renwick's permanent, comprehensive collection of 20C crafts, ranging from traditional basketry to abstract works in glass, wood, clay, metal, and fiber. The five first-floor galleries are devoted to temporary exhibits—either traveling shows or exhibits mounted by the museum itself. The Renwick's exhibits are renowned for their innovative design and sophisticated content.

★ DAUGHTERS OF THE AMERICAN REVOLUTION

Michelin map 48 J6 — *time: 1 hour*

17th and D Sts. NW. M Farragut West. Open Mon–Fri 8:30am–4pm, Sun 1–5pm; closed Sat, Federal holidays, the last 3 weeks of Apr, and Jan 1, Thanksgiving Day, Dec 25. Free admission. Guided tours (45min) Mon–Fri 10am–2:30pm, Sun 1–5pm. ♿ ☎879-3254.

This stately complex occupies an entire city block and is reputedly the world's largest group of structures owned and maintained exclusively by women. The national headquarters of the Daughters of the American Revolution (DAR), it houses an extensive collection of genealogical materials and artifacts relating to the colonial and early Republic periods through the mid-19C.

The Daughters – The DAR was established in 1890 by a group of women who were descended from Revolutionary War patriots. In the last century, the organization has achieved a national reputation for perpetuating "the memory and spirit of the men and women who achieved American Independence" and for fostering "true patriotism and love of country." Today, it is supported by more than 193,000 members belonging to chapters throughout the 50 states and abroad.

Memorial Continental Hall – This Beaux-Arts edifice was designed at the turn of the century by Edward Pearce Casey, who also collaborated on the construction of the LIBRARY OF CONGRESS. Facing the gracious expanse of the Ellipse, the original entrance is dominated by a monumental porte-cochere or carriage entry, covered by a pedimented roof. The semicircular portico that rises from the balustrated terrace on the C Street side features 13 columns, representing the 13 colonies.

The building houses 33 **period rooms** depicting parlors and studies, as well as a colonial home, tavern, church, and other historical interiors dating from the late 17C to the mid-19C. Of note are the Georgia Room, portraying the late 18C Peter Tondee Tavern in Savannah; the brick-floored Oklahoma kitchen; and the Virginia room, reproducing an 18C dining room.

The original meeting hall, an enormous room overhung by a vaulted skylight and elaborate neoclassical trim, is now the DAR library, a renowned repository of genealogical material. Author Alex Haley used these facilities while researching his 1970s classic, *Roots.*

The **DAR Museum** regularly displays ceramics, silver, glass, and textiles. Additional pieces from the permanent collection of more than 30,000 objects are placed on view in changing exhibits.

In the 1920s, having outgrown its original building, the DAR commissioned the prolific architect John Russell Pope to design **Constitution Hall**, a colossal structure whose columned, pedimented entrance faces 18th St. The building contains a U-shaped, 3,800-seat auditorium, where the Daughters meet for their annual April convention. In addition, the hall functions as a public auditorium where a variety of concerts and lectures are held.

★ DECATUR HOUSE

Michelin map 48 G6-H6 — *time: 1/2 hour*

748 Jackson Place NW. M Farragut West or Farragut North. Visit by guided tour (30min) only Tue–Fri every half hour 10am–3pm; Sat, Sun and holidays noon–4pm; closed Mon and Jan 1, Thanksgiving Day, Dec 25. Admission: $3, children under 19 and seniors $1.50. ♿ ☎842-0920.

For almost a century and a half, this sedate brick town house on the northwest edge of Lafayette Square figured prominently in the social and political life of Washington. The first home built on the square and the last to remain in private ownership, it served as the residence of military heroes and renowned statesmen.

The Decatur Years – Stephen Decatur, a 19C naval hero, had the house built in 1818. Substantial prize money from his military successes against the Barbary pirates off the coast of North Africa and against the British in the War of 1812 enabled him to commission the eminent architect **Benjamin H. Latrobe** to design a home in elegant style. The 3-story structure, 51ft wide and 45ft deep, cost Decatur $11,000. He and his wife, Susan, entertained lavishly here, but only for a brief 18 months. At the age of 41, the young commodore was killed in a duel with a discredited naval captain who believed Decatur responsible for his disgrace. Bereft, Mrs Decatur moved to a Georgetown town house *(p 107)* and rented the Lafayette Square house to a succession of dignitaries. In the 1820s, Secretary of State Henry Clay, the "Great Compromiser," lived in Decatur House, calling it "the best private dwelling in the City." After Clay, Martin Van Buren, then Secretary of State and soon to be President, occupied the house. In 1837, the hotelier John Gadsby *(p 148)* purchased it from Mrs Decatur. During the Civil War, Decatur House was appropriated by the Government as a commissary facility.

The Beale Era – Edward Fitzgerald Beale, a renowned Western adventurer, became owner of the house after the Civil War. In 1847 Beale, accompanied by his cohort Kit Carson, brought back word of California's accession to the Union. A year later, Beale again crossed the country, in a record-breaking 47 days, to officially report the discovery of gold in California.

When Beale and his wife Mary took possession of Decatur House in 1872, it was in disrepair from wartime use. Following the fashion of his day, Beale added such Victorian embellishments as sandstone trim around the entrance and windows. He also had the Latrobe fanlight and side lights around the front door removed and the first-floor windows lengthened. For two decades, the Beales were prominent members of the capital's social circles. President Grant frequently crossed Lafayette Square to visit Beale, who was one of his closest friends.

Decatur House in 1882. Watercolor by E. Vaile

National Trust for Historic Preservation

In 1902, the house passed to the Beales' son, Truxtun. He and his second wife, Marie, made Decatur House a focal point of Washington society. One of the capital's most important annual events, a dinner following the White House Diplomatic Reception, was given here for three decades. Mrs Beale, considered the city's premier hostess, continued to entertain diplomats, royalty, and statesmen even after her husband's death in 1936.

In the early 1940s, recognizing the historic significance of her home, Mrs Beale engaged the noted restoration architect Thomas Tileston Waterman to recover the Latrobe character of the house. In 1956, she bequeathed it to the National Trust for Historic Preservation, which operates it today.

Tour – Latrobe's vestibule combines domes, arches, and recesses to achieve an effect of understated elegance. Off the vestibule to the left lies the parlor, which, like the dining room adjacent to it, is decorated with furnishings appropriate to the Decatur period. Among the parlor furnishings is a *secretaire a guillotine,* so called for its sliding front panel. The room off the right side of the vestibule was used either as a bedchamber or as Decatur's office. Curving double doors, fit to the contours of the vestibule's rear wall, lead to a separate hallway and the main staircase.

The second floor is devoted to the Beale period. A small family sitting room is decorated as it was in Truxtun Beale's day, with informal furnishings and family photographs. In the two formal Victorian drawing rooms, the Beales held their famous soirees. Note the seal of California, composed of a dozen different woods, inlaid in the floor of the north drawing room.

★ OLD EXECUTIVE OFFICE BUILDING

Michelin map 48 H6 — *time: 1 hour*

17th St. and Pennsylvania Ave. NW. M Farragut West or Farragut North. Visit by guided tour (1 3/4 hour) only, Sat 9am–noon (4-week advance reservation required); closed Jan 1, Thanksgiving Day, Dec 25. Free admission. ♿ ☎395-5895.

The massive granite pile that rises like a tiered wedding cake to the west of the White House is one of Washington's foremost architectural treasures. Having survived years of derision and neglect, it has been restored to its former grandeur and houses several key government offices of the Executive branch, including the Executive Office of the President.

Second Empire Landmark – Erected between 1871 and 1888 as headquarters for Departments of State, War, and Navy, this grand building symbolized the renewed vitality of the post-Civil War Government. Its chief architect was Alfred Mullett, who had recently designed the north wing of the TREASURY BUILDING, flanking the opposite side of the White House. Rather than adopt the neoclassical vocabulary used in his earlier building, Mullett opted for the French Second Empire style, following the example of the Corcoran Gallery (now the RENWICK GALLERY) that was completed 20 years earlier on a site just across Pennsylvania Avenue. Known in the US as General Grant style because of the popularity it enjoyed during the Grant administration (1869-1877), this style is characterized by mansard roofing and prominent corner and central pavilions. Although lacking the elaborate sculpture and ornamental detailing generally adorning Second Empire edifices, the exterior is noteworthy for its vigorous play of surfaces, lines, and recesses. With 900 exterior columns, 1,572 windows, over 550 rooms, nearly two miles of corridors and 4 1/2ft-thick granite walls, this construction was Washington's largest and most lavish office building and is generally considered to be the finest surviving example of the Second Empire style in the country.

A Threatened Monument – Like many 19C works of architecture that did not fit the capital's predominating neoclassical mold (e.g., the PENSION BUILDING and the OLD POST OFFICE), the OEOB, as it is known, has evoked more scorn than admiration. By the time the edifice was completed in 1888, the Second Empire style had already passed out of fashion. In the period between the two world wars, plans were drawn up to transform the facade to resemble the numerous neoclassical edifices throughout the city. Owing to insufficient funds, these projects were never carried out; however, the building was allowed to deteriorate, and demolition seemed inevitable.

Gradually the original occupants moved to more modern quarters in various sites around the city. The Navy Department led the way soon after World War I, followed by the War Department in 1938. After the State Department's move in 1947, the Executive Office of the President appropriated the building as an annex of the adjacent White House (hence the structure's current name).

The Kennedy administration was instrumental in promoting the building's subsequent rehabilitation. The exterior was cleaned in the 1960s, and finally in 1983, a large-scale restoration project was begun to refurbish the spectacular interior. In addition to the President's office, among the most influential divisions of the Executive housed in the building today are the Office of Management and Budget, the National Security Council, and the Office of the Vice President.

Interior Highlights – The sumptuous halls, stairways, and offices, designed primarily by Mullett's successor Richard von Ezdorf, have provided a splendid work place for scores of noted government figures over the past century. Theodore and Franklin D. Roosevelt, Taft, Hoover, Eisenhower, Johnson, Ford, and Bush all maintained offices here at some point in their careers before moving into the Executive Mansion next door.

The **cast-iron detailing**, employed throughout the building for fire protection, is an outstanding decorative feature.

Executive Office of the President Libraries – Four stories of alcoves enclose the library's central reading area, which is crowned by an elegant vault pierced by a skylight. The upper three stories are adorned with intricately designed white cast-iron balconies, resembling marvelous pieces of lacework.

The 3-story law library, similar in layout to the above room, features dark cast-iron balconies. The floors of both libraries are laid with Milton tiles, which create elaborate geometric patterns.

Indian Treaty Room – Originally the Navy's library and reception room, this graceful hall contains a lacy cast-iron balcony featuring eagles, anchors, shells, and other nautical motifs.

Office of the Secretary of the Navy – The original fireplace, mirrors, and elaborately stenciled walls of this spacious suite have been restored to their former splendor. Among the four **corner domes** and two **central rotundas**, note the skylight of the **west rotunda**, covered in gold leaf and tinted in soft yellow, peach, and pale-green colors.

From photo by L. Jones

Detail of Old Executive Office Building

ORGANIZATION OF AMERICAN STATES

Michelin map 48 J6 time: 1 hour

17th St. and Constitution Ave. NW. **M** *Farragut West. Open Mon–Fri 9am–4pm; closed Federal holidays. Free admission. Guided tours (45min) available (1-week advance reservation required). Spanish language tours available. ♿ ☎458-3751.*

Conceived as a symbolic amalgam of North and South American architecture, this white marble, terra-cotta-roofed building has the gracious ambiance of a Spanish colonial villa. As the headquarters for the Organization of American States, the building serves as a forum for discussions and conferences affecting the political and economic climate of the Western Hemisphere.

The OAS – Established in 1890 as the International Union of American Republics, this organization is the oldest such alliance of nations in the world. It was created to engender peaceful relations and economic cooperation among the independent countries of the Americas. In its 100-year history, it has grown from 24 member nations to 35, the most recent to join being Canada, in 1990. The US was a charter member of the organization.

In the early 20C, Washington was chosen as the site for this headquarters building because it was the only city in which all member nations maintained permanent legations. Congress donated the tract of land, which then became international territory. In addition to housing offices of the permanent staff, the building serves as headquarters of the General Secretariat, the 700-member body responsible for OAS administration and policy implementation.

Headquarters Building – For their innovative blending of classical elements and traditional Latin motifs, Paul Cret (designer of the FOLGER SHAKESPEARE LIBRARY) and Albert Kelsey won the architectural competition to design this "House of the Americas," as it is frequently called. A gracious plaza fronts the triple-entry arches, which are flanked by allegorical statues, one depicting North America *(right)* by Gutzon Borglum (best known for his presidential profiles at Mount Rushmore) and the other, South America *(left)* by Isidore Konti.

The interior lobby is dominated by the **tropical patio**, designed after a Spanish colonial courtyard. A fountain bearing Meso-American motifs occupies the center of the patio, whose lush vegetation includes the now enormous "peace tree," a grafted fig and rubber tree planted at the building's dedication in 1910 and symbolizing the peaceful coexistence of North and South America. The coats of arms of the member nations embellish the entablature around the roofed overhang. A gallery behind the patio features changing exhibits, generally from the collection of the OAS museum *(described below)*.

On the second floor, the columned **Hall of the Americas**, an ornately trimmed and vaulted auditorium, contains three Tiffany rock-crystal chandeliers and Tiffany stained-glass windows. The adjacent Old Council Room is adorned with bronze bas-relief friezes depicting scenes in the histories of the Americas.

Museum and Grounds – Behind the main building, the Aztec Gardens display contemporary and traditional sculpture. The stuccoed loggia fronting the garden pool is the rear of a building designed by Cret and Kelsey to serve as the residence of the OAS secretary general. In 1976, it was converted to the **Art Museum of the Americas** *(open Mon–Fri 9am–5pm; closed Sat, Sun and Federal holidays. Free admission. ♿ ☎458-6016)*. In addition to occasional traveling art shows, the museum mounts rotating exhibits devoted to the works of the modern Caribbean and Latin American artists represented in its permanent collection of some 700 pieces.

At the north corner of the complex is a small stuccoed building originally designed by Benjamin Latrobe as the stables for the private estate that first occupied the site.

ST JOHN'S CHURCH

Michelin map 48 G7 time: 1/4 hour

Lafayette Square at 16th and H Sts. NW. **M** *McPherson Square. Open Mon–Sat 8am–4pm, Sun 7:30am–2pm. Free admission. Guided tours (30min) available (2-week advance reservation required). Free organ recitals Wed at 12:10pm. ♿ ☎347-8766.*

Occupying a prominent corner of Lafayette Square since 1815, this elegant structure is one of the most historic and prestigious churches in Washington. It enjoys the sobriquet the "church of Presidents," because every Chief Executive since the church's inception has worshipped here at some time while in office.

Historical Notes – In the early 19C, parishioners of the capital's only Episcopal church, Christ Church on Capitol Hill, began to consider creating a new parish in the area that was then developing around the White House. In 1815, the eminent architect **Benjamin H. Latrobe** was engaged to draft plans for the building. Latrobe's church took the shape of a Greek cross, and the finished product so pleased him that he wrote his son after the church's opening in 1816, "I have just completed a church that made many Washingtonians religious who were not religious before."

Throughout the church's history, its vestry has attempted to maintain the integrity of Labrobe's design even as the building has been expanded and altered. In 1822, a pillared porch was added to the west side, which became the main entrance, rather than Latrobe's south entrance. The bell tower was also added at this time, and the west transept extended, changing the church's shape to a Latin cross.

In 1883, another prominent architect, James Renwick, oversaw further renovation to the church, which included the addition of a Palladian window behind the altar and stained-glass windows designed by Madame Veuve Lorin, curator at Chartres Cathedral in France.

Interior – Latrobe's graceful saucered dome and lantern draw the eye to the mid-point of the low-ceilinged church. A brass plate on **pew 54** indicates the President's pew, where attending Chief Executives are seated. The kneeling stools in this and nearby pews are covered in needlepoint patterns bearing the presidential seals and the names of Presidents.

Adjoining the church on H Street is Ashburton House, a Federal-style structure (1836) that now functions as the parish house.

TREASURY BUILDING

Michelin map 48 H7 *time: 1 hour*

15th St. and Pennsylvania Ave. NW. Ⓜ Metro Center. Visit by guided tour (90min) only every Sat (except holiday weekends) 10, 10:20 and 10:40am (1-week advance reservation required; date of birth and social security number must be provided when making reservation). Free admission. ♿ ☎622-0896.

Pictured on the back of the $10 bill, the stately Treasury Building, which flanks the Executive Mansion to the east, is the seat of governmental finances and a prominent architectural landmark in its own right.

The Department of the Treasury – Established in 1789 as a department of the Executive branch, the Treasury has monitored many of the financial and quasifinancial functions of the Federal Government throughout the nation's 200-year history. The Postal Service, General Land Office (now the Department of the Interior), Departments of Commerce and Labor, and the Coast Guard all initially began as arms of the Treasury.

Today, the Treasury Building houses executive and support offices for the secretary of the treasury and other high level administrators. A number of bureaus administered by the department are housed elsewhere in the city. Among these are the BUREAU OF ENGRAVING AND PRINTING, where currency is printed; the Customs Service; the Internal Revenue Service; and the Secret Service.

Historical Notes – The first Treasury Building, designed by George Hadfield, was one of the few official buildings completed when Congress and the President officially moved to Washington in 1800. A compact Georgian structure, it stood on the site of the current building. During the British invasion of 1814, the building was burned to the ground, but was quickly replaced with a new structure designed by White House architect James Hoban. This structure, too, was destroyed in a fire set by arsonists in 1833.

The current building was begun in 1836, with the construction of the T-shaped east wing, designed by **Robert Mills**, who also created the WASHINGTON MONUMENT and the OLD PATENT OFFICE BUILDING. Mills employed brick vaulting to fireproof the interior and, in compliance with the wishes of Congress, used Aquia Creek sandstone, an ill-suited material that was also used in the construction of the WHITE HOUSE and the CAPITOL. His plan ultimately envisioned additional wings on the north and south, forming an E-shaped building with the ends open to the White House. The colossal size of the structure, and particularly the addition of the south wing, broke with the original city plan, which called for an unobstructed view along Pennsylvania Avenue between the White House and the Capitol.

In 1851, due to political wrangling, Mills was dismissed and eventually replaced by Thomas U. Walter, best known as the designer of the Capitol dome. Walter modified Mills' E-shaped structure by adding a west wing that would enclose the E in a square and create two interior courtyards. The south, west, and north additions took 14 years to complete and were supervised by the following architects, who added their own embellishments to the interiors: Ammi Young (south wing, 1855-60); Isaiah Rogers (west wing, 1855-64); and Alfred Mullett (north wing, 1867-69). Shortly after completing the Treasury Building, Mullett began work on his most celebrated project, the OLD EXECUTIVE OFFICE BUILDING, positioned on the west side of the White House.

Exterior – The granite building (the Aquia sandstone exterior and east colonnade were replaced in 1909) covers two blocks and reflects the Greek Revival style prevalent in the 1830s and 40s. The building's most distinctive feature is the Ionic colonnade of 30 monolithic columns, each 36ft high, that adorns the east facade. The south, north, and west entrances are approached by wide plazas. The south plaza contains a statue of Alexander Hamilton, first Secretary of the Treasury (1789-1795), and the north plaza, one of Hamilton's successor, Albert Gallatin (1801-1814). Both statues were designed by James Earle Fraser. Broad staircases lead from the plazas to columned and pedimented porticos. Pediments also cap the ends of the east and west facades, interrupting the roofline balustrade.

Tour – The tour follows the chronological construction of the building. The hallways in the original T-shaped east wing were conceived by Mills with Doric columns and groin- and barrel-vaulted ceilings. The more elaborately ornamented hallways of the south, north, and west wings exemplify the Greek Revival style. Cast-iron pilasters lining the hall feature eagles and a hand holding the Treasury key. Ornate cast-iron balustrades adorn the circular staircases.

The third-floor corridors serve as a portrait gallery hung with paintings of the secretaries of the treasury, arranged in chronological order. The **Secretary's Conference and Reception Rooms** have been created to reflect the decor popular in public buildings in the late 1860s-1880s. The conference room features a painting of George Washington attributed to the eminent portraitist Gilbert Stuart, and one of Salmon Chase (treasury secretary under Lincoln from 1861 to 1864), attributed to Thomas Sully.

The **Andrew Johnson Suite** has been restored to its appearance in 1865, when the suite served as the Executive Office for President Andrew Johnson following Lincoln's assassination. Johnson maintained his office in the Treasury building until Mrs Lincoln vacated the White House.

The walls and ceilings of the **Secretary Salmon Chase Suite** are lavishly decorated with stencilling, allegorical figures, and gilt detailing that dates from Chase's tenure.

The second floor is notable for the Treasurer's Office, where a decorative cast-iron **vault wall**, designed by Isaiah Rogers in 1864, is visible. The wall, incised with seals and medallions, was obscured behind other vault extensions and forgotten about for 80 years. The wall has now been restored, and its interior lining of steel balls, intended to prevent burglary, can be viewed through a wall cutaway.

The north lobby, fronting Pennsylvania Avenue, opens onto the opulent **Cash Room★**, designed by Alfred Mullett. The site of Ulysses S. Grant's inaugural reception in 1869, the impressive 72ft by 32ft chamber features immense bronze chandeliers, a coffered ceiling, and walls and floors faced in seven different marbles. A mezzanine with ornate pilasters and an elaborate bronze railing rims the room. Intended to inspire public trust in paper money, which the Government first issued in 1862, the Cash Room functioned to redeem government-issued certificates and supply commercial banks with coins and currency. It ceased operations in 1976 and is now used for official functions.

© White House Historical Assoc.; photo by National Geographic Society

White House

4

★★

Downtown

Traditionally the commercial heart of Washington, Downtown reflects the flavor of the city's past and present. Large department stores and office buildings tower above 19C shopfronts, and the process of revitalization is everywhere apparent.

19C – Conceived by planner L'Enfant to link the White House and the Capitol, **Pennsylvania Avenue** was the capital's first major thoroughfare, and as such it gave rise to the city's commercial district. In 1801, President Jefferson authorized the building of a central market on the avenue between 7th and 9th Streets, and in 1807, construction began on the ill-fated Tiber Creek canal, which was eventually covered over in the 1870s *(see p 21)*.

For much of the 19C, Pennsylvania Avenue was lined with hotels, boarding-houses, and theaters, in keeping with L'Enfant's intent that this be a thoroughfare "attractive to the learned and affording diversion to the idle." Among the diversions were the **National Theatre**, an institution still operating between 13th and 14th Streets on the Avenue, and the **Willard Hotel**, for decades Washington's premier hostelry. Established in the 1850s, the Willard has occupied several buildings on the same site. The present building (1901) was designed by H.J. Hardenberg, architect of Manhattan's celebrated Plaza Hotel.

As the city grew, F Street became the site of major government buildings and fashionable residences. North-south growth occurred along 7th Street, where 2- and 3-story brick buildings housed shops and residences. In the 1830s, 7th Street was chosen as the site for the Patent Office *(see p 90)* and became an enclave for German immigrants working in the drygoods trade. By the turn of the century, their businesses had made this street the commercial hub of Downtown.

A Century of Change – During the first half of the 20C, Downtown continued to thrive, with major new development occurring in the land bordered by Pennsylvania and Constitution Avenues. Known as **Federal Triangle**, this cluster of Classical Revival government buildings was designed as a collaborative effort by a group of eminent architects.

After World War II, Downtown declined as it lost business to suburban malls. When John F. Kennedy's inaugural parade moved down Pennsylvania Avenue, the thoroughfare was described by one cabinet member as "a vast unformed, cluttered expanse." A cabinet committee established by Kennedy in 1960 began a redevelopment process that has gradually revitalized the Avenue. At the core of this rebirth was the renovation of the OLD POST OFFICE.

In recent years, such mixed-use complexes as Hartman-Cox's Market Square (1984), near the site of the old city market, have risen on the Avenue. The Landsburgh complex *(7th, 8th, and E Sts.)*, home of the new **Shakespeare Theatre** (1992), was the result of the overhaul of several buildings. Both Market Square and the Landsburgh are part of **Pennsylvania Quarter**, the new designation for Pennsylvania Avenue's north side between 6th, 9th, and E Streets. Today, a refurbished Willard Hotel overlooks Pershing Park, a pleasant square with an outdoor cafe. Nearby **Freedom Plaza**, designed by the prestigious architectural group, Venturi, Rauch, and Scott Brown, has a large-scale copy of **L'Enfant's city plan** incised in its pavement. Anchoring the northern portion of Downtown is the **Washington Convention Center**. Its presence has encouraged the development of major hotel-office complexes in the area, including the nearby Techworld Plaza. Several museums are nearby, and 7th Street between G Street and Constitution Avenue is developing as an arts corridor with such tenants as the **Washington Project for the Arts**, a showcase for contemporary art, with an emphasis on works of local artists. The area has also become a testing ground for innovative rehabilitation of 19C commercial architecture, as seen in the Gallery Row complex at F and D Streets. On G and 9th Streets is the **Martin Luther King Memorial Library** (1972), an austere building designed by Mies van der Rohe, one of this century's most influential architects. **Chinatown**, a small stretch of restaurants and shops on H Street between 6th and 7th Streets, is recognizable by its ornate Friendship Archway.

★★ NATIONAL PORTRAIT GALLERY

Michelin map 48 H9 *time: 1 1/2 hours*

Old Patent Office Building at 8th and F Sts. Entrance on F St. M *Gallery Place. Open daily 10am–5:30pm; closed Dec 25. Free admission. Guided tours (45min) Mon–Fri 10am–3pm, Sat and Sun 11:15am.* ♿ ✂ ☎*357-2700.*

Sharing the elegant interior of the Old Patent Office Building with the NATIONAL MUSEUM OF AMERICAN ART since 1968, this museum might be thought of as the nation's family album. Modeled after its namesake in London, the National Portrait Gallery conserves some 15,000 paintings, sculptures, photographs, engravings, and drawings of "men and women who have made significant contributions to the history, development and culture of the people of the United States." To be accepted into the permanent collection, portraits must be original works of art, preferably taken from life.

A Grand Old Building – In the mid-1830s, Congress authorized a "temple of the useful arts"—a patent office—to be constructed on this site equidistant from the CAPITOL and the WHITE HOUSE. In 1836, construction began on the Greek Revival edifice designed by William Parker Elliott. The monumental and severe stone **Old Patent Office Building**★★ features a pedimented Doric portico on each of its four sides and encloses a spacious central courtyard. The distinguished architect Robert Mills (1781-1855) oversaw construction of the south wing, which was finished in 1840. (The golden sandstone used in this wing contrasts markedly with the granite employed throughout the rest of the building.) During the almost 30 years of ensuing construction, Thomas U. Walter, designer of the Capitol dome, and Edward Clark were involved in the building project.

During the Civil War, the broad corridors of the building served as a hospital for Union soldiers. Clara Barton, a Patent Office copyist and founder of the Red Cross, ministered to the wounded, as did poet Walt Whitman, who read to them from his works. In 1865, Lincoln's second inaugural reception was held here, just five weeks prior to his assassination. A benefit to raise funds for the families of Union soldiers, the gala attracted 4,000 people and took place in the immense 264ft-long, marble-pillared hall—now called the Lincoln Gallery—on the third floor of the east wing.

When completed in 1867, the building was the largest structure in the city. In addition to the patent office, it was also home, at various times, to the Department of the Interior and the Civil Service Commission. In 1958, Congress saved the building from threatened demolition and gave it to the Smithsonian Institution, which now uses it to house two museums—the National Portrait Gallery and the NATIONAL MUSEUM OF AMERICAN ART—as well as the Archives of American Art. The two museums are connected by hallway galleries.

The building's interior **courtyard**, with its cast-iron fountains and monumental pieces of sculpture, including Alexander Calder's *The Spiral,* is one of the most pleasant and tranquil spots in Downtown.

National Portrait Gallery

Self-portrait by John Singleton Copley

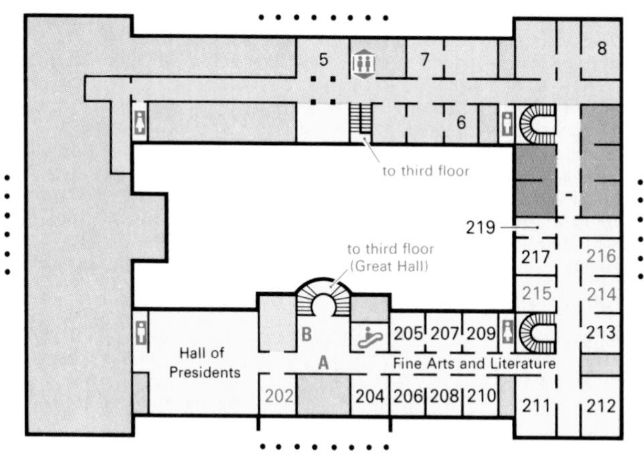

NATIONAL PORTRAIT GALLERY/
NATIONAL MUSEUM OF AMERICAN ART

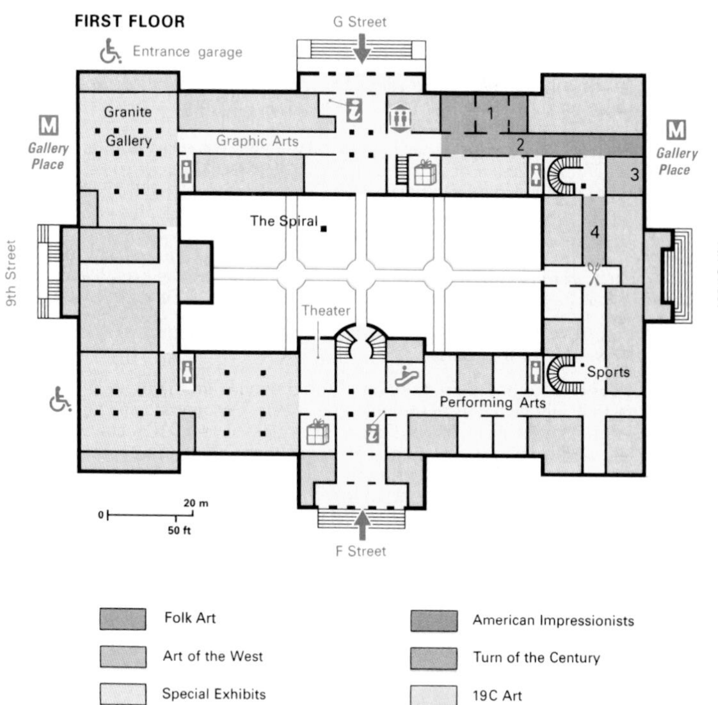

Folk Art
Art of the West
Special Exhibits
American Impressionists
Turn of the Century
19C Art

VISIT

As the gallery's vast permanent collection is displayed on a rotating basis, some of the works described below may be temporarily relocated or removed.

Begin the visit on the 2nd floor.

Second Floor – The panorama of American history unfolds on the second-floor landing, which is dominated by Gilbert Stuart's celebrated **Lansdowne portrait**★ (**A**) of George Washington (another version by Stuart hangs in the East Room of the White House). The wall to the right (**B**) is reserved for other major works by Stuart—his celebrated **Athenaeum Portraits** of George and Martha Washington (which are co-owned with the Museum of Fine Arts in Boston) are alternated every three years with Stuart's **Thomas Jefferson portrait** (co-owned with Monticello). The Athenaeum portrait is the most widely known representation of the first President, since it served as the model for the portrait that appears on the one-dollar bill.

The handsome groin-vaulted Hall of Presidents *(to the right of the landing)* provides a stately setting for the museum's series of **presidential portraits**, featuring representations in various media of the Americans who have occupied the nation's highest office. Note George P. A. Healy's oil painting of a pensive Abraham Lincoln.

Adjacent to the Hall, room 202 contains numerous engravings, paintings, and busts of George Washington.

Fourteen galleries on the opposite side of the landing present a chronological overview of prominent people and events in American history. Half of this section's L-shaped central corridor features portraits of illustrious Americans who have made noteworthy contributions to fine arts and literature. Among those depicted here are the painters John Singleton Copley *(see illustration p 90)* and **Mary Cassatt** (by the 19C French artist Degas); renowned 19C writers such as Nathaniel Hawthorne, Henry David Thoreau, Longfellow, and Emerson; as well as actors such as Edwin Booth (brother of President Lincoln's assassin), and Ira Aldridge.

The survey of the country's historical figures begins in **Colonial America** *(gallery 204)* and **The Road to Independence** *(gallery 206)*, which feature a selection of notable settlers and Founding Fathers. **The American Revolution** *(gallery 208)* contains a rare engraving of the traitor Benedict Arnold. Among the works exhibited in **The Early Republic** *(gallery 210)* are a marble bust of Alexander Hamilton, and portraits of the war heroes, Commodores Oliver Perry and Stephen Decatur *(see p 83)*.

Continue the visit in gallery 205 at the other end of the corridor.

The **Native Americans** exhibit *(gallery 205)* includes watercolors, photographs, and paintings, including four oils by the renowned painter of Indians, George Catlin. **The Expanding Frontier** *(gallery 207)* shows the adventurer Davy Crockett. Portraits in the next room highlight **Pre-Civil War Science and Invention** *(gallery 209)*. Of note is the group portrait entitled *Men of Progress* (1862), which depicts 19 Americans who made important contributions in the field of technology. The figures portrayed were painted separately and then regrouped on one canvas.

Industry, Change and Reform *(galleries 211 and 212)* introduces late 19C inventors, tycoons, and agents of social change: inventor Thomas Edison, steel magnate Andrew Carnegie, and financial giants J.D. Rockefeller and J.P. Morgan; Suffragists Susan B. Anthony and Elizabeth Cady Stanton; Chicago social worker and Nobel Peace Prize recipient (1931) Jane Addams; and Tuskegee Institute founder Booker T. Washington.

The Twenties *(gallery 213)* features several personalities from this turbulent period in American history such as Andrew Mellon, Secretary of the Treasury and founder of the NATIONAL GALLERY OF ART, and John Pershing, the first military leader since George Washington to hold the title General of the Armies.

World War II *(gallery 215)* commemorates military and other key figures who shaped American international policy in the early 20C. Gallery 219 is devoted to a rotating selection of portraits by the noted sculptor **Jo Davidson** (1883-1952), who immortalized in bronze, stone, or terra-cotta many prominent figures of his period including Clare Boothe Luce, Robinson Jeffers, and Fiorella La Guardia.

The remaining galleries and the 7th Street hallway are filled with portraits of Americans prominent in history, literature, and the arts in the last 60 years, including Carl Sandberg, Rachel Carson, Langston Hughes, and George Gershwin.

Return to the main landing. Take the twin staircases to the 3rd floor, noting the finely crafted bronze balustrade.

Third Floor – The entire south wing of the museum on this floor is occupied by the **Great Hall**, whose decor of multicolored Milton tiles, carved ceiling medallions, and a yellow and blue central skylight reflects eclectic late-19C tastes. The frieze of six relief panels illustrating sources of man's technology (fire, electricity, water, agriculture, metal fabrication, mining) is a reminder that the hall was originally designed to display miniature patent models. The hall is flanked on its long sides by mezzanines with cast-iron balustrades. An exhibit devoted to the **Civil War Period** begins on the east mezzanine *(to the left)*, which is dominated by a full-length portrait of Abraham Lincoln. Renowned figures from this period include Harriet Beecher Stowe, author of *Uncle Tom's Cabin*; the abolitionist John Brown; and Generals William Tecumseh Sherman and Ulysses S. Grant. Particularly moving is the famous **"cracked plate" photograph of Abraham Lincoln** taken on April 10, 1865, just four days before his assassination. Completing this historical survey of the Civil War is a portrait of the dashing commander of the Confederate forces, Gen Robert E. Lee.

This floor also houses the **Archives of American Art**, a noted research facility in the fields of visual arts and cultural history *(open to the public for research purposes only; for access, inquire at the information desk)*.

First Floor – The east-wing corridor is lined with paintings and photographs of popular figures from the world of **Sports** (John L. Sullivan, Ty Cobb, Jack Dempsey, Joe Louis, and others) and **The Performing Arts**, including great names in American theater, film, and music, such as Aaron Copeland, Duke Ellington, Marian Anderson, Benny Goodman, Grace Kelly, and Will Rogers. In the adjacent corridor, recently acquired works are exhibited on a rotating basis.

The vaulted galleries situated on the opposite side of the lobby are devoted to special exhibits.

The ✗ symbol indicates that eating facilities can be found on the premises of the sight.

★ NATIONAL MUSEUM OF AMERICAN ART

Michelin map 48 H9 — *time: 1 hour*

Old Patent Building at 8th and G Sts. NW. Entrance on G St. M Gallery Place. Open daily 10am–5:30pm; closed Dec 25. Free admission. Guided tours (1 hour) Mon–Fri at noon, Sat and Sun at 2pm. ♿ ✗ ☎357-2700.

Housed in the landmark Old Patent Office Building *(see description p 90)*, this museum comprises the country's oldest Federal collections of art. Its holdings cover the gamut of American art from early 18C portraiture and 19C landscapes to the free-form sculpture and large, abstract canvases of contemporary artists.

History – The museum traces its beginnings to the efforts of a Washingtonian named John Varden. In 1829, he began a collection of art, artifacts, and natural history specimens, which he displayed in his own "Washington Museum." In 1841, his collection was joined with that of the congressionally mandated National Institute. The combined collections were exhibited in the completed south wing of the Patent Office Building, alongside cases displaying inventions, including Benjamin Franklin's printing press, and an assortment of historic treasures, among them the Declaration of Independence (now in the NATIONAL ARCHIVES).

In 1862, the collection was donated to the Smithsonian Institution, which exhibited selected pieces at various times and in several buildings throughout the city, including the CASTLE, the CORCORAN GALLERY, and the NATIONAL MUSEUM OF NATURAL HISTORY. In 1906, the collection was officially designated the National Gallery of Art, but it still had no permanent home or cohesion. Even its title was short-lived, since the new museum being built on the Mall to house the Mellon Collection was officially named the National Gallery of Art in 1937.

The National Collection of Fine Arts, as it was then called, remained in the Museum of Natural History until 1968 when it was permanently installed in its original quarters—the Old Patent Office Building. Since then, the collection has increased fivefold and now includes more then 34,000 objects. It received its current name, the National Museum of American Art, in 1980, to reflect its mandate to display exclusively the works of US artists. The NMAA is also the repository for art created under Federal patronage, including the works commissioned by the Federal Art Projects.

VISIT *(Floor plan p 91)*

The National Museum of American Art displays roughly 1,000 objects from its permanent collection at any one time.

First Floor – Not to be missed in the **Folk Art** section is James Hampton's **Throne of the Third Heaven of the Nations' Millennium General Assembly** (**1**). This astounding three-dimensional work depicts the throne of God, surrounded by altarlike pulpits and offertories. While employed as a Washington janitor from 1946 to 1960, Hampton created this monumental piece from discarded furniture, bottles, and other items that he wrapped in aluminum and gold foil. The remaining galleries in this section showcase other works from the museum's 600-piece collection of 19C and 20C American folk art.

A section (**3**) at the end of the east corridor features works by Frederic Remington, John Stanley Mix, and other 19C artists who portrayed life in the **American West**. The corridor (**4**) is devoted to the early 19C paintings of American Indians by artist-anthropologist **George Catlin** (1796-1872). The museum's collection includes 445 works by Catlin.

Rotating exhibits of graphic arts are exhibited in the west corridor of this floor. The low-ceilinged **Granite Gallery**, which takes its name from the massive stone pillars that support the room's elegant vaulting, is devoted to special exhibits.

Second Floor – American Art produced in the 19C and early 20C is displayed on this floor. The three **Western scenes** by Thomas Moran *(The Chasm of the Colorado* and two views of *The Grand Canyon of the Yellowstone)*, which hang in the lounge (**5**), exemplify the monumental landscape painting of the period, a genre continued in the works displayed in the east corridor. Gallery 2-D (**6**) features the haunting visionary scenes of Albert Pinkham Ryder (1847-1917), while the gallery across the corridor (**7**) is devoted to the paintings of Ryder's contemporary, Winslow Homer (1836-1910), whose use of color and light prefigures the Impressionists. The east corridor contains later 19C art, including the paintings of John Singer Sargent and Thomas Eakins.

A special gallery (**8**) displays the neoclassical sculptures from the Florence studio of prominent 19C artist Hiram Powers.

Among the paintings on view in the galleries devoted to art of the **Turn-of-the-Century** and **American Impressionists** are the lyrically romantic works of Childe Hassam, Thomas Wilmer Dewing, John Henry Twachtman, and Julian Alden Weir, all members of "The Ten American Painters," a group of renowned Impressionists. Also shown are works by Mary Cassatt, Romaine Brooks, and Maurice Prendergast.

At the end of the west corridor, the works of prominent **18C and early 19C portraitists** Gilbert Stuart, Charles Willson Peale, and Thomas Sully are presented, as are portrait miniatures.

Third Floor – Galleries in the east corridor display American art from the 1900s to the 1940s, including pieces from the museum's extensive Federal Art Projects holdings. The cavernous **Lincoln Gallery** highlights major schools and trends in mid-to-late 20C art. The Ash Can school (Robert Henri and John Sloan) is represented, as are Abstract Expressionism (Hans Hofmann and Franz Kline), Color Field (Morris Lewis and Kenneth Noland), and Pop Art (Jasper Johns, Robert Rauschenberg, Andy Warhol). The west corridor is reserved for special exhibits.

★ FORD'S THEATRE and PETERSEN HOUSE

Michelin map 48 H8 *time: 3/4 hour*

10th St. between E and F Sts. NW. M Metro Center.

In the heart of Downtown, amid a stretch of 19C structures, stands old Ford's Theatre, where Abraham Lincoln was shot by an assassin, and Petersen House, where he died of his wound.

HISTORICAL NOTES

A Tragic Gala – On the evening of April 14, 1865, President and Mrs Lincoln attended a performance of the popular comedy *Our American Cousin* at Ford's Theatre. The capital was in a festive mood, as only five days before, Confederate Gen Robert E. Lee had surrendered to Gen Ulysses S. Grant at Appomattox, Virginia. Grant and his wife had, in fact, been in Washington on April 14 and were to have attended the theater with the Lincolns, but they made the decision to leave town earlier in the day. In their stead, Clara Harris, daughter of Sen Ira Harris, and her financé, Maj Henry Rathbone, attended. That night the theater was full of Washingtonians hoping for a glimpse of Grant, who had rarely visited the city. In preparation for the President's arrival, boxes 7 and 8 had been draped with flags and the partition between them removed to allow the presidentail party more space. The Lincoln party was engrossed in the third act of the play when **John Wilkes Booth** silently entered the box and shot the President at close range. The bullet from the small, single-shot derringer entered behind Lincoln's left ear and lodged behind his right eye. Major Rathbone immediately tried to subdue the attacker, but Booth defended himself with a large knife, stabbing the major in the left arm. Booth leapt over the balustrade of the box, but, as he did so, his feet got entangled in the draped flags and in an engraved portrait of Washington hanging on the rails. He landed off balance on the stage 12ft below, breaking a small bone in his leg with the fall. Most accounts claim that Booth then stood and flourished his knife, declaring "Sic semper tyrannis!" (Thus always with tyrants). The audience, believing that Booth's appearance was part of the play, was slow to respond. Booth mounted a horse he had sequestered in the theater alley and escaped.

Lincoln's Final Hours – Three army surgeons in the audience immediately attended the stricken Lincoln. Recognizing the seriousness of the wound, they ordered him moved to the nearest bed, and the President was carried across the street to a boarding house owned by a tailor named Petersen. He was laid in a first-floor back room then being rented by a young man in the Union Army. Due to Lincoln's height, he had to be placed diagonally across the bed. As the night passed, Cabinet ministers, physicians, and other prominent people gathered in the back parlor, while Mrs Lincoln was consoled by friends in the front parlor. Lincoln never regained consiousness. At 7:22am the following morning, he died.
After official ceremonies in Washington, Lincoln's body was taken by train to Springfield, Illinois, for burial. Along the route, he lay in state in several large cities. Abraham Lincoln was buried at Springfield's Oak Ridge Cemetery on May 4.

The Assassination Plot – A successful actor who appeared several times on the stage of Ford's Theatre, John Wilkes Booth apparently sought to achieve lasting fame for himself by what he considered his "heroic" act on behalf of the Confederacy. He was the ringleader of a band of conspirators who had initially plotted the kidnapping of Lincoln. When logistics prevented this approach, Booth hatched a plot in which he would kill Lincoln and his accomplices would assassinate other high government officials. Only Booth was successful.
Once he had inflicted the mortal wound, Booth made for the home of Dr Samuel Mudd, in the southern Maryland countryside. Mudd set his leg, and Booth continued his flight, accompanied by a fellow conspirator, David Herold. The two men crossed into Virginia and were apprehended the night of April 26 by a cavalry detachment in Port Royal, Virginia. Herold surrendered, but Booth refused, forcing his pursuers to set on fire the barn in which he was hiding. As the building burst into flames, the assassin was fatally shot through the neck by one of the soldiers.

FORD'S THEATRE *time: 1/2 hour*

Open daily 9am–5pm; closed Dec 25 and during rehearsals and performances. Free admission. ♿ ☎426-6924.

When John Ford opened the doors of this brick structure in 1863, it was one of the grandest theaters in the country, with an advertised seating capacity of 2,500. Though its facade was adorned only with arched door bays, window trim, pilasters, and an undecorated pediment, its interior was lavishly appointed. A cantilevered "dress circle," or balcony, flanked by private boxes, sloped toward the stage.
After Lincoln's assassination, the theater was ordered closed by the Federal Government. John Ford's announced intention to continue dramatic productions in the theater met with threats, so the War Department leased the building from Ford and began converting it into office space, ultimately purchasing it a year later for $100,000.
In 1893, another tragedy occurred here when collapsing floors killed 22 office workers. Thereafter, the building was used only for storage until 1932, when the Government opened it as a Lincoln museum, displaying memorabilia relating to the life of the 16th President. In the mid-1960s, Congress authorized a restoration of the building to its 1865 appearance. Ford's Theatre reopened in 1968 as both a memorial and an active playhouse.

The **box** where Lincoln sat is decorated as it was on the night of April 14, 1865, with upholstered Victorian period pieces, including the settee that had been specially place there for the President and his guests. On the balcony level is an imposing **bronze head of Lincoln** by Carl Tolpo, which was presented to Ford's in 1965.
In the basement, the refurbished **Lincoln Museum** *(same opening hours as the theater)* displays such artifacts from the assassination as Booth's derringer and the clothes Lincoln was wearing.

PETERSEN HOUSE *time: 1/4 hour*

Across the brick-paved street from the theater at 516 Tenth St. Open daily 9am–5pm; closed Dec 25. Free admission. ☏426-6924.

The simple 3-story brick row house where Lincoln died was built by William Petersen in 1850. Its three first-floor rooms, a front and back parlor and bedroom, decorated in Victorian period furnishings, are open to the public. The bloodstained pillow case on the bed was the one on which Lincoln was lying at his death.

★ FEDERAL BUREAU OF INVESTIGATION

Michelin map 48 H9-J9 *time: 1 hour*

E St. between 9th and 10th Sts. NW. Ⓜ Federal Triangle. Visit by guided tour (1 hour) only Mon–Fri 8:45am–4:15pm, every 20min (congressional visits also available—see p 162); closed Sat, Sun and Federal holidays. Free admission. ♿ ☏324-3447.

Officially known as the J. Edgar Hoover FBI Building, this immense fortress-like structure bordering Pennsylvania Avenue houses the national headquarters of the Federal Bureau of Investigation. An arm of the Justice Department, the FBI traces its beginnings to 1908, when a permanent investigative force of special agents was placed under the control of the Attorney General. In 1935, this force was designated the Federal Bureau of Investigation and its powers broadened in an effort to combat rampant gangsterism. Under the 48-year leadership (1924-1972) of Director **J. Edgar Hoover**, the bureau became the supreme Federal authority in matters of domestic crime.

Building – Stanley Gladych's design exemplifies the New Brutalism school of architecture, which features exposed concrete and little embellishment. Covering a city block, the building wraps around an interior courtyard. An exterior arcade along the perimeter is lined with rows of massive pillars. According to the FBI's own literature, the design of the building "retained the idea of a central core of files." Begun in 1963, the headquarters was completed 12 years later in 1975, at a cost of over $126,000,000. It houses nearly 8,000 workers. In addition, the FBI maintains 56 field offices and over 300 resident agencies, employing more than 9,600 agents.

Tour – The one-hour FBI tour is one of Washington's most popular attractions. A small exhibit hall contains displays on the history of the bureau and its procedures. The remainder of the tour is devoted to various research facilities housed here, such as the labs where bullet, firearm, and fiber analyses are conducted. A live firearms demonstration often concludes the tour.

★ NATIONAL MUSEUM OF WOMEN IN THE ARTS

Michelin map 48 G8-H8 *time: 1 hour*

New York Ave. and 13th St. NW. Ⓜ Metro Center. Open Mon–Sat and holidays 10am–5pm, Sun noon–5pm; closed Jan 1, Thanksgiving Day, Dec 25. Suggested contribution: $3, children and seniors $2. Guided tours (1 hour) available. ♿ ☏783-5000.

Behind this Beaux-Arts exterior is the world's only major museum devoted exclusively to the works of women artists. Local philanthropists Wilhelmina and Wallace Holladay founded the museum in 1981 as a private institution, "to encourage greater awareness of women in the arts and their contributions to the history of art." The Holladays donated their own collection to form the core of the museum's permanent holdings, which today comprise over 1,500 works by some 400 women artists. Opened in 1987, the museum displays works from the 16C to the present, covering every medium from Native American pottery to abstract sculpture.

Building – The edifice housing the museum was the Masonic temple for Washington from 1911 to the early 1980s. Its architect, Waddy B. Wood, designed the stately limestone and granite trapezoid to be "in keeping with the classic public buildings" of the capital city. Designated a National Historic Landmark in the early 1980s, the building has set the style for urban renewal in this area, influencing the architecture of such structures as the nearby office buildings at 1212 and 1201 New York Avenue. In 1983, the newly founded museum purchased the building from the fraternal order of Masons. An $8-million renovation transformed the interior into three levels of exhibit space, a library and research center, and a 200-seat auditorium, where public lectures, workshops, films, and concerts are held.
The main floor is dominated by the extensively remodeled **Great Hall**, a 2-story expanse of rose, white, and gray Turkish marble (and *faux marbre*) overhung by three crystal and gold-leaf chandeliers. The mezzanine level, which was added during the renovation, is rimmed with a heavy marble balustrade that extends along

the twin staircases on opposite sides of the hall. The gilded lions' heads topping the columns on this level and the ornate ceiling are the only features from the building's original interior. Light is admitted through the mezzanine's large arched windows.

Collection – Selected works from the permanent collection are hung in the Great Hall on a rotating basis. On the mezzanine level, sculpture and the works of silversmiths are displayed, as well as occasional changing exhibits. The second floor is generally devoted to major temporary exhibits.
The museum's third-floor galleries, ar-ranged chronologically, are devoted to works from its **permanent collection**. The earliest works (displayed in the 16-18C gallery) are primarily still lifes and portraits, characteristic of the subject matter of early women artists. The oldest work in the collection is the *Portrait of a Noblewoman* (c.1580) by Lavinia Fontana, a 16C Italian painter from Bologna who is considered the first professional woman artist. *Still Life of Fish and Cat* by Clara Peeters, a 17C Flemish artist, highlights her contributions to the development of that genre. Two still lifes of flowers are representative of the work of Rachel Ruysch, a 17C Dutch artist. This gallery also contains a portrait by the court painter of Marie-Antoinette, Elisabeth Vigée-Lebrun (1755-1842).
The 19C gallery displays works by the well-known animal portraitist Rosa Bonheur; and a still life, *The Cage,* by the famous French Impressionist, Berthe Morisot.
Among the 19C American works are an early portrait by Cecilia Beaux and *The Bath*, from a renowned series of graphics by the acclaimed Impressionist **Mary Cassatt**. Lilla Cabot Perry, who introduced the work of Monet to Americans, is represented by her *Lady With a Bowl of Violets* and *Lady in Evening Dress.*
The museum's notable collection of **19C sculpture**—a rare medium for female artists of that period—includes the works of Malvina Hoffman, Anna Vaughn, Hyatt Huntington, Bessie Potter Vonnoh, and Evelyn Beatrice Longman.

National Museum of Women in the Arts

Lady with a Bowl of Violets
by Lilla Cabot Perry

The 20C galleries feature paintings by Helen Frankenthaler, Elaine de Kooning, Lee Krasner, and Nancy Graves. The Mexican artist Frida Kahlo is represented by her powerful *Self-portrait* in homage to Trotsky.

State Shows – The museum maintains a unique grassroots program designed to showcase the works of female artists, both past and present. State committees organize these temporary exhibits, which are shown on a rotating basis in the **Gudelsky State Gallery** on the third floor.

NATIONAL BUILDING MUSEUM The Pension Building

Michelin map 48 H10 *time: 1 hour*

North side of Judiciary Square. M Judiciary Square. Open Mon–Sat 10am–4pm, Sun and holidays noon–4pm; closed Jan 1, Thanksgiving Day, Dec 25. Free admission. Guided tours (1 hour) daily 12:30pm, additional tour Sat and Sun 1:30pm. ♿ ☎272-2448.

Commonly known as the Pension Building, the colossal brick edifice bordering the north side of Judiciary Square was long considered one of the capital's most monumental eyesores. Painstakingly refurbished, this extraordinary example of 19C eclecticism now houses a museum devoted to America's achievements in the building arts.

"Meigs Old Red Barn" – In the 1880s, US Army engineer Gen **Montgomery Meigs** (1816-1892) was commissioned to design a permanent workplace for the 1,500 employees of the Pension Bureau, the Federal agency responsible for distributing government pensions to wounded veterans and survivors of persons killed in American military conflicts. Earlier in his career, Meigs had supervised the mid-19C extension of the CAPITOL and the construction of the ARTS AND INDUSTRIES BUILDING. Nicknamed "Meigs Old Red Barn," the **Pension Building★**, impressive in both its scale and design, has been a subject of controversy since its completion in 1887. Referring to the building, Union Gen William Tecumseh Sherman reputedly commented, "The worst of it is, it is fireproof."
Occupying an entire city block, the massive rectangular edifice (400ft by 200ft) contains 15,500,000 bricks and stands almost 160ft (the height of a 15-story modern building). The exterior design, with its prominent overhanging cornice and three stories of pedimented and lintelled windows, is a double-scale version of the Palazzo Farnese in Rome—the 16C architectural masterpiece partly designed by Michelangelo. The oversized "palazzo" is crowned by a curious roof structure consisting

of intersecting gable-ended clerestories, specially designed to provide abundant light within and to conserve heat in winter. Concerned with providing healthy conditions for the office workers, Meigs incorporated other technical innovations such as a sophisticated ventilation system that afforded an excellent crosscurrent between the roof, windows and the small openings below each window. The structure was made fireproof by the use of brick and metal.

The outstanding decorative feature on the building's exterior is the 3ft high terra-cotta **frieze** that extends around the entire structure above the ground-floor windows. Created by 19C sculptor Casper Buberl, the 35 panels making up this memorial to the Civil War dead depict Union infantry, cavalry, artillery, naval and medical troops on the march.

Since the transfer of the Pension Bureau to more spacious accommodations in the 1920s, the building has housed various government agencies. In the 1950s, demolition was considered, but the building's survival was ensured during the following decades, thanks to its designation as a National Historic Landmark and the decision to convert it into a museum devoted to the building and arts trades.

G. Cannon/Michelin Travel Publications

National Building Museum

Interior – Upon entering the vast interior court known as the **Great Hall**, the visitor is impressed by its staggering proportions. Measuring 116ft by 316ft, this monumental space is punctuated by eight 75ft Corinthian columns made of brick and painted to resemble Siena marble. Out of scale with the rest of the interior, these colossal pieces of solid masonry support the central roof structure, which admits abundant light. The court is flanked by two stories of elegant galleries lined with 72 Doric and 72 Ionic columns, evoking the graceful courtyards of Renaissance palaces. The third-floor parapet is ornamented by plaster replicas of the terra-cotta urns originally designed for the building. In the cornice of the hall's central section high above the colossal columns, note the 244 niches *(best seen from the upper floors)* containing life-size busts symbolizing American builders and craftsmen. Roaming through the spacious building *(the 1st and 2nd floors are open to the public)*, the visitor discovers a wealth of fine architectural detail, including deep-set brick stairways covered by pure-lined barrel and groin vaulting.

Since 1885, the Great Hall has been the setting of **inaugural balls** for 13 US Presidents, including Theodore Roosevelt, Richard M. Nixon, Jimmy Carter, Ronald Reagan, George Bush, and Bill Clinton.

The Pension Building is now the home of the National Building Museum, created in 1980 by congressional mandate to commemorate the American experience in architecture and to encourage the study and appreciation of the building arts. At present, the museum's main attraction is the building itself. On the second floor, a presentation of the building's construction and restoration is permanently displayed. The exhibit entitled "Washington: Symbol and City," featuring models of several prominent monuments, offers an overview of the development of architecture in the nation's capital. In addition to organizing temporary exhibits, the museum sponsors numerous walking tours, lectures, and programs on various aspects of building.

For information on current exhibits and activities, consult the NBM's publication, *Blueprints.*

Unless otherwise indicated, all telephone numbers given in this guide are in the 202 calling area.
When telephoning Virginia or Maryland from within Washington DC proper, dial the appropriate area code (703 Virginia, 301 or 410 Maryland) before the seven-digit number.

OLD POST OFFICE

Michelin map 48 J8 *time: 1/2 hour*

Pennsylvania Ave. and 12th St. NW. Ⓜ *Federal Triangle. Open daily Apr 15–Sept 5 8am–10:45pm, rest of the year 10am–6:15pm; closed Jan 1, Thanksgiving Day, Dec 25. Free admission.* ♿ ✗ ☎*606-8691.*

Saved from the wrecker's ball at the eleventh hour, this rejuvenated Pennsylvania Avenue landmark has been converted into a "festival market" that attracts numerous residents and tourists throughout the year.

The "Old Tooth" – The massive granite structure, which was built as the headquarters of the US Postal Service, met with public disfavor almost immediately after its completion in 1899. Designed in the then-outmoded Richardsonian Romanesque style—replete with rough-faced masonry, gabled dormers, corner turrets, and an imposing 315ft tower—the building was facetiously nicknamed "Old Tooth." The structure greatly deteriorated in the decades following the postmaster general's move to new quarters in 1934.

In 1971, the year in which the building's demolition was officially approved, various preservation groups spearheaded a popular movement that ultimately led to the building's resurrection. A $30 million federally funded restoration project (1978-1983) transformed the Old Post Office into a multi-functional complex, with office and commercial space. This widely acclaimed adaptive-use project served as a catalyst for the rehabilitation of the blighted Pennsylvania Avenue area.

Interior – The outstanding architectural feature is the central glass-roofed **courtyard** (99ft by 184ft; 160ft high) surrounded by seven floors of offices for various Federal agencies. The courtyard's first three levels accommodate a variety of eating facilities (restaurants, cafes, and fast-food stands), souvenir shops, and a stage for live entertainment. Called The Pavilion, this popular spot has been the setting for several annual festivities, including a New Year's Eve celebration.

Tower – Ascending the 315ft clock tower by means of the glass elevator *(situated in the northwest corner of the courtyard)* allows the visitor to appreciate the vastness of the courtyard. Near the summit are the **Congress Bells** donated to the US Government in 1983 to commemorate the end of the American Revolution. Cast in London in 1976, the ten bells are played for State occasions and to mark the opening and closing sessions of Congress. The observation deck, the area's second-highest public vantage point (surpassed only by the Washington Monument), offers a **view** of the surroundings.

NATIONAL AQUARIUM

Michelin map 48 J7 *time: 1/2 hour*

Dept. of Commerce Building, 14th St. and Constitution Ave. NW. Ⓜ *Federal Triangle. Open daily 9am–5pm; closed Dec 25. Admission: $2, children under 12 and seniors $.75. Shark feeding Mon, Wed and Sat 2pm, piranhas feeding Tue, Thu and Sun 2pm.* ♿ ✗ *(cafeteria open Mon–Fri 9am–2pm)* ☎*482-2825.*

This small aquarium is the nation's oldest. Established in 1873 under the auspices of the Federal Fish Commission, it has occupied various locations, including a series of ponds on the grounds of the Washington Monument. In the early 20C, the Fish Commission came under the Department of Commerce, and in 1932, the aquarium was moved to its present location in the basement of the Dept. of Commerce Building. Since 1982, the aquarium has functioned independently of the Government as a private, non-profit organization.

Its tanks house some 1,500 specimens of aquatic life, including sea turtles, lemon sharks, piranhas, moray eels, and lung fish. A touch tank allows visitors to handle such marine life as sea urchins and hermit crabs, and a theater features presentations on the underwater world.

The ***Michelin Green Guide to New England*** *spotlights the region's historical, cultural and natural attractions. Let Michelin's famous star-rating system direct you to a selection of over 800 points of interest in the area. More than 50 detailed city and regional maps are included to guide you through carefully designed walking and driving tours. The guide also contains fold-out maps of principal sights and recommended driving tours; practical information, such as helpful tips and useful addresses; and essays on New England's history, geography and artistic heritage.*

5

★★

Foggy Bottom

Once industrialized riverfront, this bottomland lying west of the White House was transformed after World War II into an administrative quarter. Today, it houses private institutions, government departments, a celebrated performing arts complex, and the city-styled campus of George Washington University.

Breweries and Gasworks – Prior to the founding of the Federal City, a small German settlement called Hamburg was located on the present site of the State Department Building. In L'Enfant's city plan *(see p 20)*, little was stipulated for this end of town except a circle—now Washington Circle—and a battlement, to be constructed on Camp Hill between what is now 23rd and 24th Streets. In the early 19C, a glassworks and brewery attracted more Germans here, but the area called Foggy Bottom—presumably because of the mists that hovered over its marshy ground—developed slowly.

One of the earliest and finest homes in the area was THE OCTAGON, built a few blocks west of the White House. On higher ground, along the K Street corridor, well-heeled Washingtonians built substantial dwellings. In 1844, a naval observatory was constructed atop Camp Hill. The original building still stands on the grounds of the Navy Bureau of Medicine and Surgery *(not open to the public)* on 23rd Steet. In 1856, the Washington Gas Light Storage Facility was built in Foggy Bottom and became a major employer, particularly for the Irish immigrants who lived in Connaught Row, south of Virginia Avenue.

The growing black population in the area managed to amass the funds to commission the renowned architect, James Renwick, to design **St Mary's Episcopal Church** for them. Established in 1886, the brick Gothic Revival church still stands at 728 23rd Street.

Two breweries—the Abner Drury Brewery and the Heurich Brewery, established by Christian Heurich *(see p 122)*—employed many of the neighborhood's German residents. Waterfront warehouses and wharves added to the industrial character of this malarial bottomland, and rows of narrow brick tenements constituted its residential core.

Transformation – In 1912, **George Washington University** moved to the northern end of Foggy Bottom, thus lending a collegial air to the streets southeast of Washington Circle. Nonetheless, throughout the first half of the 20C, the lowlands near the Potomac remained an industrial area of steadily declining fortunes and substandard housing. Then in 1947, the State Department moved into a large but graceless new headquarters building at 23rd and D Streets. At the same time, the century-old gas plant ceased operations, and Foggy Bottom took on a new respectability.

Throughout the 1950s, the neighborhood shifted from low-income industrial to middle-class professional. A series of office-residential medium-rise buildings were constructed, and in the 1960s, the Potomac shoreline became the site of the JOHN F. KENNEDY CENTER FOR THE PERFORMING ARTS. Beside it, the exuberant curves of the exclusive **Watergate complex** of condominiums and shops further graced the riverfront. In the 1970s, the complex gained national notoriety as the site of the Democratic National Committee break-in that ultimately led to President Nixon's resignation. Offsetting this modern construction, pleasant pockets of 19C row houses can still be found in the vicinity of George Washington University *(18th-25th Sts. and E-K Sts.)*. In Foggy Bottom's southern quarter are the administrative headquarters of such internaitonal organizations as the **World Bank** *(1818 H St.)* and the **Pan-American Health** and **World Health Organizations** *(both at 523 23rd St.)*, as well as numerous government departments. The north side of Constitution Avenue is lined with the dignified facades of the **Department of the Interior** (1937), the **Federal Reserve** buildings (1937), the **American Pharmaceutical Association** (1934), and the **National Academy of Sciences** (1924), on whose grounds is a compelling monument to physicist Albert Einstein.

★★ JOHN F. KENNEDY CENTER FOR THE PERFORMING ARTS

Michelin map 48 H3-H4 *time: 3/4 hour*

New Hampshire Ave. at Rock Creek Parkway. M *Foggy Bottom. Open daily 10am–midnight, Sun and holidays noon-midnight. Free Admission. Tickets must be purchased for most performances. For ticket information* *see p 171.* *Guided tours (45min) daily 10am–1pm.* ☎ *467-4600.*

Its gleaming horizontal mass dominating Foggy Bottom's riverfront, the Kennedy Center today ranks as one of the country's leading cultural institutions. Its designation as the capital's official memorial to the 34th President of the US has greatly contributed to the Center's popularity as a tourist attraction.

"A Living Memorial" – Although the idea of establishing a national cultural center in Washington dates back to the early days of the capital, it was only in 1958 that such an undertaking received congressional approval. In that year, President Eisenhower signed the National Cultural Center Act authorizing the creation of a national showplace for the arts.

A prime Foggy Bottom site comprising just under 10 acres of government property was chosen for the Center's location, and architect Edward Durrell Stone was commissioned to design the complex. Due to lack of sufficient private funds, the project lagged until early 1964 when Congress unanimously voted to designate the Center as the capital's only monument to assassinated President John F. Kennedy. Unlike the other presidential memorials erected in Washington, the John F. Kennedy Center for the Performing Arts, as the complex was renamed, was to be "a living memorial." To hasten construction of the privately funded project, Congress appropriated $23 million in Federal matching funds. In the ground-breaking ceremony that took place in December 1964, President Johnson wielded the same gold-plated shovel used by two of his predecessors to initiate construction of two other presidential monuments: the Lincoln and Jefferson Memorials. Over 40 foreign governments offered gifts—primarily works of art—to adorn the presidential memorial.

UPI/Bettmann

J.F. Kennedy by Aaron Shikler

To mark the Center's official opening on 8 September 1971, the world premiere of Leonard Bernstein's *Mass* was performed in the Opera House by a cast of 200 performers before an audience that included numerous personalities in the arts and government.

Operation of the Center – Headed by a Board of Trustees appointed by the US President, the Kennedy Center operates as a non-profit institution supported by private gifts and ticket sales. As a presidential memorial, the building and its property (excluding theater and administrative facilities) are maintained by the National Park Service.

The Center houses under the same roof six theaters of varying sizes with a total seating capacity of over 7,000, as well as a specialized library facility. Home of the National Symphony Orchestra, the Center schedules a wide spectrum of world-class entertainment in music, dance, and theater, including hit Broadway shows. Selected performances are broadcast on national television and radio. Among the acclaimed artists who have performed at the Center are Bill Cosby, Placido Domingo, Duke Ellington, Ella Fitzgerald, Rudolf Nureyev, Jason Robards, Arthur Rubenstein, Beverly Sills, Frank Sinatra, Isaac Stern, and Elizabeth Taylor.

Distinguished orchestras and opera and ballet companies, such as the Berlin Philharmonic, the Scala, the Vienna State Opera, the Metropolitan Opera and the Bolshoi, are regularly invited to perform on the Center's stages. The overwhelming success of the Center has been instrumental in propelling the capital into the forefront of the national and international cultural scene, thereby belying Washington's long-held reputation as a cultural backwater.

Exterior – The low rectangular structure (630ft by 300ft) is surrounded on all sides by a colonnade of metal piers supporting a roof terrace, above which rises the building's central section. Clad in white Carrara marble (a gift from Italy), the stark building seems to echo the overall design of the LINCOLN MEMORIAL, situated just a half mile downstream.

Interior – The two principal entrances, situated on the east facade, lead to a pair of lofty galleries clearly designed to inspire awe. The dizzying effect experienced upon entering is created by the relative narrowness of these spaces. The **Hall of States** *(north side)* displays flags of the 50 states, while the **Hall of Nations** *(south side)* is decked with flags of all foreign countries diplomatically accredited to the US. These parallel halls traverse the building's width, separating the three main auditoriums and ultimately connecting with the **Grand Foyer**, reputedly one of the largest rooms in the world (630ft long, 40ft wide, 60ft high). Occupying the entire length of the river facade, this awesome space is lined with 60ft-high mirrors (a gift from Belgium) that reflect the river terrace outside the foyer's floor-to-ceiling windows. Eighteen Orrefors crystal chandeliers (donated by Sweden) illuminate the gigantic expanse. In the central section of the foyer, note the expressive bronze **bust** of President Kennedy by Robert Berks.

The foyer serves as a vestibule to the Center's three main auditoriums: the **Opera House** (2318 seats), flanked by the **Concert Hall** (2759 seats) and the **Eisenhower Theater** (1142 seats). Renowned for their excellent acoustics, these theaters are appointed in color schemes of red, ivory, and gold and contain gifts, in the form of stage curtains, chandeliers and artwork from foreign countries that contributed to the project.

The **American Film Institute Theater** (224 seats), situated off the Hall of States, shows more than 600 movies annually and organizes festivals of film classics.

The roof-level *(accessible by elevators in the Hall of States and Hall of Nations)* houses two additional theaters, a library, restaurants, and exhibit spaces. A gift from Japan, the **Terrace Theater** *(off the north gallery)* was designed by noted architects Philip Johnson and John Burgee. This 512-seat performing space hosts concerts of chamber music as well as recitals and small-scale dance and theatrical performances. The **Theater Lab** (350 seats), designed for experimentation in sound research, is often the setting for children's entertainment.

The Performing Arts Library *(open to the public)*, also designed by Johnson and Burgee, was established by the Library of Congress as a depository for its collection of printed, visual, and audio material related to the performing arts.

★★ DIPLOMATIC RECEPTION ROOMS Department of State

Michelin map 48 J5 *time: 1 hour*

23rd St. between C and D Sts. NW. M Foggy Bottom. Visit by guided tour (45min) only, Mon–Fri 9:30, 10:30am, 2:45pm; closed Sat, Sun and Federal holidays. 2-month advance reservation required in summer, 2-4 week advance reservation required the rest of year. Free admission. ♿ ☎647-3241.

Housed in an undistinguished 1960s government office building, these reception rooms have been transformed into architectural masterpieces of 18C interior design. They are furnished with one of the most impressive collections of American decorative arts in the country.

The Renovation – When the State Department headquarters building opened in 1961, its 8th-floor rooms, used for official functions in honor of visiting dignitaries, were furnished in a stark, streamlined decor in keeping with the building's concrete-and-glass modernism. Before long, an effort called the **Americana Project**, under the Fine Arts Committee of the State Department, was begun to upgrade these reception areas.

Spearheaded by Clement E. Conger, then the department's deputy chief of protocol and curator of the White House, the project solicited private donors for contributions of funds and furnishings. Over the past three decades, it has amassed a collection of **American decorative arts★★**, from the period between 1725 and 1825, valued at approximately $50,000,000; about one-fifth of the holdings are on loan from individuals or museums.

Edward Vason Jones, a Georgia architect, donated the last 15 years of his life to redesigning the rooms in the style of great 18C American manor houses. The ornately plastered ceilings, pilasters, paneling, entablatures, and pediments complement the fine furnishings.

Tour – From the austere modernism of the building lobby, elevators ascend to the Edward Vason Jones Memorial Hall. Originally a nondescript elevator hall, it now serves as an elegant **foyer** appointed with marbelized pilasters and entablatures and rare King of Prussia gray marble floors.

Adjoining it, the **Entrance Hall** contains the Chippendale furnishings, oriental rugs, ornate paneling, and English cut-glass chandeliers characteristic of the decor throughout most of the reception rooms. The mahogany bombé, or swell-sided secretary-bookcase, in this room is the oldest dated and signed piece of bombé furniture in North America. It was made by Benjamin Frothingham of Boston in 1753.

A short passageway opens onto the **Gallery**, a long narrow room that was effectively lightened and enlarged by

W. Brown/Diplomatic Reception Rooms, US Department of State

Bombé desk and bookcase (1753)

adding Palladian windows at either end. Among the **Chippendale and Queen Anne furniture** is a bombé lowchest made in Boston about 1765 and considered one of the finest examples of its kind in the world. Also made in Boston about the same time, the blonde mahogany secretary belonged to Robert "King" Hooper, the 18C colonial shipping magnate of Marblehead, Massachusetts. A portrait of his daughter, Alice, by a young John Singleton Copley, and a later Copley of Mrs John Montresor hang here, as does John Mix Stanley's *Barter for a Bride* (c.1850), depicting Blackfoot Indians poised against a vast Montana backdrop. The five-part breakfront holds a set of Chinese Export porcelain in the Fitzhugh pattern. Ordered from England about 1800, the 65-piece set arrived in Philadelphia with an incorrect family monogram and was never used. It remained packed in its original shipping boxes until put on display here.

In the large 18C-style **John Quincy Adams State Drawing Room**, official guests are greeted by secretaries of state and other dignitaries in receiving lines. Wall paneling, door and window cornices, an elaborate mantelpiece, and oriental rugs ornament this formal room. Portraits of Mr and Mrs John Quincy Adams hang on the walls. The original **portrait of John Jay** (1784) by Gilbert Stuart is considered the finest painting in the collection. The English Sheraton tambour, or desk, where Jay signed the Treaty of Paris, Britain's formal acceptance of American Independence, is among the room's furnishings, as is the simple architectural desk on which Thomas Jefferson drafted the Declaration of Independence.

The neoclassical proportions and Doric entablature of the **Thomas Jefferson State Reception Room** reflect Jefferson's own architectural tastes. A copy of the David Anger statue of Jefferson that stands in the US Capitol occupies a pedimented niche at the end of the room. Several Jefferson portraits, including Thomas Sully's 1822 work, are on display. A fine pastel portrait of Benjamin Franklin by Jean-Baptiste Greuze also hangs here. The French Savonnerie carpet, measuring roughly 39ft by 21ft, is a reproduction of one originally made for the palace at Versailles.

The cavernous **Benjamin Franklin State Dining Room**, the most recently renovated, was redesigned by John Blatteau and completed in 1985. Red-veined scagliola columns are set off by gilded capitals and entablatures. An 8,000-pound **Savonnerie rug** in rose and gold covers the floor, and eight cutglass chandeliers flank a gilded Great Seal of the US in the ceiling. Above the mantel hangs Benjamin Franklin's favorite portrait of himself, painted by David Martin.

★ THE OCTAGON

Michelin map 48 H6 — *time: 3/4 hour*

1799 New York Ave. NW. M Farragut West. Open Tue–Fri 10am–4pm, Sat and Sun noon–4pm; closed Mon and holidays. Suggested contribution: $2, students and seniors $1, children under 12 $.50. Guided tours (40min) available. ♿ ☎638-3105. In view of the long-term restoration currently underway, certain sections may be closed temporarily and furnishings and decorative art removed or relocated.

One of Washington's earliest and finest residences, this many-sided architectural gem played a decided role in the history of the young Republic. Still retaining its Federal appearance *(see illustration p 24)*, the Octagon houses period rooms and a gallery devoted to architecture and design exhibits organized under the auspices of the American Architectural Foundation, which also administers the property.

Historical Notes – In the 1790s, George Washington, anxious to spur development of the new Federal City, convinced his friend Col John Tayloe to build a town house several blocks west of the planned President's Park (now Lafayette Square). A wealthy Virginia planter, Tayloe commissioned Dr William Thornton, first architect of the US Capitol. Thornton's task was complicated by the fact that Tayloe's lot was triangular, formed by the intersection of New York Avenue and 18th Street. In order to harmonize the house with its setting, Thornton conceived an ingenious multi-sided structure that became known as the Octagon, considered one of the burgeoning city's finest homes. The Tayloes used it as their winter residence after its completion in 1801, entertaining the capital's most influential figures here. During the August 1814 burning of Washington by the British, the French Minister, Louis Seurier, was in residence at the house, and at his request, the British spared the Octagon. The WHITE HOUSE, however, was gutted by fire, and while it was being repaired, President Madison lived in several different private homes, including the Octagon. During the Madisons' stay, from September 1814 to March 1815, peace was negotiated, ending the War of 1812. The **Treaty of Ghent**, signed by the British in Ghent, Belgium, on December 24, 1814, was brought to Washington and signed by Madison at the Octagon, on February 17, 1815.

By the time of Mrs Tayloe's death in 1855, the house and surrounding neighborhood had deteriorated. Tayloe's heirs leased the property for the remainder of the century to various groups, including the Federal Hydrographic Office. By the late 19C, it had become an ill-kept tenement, but its architectural integrity attracted the interests of the **American Institute of Architects** (AIA). In 1902, the Institute purchased the building from the Tayloe family for $30,000, moved its headquarters here, and began a meticulous restoration. In 1972, the AIA built the modern structure that wraps around the rear of the Octagon to house its offices, library facilities, and bookstore. The attractive courtyard that separates the contrasting buildings features a free-form stainless steel sculpture entitled *Triple Arc 1.*

A Six-sided "Octagon" – Though its name suggests eight sides, this brick structure is actually six-sided with a rounded front pavilion, which serves as a large entrance foyer. Beyond the foyer, the main hall is dominated by a graceful oval staircase. An "amity button" embedded in the handrail indicates that the builder and owner parted on friendly terms. Opening off the main hall are two large public rooms, furnished in Federal style. The drawing room is notable for its rare mantel of Coade stone, an artificial material produced in England from the late 18C until the mid-19C. Portraits in charcoal of Colonel Tayloe and William Thornton, by Charles de Saint-Mémin, hang on either side of the fireplace. In the symmetrical Adam-style dining room hang portraits of Dr and Mrs Thornton by Gilbert Stuart.

The circular study on the second floor is known as the Treaty of Ghent room. Madison is believed to have signed the historic document at the round mahogany table in the center of the room. The two flanking rooms are devoted to changing exhibits on architecture.

The brick-floored basement houses a kitchen and wine cellar.

DEPARTMENT OF THE INTERIOR MUSEUM

Michelin map 48 J6 *time: 1/2 hour*

Department of the Interior Building at C St. between 18th and 19th Sts. NW. M Farragut West. Open Mon–Fri 8am–5pm; closed Sat, Sun and Federal holidays. Free admission. Photo ID required to enter the building. Guided tours (30min) available (3-week advance reservation requested). ♿ ☎208-4743.

This small museum, located on the first floor of the Interior Department building, has retained the flavor of the late 1930s, when it first opened to the public.

Visit – Eight of the department's 11 bureaus—including those responsible for Mines, Indian Affairs, Reclamation, Territorial and International Affairs as well the National Park Service—have been allotted space to present exhibits consisting of artifacts, drawings, documents, diagrams, photos, and paintings. Throughout the museum, the visitor can view the attractive **dioramas** depicting historic or characteristic scenes from the nation's past, such as the meeting of Generals Washington and Lafayette at Morristown in 1780, a 19C Indian trading post in 1835, furtraders of the Upper Missouri River, the land rush in Oklahoma in 1889, and a mine disaster. The dioramas and the delightful **metal cut-outs** crowning the displays of the first two sections, were executed by artists in the 1930s.

The **Native American section**—featuring pottery, baskets, a canoe, and a headdress—presents only a small fraction of the department's rich Indian collection. In the passageway leading to the other exhibits hang four paintings by artist William H. Jackson depicting some of the earliest survey teams on assignment in the West during the second half of the 19C. Working from authentic period photographs, Jackson executed these paintings in 1938 when he was in his 90s.

Surveying equipment such as zenith and meridian telescopes used at the turn of the century as well as facsimiles of early documents granting land to homesteaders and to military personnel are on display in the section devoted to the Bureau of Land Management.

Artifacts from various Pacific Islands, such as Micronesia, the Marshall Islands, and American Samoa include wood carvings, miniature vessels, woven mats and baskets, and other indigenous crafts.

Upon leaving the museum, stop in at the shop across the hall, where contemporary Indian crafts and specialized publications are on sale.

6

★★

Georgetown

Washington's choicest neighborhood, Georgetown today is an amalgam of popular nightspots, restaurants, and shops surrounded by quiet residential streets. Predating Washington itself, this historical quarter functions as a well-preserved village, bounded on the south by the Potomac and on the east by Rock Creek. In many of its fine late-18C and 19C homes live congressional representatives, foreign dignitaries, and the capital's intelligentsia.

A Rock and a Knave – In 1703, Ninian Beall, a Scottish immigrant who acquired enormous landholdings throughout the state of Maryland, patented a 795-acre tract on which most of present-day Georgetown now stands. Beall named the tract the Rock of Dunbarton, after a geologic formation in his native Scotland. Thirty years later, George Gordon acquired, from the original patentee, an adjacent tract of land known as Knave's Disappointment. Gordon changed the name to Rock Creek Plantation and established a tobacco inspection house on it, near the confluence of Rock Creek and the Potomac River.

A small settlement, predominantly of Scottish immigrants, began to grow up here, and in 1751, the inhabitants petitioned the Maryland Provisional Assembly to establish a town. The assembly complied, appointing six commissioners to negotiate the sale of lots on a 60-acre tract encompassing the lands of George Gordon and those of George Beall, who had inherited the holdings of his father, Ninian. Though both owners were dissatisfied with conditions surrounding the sale, the lots were parcelled out and the new town formed. To this day, no clear consensus on the town's namesake—the former owners George Gordon and George Beall or King George II—has been reached by historians.

The Golden Age – Positioned at the head of the Potomac's navigable waters, Georgetown thrived in the late 18C as a port of entry for foreign goods and as an exporter of products from the fertile Ohio Valley in the West. Even during the Revolution, the town prospered as a base of supplies and munitions.

After the war, when the site for the new Federal City was being chosen, local landowners requested that George Washington consider the "lands owned by them in the vicinity of Georgetown." Though Washington did not choose the area, the town thrived during the building of the capital. Well established and respected, Georgetown was considered the "court end" of the still rough Federal city.

During this golden age, such grand manors as Evermay *(1623 28th St.)* and TUDOR PLACE dotted the hills of upper Georgetown, and elegant Federal-style town houses lined its lower residential streets. In 1789, the first Catholic institution of higher learning in the country, Georgetown College—now **Georgetown University**—was founded at the western edge of the town.

Decline and Rebirth – By the late 1820s, Georgetown found itself being eclipsed by Washington. In 1828, construction on the Chesapeake and Ohio Canal, with its eastern terminus in Georgetown, was begun in an attempt to stimulate commerce and westward migration. Ironically, just as the canal was being built, so too was the Baltimore and Ohio Railroad. The efficiency of train travel gradually brought an end to barge transport. At the same time, the advent of steam navigation, which required deeper ports than the town could provide, spelled doom to Georgetown's shipping business.

By mid-century, as the town continued its decline, residents began a movement to consolidate Georgetown and Washington, but those plans were waylaid by the coming of the Civil War.

Since Georgetown counted both Union and Confederate sympathizers among its residents, sentiments ran high among its citizenry during this period. Many of its churches and public buildings were used as hospitals for the Union wounded, and as elsewhere in Washington, the area was generally consumed with the war effort. In 1871, with the war over, Georgetown was consolidated with the District of Columbia. In order to incorporate it into Washington's gridiron street plan, its original street names were changed to the letters and numbers used elsewhere in Washington.

From the late 19C through the first half of the 20C, Georgetown fell into decline. Though its great houses remained in the hands of the wealthy, many of its old row houses were divided into apartments and rooming houses and adorned with Victorian flourishes. Only in the last 30 years has the neighborhood in general regained its prestige. Under the Old Georgetown Act of 1950, the area was declared a National Historic District. Demolition, new construction, and renovation now are subject to review by the Commission of Fine Arts.

Today, Georgetown's residential streets, with their carefully restored Federal-style and mid-19C houses, bristle with refinement and respectability. At the exclusive private parties held in these homes, much of the business of government, politics, and private enterprise is conducted. Georgetown's commercial district is concentrated almost exclusively on Wisconsin Avenue and M Street, which are lined with numerous restaurants and small trendy boutiques, as well as **Georgetown Park**, a popular large-scale urban mall. Anchoring the intersection of those two main thoroughfares is the golden dome of Riggs National Bank, Georgetown's most prominent landmark. Along the canal and the waterfront, redevelopment has generally taken the form of large brick office complexes. An exception is the riverfront showcase **Washington Harbour** (1986), a glittery complex of condominiums, offices, and shops. Its elaborately terraced and fountained courtyard affords a fine **view** down the Potomac.

The old towpath along the canal, saved through the efforts of conservationists, remains a quiet walker's thoroughfare reminiscent of the town's historic past.

Georgetown is not served by Metrorail. Because of the scarcity of parking garages and available street parking (particularly in the evening), visitors may find it most convenient to reach this area by bus. The bus line (nos. 32, 34, 36, and 38) linking central Washington to Georgetown runs along Pennsylvania Ave., M St., and Wisconsin Ave.

Tours of selected Georgetown houses and gardens are given in late April and early May. ☎338-1796.

© Fred J. Maroon 1993

2800 block of N Street

WALKING TOUR

Distance: 1 1/2 miles

Michelin map p 108 *time: 1 1/2 hours*

Begin at the corner of the towpath and 30th St. NW.

★ **C&O Canal and Towpath** – Georgetown is the terminus for the old **Chesapeake and Ohio Canal**, which runs 184.5 miles through 75 lift locks to Cumberland, Maryland. In 1971, the entire canal was designated a national park. Here, at lift lock no. 3, a **bust [1]** of Supreme Court Justice William O. Douglas commemorates his work in spearheading the movement to preserve the canal as a recreation area. *Mule-drawn barge trips (1 1/2 hours round-trip) along the canal aboard* The Georgetown *depart from 1057 Thomas Jefferson St. Jun 16–Sept 12 Wed–Sun 10:30am, 1 and 3pm with additional departure Sat 5pm. Limited service in spring and fall. Admission: $5, seniors and children $3.50. ♿ ☎472-4376.*

Continue down the towpath.

At the intersection with Thomas Jefferson Street, the brick Federal structure (c.1810) at **no. 1058** originally housed the Potomac Masonic Lodge, whose early members were present at the ceremonies for the laying of the Capitol cornerstone. The quaint **row houses** just past it along the towpath were built after the Civil War as residences for artisans and laborers.

Turn right on 31st St. and then right on M St., one of Georgetown's main thoroughfares.

Old Stone House – *3051 M St. Open Wed–Sun 8am–4:30pm; closed Mon, Tue, and Federal holidays. Free admission. ♿ ☎426-6851.* The front of this small 2-story house, one of the oldest structures in Washington, was built by Christopher Layman, around 1765. Since 1960, the National Park Service has maintained it as a museum house characterizing colonial life. Note the paneling in the dining room. A large garden in the rear offers a respite from the bustle of M Street.

© Fred J. Maroon 1993

Chesapeake and Ohio Canal

Continue east on M St.

The twin buildings at nos. 3037 and 3039 (known as the Nathan Loughborough houses) date from the turn of the 19C. The Junior League of Washington, a women's civic organization, restored them in 1963 and now uses them as its DC headquarters. The late 18C buildings at **nos. 3001** and **3003** were the home of Thomas Sim Lee, an ardent Revolutionary, governor of Maryland, and friend of George Washington. In 1951, the buildings were saved from demolition under the strictures of the newly established Old Georgetown Act *(see p 106)*.

Turn left on 29th St., then right on N St.

★ **N Street** – This handsome street contains some of the finest Federal-style architecture in the city. The elegant brick residence at **no. 2812** was built in the early 19C. Mrs Stephen Decatur is said to have lived here after her departure from DECATUR HOUSE on Lafayette Square.

Return to the corner of N and 29th Sts. and continue to 30th St.

The **3000 block of N Street** boasts many of Georgetown's most distinguished town houses. During the Civil War, it was a bastion of Southern support.
At the corner of N and 30th Streets stands the **Laird-Dunlop House** *(no. 3014)*, a brick building constructed in 1799 by John Laird, a wealthy tobacco merchant, who apparently modeled his sprawling home after residences he had seen in Edinburgh. Laird's daughter Barbara married James Dunlop, a law partner of Francis Scott Key, who penned the "Star-Spangled Banner." In 1915, Abraham Lincoln's son Robert Todd, who had been a secretary of war and minister to Britain, bought the house from Dunlop heirs. He added the attached dwelling at no. 3018.
The large house across the street at **no. 3017** was built in the 1790s by Thomas Beall, descendant of original Georgetown landowner Ninian Beall. **Jacqueline Kennedy** briefly lived here in 1963, after President Kennedy's death. The dwelling at no. 3038, with its elegant doorway and shingled dormers, is a particularly fine example of the smaller town houses built during the early 19C.

Turn right on 31st St. and left on Dumbarton Ave.

Surrounded by a lush garden and a white picket fence, the imposing residence at **3123 Dumbarton Ave.** was built by Henry Foxall, a prominent Georgetown businessman, for his daughter Mary Ann McKenney. Dating back to the early 19C, the house is considered one of the most architecturally pristine structures in the area. According to local legend, it also houses a famous Georgetown ghost—a maiden lady who came to luncheon at the McKenneys' and never left.

The yellow-brick **Dumbarton United Methodist Church** *(no. 3133)* was constructed in 1849 in the Romanesque Revival style. During the Civil War, the church was used as a hospital, and poet Walt Whitman, serving as a male nurse, ministered to the Union wounded here. The current facade was added in an 1894 renovation.

Continue across Wisconsin Ave. and turn left on O St.

Note the remnants of the old trolley track embedded in this brick-paved street.

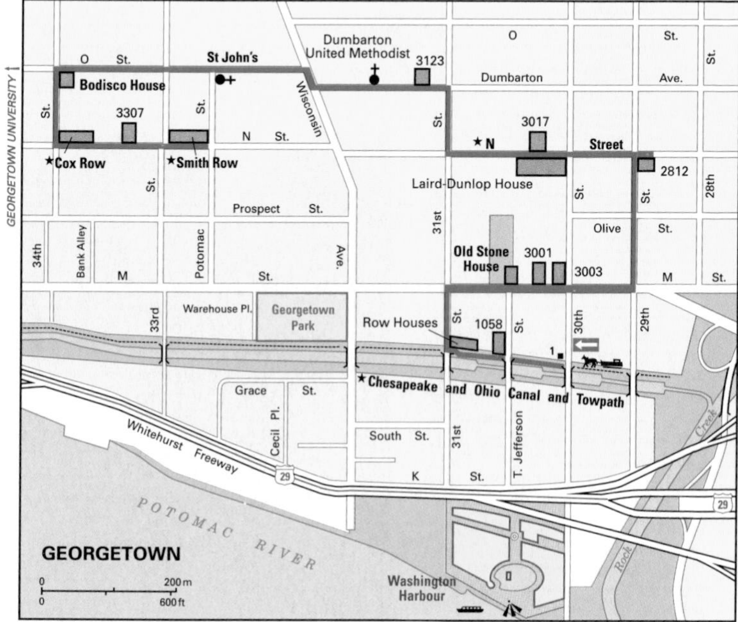

St John's Church – *3240 O St. Open Mon–Fri 9am–4:30pm, Sun 7:30am–2pm. Free admission.* ♿ ☎*338-1796.* Built between 1796 and 1804 in the Federal style, this stucco structure is the third oldest Episcopal church in Washington. Thomas Jefferson donated money for its building, and Francis Scott Key served as one of its vestrymen. In 1831, the church was abandoned due to lack of funds. Financier and art patron William Wilson Corcoran *(see p 80)* purchased it as a philanthropic gesture in 1837 and sold it back to the church several years later.

The 3300 block of O Street has a typical Georgetown mix of Federal and late 19C structures.

Bodisco House – *3322 O St.* Built about 1815, the handsome, porticoed Federal dwelling was home to Robert E. Lee's mother after she left Alexandria *(see p 150)*. The residence is most renowned, however, for the romantic tale surrounding another of its former occupants—Baron Alexander de Bodisco, the Russian minister to the US in the mid-19C. Then the structure housed the Russian legation. After the 62-year-old baron married a 16-year-old Georgetown belle, Harriott Beall Williams, he and his new bride used the house as the setting for lavish parties that became legendary. For years it was a focal point of Georgetown society.

Turn left on 34th St. and left again on N St.

★ **Cox Row** – This handsome group of five Federal houses *(nos. 3339-3327)*, adorned with swags and high, graceful dormers, was built in 1805 by Col John Cox. Georgetown's first mayor elected by popular vote, Cox held that office for 22 years (1823-1845). No. 3339 was Cox's residence for a time. In 1824, he entertained the Marquis de Lafayette in no. 3337.

Sen **John F. Kennedy** purchased **no. 3307** in 1957 as a present for his wife, Jacqueline. The Kennedys lived here until moving into the White House in 1961. This house and its twin at no. 3311 were built in 1811.

Like a number of Georgetown homes dating from the Federal period, the facade of no. 3311 has been embellished with 19C Italianate detailing (elaborate cornice and door frame, hooded window crowns with brackets).

★ **Smith Row** – An unbroken, manicured block of Federal row houses extends from nos. 3267 to 3255. Their exteriors have been little altered since they were built by Clement and Walter Smith in 1815.

★★ DUMBARTON OAKS

Michelin map 48 D2 *time: 2 hours (including gardens)*

1703 32nd St. NW between R and S Sts. Take any even-numbered 30s bus, or D2, D4, M12 bus to Wisconsin Ave. and R St. and walk one block east on R St. Open Tue–Sun 2pm–5pm; closed Mon, Federal holidays, and during inclement weather. Suggested contribution: $1. ♿ ☎342-3200.

Renowned for its outstanding collection of Byzantine and pre-Columbian art, this gracious museum and research institution is situated at the heart of what has been called "America's most civilized square mile." The 16-acre estate set on a ridge above Rock Creek Park is graced with a harmonious ensemble of buildings surrounded by beautifully landscaped gardens.

Historical Notes – In 1800 and 1801, Sen William Dorsey of Maryland purchased 22 acres on the northern edge of Georgetown from Thomas Beall, the descendant of Ninian Beall, whose vast 795-acre Rock of Dunbarton tract had once encompassed much of present-day Georgetown. Dorsey constructed the brick Federal-style home still standing at Dumbarton. He and his family lived here for only a year before personal and financial problems forced Dorsey to sell. In the ensuing decades, the property passed through a succession of prominent owners, among them Edward Linthicum, a self-made businessman who, in the 1860s, added substantial wings to the original structure, Victorianized its appearance, and renamed it "The Oaks," because of the fine stand of white oaks surrounding it.

A Marriage of Taste and Wealth – In 1920, Robert and Mildred Bliss purchased the estate. From adolescence the Blisses had known each other, because their separate, widowed parents had wed, making them stepbrother and sister. Cultured, widely traveled, and independently wealthy, the Blisses transformed Dumbarton Oaks, as they renamed it, into an elegant "country house in the city." With the help of the prominent architectural firm McKim, Mead and White, the interior was restructured and the exterior restored to its original Federal style. In 1929, a large music room was added. Working closely with Mrs Bliss, Beatrix Jones Farrand, the noted landscape architect and a personal friend of the couple, designed the extensive gardens.

Robert Bliss' career in the foreign service prevented the couple from living here until 1933. During their years abroad, they had begun an important collection of Byzantine artifacts, and once settled at Dumbarton, they continued collecting, amassing at the same time an extensive research library. A west wing was added with two pavilions and an enclosed courtyard to function as a museum open to the public.

In 1940, the Blisses conveyed the house, grounds, their Byzantine collection, a library of some 14,000 volumes, and an endowment to **Harvard University**, which maintains the estate as a research institution and museum. They also donated an adjacent 27-acre tract known as Dumbarton Oaks Park *(open daily until dusk)* to the National Park Service to be enjoyed by the public.

In 1944, the famous **Dumbarton Oaks Conferences** involving representatives from the US, the United Kingdom, China, and the Soviet Union were held at the Blisses' former home. The accords reached among the participants ultimately resulted in the creation of the United Nations.

MANSION

★★ **Byzantine Collection** – After their initial donation of artifacts, the Blisses continued to enrich the collection, as did other donors. Today, the collection numbers some 1,500 artifacts—all valuable examples of the refined artistic production of the Byzantine empire, which held sway over the eastern Mediterranean region from the 4C to 15C. The museum's collection of 12,000 Byzantine coins is one of the most complete and extensive in the world.

Byzantine Collection/Dumbarton Oaks

Gold medallion of Constantine I (c.326)

The columned interior courtyard is devoted to artifacts predating, or created on the periphery of, the Byzantine empire. Displays include Late Roman and early Byzantine bas-reliefs, Roman glass and bronze (1C-5C), textiles from Egypt and the eastern Mediterranean (6C-12C), and a 6C Syrian floor mosaic. The adjacent gallery displays 6C ecclesiastical silver from the Sion Treasury, found in present-day Turkey; Byzantine icons, lamps, and liturgical vessels, crosses, and enameled adornments.

★ **Pre-Columbian Collection** – In 1962, Robert Bliss also donated his superb pre-Columbian collection to Dumbarton Oaks and commissioned the prominent architect **Philip Johnson** to design an addition that would complement the striking objects. Johnson's concept consists of eight circular, glass-walled pavilions built around a central fountain.
Arranged by cultures, the pavilions house Olmec figurines and masks *(gallery II)*; Maya architectural reliefs and ceramics *(III-IV)*; stone yokes, and axes from Veracruz *(V)*; gold jewelry from Central America *(VI)*: pottery, gold, and tapestries from ancient Peruvian and Bolivian cultures *(VII)*; and Aztec carvings, frescoes, masks, and vessels *(VIII)*.

★ **Music Room** – This stately hall is dominated by a large stone chimney piece from the Château de Thébon (16-17C) in France's Bordeaux region. The ornately painted wooden ceiling beams are modeled on those in the 17C Château de Cheverny in the Loire Valley. Flemish and German tapestries hang on the walls, as does El Greco's *Visitation* (c.1610) *(left wall)*. The frescoes adorning the arched stair alcove *(far wall)* were painted by Allyn Cox, who executed many of the murals in the CAPITOL. During the Blisses' residency in the house, a number of famous musicians performed here, including Ernest Schelling, Ignace Paderewski, Nadia Boulanger, and **Igor Stravinsky**, whose *Concerto in E-flat*, also known as the *Dumbarton Oaks Concerto*, was commissioned by the Blisses for their 30th anniversary.
A rotating series of rare books from the permanent collection of the Garden Library is displayed in the hall to the right of the entrance pavilion.
The original brick Federal-style residence now houses research and administrative offices *(not open to the general public)*.

★★ GARDENS

Entrance at 31st and R Sts. Open Apr–Oct daily 2–6pm, the rest of the year daily 2–5pm; closed during Federal holidays and inclement weather. Admission (Apr–Oct only): $2, seniors and children $1. ☎338-8278.

In the flowering season, a map is available at the garden gate. Following the natural slope of the land, Beatrix Jones Farrand planned "a series of broad terraces leading from the strictly formal architectural character of the house through various transitions to the delightful informality of the lower garden with its loose plantings of flowering trees, shrubs, and naturalized bulbs." In addition, several "garden rooms" function as extensions of the house itself.
Today, the meticulously tended grounds include 10 acres of formal terraces devoted to such plantings as rose and herb gardens. Paths lead to secluded fountains, pools, terraces, and arbors, offset by flowering trees and shrubs. The centerpiece of the lovely **Pebble Garden** (added in the 1960s) is a shallow pool framed by rococo borders of moss and paved with a mosaic of Mexican stones arranged to represent a wheat sheaf.

To appreciate the ever-changing landscapes of Dumbarton Oaks Gardens, visit them at different times of the year. Some seasonal highlights:

- ***Mid-March through April:*** *cherry blossoms, forsythia, wisteria, azaleas, dogwood, lilacs, akebia, star magnolia;*
- ***May:*** *lilacs, clematis, roses, peonies, fringetree;*
- ***June:*** *clematis, roses, grandiflora magnolia, canna;*
- ***July through August:*** *day lilies, fuchsia, gardenias, agapanthus oleanders;*
- ***Late September through October:*** *chrysanthemums.*

★ TUDOR PLACE

Michelin map 48 E2 *time: 1 1/4 hours (including grounds)*

1644 31st St. NW. Take any no. 30s bus to Wisconsin Ave. and Q St. Walk east on Q St. and left on 31st St. Grounds open Mon–Sat 10am–4pm (no reservations necessary). Mansion visit by guided tour (1 hour) only (advance reservation required) Tue–Fri 10, 11:30am, 1 and 2:30pm, and Sat (no reservation required) hourly 10am–3pm, limited tour schedule Jan and Feb; closed Sun, Mon and Jan 1, Jul 4, Thanksgiving Day, Dec 25. Suggested contribution: $5, students and children $2.50. Grounds only $2.50. Candlelight tours offered mid-Dec. ☎965-0400.

The landmark mansion and stately grounds of Tudor Place have dominated this block of Georgetown for some 180 years. Home to the prominent Peter family for six generations, the estate now functions as a house museum and a monument to old Washington traditions.

A Residence of Distinction – Tudor Place was built as the home of Thomas Peter and his wife, Martha Custis Peter, the granddaughter of Martha Washington and the sister of George Washington Parke Custis and Nelly Parke Custis Lewis *(see table p 117)*. In 1805, with the $8,000 inheritance Martha Peter received from her step-

grandfather, George Washington, the Peters purchased an 8-acre city block in Georgetown Heights, with sweeping views of the growing capital city and the Potomac River. Dr William Thornton, family friend and first architect of the CAPITOL, was commissioned to design a home befitting the Peters' status as Washington descendants (Thornton also participated in the building of Nelly Lewis' home, WOODLAWN). Thornton's project called for a two-story central structure to be joined to the pre-existing east and west wings by means of one-story hyphens. Construction proceeded slowly, but the brick stuccoed mansion was finally completed in 1816.
At her death in 1854, Martha Peter left the estate to the youngest of the three Peter daughters, Britannia Wellington Peter Kennon, who had been widowed after only a year of marriage. During the Civil War years, Britannia, a staunch Southern sympathizer and relative of Robert E. Lee, allowed Union officers to use Tudor Place as a boardinghouse, stipulating only that "affairs of war not be discussed" in her presence. According to legend, the mistress of Tudor Place refused to receive Mrs Ulysses S. Grant as a boarder. However, Britannia willingly agreed to temporarily store the belongings of Mrs Robert E. Lee when she was forced to flee ARLINGTON HOUSE. Other illustrious 19C visitors to this respected Washington residence were the Marquis de Lafayette, Henry Clay, Andrew Jackson, Daniel Webster, and John C. Calhoun.
The estate remained in the family until the death of Armistead Peter III, in 1983, when it passed to the Tudor Place Foundation, which opened the property to the public in 1988.

The Mansion – The simple Federal-style north facade fronts a boxwood-edged carriage drive. The centerpiece of Thornton's distinctive design is the circular south portico, which stands like a columned "temple" overlooking Georgetown. The recessed semicircular wall of the portico projects into the interior, creating a striking convex glass wall in the central saloon. A number of furnishings come from MOUNT VERNON, having been purchased by the Peters when that estate's belongings were auctioned off in the early 19C. The first-floor rooms as well as the bedrooms on the upper story contain memorabilia from various eras in the family's history and do not reflect any one time period.
The 5 1/2 acres of **grounds** surrounding the house are devoted on the north side to more formal plantings, including a flower "knot," a circular garden, and a bowling green. The south lawn slopes in a broad green expanse. Against the south facade of the house is a border of old roses, a few dating from Martha Custis Peter's occupancy.

DUMBARTON HOUSE

Michelin map 48 E3 *time: 1/2 hour*

2715 Q St. NW. Take any no. 30s bus to Wisconsin Ave. and Q St. Walk east on Q St. to 27th St. Visit by guided tour (45min) only Tue–Sat 10am–12:15pm; closed Sun, Mon, Thanksgiving Day and Dec 24 to Jan 2. Admission: $3, seniors $2, children under 18 free. ☎337-2288.

Historical Notes – This brick Federal-style house is a fine example of the imposing residential architecture that predominated in upper Georgetown during the community's golden age. Built in the last years of the 18C, it quickly passed through several owners, until in 1805, it was purchased by Joseph Nourse, register of the US Treasury. When Charles Carroll became owner of the house in 1813, he named it Bellevue, a name it retained for more than a century.
In the early 20C, Georgian Revival quoins, balustrades, and other embellishments were added, and in 1915, the house was moved 100 yards north to accommodate the eastward extension of Q Street. After the move, the present east and west wings were added to the house. In 1928, the **National Society of the Colonial Dames of America,**

Georgetown Heritage Trust

Benjamin Stoddert's Children by Charles Willson Peale

a women's organization dedicated to historic preservation and education, bought the property and renamed it Dumbarton House, after the original Rock of Dunbarton tract, which once included much of present-day Georgetown. With the consultation of the eminent architectural preserver Fiske Kimball, the Dames had the house restored to its Federal appearance. Today, it serves as a house museum and the organization's national headquarters.

Visit – The exterior features a columned portico with a fanlight over the doorway and stone lintels above the windows. A sweeping staircase dominates the wide interior entrance hall, flanked by a formal library, a dining room, a music room, and a parlor. The rooms, furnished in the Federal period, display a number of pieces originally from WOODLAWN and MOUNT VERNON. Among these are china, crystal, quilts, and clothing that belonged to Martha Washington and her granddaughter Eliza Custis Law *(see table p 117)*. Also notable is a 1789 painting by Charles Willson Peale *(see illustration p 111)*. It portrays the children of Benjamin Stoddert, first Secretary of the Navy, with a view of old Georgetown and the Potomac River in the background. The second floor contains four bedrooms, also furnished predominantly in the Federal style.

OAK HILL CEMETERY

Michelin map 48 E3-E4 *time: 1/2 hour*

3001 R St. NW. Entrance at R and 30th Sts. Take any no. 30s bus to Wisconsin Ave. and R St. Walk east on R St. to 30th St. Open Mon–Fri 10am–4pm; closed Sat, Sun and Federal holidays and during funeral services. Free admission. ☎337-2835. A brochure with a detailed map of the grounds is available at the superintendent's lodge.

One of the city's oldest and most venerable cemeteries, Oak Hill occupies a wooded, rolling 25-acre tract of land along the west bank of Rock Creek. William Wilson Corcoran, financier and founder of the CORCORAN GALLERY OF ART, donated the original 15 acres of ground to the cemetery company, incorporated by Congress in 1849. James Renwick, the architect of the CASTLE and the first Corcoran Gallery (now the RENWICK GALLERY), designed the picturesque **Gothic Revival chapel** (1850) and the cast-iron gate that encloses the cemetery along R Street.

The grounds are fashioned as a garden cemetery. Most graves date to the 19C, and the tombstones and monuments are characteristic of that period. Corcoran's own grave is marked by a replica of a Doric temple, designed by 19C Capitol architect, Thomas U. Walter. Among the many other prominent citizens buried here are John Howard Payne, composer of "Home, Sweet, Home"; Dean Acheson, Secretary of State under Truman; and a number of descendants of George Washington.

7
★
Arlington Across the River

Arlington is a mixture of high rises, middle-class neighborhoods, and ethnic enclaves. Along its Potomac shoreline, a network of pleasant parkways, dotted with memorials and statues, connects Arlington to the capital.

The Beginnings – The first accounts of the lands along the Potomac came from Capt John Smith, who made an exploratory expedition up the river in 1608. He recorded an Indian village along what is now the Arlington shoreline. By the mid-17C, much of the present county had been claimed by absentee landholders. Chief among them were members of the Alexander family, after whom the town of Alexandria, established in 1748, is named.

Throughout the colonial period and into the 19C, the Arlington region was inextricably bound, both administratively and economically, to Alexandria, which served as the urban focus for the area's scattering of small farms.

Part of the Capital City – By a 1789 act of the Virginia General Assembly, land along the Potomac amounting to 34 acres and encompassing parts of what are now Arlington and Alexandria was ceded for the formation of the new Federal City. These former Virginia lands officially became the County of Alexandria of the District of Columbia. For the first half of the 15C, the current jurisdiction of Arlington was part of the capital, and yet it retained its rural character. In 1846, disillusioned with their association with the nation's capital, the county residents voted by public referendum to retrocede to Virginia.

War and Devastation – During the Civil War, Arlington's lands were occupied by Union forces guarding the southern flanks of the capital city against Confederate incursions. Forests were felled, fortresses built, and earthworks erected, all of which had a devastating effect on the land of this agrarian community. Robert E. Lee's own home, ARLINGTON HOUSE, became the headquarters for various Union commanders.

Shortly after the war ended, Virginia's adoption of a new constitution added to the community's troubles. Under the 1870 law, cities with a population of 5,000 or more became independent units, completely separate from any county jurisdiction. Alexandria thus became an entity altogether divorced from the County of Alexandria, leaving Arlington, which had come to be called "the country part of the county" to fare on its own. It took 30 years to recover from the war, but by the turn of the century, truck farms and nurseries were flourishing here. During the decade between 1910 and 1920, Arlington's population grew by 60 percent, in large part due to an influx of workers in the Word War I years. In 1920, the Virginia General Assembly recognized the county's growing prominence by changing its name from the County of Alexandria, to Arlington County, named in honor of General Lee's Arlington home.

Arlington Today – In the last six decades, Arlington has continued its phenomenal growth, largely as a bedroom community for government workers. World War II saw Arlington grow from 57,000 people in 1940 to 120,000 in 1944. Federally funded housing projects for this white-collar work force sprouted up in the southern part of the county, as did military buildings, including the enormous PENTAGON.

Some 171,000 people now live in Arlington's 25.7sq miles. While its affluent northern neighborhoods retain their traditional suburban character, the neighborhoods of south Arlington are home to many Hispanics and South Asians, who operate small specialty food stores or restaurants in the area.

★★ ARLINGTON NATIONAL CEMETERY

Michelin map 48 and map p 115 *time: 2 1/2 hours*

The cemetery is located on the Arlington side of Memorial Bridge, about 3/4 mile from the Lincoln Memorial.

Access – *Ⓜ Arlington Cemetery.* **By foot:** *The short walk across Memorial Bridge can be very pleasant in clement weather.* **By car:** *Cross Memorial Bridge to the parking lot (hourly charge) situated adjacent to the visitor center.* **By Tourmobile:** *The cemetery is included on the standard Washington tour—see p 169. Open Apr–Sept daily 8am–7pm (5pm the rest of the year). Free admission.* *☎703-697-2131.*

Touring the cemetery – The cemetery is situated on a tract comprising over 600 acres of hilly terrain crisscrossed with meandering paved routes. Car traffic is permitted only for disabled visitors and for relatives of persons interred in the cemetery. The cemetery grounds can be explored on foot (allow half a day and wear comfortable walking shoes). If you are pressed for time or do not feel up to walking, we recommend riding the special Tourmobile shuttle that operates within the cemetery making stops at the most popular sights (Kennedy gravesites, Tomb of the Unknowns and Arlington House—*see description p 116).* Tickets for the cemetery tour *($2.75, children $1.25)* can be purchased at the visitor center, behind which shuttles depart continually from opening time to a half hour prior to closing.

A sylvan retreat situated just minutes from the hubbub of the Mall, Arlington National Cemetery is the country's most revered burial ground and one of the capital's most poignant sights. This vast military cemetery, lined with endless rows of gleaming white headstones, enshrines the graves of a host of distinguished Americans.

An Act of Vindication – At the outbreak of the Civil War, ARLINGTON HOUSE was established as the headquarters for the defense of Washington, and military installations were erected in various locations around the 1,100-acre estate. As much of the early fighting took place around the capital, the need for burial space soon became evident.

In 1864, Quartermaster Gen of the Army Montgomery Meigs (architect of the PENSION BUILDING), who was responsible for overseeing the appropriation of government land for military purposes, recommended that the grounds of Arlington House be used to inter war casualties. With the approval of Secretary of War Stanton, 200 acres of the estate were designated as a burial ground, and on May 13, 1864, the first soldier, Pvt William Christman from Pennsylvania, was laid to rest there. Showing considerable vindictiveness toward Lee, whom he viewed as a traitor, Meigs ensured that the first graves were situated in the immediate vicinity of the mansion as a deterrent to the return of the Lees. In Mrs Lee's rose garden, located just south of the mansion, a large vault was constructed to hold the remains of 2,111 unidentified soldiers. Meigs himself, who died in 1892, was eventually buried at Arlington.

In 1883, following a Supreme Court decision that the Arlington estate should be returned to the Lees, the family accepted a financial compensation of $150,000 rather than demanding the restitution of the estate, which by that time contained the remains of some 16,000 war casualties. In that same year, Arlington became the official national cemetery of the US.

A National Shrine – The cemetery now comprises 612 acres and contains the graves of over 200,000 military personnel and their dependents. Among those laid to rest in the cemetery's rolling hills are veterans of every armed conflict in which the US has participated since the Revolutionary War.

L. Moore/Uniphoto

Headstones at Arlington Cemetery

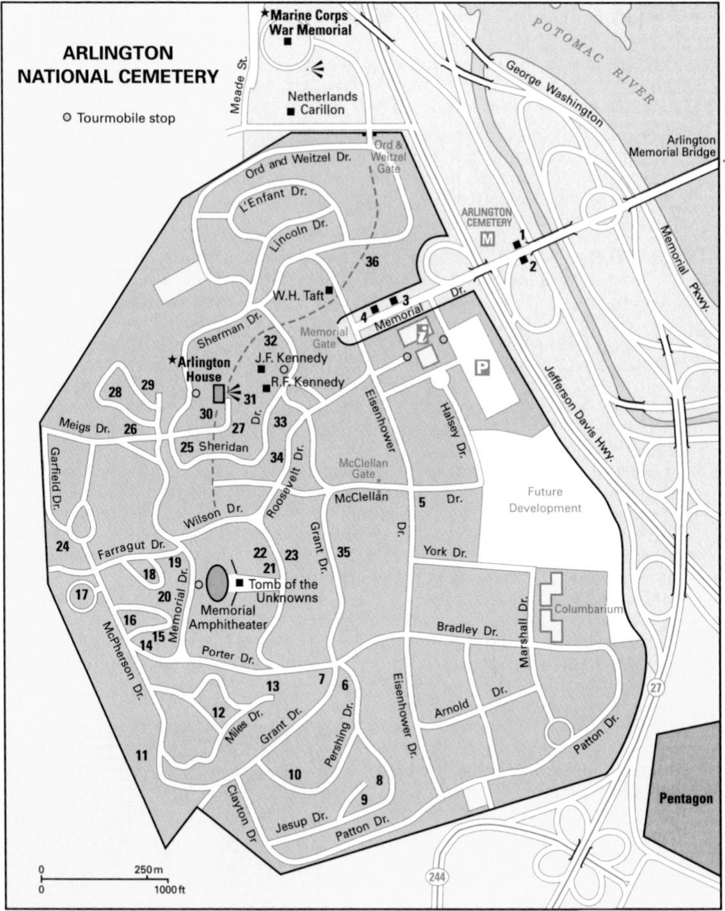

1 Seabees Memorial
2 United Spanish War Veterans Memorial ("The Hiker")
3 Adm Richard E. Byrd Memorial
4 101st Army Airborne Division Memorial
5 Memorial to service personnel killed in Beirut, 1983
6 USS Serpens Memorial
7 Mary Roberts Rinehart: mystery writer, war correspondent
8 William Jennings Bryan: Secretary of State
9 US Coast Guard Memorial
10 John P. Pershing: General of the Armies
11 Argonne Cross (dedicated to Americans killed in France during WWI)
12 V. Grissom and R. Chaffee: Apollo I astronauts
13 Walter Reed: instrumental in combating yellow fever
14 Nurses Memorial
15 John Foster Dulles: Secretary of State
16 Rough Riders Memorial
17 Confederate Monument
18 USS Maine Memorial
19 Shuttle Challenger Astronauts Memorial
20 Memorial to service personnel killed in the attempt to rescue US hostages in Iran, 1980
21 Frank Reynolds: broadcast journalist
22 Joe Louis: heavyweight boxing champion
23 George C. Marshall: General, Secretary of State
24 James Parks: Arlington House slave
25 Claire L. Chennault: Commander of the WWII Flying Tigers
26 Montgomery Meigs: Quartermaster General, engineer, architect
27 Johnny Clem: youngest soldier in the US Army
28 Anita Newcomb McGee: first woman Army surgeon
29 Tomb of the Unknown Dead of the War of 1812
30 Tomb of the Unknown Civil War Dead
31 Pierre Charles L'Enfant: planner of Washington DC
32 Oliver Wendell Holmes Jr: Supreme Court Justice
33 Richard E. Byrd (grave): Polar explorer
34 George Westinghouse: inventor
35 Dashiell Hammett: detective novelist
36 Medgar Evers: civil rights leader

Two US Presidents are buried in Arlington Cemetery: President **William H. Taft** (1857-1930) and President **John F. Kennedy** (1917-1963), whose simple grave is marked by an eternal flame. The grave of **Robert F. Kennedy** (1925-1968), marked by a white cross, lies close to that of his older brother.

Designed by Carrère and Hastings, the 5,000-seat **Memorial Amphitheater** (1920) is used for special ceremonies such as Memorial Day and Veterans Day services. As the country's most prestigious burial ground, Arlington Cemetery has been chosen to house numerous **memorials** dedicated to special groups or particular events in the nation's history. These memorials, which are scattered throughout the cemetery, include group headstones, statues, plaques, and even trees. Particularly moving is the **Tomb of the Unknowns** *(located behind Memorial Amphitheater)*, containing one soldier from each of the two world wars, and from the Korean and Vietnam Wars. The remains of these four soldiers will be forever unidentified so as to represent symbolically all the men and women who lost their lives in those conflicts. The cemetery's most prominent memorial, ARLINGTON HOUSE *(see description p 116)*, occupies a hilltop site dominating the cemetery.

★ ARLINGTON HOUSE/THE ROBERT E. LEE MEMORIAL

Map p 115. Time: 1/2 hour.

The mansion is situated on the grounds of Arlington National Cemetery. For access see p 114. Open Apr–Sept 30 daily 9:30–6pm (4:30pm the rest of the year); closed Jan 1, Dec 25. Free admission. P ♿ ☎*703-557-0613.*

Surrounded by the white headstones of Arlington Cemetery, the dignified mansion that has been designated the official Robert E. Lee Memorial tops a high bluff overlooking Washington. Lee, hero of the Confederacy, called this his home for 30 years. Here, he wrote, "my affections and attachments are more strongly placed than at any other place in the world."

The Custises – Arlington House, as the mansion is commonly known, was built by George Washington Parke Custis, whose father, John, was the son of Martha Washington by her first husband. When John Custis died during the Revolution, George and Eleanor (Nelly), the youngest of his four small children, were brought to MOUNT VERNON and raised by the Washingtons. Young George Custis spent his childhood among the Washingtons' illustrious circle of acquaintances.

Washington died in 1799 and Martha in 1802. Mount Vernon passed to Bushrod Washington, a nephew of George Washington, and the 21-year-old Custis moved to an 1,100-acre tract of land his father had left him across from the newly established Federal City.

At once Custis began planning a mansion worthy of housing what he called the "Washington Treasury"—the Mount Vernon memorabilia he had acquired through inheritance or by purchase. The architect chosen to draw up the plans was George Hadfield, who supervised part of the construction of the early CAPITOL. Hadfield's building, incorporating the lines of a Doric temple, was the area's first example of the Greek Revival style, which gained considerable popularity in the early 19C. Though he had limited funds, Custis proceeded with construction, using bricks made from clay on the estate and timber from its forests. By 1804, he had completed the south wing, and in the same year he married Mary Lee Fitzhugh. About this time he also renamed his estate Arlington, after a Custis family property in Northhampton County, Virginia. The mansion was completed in 1818.

Sophisticated and talented, Custis was a poet, playwright, and painter. Much of his skill and enthusiasm went to perpetuating the memory of his guardian and idol, George Washington. A gregarious and gracious gentleman, Custis opened the grounds of the estate to picnickers coming by ferry from Washington.

National Park Service

Robert E. Lee

The Lees – Robert E. Lee, a distant relative of the Custises, grew up in nearby Alexandria *(see p 149)* and visited their home often as a boy. In 1831, he and Mary Anna Randolph Custis, the Custises' only surviving child, were married at Arlington House. For the next 30 years, the Lees were posted to different locations, as Robert pursued his military career. During this time they considered Arlington House their true home and spent many winters here. Arlington House was the birthplace of six of the seven Lee children. At the Custises' death, title to the house passed to the Lees. In January 1861, fearing the consequences of mounting hostilities between the North and South, Lee wrote to a friend, saying "there is no sacrifice I am not ready to make for the preservation of the Union, save that of honour." Three months later, on April 18, he was called to BLAIR HOUSE and offered the command of the Union troops. He refused, and on April 20 at Arlington House, he wrote his letter of resignation from the US Army. On April 22, he left Arlington House for Richmond, Virginia, where he accepted command of the Virginia forces. He would never return to his beloved home again.

Confiscation – In May 1861, Union troops crossed the river to Virginia and quickly made the strategically located Arlington House into the headquarters for the Army of the Potomac. Throughout the war, the estate grounds were turned into fortifications and earthworks, and ultimately into a national cemetery for the Civil War dead *(see* ARLINGTON NATIONAL CEMETERY *p 114).*

In 1864, Arlington House was claimed by the Federal Government due to a dubious tax law, which required that Mrs Lee pay a $92 property tax in person. Mrs Lee, in poor health, chose not to travel to Washington, sending a cousin instead. The Government refused payment from the cousin, seized the property, and offered it up for public auction. As no bidders were forthcoming, the Government bought it for $26,800. After a legal battle that was decided by the Supreme Court, the Lees' eldest son, George Washington Custis Lee, won a suit for the return of the property. In 1883, Lee accepted the congressional appropriation of $150,000, based on the

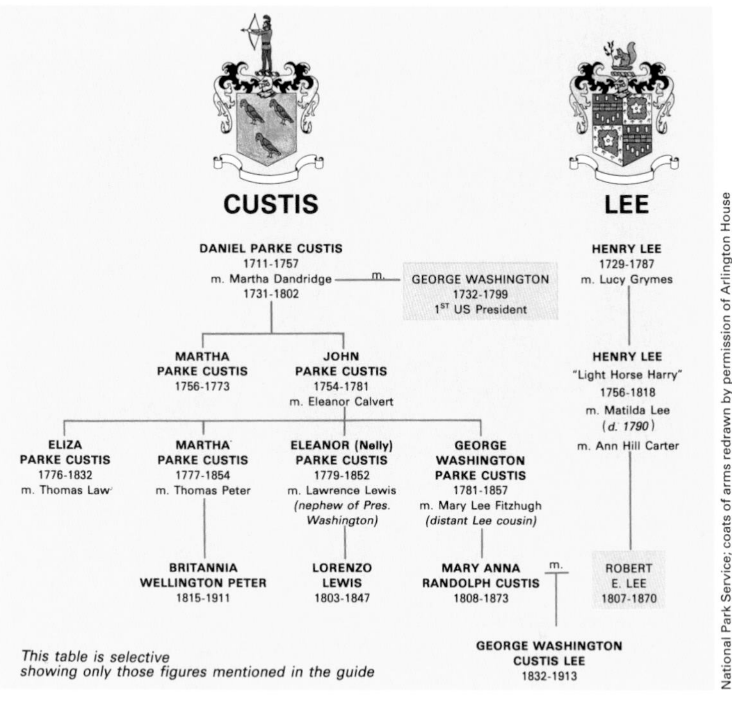

National Park Service; coats of arms redrawn by permission of Arlington House

estate's market value, rather than reclaiming the land, which by then had the character of a cemetery. Congress designated the house a national memorial to Robert E. Lee in 1925, and the National Park Service began administering it in 1933.

Visit – The mansion commands an exceptional **view★★** of Washington, with Memorial Bridge stretching to the Lincoln Memorial in the near distance and the whole panoply of the city beyond it. The main facade, with eight large Doric columns supporting an unadorned pediment, provides a gracious entrance to the off-white stucco structure.

Interior – Off the entrance hall to the right is the family parlor, where the Lees were married. Over the simple mantel is a portrait of a young Mary Custis painted by Auguste Hervieu just prior to her marriage. The room, and most of the rest of the house, is furnished with period pieces from the first half of the 19C.
In the dining room, adjacent to the family parlor, the table setting includes pieces of the Lee family porcelain and silver. Across the hall, the spacious "white parlor" holds crimson-upholstered Victorian chairs and settees chosen by the Lees. Copies of portraits of a dashing young Lee and his wife, done in 1838, hang over the room's mantels. Beyond the parlor is the well-lit room that served as an artist's studio for George W. P. Custis and for Mary Lee, who, like her father, was a painter. On an easel rests Custis's *Battle of Monmouth, New Jersey*, which hung in the US Capitol for several years. The five bedrooms and two dressing rooms on the upper floor housed the Lees and their seven children. It was in his bedchamber that Lee drafted his resignation from the Union Army.

On the lawn in front of Arlington House is the **tomb of Pierre L'Enfant**, whose remains were moved here in 1909. A marble plaque incised with his original city plan for Washington commemorates his unique contribution. A small museum *(behind the house and to the north)* features exhibits highlighting Lee's career.

★ MARINE CORPS WAR MEMORIAL Iwo Jima Memorial

Michelin map 48 and map p 115 *time: 1/4 hour*

The memorial is located in a park off N. Meade St. north of Arlington Cemetery.

Access – M *Arlington Cemetery or Rosslyn.* **By car**: *Leave Washington via Memorial Bridge heading towards US-50 West and follow signs to the memorial and Fort Meyer. To reach the memorial from the grounds of Arlington Cemetery, exit by the Ord and Weitzel Gate. The memorial is open 24 hours a day.*

This striking sculpture, honoring all US Marines who have lost their lives in military duty, ranks as one of the nation's most famous war memorials. Its prominent location across the Potomac in near-perfect alignment with the Mall's principal axis visually links the memorial to the heart of Washington.
The sculpture depicts six Americans raising the Stars and Stripes on Mount Suribachi in 1945 during the assault of the Japanese-controlled island of Iwo Jima (hence the memorial's popular name). The capture of this strategically located island is considered one of the Marines' greatest victories and marked a turning point

W. Clark/National Park Service

Marine Corps War Memorial

in the American campaign in the Pacific. Based on **Joseph Rosenthal's** Pulitzer Prize winning war photograph, the memorial was designed by Horace W. Peaslee and sculpted by Felix de Weldon. The work's poignancy is further intensified by the incessant waving of the US flag that rises from the bronze statue group.

From June through August, the traditional **US Marine Corps Sunset Parade** is held here every Tuesday *(7–8:30pm)* at the Marine Corps War Memorial. *Free transportation is provided to the parade from the Arlington Cemetery parking lot.*
The nearby tower, known as the **Netherlands Carillon**, is a gift from the Dutch people in appreciation of American assistance during and after World War II. Reminiscent of the pure geometrical style of the 20C Dutch masters Rietveld and Mondrian, this lofty metal structure contains 49 bells of various dimensions. **Carillon concerts** are given here from April to September. *For further information about the Sunset Parade and concerts ☎703-285-2598.*

The grounds of the US Marine Corps Memorial and the Netherlands Carillon afford spectacular **vistas★★** of the Mall area. The eye is drawn across the Potomac past the LINCOLN MEMORIAL and the WASHINGTON MONUMENT to the dome of the CAPITOL in the distance.

PENTAGON

Michelin map 48 P3-P4 *time: 1 1/2 hours*

I-395 at Washington Blvd. M Pentagon. Visit by guided tour (1 1/2 hours) only, Mon–Fri 9:30am–3:30pm on the half hour (visitors must show a photo ID); closed Sat, Sun, and Federal holidays. P ♿ ☎703-695-1776.

The heartbeat of the American military establishment, this enormous pentagonal building houses the offices of the highest authorities of the armed services—the secretary of defense and the joint chiefs of staff (Army, Navy, and Air Force)—all of whom answer to the Commander-in-Chief, the President of the US.
Conceived during World War II, the Pentagon combined for the first time all of the branches of the Department of War, as it was then called, under one roof. Army engineers were given one weekend in July 1941 to design the building, on the Arlington shore of the Potomac. Since the lot on which the building was to be constructed was five-sided, they devised a pentagonal shape. Though the new structure was not ultimately constructed on the original lot, the five-sided shape was retained. Built of reinforced concrete faced with limestone, the 5-story Pentagon was completed in 16 months.

Some Statistics – The Pentagon contains 6 1/2 million sq ft, making it the largest single-structure office building in the world. Its interior comprises five concentric circles that enclose a 5-acre central courtyard. Each of its five sides is larger than the CAPITOL, and together they contain 17 1/2 miles of corridors. Some 20,000 personnel, roughly half of whom are military, work here in round-the-clock shifts.

Visit – An introductory film explains the history of the construction of the Pentagon. The remainder of the tour walks visitors through office corridors displaying military art (battle scenes, portraits of high-ranking officers) and the **Hall of Heroes**, where the names of those who have received the Congressional Medal of Honor are listed.

8
★
Dupont Circle

At the turn of the century, this was the preferred neighborhood of Washington's monied elite. Back in vogue today, the Dupont Circle area boasts many of the city's finest boutiques, galleries, restaurants, and cafes.

From Swamp to Swank – During the city's early history, this area was known as the "Slashes," a tract of swampland dotted with shanties and separated from the rest of the city by a tributary of Rock Creek called Slash Run. It was during the early 1870s' public works projects overseen by Alexander "Boss" Shepherd *(see p 22)* that the Dupont Circle area developed. Shepherd diverted Slash Run into an underground sewer system, and, in compliance with L'Enfant's original city plan, laid out streets radiating from Pacific (now Dupont) Circle.

The improvements attracted the interests of an informal group of real estate investors that included Sen William Stewart of Nevada. In 1873, he began constructing an elaborate home on the circle between Massachusetts and Connecticut Avenues. Stewart's Castle (sometimes called Stewart's Folly because it stood alone in this undeveloped area) was an extravagant Second Empire estate, complete with a stable of Thoroughbreds. The mansion was razed in 1901; since 1924, a branch of Riggs Bank has stood on the site.

In 1874, the British Legation constructed its own impressive Second Empire structure at the corner of N Street and Connecticut Avenue. For the next decade and a half, however, few other substantial structures were built, and the side streets in the area developed as a modest working-class neighborhood. Not until the 1890s did the area become a "millionaires' colony," peopled mostly by Americans who had made fortunes elsewhere and choose to settle in the nation's capital. Typical of these millionaires was Levi Leiter, a Chicago department store magnate who, in 1891, built a 55-room mansion on the circle's north side.

In the early 20C, Massachusetts Avenue became a corridor of elegant Beaux-Arts palaces. The Virginia architect Waddy B. Wood designed more than 30 mansions in this area and in **Kalorama**, another prestigious neighborhood just northwest of Dupont Circle.

As the mansions rose along the avenue, the working-class houses on the side streets gave way to stylish brick row houses. In addition to private residences, a number of foreign missions were built in the area.

20C Vicissitudes – In the 1920s, the character of Dupont Circle gradually began to shift toward the commercial, and a number of the fine homes were torn down in order to build office and retail space. With the Depression of the 1930s, the flamboyant lifestyle of the old Massachusetts Avenue residents reached an end, and in the following decades, the area gradually lost its cachet as a neighborhood of the fabulously rich. By the 1950s, many of the mansions were occupied by private clubs and businesses, and the row houses had been converted into boardinghouses. During the 1960s, these dwellings became the homes of student activists and "hippies," as Dupont Circle became a haven of the counterculture.

The tax reform act of 1969 encouraged the demolition of old buildings and led to the loss of many of the area's surviving grand structures. To counter the razing, citizens groups petitioned the city to provide legal protection for the Dupont Circle environs. In 1978, the streets around the circle and north to T Street were designated a historic district. Now the neighborhood's renovated 19C row houses are once again home to professionals, and great efforts have been made to preserve the elegant old mansions that still grace Massachusetts Avenue. Galleries, cafes, shops, and museums make this area attractive to visitors.

WALKING TOUR

Distance: 1 1/4 miles

Map below *time: 1 1/2 hours (not including visits)*

M Dupont Circle-19th St. exit. Begin the tour at the circle.

Dupont Circle – Situated at the junction of five thoroughfares—Massachusetts, Connecticut, New Hampshire Avenues, 19th, and P Streets—this bustling intersection has become a focal point of the city's Northwest quadrant, true to the vision of planner Pierre Charles L'Enfant. It is here that the Frenchman's proposed arrangement of streets and avenues converging on a central green with a monument at its center can best be appreciated.

Originally known as Pacific Circle, owing to its location in the western section of the city, it was renamed in 1884 to honor Rear Adm Samuel F. Du Pont (1803-1865), the Civil War hero who directed Union naval operations along the south Atlantic coast. A bronze statue of Du Pont stood in the center of the circle until 1921, when the hero's family transferred the memorial to Wilmington, Delaware. Shortly thereafter, the Du Ponts replaced the statue with the marble **fountain** that now occupies the center of the circle. Designed in 1921 by Daniel Chester French, sculptor of the celebrated statue of Abraham Lincoln in the LINCOLN MEMORIAL, the fountain consists of a wide basin resting atop a central pillar adorned with figures symbolizing the sea, wind, and stars—references to Du Pont's naval career.

During the 1960s and 70s, Dupont Circle gained prominence as a major gathering place for the counterculture and political activists. Today, this busy urban park is frequented by a representative cross section of Washington's diverse residential population, making this one of the capital's best outdoor spots for people watching.

Cross over to Massachusetts Ave. south of P St. on the east side of the circle.

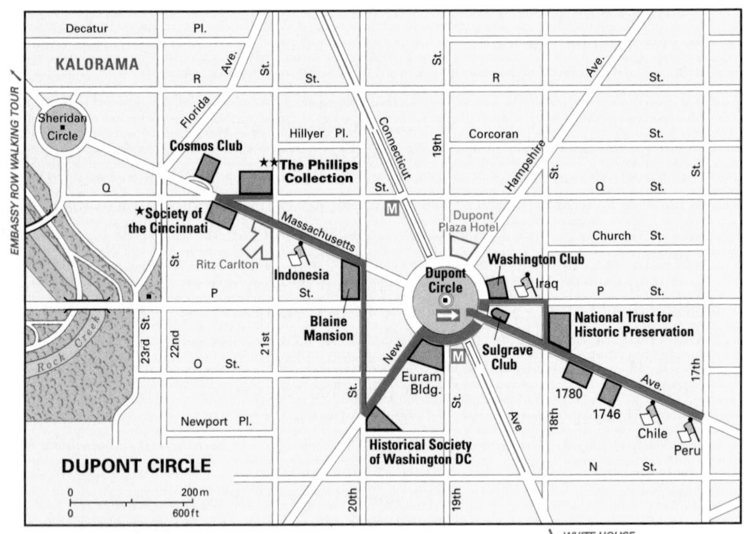

Sulgrave Club (Wadsworth House) – *1801 Massachusetts Ave. NW. Not open to the public.* This buff brick mansion, with a semidetached bow window overlooking the circle, was the residence of Herbert and Martha Wadsworth, wealthy landowners from upstate New York. Constructed around 1900 (architect unknown) on a choice triangular lot, this elegant 2-story structure is crowned by a roof balustrade and features a Palladian window above the principal entrance *(on Massachusetts Ave)*. A gilded ballroom on the second floor was the scene of lavish social gatherings attended by prominent Washington personalities.

In 1918, Wadsworth donated his residence to the Red Cross, which occupied the mansion until 1932. At that time it was sold to a group of Washington ladies who established the Sulgrave Club, one of the city's private social clubs.

Continue on Massachusetts Ave. to the corner of 18th St.

The 1700 block of Massachusetts Avenue contains four buildings by **Jules Henri de Sibour** (1872-1938). Born into an aristocratic French family and trained at Yale and at the Ecole des Beaux-Arts in Paris, de Sibour settled in Washington where he designed several palatial residences for the capital's monied classes.

National Trust for Historic Preservation (McCormick Apartments) – *1785 Massachusetts Ave. NW. The lobby is open to the public Mon–Fri 9am–5pm. ♿ ☎673-4000.* The 5-story edifice that dominates the intersection of Massachusetts Avenue and 18th Street was the city's most luxurious apartment building and perhaps de Sibour's finest commission. Completed in 1917, the building takes its name from the original owner Stanley McCormick, son of Cyrus McCormick, inventor of the reaper and founder of the International Harvester Company. The two principal facades, gracefully articulated by means of the rounded corner entrance, are accented by a rusticated first story, bas-reliefs panels, and a balcony with cast-iron railings that crowns the cornice. The steep mansard roof is lined with chimneys and pedimented dormers adorned with characteristic Beaux-Arts ornamentation.

The building's original interior reflected the fabulous lifestyle of the early 20C millionaires. Each floor was occupied by a single apartment (except the ground floor, which was divided into two). The average apartment contained six bedrooms and measured 11,000sq ft, with ceilings over 14ft high. Among the numerous amenities were a wine closet, a silver vault, a central vacuuming system, and a laundry chute leading to individual washing machines in the basement. The building could accommodate more than 40 live-in servants.

The building's most illustrious occupant was financier and Secretary of the Treasury Andrew Mellon *(p 48)*, who rented the fifth-floor apartment in the 1920s and 30s. In 1936, the art dealer Joseph Duveen leased the apartment below Mellon's and filled it with Old Master paintings and sculptures in the hopes of selling the works to Mellon, whose own quarters already housed some of the finest works of European painting in this country. Duveen gave his upstairs neighbor an apartment key so that the avid collector could appreciate the art at his leisure. Mellon eventually agreed to purchase 24 paintings and 18 sculptures for a total of $21 million. The masterpieces that once graced the walls of these apartments formed the core of the world-renowned collection of the NATIONAL GALLERY OF ART that Mellon founded in Washington DC in 1937.

Among the other privileged tenants to have enjoyed these sumptuous quarters were Robert Woods Bliss, founder of DUMBARTON OAKS; and Mrs Perle Mesta, US ambassador to Luxembourg and leading Washington hostess.

Since the 1950s, the building has housed the offices of various public and private organizations. Today, the landmark building is the headquarters of the National Trust for Historic Preservation.

Continue east on Massachusetts Ave.

Across the street stands **no. 1780**, built by de Sibour in 1922 for the Ingalls, another wealthy Washington family. The building has been remodeled to accommodate the Yater Clinic, which has occupied the site since the 1950s.

The 5-story limestone and brick mansion at **no. 1746** was commissioned in 1906 by Clarence Moore, a West Virginia tycoon who perished on the ill-fated *Titanic* (1912). The building housed the Canadian diplomatic mission from 1927 until 1988, when the embassy moved into more spacious quarters in the colossal limestone building opposite the National Gallery of Art at 501 Pennsylvania Avenue NW.

The unadorned brick and sandstone building (1889), now the **Chilean chancery** *(no. 1732)*, was constructed as a private residence by local architect Glenn Brown. The building served as the headquarters of the Washington chapter of the Daughters of the American Revolution (DAR) from 1940 to 1973.

The dignified mansion at the corner of Massachusetts Avenue and 17th Street, now the **Peruvian embassy** *(no. 1700)*, was designed by de Sibour in 1910 for the widow of Beriah Wilkins, a congressman from Ohio and editor and publisher of *The Washington Post*. The imposing facade, composed of a slightly projecting central section flanked by a pair of wings set at oblique angles, is reminiscent of a Renaissance palazzo.

Walk back up Massachusetts Ave. towards Dupont Circle, turn right on 18th St. and left on P St.

On the corner of P and 18th Streets, note the **embassy of Iraq** *(1801 P St.)*, a tan brick structure with Richardsonian detailing. Completed in 1893, this former residence was designed by the architectural firm Hornblower and Marshall.

Continue on P St. to Dupont Circle.

Washington Club (Patterson House) – *15 Dupont Circle NW. Not open to the public.* This ornate white marble and terra-cotta mansion, which resembles a Mannerist palazzo, was built in the early years of the 20C by Stanford White of the noted New York firm McKim, Mead and White. Commissioned by the Chicago socialite Mrs Robert Patterson, this opulent residence was yet another setting for lavish entertaining in the capital. The Patterson's daughter, Cissy (1884-1948), publisher of *The Washington Times-Herald*, assumed the role of the capital's premier hostess during the 1930s and early 40s.

During the renovation of the WHITE HOUSE in the summer of 1927, Patterson House served as the temporary residence of President and Mrs Coolidge. During their stay, the Coolidges hosted the nation's hero, Charles Lindbergh, just back from his historic transatlantic flight. For three days, immense crowds gathered in Dupont Circle to hail the young aviator, who greeted them from the first-floor loggia.

From photo by M. Kowicki

Washington Club

In accordance with the terms of Cissy Patterson's will, the family's Washington residence was donated to the Red Cross after her death in 1948. Three years later, the mansion was sold to the Washington Club, the elite women's organization that now occupies the building.

Walk clockwise along the circle.

Note the **Euram Building** at 21 Dupont Circle. Designed in 1971 by the Washington architectural firm Hartman-Cox, this glass, brick, and concrete office building enclosing a handsome courtyard is one of the capital's most innovative works of contemporary architecture.

Turn left on New Hampshire Ave. and continue one block to the intersection of New Hampshire Ave., 20th St., and Sunderland Pl.

Historical Society of Washington DC (Heurich Mansion) – *1307 New Hampshire Ave. NW. Visit by guided tour (1 hour) only, Wed–Sat noon–3:00 pm on the hour; closed some holidays. Admission: $3.00, seniors $1.50, children under 18 free. ♿ ☎785-2068.* This landmark Richardsonian Romanesque building is one of the city's best-preserved house museums and a resource center for the study of the capital's history. The imposing mansion (1892-94) was commissioned by Christian Heurich, the German-born founder of a prosperous brewery that stood on the present site of the KENNEDY CENTER in Foggy Bottom.

The building's exterior features—massive brownstone and brick walls, rounded arches, and a prominent corner tower—are characteristic of the Richardsonian Romanesque style. The entrance is highlighted by a stone carriage porch supported by squat coupled columns with elaborately carved capitals. Two fanciful gargoyles projecting from the porch's crowning balustrade stand guard over the entrance driveway. Constructed of poured concrete, the building is one of the earliest fireproof residences in the city, owing to the insistence of Heurich, whose brewery had been seriously damaged by fire.

The house remained in the Heurich family until 1956, when Heurich's descendants donated the building along with its furnishings to the Columbia Historical Society (later renamed the Historical Society of Washington DC). The society, founded in 1894 "to preserve, collect and teach the history of the nation's capital," established its headquarters here and maintains the property as a house museum.

Interior – The ornate period rooms, designed by a New York decorator, reflect the eclectic tastes of its owners. Carved oak and mahogany woodwork abounds alongside a profusion of painted, plastered, and stencilled decoration.

The entrance foyer features a staircase with onyx risers, marble treads, and a cast bronze balustrade. A charming musician's loggia opens onto three of the adjoining rooms: a sitting room and two formal parlors with late 19C French-style furniture. Beyond the parlors are the intimate music room, the formal dining room (note the remarkable coffered oak ceiling), and a spacious conservatory. The breakfast room in the basement, resembling a ratskeller, or German tavern, was the homey setting where the Heurichs gathered for informal meals. The bedrooms on the second floor contain many original furnishings and fixtures, numerous family portraits, and personal objects.

The third and fourth floors accommodate the Historical Society's research collections *(accessible to the public Wed, Fri, Sat 10am–4pm; closed some holidays. ☎785-2068)* numbering over 100,000 manuscripts, books, photographs, prints, maps, and other materials pertaining to the social history of the capital. Small changing exhibits on local history are presented in a gallery on the first and on the third floors. In the warm season, the mansion's tranquil garden *(accessible from Sunderland Pl., open Tue–Fri 10am–4pm; closed holidays)* is a pleasant urban oasis, where many of the neighborhood's office workers relax during lunch hour.

Upon leaving the building, cross over to 20th St. and continue north to the corner of Massachusetts Ave.

Blaine Mansion – *2000 Massachusetts Ave. NW. Not open to the public.* Erected in 1881, this severe brick edifice with an elaborate roof design is Dupont Circle's oldest surviving mansion. It was built as the Washington residence of **James G. Blaine** (1830-1893), co-founder of the Republican Party, member of Congress, secretary of state under two administrations (Garfield and Harrison), and unsuccessful Republican candidate in the 1884 presidential election (against Grover Cleveland). Displeased with the vastness and high maintenance costs of their home, the Blaines leased it to the Chicago businessman and real estate baron Levi Leiter in 1883 for the record annual sum of $11,500. Leiter remained in the mansion until the early 1890s, when he moved to the stately residence he had built on the north side of Dupont Circle (demolished in 1947; the Dupont Plaza Hotel now occupies the site). The prolific inventor George Westinghouse purchased the Blaine mansion in 1901 and lived there until his death in 1914.

Over the years, the building's interior and exterior have been considerably altered. Originally a free-standing structure with entrances on the three surrounding streets, the building is now flanked on its P Street side by an unattractive row of 1-story shops, and the wooden carriage porch (slightly transformed) on Massachusetts Avenue now serves as the main entrance. Since the late 1940s, professional offices have occupied the building.

Continue west on Massachusetts Ave.

Indonesian Embassy (Walsh Mansion) – *2020 Massachusetts Ave. NW. Visit by guided tour (30min) only, Mon–Fri 9am–4pm (2-week advance reservation required); closed Sat, Sun, and Federal and Indonesian holidays. Free admission.*

As the sight is often closed for special events, it is advisable to call before visiting. ♿ ☎*775-5306.* This fabulous turn-of-the-century mansion was built by Thomas Walsh, an Irish immigrant who struck it rich in the Colorado goldfields. After moving his family to Washington, Walsh commissioned Henry Andersen, a Danish-born architect, to design a mansion befitting his vast wealth. He had made about $45 million from the sale of his Camp Bird Mine in Colorado.

During the Theodore Roosevelt administration, the Walshes were prominent social figures, using their palatial home as the setting for parties whose lavishness became legendary. At Mrs Walsh's death in 1932, the house passed to her daughter Evalyn. Married to Edward Beale McLean, whose family owned *The Cincinnati Enquirer* and *The Washington Post*, Evalyn Walsh McLean was a Washington socialite, now remembered as the last private owner of the celebrated Hope Diamond (on view in the NATIONAL MUSEUM OF AMERICAN HISTORY). In 1951, she sold the home to the Indonesian government.

The Mansion – A balustraded terrace, a second-story loggia, ornate limestone trim, bay swells, and a red-tiled mansard roof adorn the tan brick exterior of the mansion. The carriage porch extending from the west side of the house is balanced on the east by a semicircular conservatory with stained-glass trim.

The arched double doors of the entrance portico open onto a sumptuous hall, three-stories high and topped by a stained-glass skylight. An Art Nouveau banister of mahogany sweeps up from floor to floor, its ornate woodwork repeated in the balustrades that line the open promenades on each floor.

In the Louis XVI drawing room, now partially filled by a stage for embassy functions, rose damask walls are embellished with gilt-and-white pilasters and arched woodwork. Elaborate plaster flourishes ornament the ceiling, in the center of which is a mural entitled *Eternity of Angels*.

The adjoining music room contains dark mahogany wainscoting and trim that is echoed in the woodwork of the pipe organ. Inset wall cabinets now display traditional Indonesian crafts, such as shadow puppets and Balinese wood carvings.

The building at 2100 Massachusetts Ave., across 21st Street has housed the prestigious Ritz Carlton Hotel since 1982.

Continue west on Massachusetts Ave.

★ **Society of the Cincinnati (Anderson House)** – *2118 Massachusetts Ave. NW. Open Tue–Sat 1–4pm; closed Sun, Mon and Federal holidays. Free admission.* ♿ ☎*785-2040.* This distinguished edifice is the headquarters of the venerable Society of the Cincinnati. A bastion of tradition, the society displays an impressive collection of Revolutionary artifacts and preserves its opulent building as a house museum reflecting the era of early 20C grandeur.

The Society – Founded in 1783 by former officers of the Revolution, this patriotic organization can claim George Washington as its first president-general. Named for Lucius Quinctius Cincinnatus, a 5C Roman military hero and farmer, the society extols the ideal of the soldier returning to productive civilian life and spearheaded the establishment of military pensions in America. Membership passes, by tradition and charter, through the line of eldest sons.

The Andersons – Larz Anderson, who had the house built, was descended from a founding member of the Society of the Cincinnati and was a member himself. A career diplomat, Anderson served as minister to Belgium and ambassador to Japan. He shared with his wife, Isabel Weld Perkins, a Boston heiress, an interest in travel and collecting, as reflected in the furnishings of this impressive 50-room residence. Designed by the firm of Little and Brown, the mansion was built between 1902 and 1905 at a cost of $800,000. After his retirement, Anderson and his wife entertained here, often hosting official state dinners. At Anderson's death in 1937, Mrs Anderson donated the house to the Society of the Cincinnati.

The Mansion – Arched carriage gates lead into a walled courtyard dominated by the elegant rounded portico. Flags and pennants motifs adorn the tympanum of the roof-level pediment. Inside the front hall is a bust of Washington by Thomas Crawford, who designed the statue of Freedom that tops the dome of the CAPITOL. The small room to the right is lined with late Renaissance choir stalls. On the wall above is a frieze by Henry Siddons Mowbray, which depicts awards bestowed on the Andersons and on the society. In the billiard room hang military portraits by such eminent 18C and 19C American artists as Gilbert Stuart, John Trumbull, and George Catlin. The great stair hall contains cases with battle dioramas, detailed French miniatures of soldiers, and other memorabilia.

A late 19C painting, *The Triumph of the Dogaressa Anna Maria Foscari in the Year 1424*, by Jose Villegas y Cordero, dominates the staircase landing. On the second floor, the reception room is notable for its sienna and white marble floor bearing the pattern of the Greek key. The allegorical wall and ceiling friezes in this room were also painted by Mowbray. An ornately paneled Louis XV-style parlor displays jade trees from the Andersons' Ch'ing Dynasty collection. Among the furnishings in the adjoining English parlor are Hepplewhite pieces, English portraiture, and Chinese porcelains from the 16C to 19C. The long corridor known as the Olmsted gallery contains Oriental antiques and Italian paintings, while the formal dining room is decorated with early 17C Belgian tapestries. This room opens onto a musicians gallery, overlooking the grand **ballroom** and supported by twisted columns of Verona marble. Over the ballroom mantel is a portrait of Gen Henry Knox, considered the society's founder. Arched doors lead from the ballroom into a charming solarium that overlooks a gracious, walled sculpture garden. A reflecting pool faced by an 18C statue of a Japanese Buddha gives the garden an Oriental appearance.

Cross Massachusetts Ave.

Cosmos Club (Townsend House) – *2121 Massachusetts Ave. NW. Not open to the public.* Set behind a landscaped entrance driveway, this dignified limestone mansion is the headquarters of one of the country's most exclusive social clubs. In 1899, Richard Townsend, the president of the Erie and Pittsburgh Railroad, and his wife, Mary, heiress to the Pennsylvania Railroad fortune, commissioned the renowned architectural firm Carrère and Hastings to design a palatial residence appropriate to their social position and grand lifestyle. The architects received strict instructions to integrate the site's pre-existing brick house into their plan because Mrs Townsend had been warned by a fortune-teller that calamity would strike if she were to settle into a brand new house. Despite the precautions taken, Mr Townsend died from a riding accident in 1902, the year following the house's completion. In accordance with the Townsend's request for a house in the style of the 18C Petit Trianon at Versailles, the architects designed a central facade composed of three bays separated by colossal pilasters and crowned by a roof balustrade. A mansard roof punctuated by dormer windows constitutes the fourth floor. The 2-story wings that flank the central section lend balance to the design.

Mrs Townsend gained fame among the capital's affluent circles for the extravagant manner in which she entertained in her splendid Massachusetts Avenue residence. In the 1930s, the mansion was home to the Townsends' daughter, Mathilde, and her second husband, Sumner B. Welles, under secretary of state during most of the Roosevelt administration. The Welles hosted President and Mrs Roosevelt for several weeks in January 1933 before the First Family moved to the White House. In 1950, the residence was purchased by the Cosmos Club, a social club founded in 1878 for men of distinction in the fields of science, literature, and the fine arts. Inscribed in its prestigious register are the names of three US Presidents and over 80 Nobel and Pulitzer Prize recipients.

Continue one block east on Q St. to the corner of 21st St.

★★ THE PHILLIPS COLLECTION

1600 21st St. NW. M Dupont Circle. Open Mon–Sat 10am–5pm, Sun noon–7pm; closed Jan 1, July 4, Thanksgiving Day, Dec 25. Admission: $6.50, students and seniors $3.25, children under 18 free. Guided tour (1 hour) Wed and Sat at 2pm. ♿ ✗ ☎*387-2151.*

On a quiet corner a few steps from the bustling shops and restaurants along Connecticut Avenue stands a small museum of great distinction. The Phillips Collection, the nation's oldest museum of modern art, exhibits outstanding works by prominent American and European artists in an intimate setting.

The Collector – The grandson of one of the co-founders of the Jones and Laughlin Steel Co, **Duncan Phillips** (1886-1966) developed an interest in art during his studies at Yale and in the course of his numerous travels abroad. In 1908, Duncan and his brother, James, began expanding the small private collection that hung in the family's unpretentious brick and brownstone home built by the firm of Hornblower and Marshall in 1896. Following James' death in 1918—only 13 months after the death of his father—Duncan devoted himself to transforming the family's private collection into a public memorial to his beloved father and brother. In the fall of 1921, eight years before the founding of the Museum of Modern Art in New York City, the Phillips Memorial Art Gallery, occupying two rooms of the family home, opened to an appreciative public.

That same year Phillips married Marjorie Acker, a talented painter in her own right, and the couple embarked on an active period of collecting. During the 1920s, they acquired many of the collection's most famous paintings, including Renoir's *The Luncheon of the Boating Party*, which was purchased for the record sum of $125,000 in 1923. By 1930, the collection had assumed its basic form, containing paintings by all the major French Impressionists, post-Impressionists, and Cubists as well as outstanding works by several 17C and 18C masters including Goya, El Greco, and Chardin. In 1931, Phillips and his family moved out of their home in order to provide additional space for the expanding collection, which by that time comprised some 600 works. A new wing was added in 1960, and the following year, the museum was renamed The Phillips Collection. From 1987 to 1989, the renovation and expansion of the wing (renamed the Goh Annex) was undertaken to improve exhibition conditions.

The Collection – Throughout his life, Duncan Phillips eschewed the cold formality of the art establishment. The couple relied on their judgement and taste, rather than the advice of curators or art dealers. The collector did not adhere to any one specific doctrine or school of art and largely avoided the avant-garde and cult movements of the day. Although Phillips concentrated primarily on modern art, he frequently juxtaposed 19C and 20C works with Old Masters paintings to suggest sources from which modern artists might have sought inspiration. In fact, Phillips conceived his collection as "a museum of modern art and its sources."

The Phillips Collection is, in every respect, a reflection of its creator. Most of the museum's 2,500 works, primarily from the 19C and 20C, were selected by Phillips and his wife. Artists represented in the collection include Daumier, Degas, Cézanne, Monet, Bonnard, Van Gogh, Matisse, Klee, and Picasso along with noted American painters such as Ryder, Marin, Dove, O'Keeffe, and Tack.

Paintings are hung in simply yet tastefully furnished rooms to create an informal domestic setting that Phillips considered conducive to the appreciation of art. The works, which are rotated frequently, are not arranged chronologically, but earlier pieces are generally found in the ground-floor rooms, including the foyer with its dark oak staircase and molding, and the house's largest room, the oak-paneled

Music Room, which features a ceiling decorated with raised plaster medallions. Added to the house in 1907 as a library, this room is a congenial setting for Sunday concerts *(performed at 5pm Sept–May)*. The second floor contains additional gallery space for the permanent collection and a room devoted exclusively to the delightful works of the renowned Swiss painter **Paul Klee** (1879-1940). The Goh Annex, restored in 1989, is linked to the original building by two glass enclosed walkways. Above the annex's street level entrance hovers the bas-relief of a bird in flight (which has been adopted as the museum's emblem), based on a work by Georges Braque, one of Phillips' favorite painters. Among the works displayed on a rotating basis in the annex are paintings from the popular **Bonnard Collection**, reputed to be the largest in the country. A small gallery on the first floor displays four important works by Abstract Expressionist **Mark Rothko** (1903-1970), known for his hauntingly simple canvases of large expanses of color. On permanent exhibit in a second-floor gallery is the museum's most renowned treasure: *The Luncheon of the Boating Party* (1881) by Renoir. The third-floor galleries are devoted to temporary exhibits.

Collection Highlights

The Repentant Peter	**El Greco**	c.1600
A Bowl of Plums	**Chardin**	c.1728
Self-portrait	**Cézanne**	1878-80
The Luncheon of the Boating Party	**Renoir**	1881
Miss Van Buren	**Eakins**	1886-90
The Blue Room	**Picasso**	1901
The Palm	**Bonnard**	1926
Ranchos Church	**O'Keeffe**	c.1930
Arab Song	**Klee**	1932
Painting No. 9	**Mondrian**	1939-42
Ochre and Red on Red	**Rothko**	1954

The Phillips Collection

Ochre and Red on Red by Mark Rothko

The annual Dupont-Kalorama Museum Walk Day, held on the first Saturday in June, is a neighborhood festival featuring musical performances, special exhibits and activities and tours of local museums and cultural institutions. Sights open to the public free of charge on that day include the HISTORICAL SOCIETY OF WASHINGTON DC, SOCIETY OF THE CINCINNATI, ***and*** THE PHILLIPS COLLECTION. ***For information ☎667-0441.***

9
Embassy Row

Embassy Row is the popular name of the two-mile portion of Massachusetts Avenue between Scott Circle and Observatory Circle, where some 50 diplomatic missions are concentrated. The buildings housing the chanceries (the embassy proper) and the ambassador's residences (which may be separate from the chancery) are recognizable by the colorful flags or plaques that generally adorn their facades. The area from 22nd Street to Observatory Circle is considered the most distinctive and elegant segment of Embassy Row.

Historical Notes – The portion of Massachusetts Avenue beyond 22nd Street developed in the first decade of the 20C as an extension of the exclusive Dupont Circle residential enclave *(see p 119)*. Situated on a wooded ridge overlooking a large expanse of Rock Creek Park, this pristine area offered spacious and relatively inexpensive lots well suited to the construction of the palatial residences fashionable in the early 20C before the advent of income tax. By 1915, the area around Sheridan Circle was home to some of the capital's wealthiest residents.

The 1929 stock-market crash and the ensuing Depression marked a turning point in the lifestyles of affluent Americans. Unable to maintain their sumptuous homes, the area's residents were forced to set up household in more modest quarters. In 1931, the governments of Great Britain and Japan led the way in the area's development as a diplomatic quarter by constructing new embassy compounds in the upper reaches of Massachusetts Avenue beyond Sheridan Circle. They were soon followed by several diplomatic missions and private firms, which purchased former private residences along the avenue. Before long the two-mile stretch between Scott Circle and Observatory Circle, dubbed Embassy Row, supplanted the Meridian Hill district around 16th Street NW as the capital's premier diplomatic quarter.

In the building boom that followed World War II, some of Embassy Row's buildings were sacrificed to make way for intrusive modern structures, but the avenue's upper portion (north of Florida Avenue) has managed to conserve its elegant character.

In **Kalorama**, the pleasant residential neighborhood situated north of Florida Avenue between Massachusetts and Connecticut Avenues, additional diplomatic missions have been established in reconverted upper-middle class dwellings.

Beaux-Arts Architecture – Like the adjoining Dupont Circle area, the upper portion of Embassy Row preserves a concentration of outstanding private residences designed in the Beaux-Arts style. Derived from the preeminent art academy in Paris, the Ecole des Beaux-Arts, this term, as applied to American architecture, generally refers to the wide gamut of classically inspired styles advocated by the Ecole in the second half of the 19C. Among the scores of Americans who trained in Paris during this period were the Washington-based architects George Oakley Totten, Jr (1866-1939), Waddy B. Wood (1869-1944), Nathan C. Wyeth (1870-1963), and Jules Henri de Sibour (1872-1938). The returning expatriates imported the grandiose European styles that satisfied wealthy Americans' appetites for edifices reflecting their aspirations and opulent lifestyles. These styles included the Chateauesque and Georgian and Renaissance Revivals, but the most popular Beaux-Arts style was derived from tall apartment buildings that rose in Paris' elegant residential quarters at the turn of the century. The American edifices were characterized by symmetrical design, exuberant decorative details (swags, garlands, carved panels, ornamented keystones and brackets), a rusticated first floor generally with an entry canopy, and a mansard roof rising above a stone balustrade.

WALKING TOUR *Distance: about 1 1/4 miles (not including visits)*

Map below

time: 2 hours

The following walking tour describes the most noteworthy portion of Embassy Row—Massachusetts Avenue between 22nd Street and Observatory Circle. Part of Massachusetts Avenue below 22nd Street is included on the Dupont Circle walking tour *(see p 120)*. Unless otherwise specified, all sights described or mentioned on the tour are located on Massachusetts Avenue, NW.

Access to Embassies – *Consulates and ambassadors' residences are usually open for official business only. The general public can visit selected embassies on a special tour organized annually in early May to benefit Goodwill Industries. The self-guided tour (11am–5pm) includes free shuttle bus service to the participating embassies and refreshments. Tickets: $25. For information ☎636-4225.*

M *Dupont Circle. Begin the tour at the corner of Massachusetts Ave. and 22nd St.*

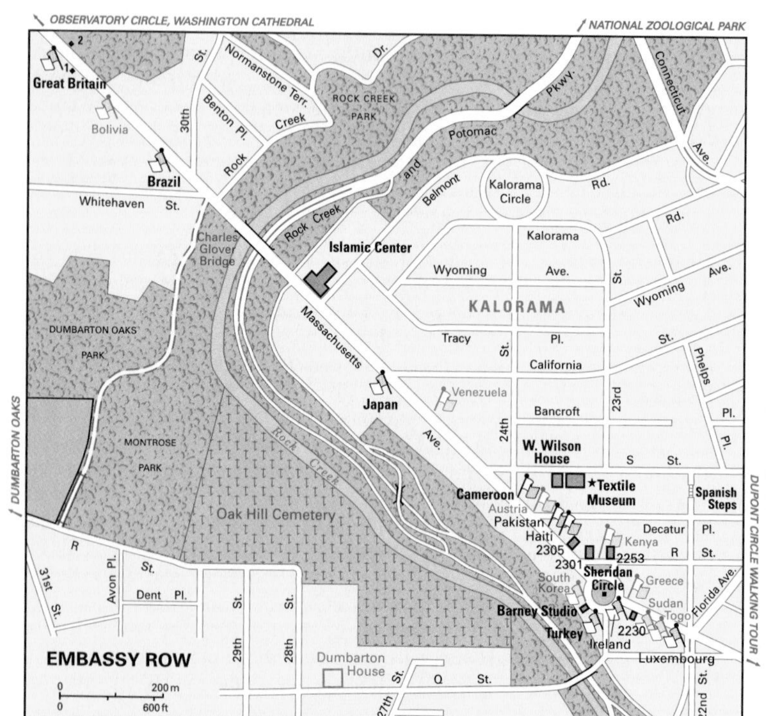

2200 Block – This gently sloped portion of Massachusetts Avenue, flanked by attached town houses, provides a pleasant entry to Sheridan Circle, situated on a rise to the northwest. Occupying a choice corner lot, the limestone mansion at no. 2200, which today houses the **embassy of Luxembourg**, was designed by Jules Henri de Sibour for Alexander Stewart (1829-1912), a lumber magnate and congressman from Wisconsin. Completed in 1909 at a cost of approximately $92,000, the building incorporates characteristic Beaux-Arts features: symmetrical design, a rusticated first floor, arched windows, and a mansard roof rising above a stone balustrade. The embassies of Togo and the Sudan are located at nos. 2208 and 2210 respectively. At **no. 2230** stands the smallest of the four Embassy Row residences built by the prolific Washington architect George Oakley Totten, Jr. Completed in 1907, this brick-faced row house was designed in the so-called Chateauesque manner—an eclectic style briefly in vogue around the turn of the century. Derived from large-scale 16C European princely estates, Chateauesque buildings are characterized by gabled dormers, steeply pitched hipped roofs, and balconies carved with reliefs or tracery. With elegant facades on both Massachusetts Avenue and Sheridan Circle, **no. 2234** was erected in 1909 as a private residence by William Cresson (1873-1932), an architect-turned-rancher, diplomat, and eventually law professor. Cresson's training at the Ecole des Beaux-Arts is reflected in the building's overall design and ornamental details. Since 1949, the building has housed the embassy of Ireland. The free-standing structure across the avenue at no. 2221 is the embassy of Greece.

Sheridan Circle – Originally called Decatur Circle in honor of the early 19C naval hero Commodore Stephen Decatur *(see p 83)*, the park was renamed in 1890 after Gen Philip H. Sheridan (1831-1888), leader of the Union cavalry. Sheridan is known for his victory in the Shenandoah Valley on October 19, 1864, and for his role in bringing about General Lee's surrender at Appomattox in 1865. Dedicated in 1908, the vigorous bronze equestrian **statue** of Sheridan at the park's center was designed by Gutzon Borglum, renowned for the colossal presidential profiles at Mount Rushmore.

A harmonious 19C addition to L'Enfant's plan for the capital, this circle with its well-tended park rimmed with age-old ginkgo and linden trees provides a graceful setting for the surrounding palatial mansions and town houses. At **no. 2301**, the striking 4-story mansion with a convex facade and monumental Palladian arch that dominates the circle's north side, is the residence of the Egyptian ambassador.
Other embassy buildings facing the circle are the residence of the ambassador of the Philippines at **2253 R St.** and the embassies of Kenya *(2249 R St.)* and South Korea *(2320 Massachusetts Ave.)*.

Continue to the corner of 23rd St. and Sheridan Circle.

Embassy of Turkey (Everett House) – *1606 23rd St.* Reputedly Embassy Row's most sumptuous mansion, this grandiose structure (1910-1915) was the home of Edward H. Everett, multi-millionaire industrialist and inventor of the fluted soft-drink bottle cap. The costly residence (1915 tax assessment: $230,000) was designed by George Oakley Totten, Jr.
The glass-covered carriage porch, the semicircular columned portico, and the balustrade crowning the roof lend an air of opulence to the structure. Totten added an exotic touch by incorporating a colonnaded porch above the south wing. Instructed to spare no expense in the decoration of the house, the architect created a building befitting the grand lifestyle of the Everetts.
The interior, richly appointed with carved wood paneling and inlaid floors, featured an indoor swimming pool and a fabulous ballroom with walls hung with gold thread damask. Mrs Everett, an opera singer, hosted a concert series known as "Evenings with Music," a coveted social event featuring world-renowned divas and attended by Washington's cultural elite. The Turkish embassy was established in the mansion in 1936.

Continue clockwise along the circle.

Barney Studio House – *2306 Massachusetts Ave. Not open to the public.* Rather modest by Embassy Row standards, this charming town house tucked away on the southwestern rim of Sheridan Circle played a pivotal role in the cultural life of Washington at the beginning of this century.
Built about 1902 by Waddy B. Wood, this 5-story structure inspired by Spanish colonial architecture (stucco facade, quatrefoil windows, curved parapet, and red tile roof) was the home of Alice Pike Barney (1857-1931), one of the city's most enterprising and creative women. Painter, playwright, and trendsetter, Barney established her studio-home to serve as one of the capital's earliest private artistic centers. During Barney's lifetime, the studio provided the setting for much-needed cultural events including art shows, small theater presentations, poetry readings, musical performances, and informal parties. In 1960, the building was donated to the Smithsonian Institution by Barney's two daughters. Natalie Clifford Barney (1876-1972), Alice's eldest daughter, spent most of her life in Paris where she hosted a celebrated salon frequented by renowned artists and literary figures, including many American expatriates.

Continue north on Massachusetts Ave. (right side).

2300 Block – Occupying adjacent lots just steps away from Sheridan Circle, the handsome Beaux-Arts mansions at **nos. 2305** and **2311** were designed between 1909 and 1910 by the Paris-trained architect Nathan Wyeth (who also drew up the plans for the Key Bridge linking Georgetown with Arlington). Sold to the Chilean government in 1923, no. 2305, with its gracefully curved central section and roof balustrades, is the ambassador's residence. No. 2311, faced with colossal Corinthian pilasters and surmounted by a steeply pitched mansard roof, was owned by the Nationalist government of China (Taiwan) from the 1940s to the 1970s; it was subsequently purchased by the government of Haiti.
Located on a prominent triangular lot on the corner of Massachusetts Avenue and Decatur Place, the magnificent mansion now housing the **embassy of Pakistan** *(no. 2315)* boldly completes this distinguished block. The stucco Beaux-Arts pile, built in 1909 for the Moran family by George Oakley Totten, Jr, is dominated by an imposing round tower, adorned with limestone and terra-cotta detailing—oval cartouches, swags, and bas-relief decorative panels.

Pakistan Embassy

From photo by C. Laboy

Cross Decatur Pl. and continue past the Austrian embassy (no. 2343) to the intersection of Massachusetts Ave. and 24th St.

Embassy of Cameroon (Hauge Mansion) – *No. 2349.* This prominently situated limestone "chateau" was the first of the four Embassy Row residences designed by George Oakley Totten, Jr (the three other buildings—2230 Massachusetts Ave. and the Turkish and Pakistan embassies—are described on *pp 128 and 129).*
Christian Hauge, Norway's first minister to the US, commissioned the building to serve as both private residence and his government's legation offices. However, in 1908, less than a year after the mansion's completion, Hauge died accidentally in Norway. For 19 years thereafter, it was the home of Hauge's American wife, Louise, a prominent East coast socialite. Like the sumptuous Sheridan Circle mansion of the Everetts (now the embassy of Turkey), Mrs Hauge's residence was, according to a local newspaper, "the scene of much of Washington's most brilliant entertaining."
After almost 40 years as the Czechoslovakian foreign mission, the mansion was sold to the Cameroon government in 1972.
The Hauge mansion is architecturally significant as the city's finest example of the Chateauesque manner. Much bolder in scale and design than the row house at 2230 Massachusetts Avenue that Totten designed about the same time, this freestanding structure is based on the 16C French chateau Azay-le-Rideau, in the Loire Valley. The mansion's outstanding architectural feature is the imposing rounded tower with its candle-snuffer roof. Like the nearby Pakistan embassy *(no. 2315),* this building displays Totten's skillful and dramatic handling of irregular corner lots.

Turn right on 24th St. and right again on S St.

Woodrow Wilson House – *2340 S St. Open Tue–Sun 10am–4pm; closed Mon and Federal holidays. Admission: $4, students and seniors $2.50, children under 7 free. Guided tours (1 hour) available. ♿ ☎387-4062.* The 28th President of the US chose this residence as his place of retirement upon completing his second term in the White House in 1921. The brick Georgian Revival town house, designed in 1915 by Waddy B. Wood, was described by Wilson's wife as "an unpretentious, comfortable, dignified house fitted to the needs of a gentleman's home."
The house has been converted into a **museum**, which preserves the lifestyle of an upper middle-class family in the 1920s and serves as a window on the family life of the President who lead the US through World War I and into a position of world leadership.

Continue on S St.

★ **Textile Museum** – *2320 S St. Open Mon–Sat 10am–5pm, Sun noon–5pm; closed Federal holidays. Suggested contribution: $5. Guided tours (1 hour) available. ♿ ☎667-0441.* Founded in 1925 by George Hewitt Myers, this small private museum occupies a pair of elegant townhouses built by two renowned Washington architects. The building serving as entrance to the museum was designed in 1913 by the prolific John Russell Pope as a private home for Myers. In 1908, the adjoining house was designed by Waddy B. Wood, who later constructed the adjacent WOODROW WILSON HOUSE *(see above).*
The museum focuses on the collection, study, and preservation of handmade textiles and carpets. Its holdings comprise over 14,000 textiles and 1,400 rugs primarily from the Near and Far East and South America, including an outstanding **pre-Columbian collection** from Peru.
Changing exhibits present textiles from the US and abroad.
Less than a block east, the **Spanish Steps**, which connect S Street with Decatur Place, offer a quiet spot to sit and enjoy the lion-head fountain and seasonal plantings.

Return to Massachusetts Ave.

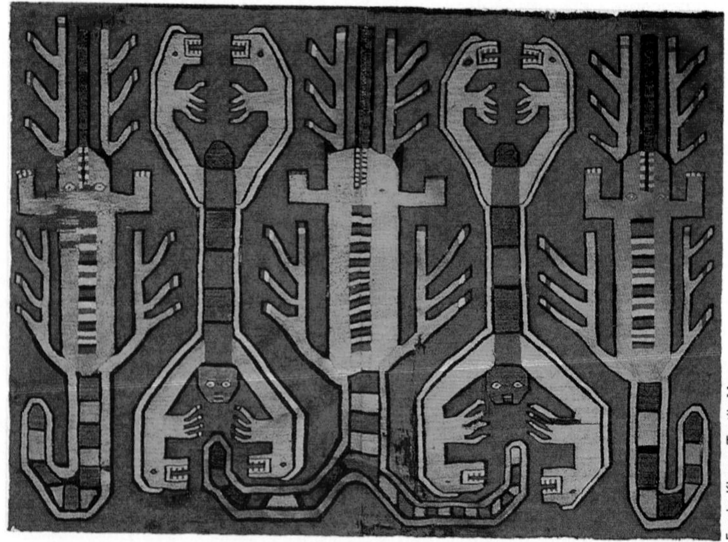

Franko Khoury/Textile Museum

Peruvian Nasca tunic fragment (c.700 AD)

Note the embassy of Venezuela *(nos. 2443-2445)*, a low complex of white buildings on impeccably maintained grounds.

Cross the avenue.

Embassy of Japan – *2520 Massachusetts Ave.* This handsome Georgian Revival structure dominating a tree-lined cobblestone courtyard was built in 1931 for the Japanese government. The design, conceived by the architectural team Delano and Aldrich and reputedly approved by Emperor Hirohito, contains a hint of Oriental aesthetics in the delicately curved roof line and the "rising sun" that emerges from the balcony recess over the front entrance. The starkly modern chancery building to the right was added in 1986.

Continue on the opposite side of the avenue.

The Islamic Center – *2551 Massachusetts Ave. Open daily, except Fri 10am-5pm. Free admission. Guided tours (1 hour) available (1-week advance reservation required). Proper attire is required while visiting the mosque: arms, legs (and women's heads) must be covered and shoes removed. ☎332-8343.* This long white edifice, surmounted by a slender minaret, serves as a place of worship and instruction for the metropolitan area's sizeable Islamic population (estimated at 65,000). Built between 1949 and 1957 with funds and materials donated primarily by the governments of Islamic countries, the center houses one of the first mosques in the US.

Operation of the Center – A board of governors, composed of the heads of Islamic diplomatic missions in Washington, sets policies and provides guidance for the center's activities. In accordance with Muslim practice, prayer services are held five times daily: before sunrise, after noon, in the late afternoon, immediately after sunset, and before retiring for the night. The call to prayer, traditionally chanted from a raised place by the *muezzin*, can be heard *(10am–5pm only)* from the loudspeaker installed on the minaret. Every Friday, the Muslim's holy day, the faithful meet for congregational prayers. Marriages and funerals are also performed in the mosque. Through its publications and a program of lectures, seminars, language and religious classes, the Islamic Center strives to meet the needs of its congregation and to promote better understanding of Islam among Americans of all faiths.

Visit – The limestone construction incorporates characteristic features of Islamic architecture including horseshoe arches, roof cresting, and a minaret, which reaches a height of 160ft. The 2-story buildings facing Massachusetts Avenue house the library and the administrative offices. The double row of arches linking the two buildings leads to a small courtyard enclosing a pink marble fountain, which serves as a sort of atrium to the mosque. From this point the visitor should note the oblique alignment of the mosque's facade. This curious configuration is explained by the fact that, like all mosques, this building is oriented in the direction of Mecca. The **mosque** proper is an open square space flanked by colonnades richly ornamented in a profusion of calligraphy, and geometric and floral patterns (the Koran forbids the representation of human or animal forms). The lower parts of the walls are faced with 7,000 blue tiles donated by the Turkish government. The gifts from Egypt include the 2-ton copper chandelier in the center of the mosque, and the carved wood pulpit or *minbar*. To the left is the *mihrab*, the niche that indicates the direction of the holy city of Mecca to which the faithful pray. The silk rugs were donated by the last Shah of Iran.

Cross the Charles Glover Bridge, a 420ft long single-span construction (1940) that rises 75ft above a heavily wooded section of Rock Creek Park.

Continue to the corner of Whitehaven St.

Embassy of Brazil – *3000 Massachusetts Ave.* This handsome edifice, set back on a spacious lawn, was built in 1909 for an American diplomat by John Russell Pope. Inspired by Italian Renaissance palaces, the renowned architect designed four elegantly proportioned stories topped with a prominent cornice. The sober facade is punctuated by a recessed entry graced with two pairs of columns. The building, which was purchased by the Brazilian government in 1934, today serves as the ambassador's official residence.

The dark-glass rectangular structure resting on concrete legs at **no. 3006** houses the chancery. Erected in 1971 by the Brazilian architect Olavo Redig de Campos, it is noteworthy as one of the few buildings of contemporary design constructed on Embassy Row.

Continue beyond the embassy of Bolivia *(nos. 3012-3014)* to the **Winston Churchill statue [1]** on the left. One of the greatest public figures of the 20C, Prime Minister Churchill was given honorary American citizenship in 1963 by President John F. Kennedy. Three years later, this statue by William McVey was unveiled. The realistic work depicts Churchill with his familiar attributes—cane and cigar—and his hand raised in the "V for Victory" salute. The location of the statue was carefully chosen to symbolize Churchill's American and British attachments: the statue's right foot is placed on American soil (Churchill's mother was born in the US), while his left foot is resting on the property of the British embassy.

British Embassy – *3100 Massachusetts Ave.* Completed in 1931, this embassy complex was the first to be erected in the area north of Sheridan Circle, thereby leading the way for the avenue's subsequent transformation into Embassy Row. Designed by the period's leading British architect **Sir Edwin Lutyens** (1869-1944), this sprawling compound resembles an early 18C English country estate. The building facing the avenue is the main chancery—a U-shaped brick structure trimmed in white stone with steep roofs accented by tall chimneys. The ambassador's residence is linked to the rear of the chancery (the two chimneys rising above the chancery's roof are the only parts of the residence visible from the avenue). Traditional and elegant, the embassy is a stately presence among embassies in Washington. Its social functions, often charity benefits, are among the most popular in diplomatic circles. The nondescript office building rising to the west of Lutyens' building is the chancery annex. In 1957, the cornerstone for this addition was laid by Queen Elizabeth during her visit to the US. The circular glass capsule near the entrance gate is a multifunctional space primarily for conferences.

Opposite the embassy is the **Kahlil Gibran Memorial [2]**, a 2-acre landscaped site in Normanstone Park commemorating the author of *The Prophet*. At the entrance, a bronze head of the Lebanese-born American (1883-1931) rests on the curved wall above a small pool. Paved walkways rise to a circular, fountained terrace where his writings are inscribed on limestone benches.

The annual Dupont-Kalorama Museum Walk Day, held on the first Saturday in June, is a neighborhood festival featuring musical performances, special exhibits and activities and tours of local museums and cultural institutions. Sights open to the public free of charge on that day include the WOODROW WILSON HOUSE ***and the*** TEXTILE MUSEUM. ***For information ☎667-0441.***

Mountains and Clouds by Alexander Calder

MONUMENTAL SCULPTURE IN THE CAPITAL

The following is a selection of noteworthy works of modern sculpture adorning the public spaces of Washington DC *(see also* **MEMORIALS** *pp 178-179)*:

Works by Alexander Calder

- **Mountains and Clouds** *(see illustration above)*. Atrium of the Hart Senate Office Building, Constitution Ave. and 2nd St. NE.
- **Mobile** (untitled) *(p 54)*. Atrium of the National Gallery's East Building.
- **The Gwenfritz** *(p 59)*. Constitution Ave. and 14th St. NW on the grounds of the National Museum of American History.
- **The Spiral** *(p 90)*. Courtyard of the Old Patent Office Building.

Infinity *(p 59)* by Jose de Rivera. Outside the Mall entrance of the National Museum of American History.

The Awakening by J. Seward Johnson. A striking aluminum sculpture depicting a giant emerging from the ground. Hains Point in East Potomac Park SW.

The plaza and the sculpture garden of the Hirshhorn Museum *(p 62)* provide an open-air showcase for works by prominent modern artists such as Rodin, Matisse, Calder, Moore, Maillol, and Smith as well as pieces by contemporary sculptors.

10
Anacostia and the Eastern Riverfront

Decidedly off the beaten track, the banks of the Anacostia River host several historic military installations and the Southeast neighborhood known as Anacostia, an area rich in black history.

Beginnings – The Nacotchtank Indians inhabited the area along the east branch of the Potomac River when Capt John Smith explored it in 1608. Later explorers misheard Nacotchtank as "Anacostia," the name now applied to the eastern branch of the Potomac and its southeast shore. Throughout much of the 17C, this area was in the hands of large landholders. By mid-century, lucrative tobacco plantations, worked predominantly by black slaves, dotted the riverfront. The incidence of escaped slaves here was high, as they were given refuge by local Indians.

When the Federal District was formed in 1790, the area was incorporated into it as a part of Washington County. Thomas Jefferson had recommended that the land south and east of the Eastern branch, now the Anacostia River, be included in the district, as it offered a strategic position from which to defend the city militarily. Both Jefferson and planner L'Enfant expected the shores of the Anacostia River to become a naval bastion for the capital and its commercial hub. Though lower Southeast did not develop commercially, it did become the site of military installations, the first being the NAVY YARD, established on the north bank of the river in 1799. The US Arsenal (on the present-day site of FORT MCNAIR) was established in 1803 on the peninsula known as Greenleaf Point, at the confluence of the Anacostia River and Washington Channel. By the late 18C, tobacco had depleted the soil in this area and farmers turned to such crops as wheat, corn, and maize. With the demise of the labor-intensive tobacco economy, slaves were increasingly given, or allowed to buy, their freedom, and the area had a large population of freed blacks by the early 19C. In addition, the liberal attitude of the Federal circuit court of Washington County toward black landownership and the rights of blacks to claim their freedom encouraged many freemen to settle here.

The First Suburb – In the 1850s, the area took on a suburban tenor with the establishment of a community called Uniontown, whose row houses still stand along U, V, and W Streets east of Martin Luther King Jr Avenue. Along with the nearby NAVY YARD, the US Government Insane Asylum (now St Elizabeth's Hospital), which opened in 1855, provided employment opportunities. Eventually people seeking relief from the congested city moved to what promoters called "the most beautiful and healthy neighborhood around Washington."

In 1862, Congress enacted a bill emancipating slaves in the District and compensating their owners. Soon thereafter the country was at war and 11 forts were erected in Anacostia and along the eastern riverfront. Most were dismantled after the war, and their grounds now serve as public parks. After the war, a Freedman's Bureau was established under Gen O.O. Howard, for whom Washington's Howard University is named. The bureau quietly purchased the 375-acre Barry Farm in Anacostia in 1867 and resold plots to black families eager to own land. Within a year, 500 families lived here. In 1877, **Frederick Douglass**, the nation's most prominent black spokesman, moved to Anacostia *(see p 134)*.

The area remained sparsely populated until the 1920s and 30s, when additional housing developments were constructed. Throughout the first half of the 20C, Anacostia's demographics reflected a mix of black and white working-class residents, living in single-family homes. Low-income housing projects built here in the 1950s and 60s shifted the population so that, by 1970, the area was predominantly black (86 percent).

In recent decades, the area has suffered the serious social and economic problems afflicting many city neighborhoods. In 1986, however, the District Government designated Anacostia one of three development zones for the city, and a line of the Metro has been extended into the area.

★ FREDERICK DOUGLASS NATIONAL HISTORIC SITE

Map p 165 BZ *time: 1 hour*

1411 W St. SE. Access by car: From Downtown cross the 11th St. Bridge to Martin Luther King Jr Ave., turn left on W St. Accessible by Tourmobile in summer (p 169). Visit by guided tour (1 hour) only Apr 15–Oct 15 daily 9am–5pm (4pm the rest of the year). Tours given on the half hour, introductory film on the hour; closed Jan 1, Thanksgiving Day, Dec 25. Free admission. ☎426-5961.

Known as Cedar Hill, this quaint Victorian house was the last residence of black statesman, orator, and abolitionist, Frederick Douglass. The estate tops a grassy, shaded knoll overlooking the Anacostia River, and the Mall area beyond, and serves as a perpetual monument to Douglass' ideals and spirit.

Father of the Civil Rights Movement – Born into slavery in Talbot County, Maryland, about 1818, Frederick Douglass, christened Frederick Augustus Washington Bailey, was the son of a black mother and an unidentified white father. As a boy, he worked as a house servant in Baltimore, where he was taught the rudiments of reading and writing by the household's white mistress. However, as a young man he was sent to work in the fields and suffered physical deprivation and abuse at the hands of a notorious slave manager. Later, his owner allowed him to leave the fields and learn the trade of ship's caulker.

Frederick Douglass

In 1838, Douglass escaped bondage and fled north, settling with his wife Anna Murray in New Bedford, Massachusetts. In 1841, he became involved with the Massachusetts Anti-Slavery Society and was soon a respected and well-known abolitionist and publicist. Soon after the publication of his first autobiographical work, *Narrative of the Life of Frederick Douglass, An American Slave,* in 1845, Douglass departed for Europe. While abroad, Douglass became a free man thanks to English sympathizers and friends who purchased his freedom in 1846. During the Civil War, Douglass exerted his efforts in recruiting black troops and in persuading Lincoln to legally end slavery. After the war, he was involved with Reconstruction and moved to Washington, first settling in a row house on Capitol Hill, then in 1877, on his Cedar Hill estate. During his years in Anacostia, Douglass received several presidential appointments to serve in District government. In 1882, his wife died, and in 1884, his remarriage to Helen Pitts, a white woman, caused controversy, but did not ultimately detract from Douglass' influence as a powerful spokesman for civil rights. In 1895, after attending a women's rights meeting, Douglass died suddenly of a heart attack at his home.

Cedar Hill – The neat white house with its broad columned front porch was originally built as a speculative property in the late 1850s by John Van Hook, one of the developers of the area's first planned residential community, Uniontown. When Douglass purchased the nine-acre estate from Van Hook, the house had never been lived in. Douglass expanded the property to 15 acres and added seven rooms to the rear of the house.

In 1900, Douglass' widow, Helen, founded the Frederick Douglass Memorial Association, which, in conjunction with the National Association of Colored Women, opened the house for public tours. In 1962, the house was donated to the National Park Service, which restored the estate and opened the historic site to the public.

The house is decorated with Victorian furnishings and memorabilia, most of which belonged to the Douglass family. The ground floor consists of a formal parlor and a family parlor, a dining room, kitchen, Douglass' study, and a pantry and washroom. Note the rare Douglass portrait by Sarah James Eddy in the formal parlor. Douglass sat for the artist during a visit to Massachusetts. The five bedrooms on the second floor include those of Douglass and his two wives, as well as two guest rooms. Behind the house, a small reconstructed stone building served as a second study, which Douglass called "the Growlery."

It [Washington] is our national center. It belongs to us, and whether it is mean or majestic, whether arrayed in glory or covered with shame, we cannot but share its character and its destiny.

Frederick Douglass, 1877

ANACOSTIA MUSEUM

Map p 165 BZ time: 1/2 hour

1901 Fort Place SE. Access by car: From Downtown cross the 11th St. Bridge to Martin Luther King Jr Ave., turn left on Morris Rd., which becomes Erie St. before ending at Fort Pl. Open daily 10am–5pm; closed Dec 25. Free admission. Guided tours (1 hour) daily at 10, 11am, 1pm. 🅿 ♿ ☎*287-3369.*

Located on the high ground of old Fort Stanton, a Civil War fortress now converted into a public park, this museum was conceived by the Smithsonian Institution as a neighborhood museum.

Since its inception in 1967, the museum has moved from its original Anacostia location to its present site and expanded its focus to encompass more broadly the African-American heritage. It features changing exhibits on black history, culture, and achievements.

CONGRESSIONAL CEMETERY

Michelin map 48 L16-M16 time: 1/2 hour

1801 E St. SE. Ⓜ *Potomac Ave. Open daily 9am–5pm. Free admission. Guided tours (1-2 hours) available (2-day advance reservation requested).* 🅿 ☎*543-0539.*

Established in 1807 by a group of private investors, this grassy site above the Anacostia River was intended to serve as the burial grounds for the new Federal City. In 1812 the cemetery was deeded to nearby Christ Church, whose vestry in turn allocated 100 plots for the burial of members of Congress, adding a further 300 in 1823. Congress bought more sites, provided funds for walls, a gatekeeper's house, vaults, and other improvements, and in the process added its own name, Congressional Cemetery, to the appropriating legislation.

Many prominent individuals involved with the history of the nation are buried on the 32-acre grounds. Notable among these are the Civil War photographer Mathew Brady; the "March King" and composer John Philip Sousa (who was born in nearby Anacostia); Push-ma-ta-ha, a Choctaw chief who served with Andrew Jackson in the War of 1812; and three architects who played important roles in the development of the Federal City: William Thornton *(p 24)*, Robert Mills *(p 24)*, and George Hadfield.

In addition, more than 70 former members of the House and 20 former senators lie here. The graves of congressmen who died in office are uniformly marked by distinctive sandstone monuments, clustered in two locations in the cemetery. From 1839 to 1875, these monuments were also erected as cenotaph ("empty grave") markers in memory of congressional members buried elsewhere.

WASHINGTON NAVY YARD

Michelin map 48 N13-N14 time: 1 1/2 hours

9th and M Sts. SE. Ⓜ *Navy Yard. A photo ID is required to enter the Navy Yard. The grounds are open 24 hours a day.*

Historical Notes – In 1799, the first Secretary of the Navy, Benjamin Stoddard, authorized this shipbuilding yard as the US Navy's first shore facility. The prominent architect Benjamin H. Latrobe was commissioned to design the complex. The Navy Yard expanded rapidly until the British occupation of Washington in 1814. At that time, the yard's commandant, Capt Thomas Tingey, ordered the facility burned down, to avoid its takeover by the enemy. The yard was rebuilt and continued ship production until the mid-1850s, when it increasingly turned to ordnance manufacture. By 1886 it had become known as the Naval Gun Factory. In both world wars its involvement in weaponry production necessitated further expansion. The facility ceased operation in 1961 and now serves primarily as an administrative center and as a historic precinct used ceremonially as the "Quarterdeck of the Navy."

Navy Museum – *Entrance on Sicard St. Open Memorial Day–Labor Day, Mon–Fri 9am–5pm, Sat, Sun and holidays 10am–5pm; the rest of the year Mon–Fri 9am–4pm, Sat, Sun and holidays 10am–5pm; closed Jan 1, Thanksgiving Day, Dec 24, Dec 25. Free admission. Guided tours (1 hour) available (2-week advance reservation required)* 🅿 ♿ ✗ ☎*433-2651. (Mon–Fri).* Housed in a cavernous workshop of the former gun factory, this exhibit hall was opened in 1963. Its permanent displays of naval memorabilia, dioramas, ordnances, and equipment interpret the history of the US Navy from the Revolutionary War through the Space Age. Among the highlights of the museum are an extensive collection of scale model ships, including a 25ft-long, elaborately detailed model of a World War II landing craft (LSM); the fighting top from the USS *Constitution*; a World War II Corsair plane; and the bathyscaphe *Trieste,* which carried two men to a depth of 35,800ft underwater in 1960. A number of gun mounts on display may be manipulated by visitors. A gallery to the left of the museum entrance features changing exhibits.

The **museum annex**, located in one end of the old experimental model basin, contains several examples of rare submarines, such as the so-called *Intelligent Whale,* a Civil War submersible, and the German Seehund, a midget sub. Missiles and related military equipment are also exhibited.

Permanently docked near the annex at Pier 2 is the **USS Barry**, a destroyer maintained for public display. The below-deck living and working quarters are open to the public.

Marine Corps Museum – *Located in the Marine Corps Historical Center, Parsons Ave. near the 9th St. gate. Open Mon–Sat 10am–4pm, Sun noon–5pm; closed Dec 25. Free admission. Guided tours available upon request.* P ♿ ☎*433-3267.* This museum displays weaponry, uniforms, medals, papers, musical artifacts, and memorabilia related to the history of the Marine Corps. Interpretive exhibits on major battles are also featured.

At 8th and M Streets, note the Greek-Revival brick **entrance gate** with iron grillwork designed by Benjamin H. Latrobe in 1804 *(admittance through this gate is restricted to authorized personnel).*

FORT LESLEY J. McNAIR

Michelin map 48 P10-R10 *time: 1/2 hour*

4th & P Sts. SW. M *Waterfront or bus no. 60, 70 or M2 from central Washington. Since the fort is an active military base, buildings are open only to military personnel. Visitors are allowed to drive or stoll around the grounds.* P ♿.

Strategically positioned at the confluence of the Anacostia River and Washington Channel, this complex, dating back to 1794, is one of the nation's oldest military installations in continuous operation. Known by various names over the years—Turkey Buzzards Point, Fort Humphreys, and the US Arsenal—the post was renamed Fort Lesley J. McNair in 1948 in honor of the commander of the Army Ground Forces who was killed in Normandy in 1944.

It was on this site in 1865 that four of John Wilkes Booth's alleged fellow conspirators in the Lincoln assassination plot were imprisoned and hanged. One of them, Mary Surratt, was the first American woman executed by Federal order. At the turn of the century, Maj Walter Reed, who was instrumental in identifying the carrier of yellow fever, conducted research in the fort's military hospital.

Today Fort McNair, which occupies a 98-acre site, is the headquarters of the US Army Military District of Washington and the home of the prestigious National Defense University.

Visit – Resembling a university campus more than a fort, the post is laid out in a long quadrangle with a central esplanade bordered by rows of neat brick houses that serve as residences for officers and enlisted personnel. At the southern tip of the grounds rises the **National War College** (1907) an imposing brick structure designed by McKim, Mead and White.

The waters of the Anacostia and Washington Channel provide an attractive backdrop to the impeccably maintained grounds and buildings. From various points along the quadrangle, there are pleasant **views** of East Potomac Park across the channel. Among the other noteworthy institutions on the post are the Industrial College of the Armed Forces and the **Inter-American Defense College** (1962), which trains senior officers from 19 countries in the Western Hemisphere.

Additional Sights in DC

★★ WASHINGTON CATHEDRAL

Michelin map 48 A1 — *time: 1 1/2 hours*

Massachusetts and Wisconsin Aves. NW. Take any no. 30s bus to the intersection of Wisconsin and Massachusetts Aves. Open first Mon in May–Labor Day, Mon–Fri 10am–9pm (4:30pm Sat and Sun), rest of the year daily 10am–4:30pm. Suggested contribution: $2, children $1. Guided tours (45min) Mon–Sat 10am–3:15pm, Sun 12:30–2:45pm (no tours are given during services). ☎*537-6200. Organ recitals Sun 5pm (4:45pm in summer); carillon recitals Sat 12:30pm (5pm in summer).*

Officially named the Cathedral Church of Saint Peter and Saint Paul, the imposing Gothic-style edifice, overlooking the city from its 57-acre site on Mount St Alban, is popularly known as Washington Cathedral or National Cathedral. This magnificent 20C anachronism—replete with flying buttresses, dizzying vaulting, gargoyles, and stained-glass windows—was raised to celebrate Christian faith as well as the American nation and key figures and events in its history.

A Long Time Coming – The inspiration for a national cathedral dates back to the beginning of the Republic. In his grand plan for the capital, planner Pierre Charles L'Enfant proposed "a great church for national purposes," but the idea won little initial support, the new nation being committed to the separation of church and state. Finally in 1893, Congress chartered the Protestant Episcopal Cathedral Foundation and authorized the building of the cathedral complex. Since no Federal funds were allocated for the project, support had to be provided exclusively by private contributions. Under the tireless leadership of the Right Reverend Dr Yates Satterlee, first Episcopal Bishop of Washington, the foundation was able to purchase the Mount St Alban site at the turn of the century. Satterlee shaped both the philosophy and the design of the cathedral. He insisted that the cathedral welcome all, regardless of faith or nationality, and that it be built in what he considered the only truly Christian architectural style—Gothic. He envisioned "a genuine Gothic

S. Brimberg/Washington National Cathedral

Interior of Washington Cathedral

cathedral on this side of the Atlantic that will kindle the same religious, devotional feelings and historic associations that are awakened in the breasts of American travelers by the great Gothic cathedrals of Europe."

Construction – The foundation stone was laid by President Theodore Roosevelt on September 29, 1907 before a crowd of 10,000. In 1912, the first service was celebrated in Bethlehem Chapel, and services have continued in the cathedral every day since. Interrupted only by world wars and intermittent financial difficulties, construction was carried out primarily under the supervision of Philip Hubert Frohman, the project's chief architect from 1912 to 1971. The cathedral, built primarily of Indiana limestone, was erected by applying traditional techniques known to medieval European masons. However, work was accelerated by the use of pneumatic tools, and modern cranes were employed to lift the blocks and carved stonework into place. Thousands donated time and energy as well as money toward the construction, embellishment and furnishing of the cathedral, and the landscaping of its grounds.

In a ceremony held on September 29, 1990—exactly 83 years after the laying of the foundation—the final stone was set in place on the St Paul Tower *(south side of main facade)* in the presence of President George Bush.

A National Cathedral – Although the cathedral is administered by the Episcopal Church, it strives to extend its reach across the nation, beyond religious and state boundaries. Constructed largely from funds provided by Americans nationwide, the cathedral continues to receive support from members of the National Cathedral Association throughout the US. Every US President since Theodore Roosevelt has visited the cathedral. In 1989, President Bush's inaugural prayer service took place here. Holiday services are often broadcast to a national audience, and the cathedral has hosted several special memorial services such as those organized for the Vietnam War casualties, the Iran hostages, and the Americans killed in the Persian Gulf conflict. Great religious leaders from the US and abroad have preached their messages in this place of worship, and several prominent figures are among the more than 100 Americans interred in the cathedral.

Exterior – Modeled after 14C English Gothic cathedrals, this massive structure is among the world's ten largest churches in size and second in the US after St John the Divine in Manhattan *(see Michelin Green Guide to New York City)*. From west facade to apse, the construction measures 514ft long. Crowning the crossing, the **Gloria in Excelsis Tower**, with its 53-bell carillon and 10-bell peal, rises 301ft and dominates the skyline of much of northwest Washington.

The **west facade**, designed by Frohman, is flanked by two identical towers dedicated to St Peter *(left)* and St Paul *(right)*. The carved tympanum above the central portal was designed by Frederick Hart, also known for his VIETNAM VETERANS MEMORIAL sculpture group on the Mall. Hart's interpretation of Creation is a swirl of human figures emerging from nothingness. The bronze gates of the central portal are finely decorated with scenes from the lives of Abraham and Moses, and a statue of Adam adorns the portal's *trumeau* or central pillar. The centerpiece of the facade is the 26ft rose window—an abstract composition of 10,500 pieces of glass that celebrates the creation of light, by stained-glass artist Rowan LeCompte.

Designed to carry rainwater away from the walls, the gargoyles and grotesques around the flying buttresses that support the vaulting of the nave reflect the whimsies that carvers were occasionally allowed to indulge in. With the help of binoculars, the visitor can spot these fanciful creatures. On the St Peter tower glowers a sculpture of Darth Vader from the film *Star Wars*.

Interior – The narthex, just inside the west entrance, is noteworthy for the inlaid seals of the 50 states and the District of Columbia that embellish its floor. The cathedral's vast proportions can be best appreciated upon entering the nave from the narthex. The nave extends approximately 565ft to the high altar. The nave's walls are divided into three levels: an arcade of pointed arches; the gallery or triforium, which bears the state flags; and the upper section pierced with windows (the clerestory). The vaulted ceiling soars 102ft—about ten stories high. Side aisles flank the nave, and a series of bays opens onto the aisles.

The first pair of bays honors two famous Presidents: Abraham Lincoln *(to the left of the entrance)* and George Washington *(right side)*. Halfway down the right aisle *(over the 5th bay)*, the cathedral's most popular stained-glass window, the **Space Window**, commemorates the first manned lunar landing in 1969. A genuine moon rock is fitted in the center of the large red disc representing the moon. Just past the Space Window is the tomb of President Woodrow Wilson, adorned with symbols such as the crusader's sword representing his crusade to secure world peace after World War I.

Continue to the crossing and look back at the west facade to appreciate the blazing colors of the rose window *(best viewed in the late-afternoon light)*. The four colossal pillars in the crossing provide support for the Gloria in Excelsis tower. Note the massive pulpit, built of stone from Canterbury Cathedral. From this pulpit, still used every Sunday, the Rev Martin Luther King, Jr delivered his last Sunday sermon.

Above the high altar, the Jerusalem altar, is the **Ter Sanctus reredos**, an intricately carved stone wall dominated by a representation of Christ in Majesty surrounded by smaller sculptures of prophets and saints. To the left of the altar, note the Glastonbury Cathedra, a bishop's throne built of blocks from Glastonbury Abbey in England.

To the right of the choir, just past the crossing, the War Memorial Chapel commemorates those who lost their lives for the nation. A statue of a young Jesus welcomes visitors to the Children's Chapel, with furnishings scaled-down for youngsters.

Crypt – *Access by the staircase on the north side of the choir.* Unlike crypts in medieval churches, which are generally limited to the area below the chancel, this vast underground labyrinth extends under the entire main floor. Of particular note are a group of chapels dedicated to the birth (Bethlehem Chapel), death, and resurrection of Jesus.

Among the notable Americans interred here are Helen Keller (1880-1968) and her teacher Anne Sullivan. A commemorative plaque honoring the two women can be seen in the Chapel of St Joseph of Arimathea situated just below the crossing. The crypt also houses the cathedral's visitor center.

Observation Gallery – *7th floor. Open daily 10am–4:30pm. Take either of the elevators in the narthex flanking the main entrance.* The enclosed gallery provides a **panorama** of Washington and its surroundings. The gallery's 70 windows also reveal a bird's-eye view of the flying buttresses that support the nave. A slide show and a small exhibit illustrate the history of the cathedral.

Grounds – The lushly landscaped 57-acre site on which the cathedral stands, also known as the close, comprises three schools, a college for clergy and the **Bishop's Garden** *(south side of the cathedral)*, which provides a fragrant haven of herbs, flowers, and boxwood.

★★ HILLWOOD

Map p 164 AY *time: 2 hours*

4155 Linnean Ave. NW. Access: M Van Ness (1/2 mile from Hillwood). By bus: L2 or L4 along Connecticut Ave. to Tilden St. (1/2 mile from Hillwood). Grounds open Tue–Sat 11am–3pm (no reservations necessary). Mansion visit by guided tour (2 hours) only Tue–Sat 9am, 10:30, noon, 1:30pm, 3 (reservations required); closed Sun, Mon, Federal holidays, and the month of Feb. Admission: $10, children $5 (under 12 not admitted); grounds only $2. P ♿ ✗ ☎686-5807.

On a placid residential street above Rock Creek Park lies the 25-acre estate of **Marjorie Merriweather Post** (1887-1973), heiress to the Post cereals fortune. A renowned businesswoman, hostess, and philanthropist, Mrs. Post was also an avid collector. She transformed Hillwood, her final home, into a showcase for her extraordinary acquisitions. Though the columned brick mansion is somewhat unremarkable in both scale and appearance, its interior is lavishly decorated with 18C and 19C French furnishings. Displayed in its many vitrines and wall cabinets is the most extensive collection of **Russian decorative arts★★★** outside Russia.

Hillwood Museum

Imperial Easter Egg (1892) by Carl Fabergé

Treasures of the Tsars – Marjorie Post Davies accompanied her third husband, Joseph E. Davies, when he served as ambassador to Moscow, from 1937 to 1938. The timing was propitious. In the late 1930s, the Soviet government began selling art confiscated from the imperial family, aristocracy, and church during the Revolution of 1917. The Davies were among the last to be able to purchase some of these treasures in the commission shops of Moscow and Leningrad. Thus began Mrs Post's affection for what she called "this gay Russian art."

The objects she collected during her sojourn in Moscow make up only about 20 percent of the collection she ultimately amassed. Hillwood's treasures illustrate more than 200 years of Russian decorative arts, from the reign of Peter the Great (1682-1725), who introduced a backward Russian court to the refined aesthetics of Western European art, to the days of the last tsar, Nicholas II (1868-1918), when jeweler Carl Fabergé created the fabulous Easter eggs and other precious bibelots that delighted an extravagant nobility.

Tour – *The tour begins with a film (30min).* The front hallway, with its rock crystal chandelier, its four 18C French marquetry commodes, Sèvres porcelain, and 20 portraits of Romanov royalty, gives a foretaste of Hillwood's regal exuberance.

Off the hall, the small **Icon Room★★** contains the finest Fabergé pieces in the collection, including elaborate boxes, clocks, and two of the 50-some **Imperial Easter Eggs** commissioned by the royal family as presents for one another. A 19C **diamond nuptial crown** is the only such *objet d'art* known to exist outside Russia. In addition to many superb icons, other ecclesiastical pieces, such as jeweled gold chalices and incense burners, are exhibited.

The small, octagonal **Porcelain Room** is lined with lighted wall cases containing dinner services commissioned by Catherine the Great (1762-1796) and produced in the Moscow factory established by the Englishman Francis Gardner. The oldest of the porcelains is a simple white pattern with pink rosettes, commissioned by Elizabeth I (daughter of Peter the Great) from the Imperial Russian Porcelain Factory she established in 1744.

Three large reception rooms occupy much of the first floor: the **French drawing room** is elaborately appointed in Mrs Post's favorite style, Louis XVI; the **dining room**, with its changing table settings, features an exquisite inlaid marble Florentine table capable of seating 30 guests. The long pavilion at the northwest end of the house was used as a small movie theater and for square dancing, an activity Mrs Post enjoyed. Note the large painting of *The Boyar Wedding* (1883), by Konstantin Makovsky. The chalices and other decorative pieces depicted in the painting are similar to pieces on display throughout Hillwood. The **Vestment Hall** off the kitchen contains Russian Orthodox robes brocaded with silver and gold threads and an exquisite 24-carat **gold chalice** commissioned by Catherine the Great.

The bedrooms on the second floor include Mrs Post's Louis XVI room and an Adam-style guest room with blue-and-white Wedgwood jasperware. On this floor a rotating exhibit from Mrs Post's lace collection is generally displayed, along with selected items from her wardrobe and jewelry.

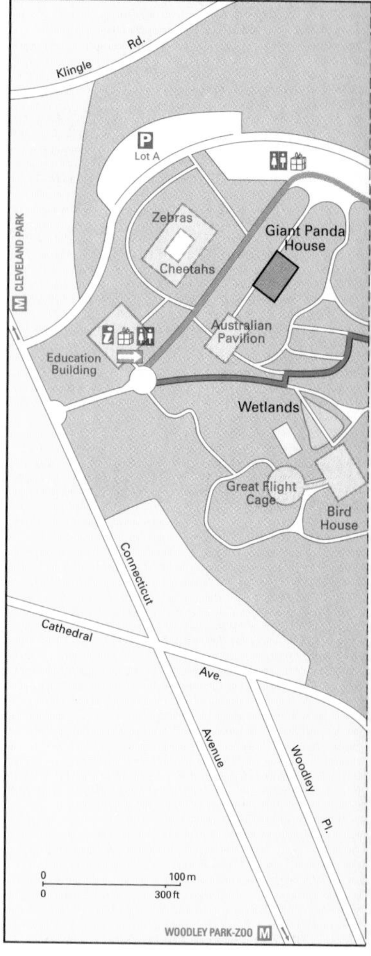

Grounds – *To locate points of interest on the grounds, consult the map distributed at the entrance gate.* Several gardens surround the mansion, including an informal flower garden, a formal French parterre planted in boxwood; a rose garden encircling a pillar marking Mrs Post's grave, and a Japanese garden complete with a waterfall and arched bridge. Wooded paths connect the gardens and encircle the sweep of lawn on the mansion's south facade. Two dependencies also lie in the wooded area south of the mansion. The log **dacha**, a replica of a Russian-style cottage, was built by Mrs Post to house part of her collection of Russian decorative art. The **Indian building**, a rustic wood cabin modeled on Adirondack architecture, displays the Indian basketry, rugs, pottery, and silver objects that formerly decorated Mrs Post's Adirondack camp.

★ NATIONAL ZOOLOGICAL PARK

Michelin map 48 A4-A5 *time: 2 hours*

3001 block of Connecticut Ave. NW. Main entrance at Connecticut Ave.; other entrance at Beach Drive (Rock Creek Parkway) and Harvard St. M *Woodley Park-Zoo or Cleveland Park. Grounds open Apr 15–Oct 15 daily 8am–8pm (6pm the rest of the year). Buildings open daily 9am–4:30pm; closed Dec 25. Free admission. Guided tours (2 hours) available mornings only (3-week advance reservation required). Audio tours ($3) also available.* P ♿ ✗ ☎*673-4800.*

Created in 1887 as the Department of Living Animals, the precursor of this zoo was originally located on the Mall and featured such indigenous American mammals as bison, mule deer, and lynx. In 1889, Congress appropriated funds for the creation of a true zoological park, to be administered by the Smithsonian Institution. A 166-acre tract above Rock Creek Park was purchased, and renowned landscape architect Frederick Law Olmsted laid out plans for the new zoo, but because of disagreement among zoo administrators, Olmsted's project was only minimally realized.

Though it was an immediate popular success, the zoo was constantly plagued with financial problems. Not until 1964, when appropriations for it became part of the overall Smithsonian Institution budget, was the zoo able to revamp and modernize its facilities. Today, it functions as a "biopark," with plants and landscaped environments an integral part of its concept. In addition to exhibiting some 5,000 wild animals, the National Zoo serves as a research institution devoted to the study, preservation, and breeding of threatened species.

Visit – In recent years, parts of Olmsted's original design have been implemented, and today, the **Olmsted Walk** forms a continuous path through the zoo's numerous state-of-the-art exhibits. The highlight of this walk is the zoo's most famous inhabitant—Hsing-Hsing—the **giant panda** donated by the People's Republic of China in 1972. Also on view are big cats, primates, and large African ungulates (hippos, rhinos, giraffes, and elephants). The zoo's oldest building, the quaint **Monkey House**

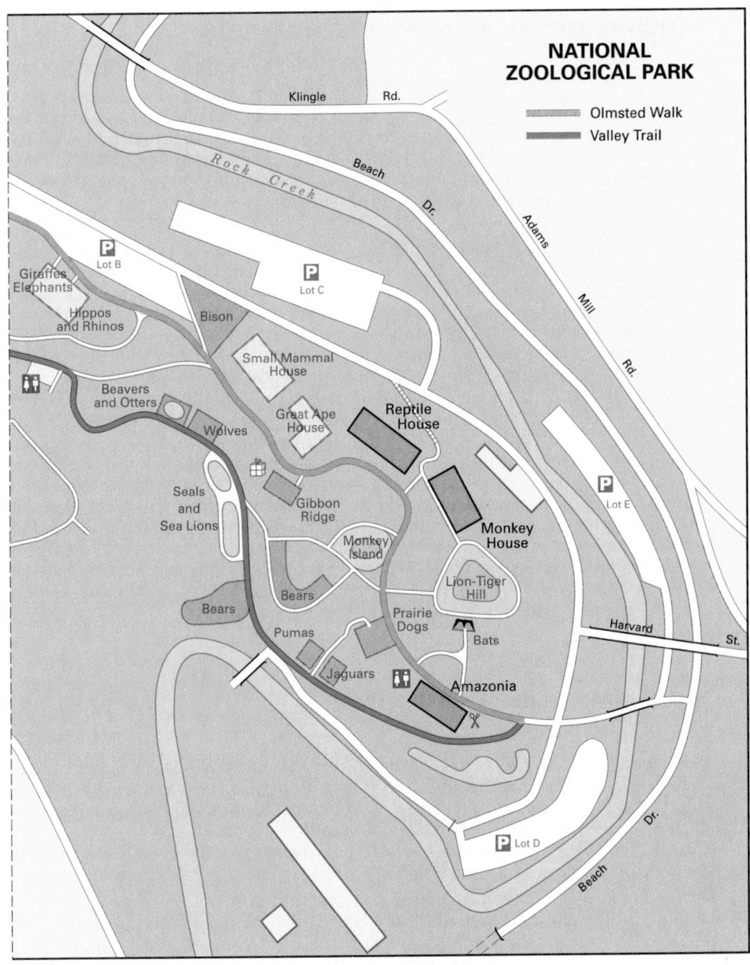

(currently under renovation), was completed in 1906. Adorned with fanciful bas-reliefs of animals, the Byzantine-style **Reptile House** (1929) was voted "the outstanding brick building in the Eastern US" by the American Institute of Architects. Behind the Reptile House, the largest lizard in the world, the Komodo dragon, resides in a specially constructed enclosure.

The **Valley Trail** follows the wooded fringe of the zoo, where outdoor enclosures feature wolves, birds, hoofed animals, seals, and sea lions. More than 40 species of waterfowl frequent the **Wetlands**, a natural setting of grasses and aquatic plants. The trail leads to the **Amazonia** exhibit, where a tropical forest river habitat covering 15,000sq ft has been re-created. Unusual fish, a rainforest sustaining a variety of animals and 358 plant species, and a simulated biologist's field station complete the exhibit. An educational gallery contains interactive exhibits on rainforest biology and lessons in environmental impact.

★ NATIONAL GEOGRAPHIC SOCIETY EXPLORERS HALL

Michelin map 48 G6 — *time: 3/4 hour*

17th and M Sts. NW. Ⓜ Farragut West or Farragut North. Open Mon–Sat 9am–5pm, Sun 10am–5pm; closed Dec 25. Free admission. ♿ ☎857-7588.

The National Geographic Society's century-long support of explorers, archaeologists, oceanographers, and other scientists is showcased in this museum. Housed in the Geographic's three-building headquarters complex, the hall occupies the ground floor of a 10-story marble-and-glass structure designed by Edward Durrell Stone, architect of the KENNEDY CENTER, and opened in 1964.

One side of the hall *(to the left of the reception desk)* is devoted to an interactive science center known as **Geographica**. Installed during the National Geographic Society's bicentennial in 1988, the center's high-tech exhibits highlight research into the origins of early humans, undersea archaeology and exploration, botany, and astronomy. An enormous unmounted **globe**—11ft along the polar axis and 34ft in circumference, said to be the largest in the world—is the centerpiece of a 72-seat amphitheater where the hall's popular Earth Station One program is held. Simulating space flight through special effects, the interactive program looks at Earth from above. The right side of Explorers Hall features changing exhibits whose contents may be cultural as well as geographic or scientific.

KENILWORTH AQUATIC GARDENS

Map p 165 BY *time: 1/2 hour*

Anacostia Ave. and Douglas St. NE. Access: M Deanwood. By car: Drive northeast on New York Ave., turn right on Kenilworth Ave. (Rte 295) and follow signs. Open Apr–Sept daily 7am–7pm (5pm rest of the year). Free admission. ☎426-6905. The blooms are most spectacular in the morning. Seasonal highlights: Water lilies in Jun and Jul; tropical plants in Jul and Aug. A brochure on the gardens, with a map of the ponds, is available at the visitor center.

Located on tidal marshland along the eastern bank of the Anacostia River, this peaceful haven in Northeast Washington comprises some 40 diked ponds devoted to the cultivation of water lilies, lotus, and other aquatic plants. Walter B. Shaw, a Civil War veteran, began the gardens in 1880 for his private enjoyment. The lilies he grew multiplied so prolifically that he soon began commercial cultivation.

During the 1920s, the Shaw family gardens were a popular destination for Washingtonians on Sunday outings and were visited by such luminaries as Presidents Wilson, Harding, and Coolidge. In the 1930s, a dredging project proposed by the Army Corps of Engineers threatened the survival of the ponds. To save them for public enjoyment, the Department of Interior purchased them in 1938. The 12-acre tract is currently administered by the National Park Service.

Among the park's exotic flora are the **Victoria amazonica**, a water lily whose platter-shaped leaves grow as large as 6ft across, and the **East Indian Lotus**, grown from seeds estimated to be hundreds of years old. In 1951, seeds for this rare plant were discovered in a dry lakebed in Manchuria and subsequently germinated by the Park Service. They are believed to have been 350 to 575 years old, making them among the oldest viable seeds discovered to date. These ancient lotus plants can be viewed in the pond directly behind the visitor center. The Victoria lilies are located in a pond at the far western end of the gardens near the Anacostia River.

NATIONAL ARBORETUM

Michelin map 48 E17-E18 *time: 2 hours*

3501 New York Ave. NE. Access by car: From Downtown drive northeast on New York Ave. and enter service road on right after crossing Bladensburg Rd. Other entrance at 24th and R Sts. NE. Open Mon–Fri 8am–5pm, Sat and Sun 10am–5pm; closed Dec 25. Free admission. ☎475-4815.

The arboretum is designed to be toured by car. Nine miles of paved roads lead past the various gardens, collections and designated parking areas along the route.

One of the largest arboretums in the country, this federally owned 444-acre tract situated on the gentle slopes of Mount Hamilton provides a tranquil respite from the warehouses and thoroughfares of surrounding Northeast Washington. Established by Congress in 1927, the arboretum did not become a reality until 1946-1947, when the first plantings of azaleas were made. It opened to the public in the early 1950s. Today, its hills and valleys are covered in evergreens, wildflowers, and such flowering trees and shrubs as azaleas, rhododendrons, and dogwoods, whose spectacular blossoms traditionally attract numerous visitors.

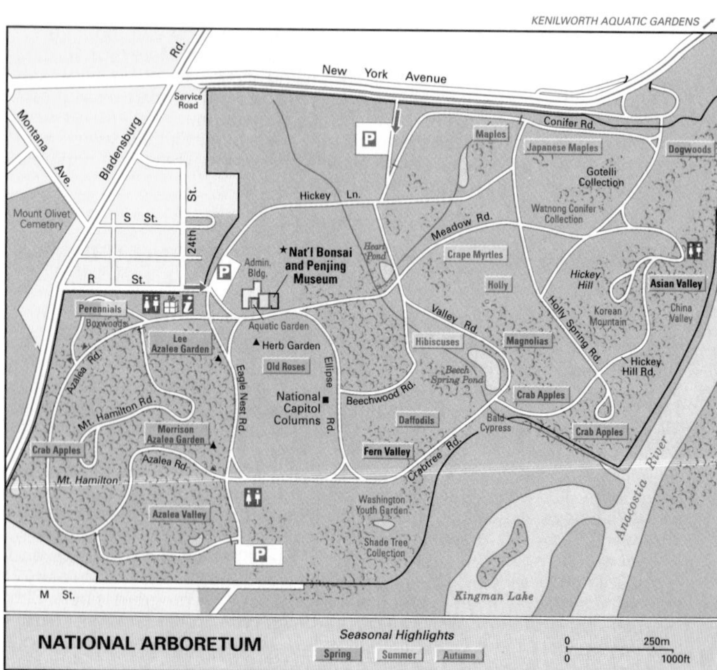

E. Neumann/National Arboretum

National Arboretum in spring

Outstanding Collections – The walled Japanese garden complex, behind the modern administration building, comprises several small gardens and the **National Bonsai and Penjing Museum★** *(open 10am–3:30pm)*, renowned for its outstanding collection of Japanese, Chinese, and American Bonsai.
The 2-acre **Herb Garden** comprises a formal 16C English "knot" garden; a rose garden with more than 80 varieties of "old" roses; and ten specialty gardens, where herbs are grouped according to their uses throughout history. Atop a bluff stand the **National Capitol Columns**, which originally flanked the east entrance of the CAPITOL prior to its expansion in the late 1950s *(see illustration p 31)*.
Pleasant stops along the drive include **Fern Valley**, the picturesque **Asian Valley**, and the **Gotelli collection**, considered one of the finest groupings of dwarf conifers in the world.

As both the NATIONAL ARBORETUM ***and the*** KENILWORTH AQUATIC GARDENS ***are located in the same far-flung corner of the Northeast quadrant, we recommend that you visit them on the same day by car. Tour the Aquatic Gardens in the morning when blooms are best, and continue to the Arboretum.***

NAT'L SHRINE OF THE IMMACULATE CONCEPTION

Map p 165 BY *time: 3/4 hour*

4th St. and Michigan Ave. NE. Ⓜ Brookland CUA. Open Apr–Oct daily 7am–7pm (6pm rest of the year). Guided tours (1 hour). Free admission. ⓟ ♿ ✕ *☎526-8300.*

A 20C blend of Byzantine and Romanesque styles, this massive Roman Catholic church is the official national tribute to Mary, the Mother of Christ and the Patroness of the US.

A Church for a Patroness – Official papal recognition of Mary as this country's patroness dates back to 1846, but it was not until 1914 that the plan for a national church for American Catholics was formulated, approved, and a design chosen. Construction of the crypt church began in 1920, and services have been held there since 1927. The shrine was dedicated in 1959.

Exterior – Constructed of brick, granite, tile, and concrete, the shrine features the customary Latin cross design. Its dome is 108ft in diameter and 237ft in height to the summit of the cross. The dome's exterior is gold-leafed and adorned with blue, gold and red tiles depicting Marian symbols. The **Knights' Bell Tower**—a gift from the Knights of Columbus—surmounted by a 20ft gilded cross, stands 329ft high. It houses a carillon comprising 56 bells cast in Annecy, France.

Interior – The church's nave rises 100ft and measures 58ft in width. Some 200 windows, including three rose windows accented in gold and amethyst, illuminate the sanctuary. The main altar is dominated by a monumental mosaic group depicting Christ in Majesty.
The mosaic in the chancel dome, the Descent of the Holy Spirit, was designed by Parisian artist Max Ingrand; it is the largest mosaic in the shrine. A series of 17 chapels line the east and west sides of the upper church. Note especially the chapels dedicated to Our Lady of Czestochowa of Poland, Our Lady of Guadalupe of Mexico, and Our Lady's Miraculous Medal on the west side.
Among the richly adorned chapels in the **crypt**, note the Mary Altar *(below the main altar)*, made of a block of golden Algerian onyx. The side chapels are dedicated to saints, martyrs, the Good Shepherd, Our Lady of Bistica, and Our Lady of Lourdes.

B'NAI B'RITH KLUTZNICK MUSEUM

Michelin map 48 F6 *time: 1/2 hour*

1640 Rhode Island Ave. NW. M Farragut North or Farragut West. Open Mon–Fri and Sun 10am–5pm; closed Sat, Federal and Jewish holidays. Suggested contribution: $2, children $1. Guided tours (1 hour) available. ♿ ☎857-6583.

Located on the ground floor of B'nai B'rith International, the world's oldest Jewish service organization, this museum houses an extensive collection of Judaic ceremonial, folk, and fine art. Changing exhibits from the permanent collection feature antique and contemporary ritual objects, such as Torah implements, spice boxes, Esther scrolls, Hanukkah menorahs, and kiddush cups. Photographic and other temporary exhibits are presented in the gallery to the left of entrance hall.

NAT'L MUSEUM OF HEALTH AND MEDICINE

Map p 164 AY *time: 3/4 hour*

Walter Reed Army Medical Center, 6825 16th St. NW. Drive north on 16th Street; take the first right after Aspen St. into the compound. At the circle, take the second right (14th St). Turn right at stop sign. Museum is first building (no. 54) on left. Open daily 10am–5:30pm; closed Dec 25. Free admission. Guided tours (30min) by advance appointment. P (obtain permit from receptionist) ♿ ☎576-2348. A floor plan is mounted on the wall near the gallery entrance. Some exhibits are not for the faint-hearted.

Housed in an undistinguished building on the grounds of the Walter Reed Army Medical Center, renowned for its Presidential patients, this small museum depicts medical progress through displays ranging from Revolutionary War amputation implements to the medicinal leeches of modern microsurgery. Begun during the Civil War by US Surgeon Gen William Hammond, the museum has advanced scientific knowledge through staff research conducted during wartime, epidemics, and national tragedies such as the Lincoln and Garfield assassinations. As curator, **Maj Walter Reed** (US Army Surgeon 1851-1902) and his team identified the carrier of yellow fever, paving the way for the disease's control. In 1909, Maj Frederick Russell successfully tested a vaccine for typhoid at the museum. Today, the institution fosters public education through permanent and changing exhibits on contemporary health concerns, such as AIDS and heart disease.

Highlights of the visit are photographs of Civil War injuries before-and-after facial reconstruction, a microscope collection dating from late the 16 to 20C, and such curiosities as a hat struck by lightning and microscope slides of Ulysses S. Grant's tumor.

US NAVAL OBSERVATORY

Michelin map 48 C2 *time: 2 hours*

3450 Massachusetts Ave. NW. Drive north on Massachusetts Ave. past Embassy Row to visitors gate at Observatory Circle. Visit by guided tour (2 hours) only Mon evenings at 8:30pm (limited to first 90 visitors). Closed Memorial, Labor, and Columbus Days. Free admission. P ☎653-1507.

Originally established in 1830 in Foggy Bottom *(p 99)*, the observatory was the first true sciencific agency in the country. With its 26in telescope, Asaph Hall discovered the two moons of Mars in 1877. To avoid the detrimental noise, light, and vibrations of the Foggy Bottom area, the observatory was moved in 1893 to a more secluded location on the upper portion of Massachusetts Avenue. The main buildings were designed by noted architect Richard Morris Hunt.

Since 1974, a white brick Victorian structure initially built on the observatory grounds as the superintendent's house has served as the official residence of the Vice President of the US *(not open to the public)*.

The **Master Clock** of the US, actually several rows of atomic clocks, is included on the tour. Visitors are given an opportunity to view the sky through a 12in telescope.

MAY WE SUGGEST FOUR MORE WAYS TO IMPROVE YOUR JOURNEY?

SET OUT ON A NEW SET

For the best the road has to offer, drive the best tires for the road. Michelin® makes them for whatever you drive.

PERFORMANCE TOURING CARS

Our MXV4™ brings out more performance and comfort in your performance touring car. You'll get a combination of responsive handling and ride only Michelins can provide, thanks to our exclusive Bead Tension Structure™. Plus all-season grip so superior, we call it Climate Control.

MXV4 offers the perfect blend of performance and comfort.

FAMILY CARS

With its breakthrough 80,000 Mile Treadwear Limited Warranty, our all-season XH4® may last as long as you own your family car. And the Michelin MX4® offers another reassurance families will value. Unequaled wet traction in an all-season tire that helps keep you going no matter what the weather brings.

The world's first 80,000-mile tires reflect Michelin's technological leadership.

The Michelin MX4 delivers unequaled wet traction with a proprietary rubber compound and three water channeling grooves.

OF MICHELIN® TIRES.

Michelin Higher Performance Tires are original equipment on some of the world's fastest cars.

HIGH PERFORMANCE CARS

With Michelin XGT® Series tires you'll boldly experience the outer performance limits engineered into your high performance car. Special belt technology delivers superb high-speed stability. And Bead Tension Structure ensures crisp steering response while it filters out road harshness. Our XGT Series tires deliver performance so outstanding we call them The Higher Performance Tires.™

LIGHT TRUCKS

Michelin LTX Series tires deliver rugged performance with no compromise in ride comfort.

If you drive a light truck – a pickup, van, or sport utility vehicle – Michelin can enhance its performance, too. Our LTX® Series tires set a new standard of durability. And blend traction with quiet comfort like no light truck tires before them.

You've got our Guide. Now, add our tires. And enjoy all the pleasures of the road.

MICHELIN®
BECAUSE SO MUCH IS RIDING ON YOUR TIRES.®

GREEN GUIDE. TRAVELER'S CHECKS. AND A SET OF NEW MICHELINS.

Year after year, Michelin tires rank number one in customer satisfaction.
See your Yellow Pages® for the Michelin Dealer nearest you.

Excursions

As the focus of this guide is Washington DC, we have limited our selection of excursions to those nearby sights whose history is closely related to that of the capital. The four excursions described in the following pages are concentrated within a 22-mile radius south of Washington and are easily accessible by car or by public transportation. The well-organized visitor can take in two or more excursions in the same day *(expect long entry lines at* MOUNT VERNON *during the tourist season).*

For those interested in longer excursions, the area offers a wealth of possibilities, including Baltimore (40 miles from DC), Annapolis (36 miles), and the vast Chesapeake Bay region in Maryland; and Manassas (132 miles), Fredericksburg (53 miles), and Monticello (near Charlottesville—115 miles) in Virginia.

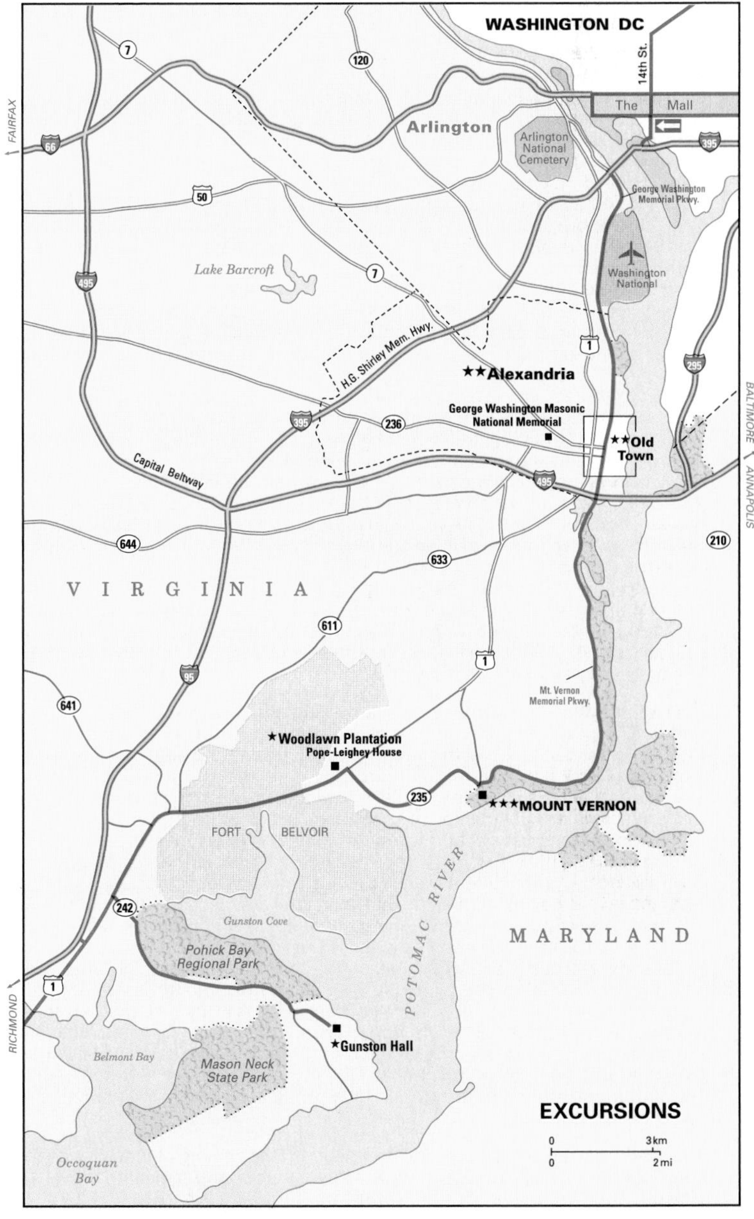

★★ ALEXANDRIA

Map p 145 *time: 1/2 day*

Access – *Alexandria is located on the west bank of the Potomac River, 6 miles southeast of Washington.* **By car:** *Leave Washington by the 14th St. Bridge, take exit 11A (for National Airport), and continue south on the George Washington Memorial Parkway. One-day (24 hour) visitor's parking permit is available at* RAMSAY HOUSE VISITORS CENTER *(King and Fairfax Sts).* **By public transportation:** *Take Metro to King Street Station, then board an eastbound Dash bus no. AT 2 or AT 5.*

Though it is situated just a few miles down the Potomac from the nation's capital, this enclave of historic homes and churches set amid tree-shaded brick walks retains its colonial charm and an atmosphere of slow-paced southern gentility. Alexandria's past is intimately bound with the founding of the country and with such preeminent Americans as George Washington, George Mason, and Robert E. Lee.

A Prosperous Seaport – The area now called Old Town Alexandria traces its beginnings to the early 1700s, when a tobacco warehouse on the waterfront, near what is now Oronoco Street, spawned a small settlement. Prominent Scottish tobacco merchants and Virginia tobacco planters joined to petition the Virginia General Assembly to establish a town in the area, and in 1748, the assembly granted their request, stating that such a town "would be commodious for trade and navigation and tend greatly to the best advantage of frontier inhabitants." The 60-acre tract on which the town was to be sited belonged to members of the Alexander family, and thus the new town was named Alexandria.

The new town was laid out in the grid pattern characteristic of 18C urban planning. Seven streets ran west from the river, bearing, as was typical of the day, the titles of royalty—Duke, Prince, King, Cameron (named for Virginia's Lord Fairfax, the Baron of Cameron), Queen, Princess, and Oronoco (after the original tobacco wharf). The three north-south cross streets were named Water, Fairfax, and Royal Streets. Sale of the 84 half-acre lots was placed under the authority of 11 trustees, and on July 13, 1749, a public auction was held. Over a two-day period, 42 lots were purchased. The Spanish *pistole,* the most available hard currency at the time, was the predominant means of payment. Following stipulations laid down by the General Assembly, no bidder was allowed more than two lots and, to ensure the growth of the town, a dwelling had to be erected within two years of purchase.

For the next quarter century, Alexandria flourished as a rambunctious colonial seaport and trading center. It was a mixture of warehouses, shipyards, taverns, small clapboard dwellings, and impressive Georgian mansions, like that of John Carlyle, one of the Scottish immigrants whose traditions still flavor aspects of Old Town. By 1763, the port had outgrown its original space and was beginning to expand westward, adding more cross streets. It also grew eastward by filling land on the marshy Potomac shoreline around present-day Union Street.

Growth abruptly ended with the coming of the Revolution in 1775. During the war, Alexandria was a pivotal meeting point for such patriotic leaders as George Mason, whose plantation, GUNSTON HALL, was in the area, and George Washington, who maintained a small house in town and a large plantation, MOUNT VERNON, eight miles down the Potomac.

The townspeople themselves were divided during the Revolution: some were ardent patriots, while others resented the economic havoc war was playing with their lives. Battle threatened them only once, when a contingent of British ships sailed up the Potomac, fired a few shots, then left. At the height of the war, in 1779, Alexandria was incorporated as a town.

Part of the New Capital – With the coming of peace, Alexandria's prosperity returned, and in 1789 its fortunes took a monumental turn when it was ceded by Virginia for the formation of the new Federal City. Congress officially accepted it as part of the District in 1801.

Alexandria's prospects were curtailed, however, by a congressional amendment that prohibited the construction of any Federal buildings on the Virginia side of the river. Historians believe that this amendment was enacted at the instigation of President Washington, who owned Alexandria lands and feared allegations of favoritism. Though no government buildings actually went up on Alexandria soil, the town had its heyday during the building of the new capital. Taverns, hostelries, and businesses flourished, and the port became a major exporter of wheat, which had taken the place of tobacco as Virginia's cash crop.

In the early decades of the 1800s, Alexandria's fortunes declined as it lost trade to growing commercial centers in nearby Georgetown, Richmond, and Baltimore. The town also incurred heavy debts in the building of the Alexandria Canal, which failed to stimulate the trade expected. Suffering economically from their association with the capital city and without representation in Congress, Alexandrians became disillusioned with their status as citizens of the nation's capital. In 1846, the County of Alexandria retroceded to Virginia, with whom it had always maintained strong social and political ties.

The Civil War Years – From 1850 to 1860, with the coming of industrialization, a cotton gin and locomotive factory were built in town, and Alexandria once again thrived. Then Federal troops moved in and occupied the town in 1861 for the duration of the Civil War, converting public buildings into Union hospitals and constructing a fort on Shooter's Hill, now topped by the granite tower of the GEORGE WASHINGTON MASONIC NATIONAL MEMORIAL. While the town suffered under Union occupation, Robert E. Lee, whose BOYHOOD HOME still stands in Old Town, led the Confederate Army.

Mariners' Museum, Newport News VA

Bird's-eye view of Alexandria in 1863

In 1870, soon after the war's end, Alexandria became an independent city, separate from the county of the same name (now called Arlington). Over the decades, it spread west, annexing parts of the old county as it grew. Not until World War I did the town experience any real prosperity again, when the Federal Government constructed a torpedo factory on the waterfront.
During World War II, Alexandria benefited from the growth that infected the entire metropolitan area. Today, the city encompasses 15.75sq miles, with a population of 111,000.

Elegant Enclave – In recent decades, the Old Town quarter of the city has paid increasing attention to its architectural heritage, fostering its image of genteel provincialism. The city government carefully monitors the appearance of buildings in the historic district, which in 1969 was placed on the National Register of Historic Places.
Since the 1960s, gentrification has overtaken what had been the working-class neighborhoods of Old Town. Professionals, lured by Alexandria's cachet, have bought and renovated the small colonials and elegant Georgians. Many now display the official metal plaques that designate buildings "of historic or architectural significance."
Today, the city's waterfront is graced with parks, and restaurants and boutiques line King and Washington Streets. At the foot of King Street, the **Torpedo Factory** *(map p 149)* has undergone a much acclaimed urban renovation and now serves as an extensive art center, housing the shops and studios of visual artists.

★★ **OLD TOWN** *Walking tour. Distance: 4 miles. Map p 149. Time: 3 hours (not including guided tours).*

Begin at the corner of King and N. Fairfax Sts.

Ramsay House Visitors Center – *221 King St. Open daily 9am–5pm; closed Jan 1, Thanksgiving Day, Dec 25. ☎703-838-4200.* The north portion of this colonial clapboard incorporates the remains of the oldest structure in Old Town. Built in 1724 by William Ramsay, a Scottish merchant, the small house was moved to Alexandria soon after the town's founding. It now functions as the official visitors and convention center.

Turn left on S. Fairfax St.

Stabler-Leadbeater Apothecary Museum – *105-107 S. Fairfax St. Open Mon–Sat 10am–4pm; closed Sun and Jan 1, Thanksgiving Day, Dec 25. Admission: $1, children under 12 free. ☎703-836-3713.* An apothecary from 1792 to 1933, this shop has been restored to its mid-19C appearance. Shelving, cases, glass bottles, and equipment used for preparing medicines and remedies are from the original store, which served as a major supplier of pharmaceuticals in the area.

Market Square – Now modernized and dominated by a steepled city hall (1873), this square has served as the city's focal point since the mid-18C. It has been the setting for many historic gatherings, including Washington's drilling of his Revolutionary troops.

★ **Carlyle House** – *121 N. Fairfax St. Visit by guided tour (45min) only Tue–Sat every half hour 10am–4:30pm, Sun noon–4:30pm; closed Jan 1, Thanksgiving Day, Dec 24, 25. Admission: $3, children 11-17 years and students $1. ♿ ☎703-549-2997.* Modeled after a Georgian manor house, this free-standing stone construction was built by John Carlyle, one of the Scottish entrepreneurs instrumental in founding Alexandria. Carlyle came to Virginia in 1741 as an agent for an English merchant, but he soon established his own trading concerns. His marriage in 1747 to Sarah Fairfax, daughter of one of the colony's most influential men, further secured Carlyle's fortunes and position. He became a friend of George Washington, a founding trustee of the town, and a respected merchant and builder. His impressive mansion, completed in 1753 and surrounded by stables, sheds, dependencies, and a warehouse, dominated the Alexandria waterfront for several decades before the swampland along the Potomac was reclaimed in the second half of the 18C.

The mansion's hour of glory came in April 1755, when the British general Edward Braddock, en route to his ill-fated campaign against the French and Indians, headquartered himself here. During his stay, he commissioned George Washington to serve with him in the campaign, and he held the historic **Governor's Council**. At this unprecedented meeting, five colonial governors met with Braddock in Carlyle House. He petitioned them both for advice on military strategy and for financial support from their local assemblies. The governors' contention that the colonists would refuse to provide funds to the British was an early sign of tension between England and the colonies.

When Carlyle died in 1780, his property passed to his daughter Sarah and her husband, William Herbert. After the Herberts' tenure, the house was sold out of the family. In 1970, the Northern Virginia Regional Park Authority purchased Carlyle House and began a six-year renovation to restore it to its colonial appearance.

From photo Alexandria Conv. & Visitors Bureau

Carlyle House

Mansion – The 2-story building, with a projecting central section and prominent quoin (or corner) stones, is topped by a graceful hipped roof punctuated by a pair of chimneys. Inside, the mansion is authentically decorated in the style fashionable to its period. The popular tones of the day (verdigris green, blue verditer and Prussian blue) predominate throughout the house. Note the fine woodwork cornices, pediments, and paneling in the first-floor study and main parlor, the only two rooms that have retained their original architecture.

The second floor has bedrooms and an architectural exhibit room, where the restoration process is explained in captioned photographs, and a section of the original rubble-and-mortar walls of the house is exposed. On the basement level is a servant's work room with various utensils of the day.

A formal garden behind the house is laid out in parterres with brick walkways *(no admission charge).*

Bank of Alexandria (Signet Bank) – *133 N. Fairfax St.* This recently restored brick Federal structure is the oldest building (1807) in Virginia that has been continually used as a bank. Ramsay's son-in-law, William Herbert, served as the bank's second president and a director.

Turn left on Cameron St.

The row houses in the **300 block (A)** of Cameron Street, representative of the early to mid-19C architecture of the area, now house the kinds of storefront boutiques for which Old Town is noted. No. 309 has a picturesque side courtyard and loggia.

★ **Gadsby's Tavern Museum** – *134 N. Royal St.* This is one of the most celebrated hostelries from the early days of the country. Functioning now as a museum and restaurant, it is actually two joined brick structures: the 2-story Georgian-style tavern dates back to about 1770; the 3-story Federal-style construction was built as a hotel in 1792 by John Wise, a local businessman. Englishman John Gadsby leased the larger building from Wise in 1796, and in 1802, Gadsby also took over the smaller one, which he operated as a coffee house. The Federal-style building became the renowned Gadsby's Tavern, considered the finest public house in the new capital. While the Federal City was being built across the Potomac, Gadsby's Tavern frequently entertained its officialdom—the Jeffersons, the Adams, and George Washington himself, whose town house was just a block away at 508 Cameron Street *(see p 149)*. For years, an annual gala celebrating Washington's birthday was held in Gadsby's ballroom.

The buildings functioned as a tavern until 1878. They were restored to their original appearance in 1975 and reopened in 1976. The ground floor of the Federal-style building is leased as a commercial restaurant, serving meals in the re-created ambience of a late 18C tavern. Much of the rest of the two buildings is devoted to a museum re-creating the tavern as it appeared in Gadsby's day.

Museum – *Visit by guided tour (30min) only Apr 1–Sept 30 Tue–Sat every 15min 10am–5pm, Sun 1pm–5pm (11am–4pm rest of year, same Sun hours); closed Mon and Federal holidays. Admission: $3, students and children 11-17 $1. ♿ ✗ ☎838-4242.* The first floor consists of an entrance hall and two public rooms. The larger room to the left is set as a dining room, with furnishings and food appropriate to the late 18C. The small dining room to the right contains a table set as it would have been for one of the private dinners that often took place there.

A large assembly hall dominates the second floor of the older building. Furnished with only a few chairs, this room was used by merchants to show their wares and by itinerant dentists to treat patients, as well as for social events.

Gadsby's famous **ballroom**, which occupies much of the second floor of the Federal building, was the scene of many elegant soirees. Its original paneling is now conserved in the Metropolitan Museum of Art in New York. A musicians' gallery is cantilevered out over the ballroom.

The canopied beds and pleasant decor of the two bedchambers on this floor contrast sharply with the spartan accommodations in the small third-floor bedrooms, where travelers sometimes slept two or three to a bed.

Return to Cameron St. and continue west.

The modest clapboard building at **508 Cameron Street** is a recent reconstruction of the town house George Washington built as a convenient in-town office and lodging.

Turn right on N. St Asaph St.

At the intersection with Queen Street, note **523 Queen Street** *(the second house from the corner)*, one of the smallest houses in Old Town. Among the quaint mid-19C clapboards in the 300 block of N. St Asaph Street is an example of a **flounder house** *(no. 311)*. This vernacular architectural style, which dates from the first half of the 19C, derives its name from the flat, windowless side of the house, resembling the eyeless sides of flounder fish. There are about 20 such structures still standing in Old Town.

At the next intersection, note Princess Street *(on the left)*, which has its original cobblestone paving. The cobbles often came across the Atlantic as ballast for ships.

Continue to the corner of Oronoco St. and turn left.

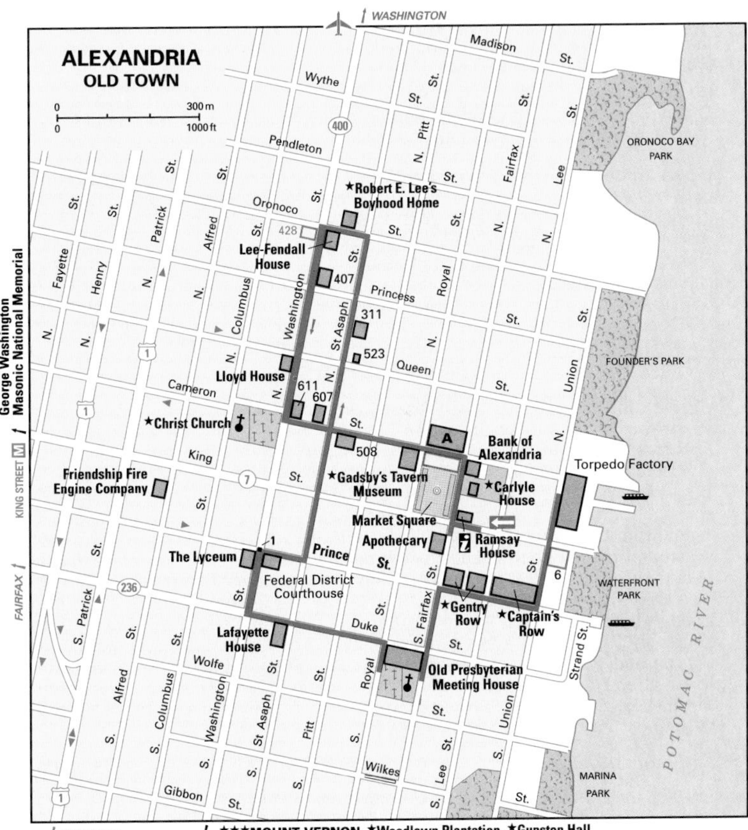

★ **Robert E. Lee's Boyhood Home** – *607 Oronoco St. Visit by guided tour (30min) only Mon–Fri 10am–3:30pm, Sun 1pm–3:30pm; closed Dec 16–Feb 1, Easter Sunday, and Thanksgiving Day. Admission: $3, students 11-17 $1, children under 11 free. As the sight is often closed for special events, it is advisable to call before visiting. ☎703-548-8454.* Constructed in 1795 by John Potts, a business acquaintance of George Washington, this gracious Federal town house soon became the residence of William Fitzhugh, a close friend of Washington.

Here, in 1804, Fitzhugh's daughter Mary married Washington's ward and the squire of ARLINGTON HOUSE, George Washington Parke Custis *(see table p 117)*.

In 1812, "Light-Horse Harry" Lee, a Revolutionary War hero, friend of Washington, and father of Robert E., rented the house from the Fitzhughs, relatives of his second wife, Ann Carter.

Soon after, Lee was wounded in a Baltimore riot. Crippled by his wounds and virtually bankrupt save for his wife's income, he sailed to Barbados in the Caribbean, reputedly to recover his health. Six-year-old Robert never again saw his father, who died away from home five years later.

Widowed and invalided by arthritis, Ann Carter Lee relied heavily on her fourth child and youngest son, Robert. The family lived here until 1825, with the exception of a four-year hiatus, during which William Henry Fitzhugh was in residence, and the Lees occupied another Lee family property at 407 N. Washington Street *(see below)*. Robert left his boyhood home in 1825 to become a cadet at West Point Military Academy. Unable to maintain a household without his help, Mrs Lee moved to Georgetown *(see p 108)*.

Mansion – A spacious L-shaped brick structure, the house, along with 609 Oronoco Street, is part of an unusual 18C duplex design. Opening off a wide entrance hall are a music room and dining room, decorated in period furnishings. A narrow back hall leads to a morning room and kitchen. On the wall of the elegant main staircase hang five pastel portraits of Lee by contemporary artist David Silvette. They depict the general over the course of 40 years. The second floor contains bedrooms furnished as they would have been in the Lee years.

The intersection of Oronoco and Washington Streets is known as "Lee Corners" due to the cluster of Lee family residences. The stately Georgian building at 428 N. Washington Street was the home of Light-Horse Harry's brother Edmund Jennings Lee, mayor of Alexandria from 1815 to 1818.

Lee-Fendall House – *614 Oronoco St. (Enter on Washington St.) Visit by guided tour (30min) only, Tue–Sat 10am–3:45pm, Sun noon–3:45pm; closed Mon and Federal holidays. Admission: $3, students 11-17 $1, children under 11 free.* P *☎703-548-1789.* This large clapboard was built in 1785 by Philip Richard Fendall, a distant Lee relative who bought the half-acre lot from Light-Horse Harry Lee. Fendall was married to three different Lee women, and members of the Lee family continually lived in the house until 1904. From 1937 to 1969, it was the residence of the famous labor leader John L. Lewis. Today, the house is decorated in early 19C style, with many authentic Lee pieces.

Continue down N. Washington Street, noting the house at **no. 407**. Built by Charles Lee, another brother of Light-Horse Harry, this was the home young Robert E. Lee lived in with his mother from 1817 to 1820.

Lloyd House – *220 N. Washington Street Open Mon–Fri 9am–6pm (5pm on Sat); closed Sun, Jan 1, Jul 4, Labor Day, Columbus Day, Thanksgiving Day, Dec 25. Free admission. ♿ ☎703-838-4577.* John Wise, who established GADSBY'S TAVERN, built this attractive late Georgian brick edifice as his residence in 1797. In the early 19C, a succession of prominent Alexandrians lived in the house, including Benjamin Hallowell, a Quaker school master who briefly tutored Robert E. Lee. In 1832, the house was purchased by John Lloyd, whose wife, Ann Lee Lloyd, was a first cousin of Robert E. Lee. The house remained in the Lloyd family until 1918. In 1976, it became part of the Alexandria library system. Both floors of the house function as a library devoted to Virginia history and genealogy.

★ **Christ Church** – *Corner of N. Washington and Cameron Sts. (Enter walled graveyard from Washington St.) Open Mon–Sat 9am–4pm, Sun 2–4:30pm; closed holidays, Good Friday, the day after Thanksgiving Day, Dec 24. Free admission. Guided tours (15min) available. As the church may be closed for private use, it is advisable to call before visiting. ♿ ☎703-549-1450.* Encircled by a high wall, the church grounds provide a peaceful haven where trees shade 18C grave markers. In the simple brick and stone structure, with its pepperpot steeple, both George Washington and Robert E. Lee worshipped. By tradition, 20C Presidents have come here to worship in Washington's pew the Sunday nearest February 22, his birthday. Construction of the church began in 1767, but for unknown reasons, the original builder did not complete the job. It was John Carlyle *(see p 147)* who finished the church in 1773, and in 1774 a member of the Alexander family, after whom the town was named, gave the parish vestry the acre of land on which the church is situated. In the church's unadorned and luminous interior a raised wine-glass pulpit and a large Palladian window provide the focal point. Silver plates mark the **pews** of Washington *(no. 60)* and Lee *(no. 46)*.

Return to Washington St., cross and walk down the 600 block of Cameron St.

In 1811, the Georgian brick at **611 Cameron Street** was home to Light-Horse Harry Lee and his family, including his three-year-old son Robert. Thomas, the ninth and final Lord Fairfax, lived in the imposing Federal-style structure at **no. 607** in the 1830s.

Turn right on S. St Asaph St. and walk two blocks, past the intersection with King St., the main shopping street in Old Town. Turn right on Prince St.

The large brick structure with Palladian windows at the corner of Prince and Washington Streets is the **Federal District Courthouse** for Virginia's Eastern District. A number of nationally publicized trials, particularly involving Pentagon espionage, have been heard here.

The statue (1889) **[1]** dominating the intersection of Washington and Prince Streets commemorates Alexandria's Confederate dead.

Cross Washington St.

The Lyceum – *201 S. Washington St. Open Mon–Sat 10am–5pm, Sun 1–5pm; closed Jan 1, Thanksgiving Day, Dec 25. Free admission.* P ♿ *☎703-838-4994.* In 1834, Benjamin Hallowell *(see* LLOYD HOUSE *above)* interested his fellow citizens in founding a lyceum, or cultural center, in Alexandria, and five years later this Greek Revival structure was built to house a library, lecture rooms, and natural history exhibits. Many prominent 19C figures spoke here, including the renowned orator Daniel Webster. After decades of disrepair, the building was restored in 1974. Today, it houses a museum featuring changing exhibits on state and local history.

Continue one block south on Washington St., then left on Duke St. one block to S. St Asaph St.

Lafayette House – *301 S. St Asaph St. Not open to the public.* Built about 1815 by a prosperous shipping agent, this 3-story brick building, with an elegant double doorway topped by a fanlight and flanked by lunettes, is a fine example of a Federal-style town house. In 1824, the Marquis de Lafayette stayed here during a state visit.

Continue down Duke St. two blocks to S. Royal St. Turn right and enter the brick gate marked no. 316.

Old Presbyterian Meeting House – *Between 300 block of S. Royal and S. Fairfax Sts. Open Mon–Fri 8:30am–4:30pm, Sunday services at 8:30am and 11am. Free admission. ♿ ☎703-549-6678. If the meeting house is locked, apply to the church office in the flounder house at 316 S. Royal St.* The old flounder house manse on the left inside this walled churchyard was built in 1787. The graveyard beyond contains markers for John Carlyle; Dr James Craik, the surgeon general of the Continental Army; and other prominent Alexandrians. The sarcophagus enclosed by a wrought-iron rail on the north commemorates an unknown soldier of the Revolution. *(The box beside the sarcophagus plays a videotape on the church's history.)*

Church – Alexandria's many Scottish immigrants established this church in 1772, contracting John Carlyle to oversee its building. Completed in the mid-1770s, it was the sight of celebrations for Alexandria's Masons. In 1799, at Washington's death, the church bell tolled continuously for four days, and his public funeral service was preached here, "the walking being bad to the Episcopal Church." In 1835, lightning struck the steeple, and the ensuing fire virtually destroyed the church. Within two years, it was rebuilt essentially to its present state.

From the church entrance continue up S. Fairfax St. then right on Prince St.

Prince Street – The brick-paved 200 block of Prince Street is known as **Gentry Row★**, due to its dignified 18C structures. Considered one of the finest examples of this architectural period in Virginia, **no. 207** is believed to contain elements of a town house built by the George William Fairfaxes, Washington's close friends. At nos. 211 and 209 lived two of Washington's physicians, Dr Elisha Cullen Dick and Dr James Craik. The stuccoed, salmon Greek Revival **Athenaeum** (1851-1852) on the corner was built as the Old Dominion Bank and now functions as a gallery for the Northern Virginia Fine Arts Association *(open Sept 2–Jun 14 Wed–Sat 11am–4pm, Sun 1–4pm; closed Sept 1–Jun 15, Jan 1, Thanksgiving Day, Dec 25, and when reserved for private use. Free admission. ☎703-548-0035).*
The architecture changes abruptly along the roughly cobbled 100 block of Prince Street. Known locally as **Captain's Row★**, the street may derive its name from the 18C sea captain John Harper, who owned much of the land along the north side of the street. A preponderance of small residences were built here in the late 18C and early 19C, when the street bordered the Potomac River. Many of the original houses were destroyed in an 1827 fire, but the block retains a seafaring flavor.

Turn left on S. Union St.

The building on the corner *(6 King St.)* is an early 19C brick-and-stone warehouse. End the tour at the **Torpedo Factory** *(see description p 147)*.

ADDITIONAL SIGHTS *Map p 149*

George Washington Masonic National Memorial – *101 Callahan Dr. Ⓜ King Street. Open daily 9am–5pm; closed Jan 1, Thanksgiving Day, Dec 25. Free admission. Guided tours (1 hour) 9:30am–4pm. Ⓟ ☎703-683-2007.* Crowning historic Shooter's Hill, this memorial to George Washington, the first Master of Alexandria's Masonic Lodge, is a city landmark, anchoring the western end of Old Town. The large granite building, topped by a tiered tower, is modeled after one of the seven ancient wonders of the world—the lighthouse on the island of Pharos near Alexandria, Egypt. Begun in 1923, the memorial was built in increments over the course of 40 years.

Freemasonry – Reputedly the world's largest and oldest global fraternal order, Freemasonry had its origins in the stonemason guilds of the late Middle Ages. Its official founding, however, was in England in 1717. Established in the American colonies in the late 1720s, it was embraced by prominent leaders of the Revolutionary period. Fourteen US Presidents have also been Masons.
Though Freemasonry is not a secret society, as is often believed, it does maintain secrecy concerning its ritual practices, which continue to symbolically use architectural concepts and implements recalling stonemasonry. The memorial embodies many of these symbolic elements, such as the use of the five orders of architecture: Doric, Ionic, Corinthian, Composite, and Tuscan.

Visit – Passing through the imposing columned portico, visitors enter **Memorial Hall**, dominated by a 17ft-high bronze **statue** of Washington. On either side of the hall are two 46ft-long murals by artist Allyn Cox, who executed several other murals in the memorial, as well as in the CAPITOL. The mural on the left depicts Washington at the Masonic ceremony for the laying of the Capitol cornerstone; the mural on the right shows Washington with his fellow Masons at a religious service in Philadelphia's Christ Church.

The **Replica Room** *(down the hall to the left of Cox's cornerstone mural)* contains Windsor chairs and other furnishings originally in the late 18C Alexandria-Washington Lodge in Old Town. It also displays various Masonic articles associated with George Washington, including the silver trowel and the Masonic apron he used while laying the Capitol cornerstone.

The **Assembly Room** *(one floor below Memorial Hall)* has eight polished green granite columns that act as structural supports for the entire memorial. The 350-year-old Persian Royal Meshed rug here measures 30ft by 50ft, supposedly the world's largest rug made on a single loom.

The 7-story tower houses a **museum** of Washington memorabilia, a library *(open by appointment only)*, and five small floors, each devoted to a different order or type of Masonry, such as the Knights Templar, Royal Arch, and Grotto Masons. These chambers are decorated in the Persian, Egyptian, Hebraic, and medieval motifs symbolic of the specific orders.

The top level opens onto an observation deck, with a **view** of Old Town and the Potomac River.

Friendship Fire Engine Company – *107 S. Alfred St. M King Street. Open Thu–Sat 10am–4pm, Sun 1–4pm; closed Mon–Wed and Jan 1, Thanksgiving Day, and Dec 25. Free admission. Guided tours (30min) available. ♿ ☎703-838-3891.*
Organized in 1774, the Friendship Fire Company lists among its honorary volunteers statesmen, governors, and Presidents, including George Washington himself. The current brick firehouse, with its quaint cupola, was completed in 1857.

Though the company ceased active fire fighting in the early 1870s, the Friendship Veterans Fire Engine Association has continued to maintain a historic and ceremonial function.

Now the property of the city, the recently restored building features a first-floor exhibit room devoted to 18C and 19C fire-fighting equipment, including leather buckets and speaking trumpets. The meeting room on the second floor displays memorabilia relating to the company's social role in the community.

★★★ MOUNT VERNON

Map p 145

time: 1 1/2 hours

Access – *Mount Vernon is located 16 miles south of Washington.* **By car**: *Leave Washington by the 14th St. Bridge, take exit 11A (for National Airport) and continue south on the George Washington Memorial Parkway. Average round-trip driving time from Downtown: 1 hour.* **By public transportation**: *Take Metro to Pentagon or National Airport stations, then board bus no. 11P, 11H or 11Y for Mount Vernon.* **By Tourmobile** *(p 169): Sightseeing buses run several times daily.* **By boat**: Potomac Spirit *makes two excursions daily from mid-Mar–Oct; schedule varies in winter months. Departures from Pier 4, at 5th and Water Sts. SE. ☎554-8000.*
Open Apr–Aug daily 8am–5pm, Nov–Feb daily 9am–4pm (5pm Mar, Sept, Oct). Admission: $7, seniors $6, children 6-11 $3, under 6 free. P ♿ ✗ ☎703-780-2000. A map of the estate is distributed at the ticket booth.

America's most visited historic house, Mount Vernon sits on a grassy, shaded slope overlooking the Potomac River. Here, George Washington, the private man, escaped the rigors of public office and enjoyed the life of a successful Virginia planter.

HISTORICAL NOTES

The Mount Vernon property came into the Washington family in 1674, through a land grant from Lord Culpeper to John Washington, George's great-grandfather. The land passed through several descendants before Augustine Washington bought it from his sister in 1726.

In 1735, Augustine moved his family, which included 3-year-old George, from Westmoreland County to the newly purchased Potomac property, then called Little Hunting Creek Plantation. The family spent four years here before again moving to a farm on the Rappahanock River. Records of the period, though sketchy, indicate that Augustine probably built the central section of the Mount Vernon mansion during that early stay.

In 1740, Augustine deeded the Potomac property to his son Lawrence, George's elder half-brother. Lawrence renamed his 2,500-acre estate Mount Vernon, after a British admiral he had come to respect while serving in the Royal Navy. In 1743, when George was 11, his father died, and he came increasingly under the influence of his brother Lawrence. Married to Anne Fairfax, the daughter of William Fairfax, one of Virginia's wealthiest landowners, Lawrence moved in prestigious circles. George, whose upbringing until that time had been more practical than formal, was exposed to genteel colonial society at Mount Vernon.

As a young man Washington spent several years surveying uncharted areas of western Virginia. When Lawrence died in 1752, the 20-year-old George took over the management of Mount Vernon, leasing it from Lawrence's widow. Though he eventually became the nation's greatest hero and its first President, Washington considered farming the "most delectable" occupation. "It is honorable," he wrote, "it is amusing, and, with judicious management, it is profitable."

The Gentleman Farmer – In 1759, after having distinguished himself in the French and Indian War, Washington married Martha Dandridge Custis, a widow with two children, John (Jacky) and Martha (Patsy). With his marriage to Martha, who owned some 15,000 acres in the Tidewater area near Williamsburg, Washington became one of Virginia's largest landowners. To accommodate his new family, Washington redecorated the simple 1 1/2-story farmhouse at Mount Vernon and added a full story to it. In 1761, his brother Lawrence's widow died, making Washington the legal owner of the 2,126-acre estate. Over the years, he increased Mount Vernon's holdings to more than 8,000 acres, divided into five independent but adjoining farms worked by some 200 slaves. Washington believed that farms should be self-sufficient, and to that end he constructed outbuildings for such activities as blacksmithing, shoemaking, weaving, and fish salting.

Washington enjoyed entertaining at Mount Vernon and was active in the social life of nearby Alexandria, where he owned a small town house *(see p 149)*. In 1773, he began an ambitious enlargement of Mount Vernon, adding 2-story additions to the north and south sides of the house, the piazza on the east, the cupola, and the curving colonnades. The project took almost 15 years to complete.

The Public Years – In 1774, Washington was elected one of Virginia's delegates to the First Continental Congress meeting in Philadelphia to protest British injustices. A year later, the Second Continental Congress unanimously voted him head of its military forces, a position that would keep him engaged in war and, for the most part, away from Mount Vernon, until 1783.

Returning home from the Revolution, Washington set about rejuvenating his farms and finances, which had suffered during the war. His fortunes were further drained by an endless stream of house guests, many of them uninvited strangers, who came to Mount Vernon to visit the famous general. For the next six years, Washington devoted himself to farming, experimenting with crop rotation and introducing new plant varieties. He took great pleasure in his wife's two grandchildren, Eleanor (Nelly), and George (Little Wash). The Washingtons brought the two orphans to live at Mount Vernon after their father, Martha's son John, was killed in the American Revolution.

From 1789 to 1797, Washington served as the country's first President. During his two terms, he managed to return to Mount Vernon on 15 occasions, sometimes for only a brief visit and at other times for several months. Refusing public demands that he serve a third term, Washington retired for a final time to Mount Vernon in March 1797.

The Final Years – The last two years of his life were spent once more as a planter. On December 14, 1799, having spent a snowy day overseeing work on the grounds, Washington contracted quinsy, an acute inflammation of the throat. Doctors administered gargles and bled him four times with leeches but to no avail. "I die hard," Washington said, "but I am not afraid to go." A day later, he passed away in his bed, at the age of 67. His body was interred in the old family burial vault overlooking the river. Two years later, Martha Washington was buried beside her husband.

After Washington – After Martha's death, the mansion passed to Bushrod Washington, a nephew and Supreme Court justice. He bequeathed it in turn to his nephew, John Augustine Washington. When the latter's son, John Augustine Jr., came into possession of Mount Vernon in 1850, the estate was no longer agriculturally productive. Realizing the need to preserve the home and without the means to do so himself, John Washington sought to sell it either to the Federal Government or to the state of Virginia, but neither was in a position to buy it. Instead, a woman in South Carolina, Ann Pamela Cunningham, began a grassroots effort to save the historic house. In 1853, she founded the Mount Vernon Ladies Association, the first historic preservation society operating on a national level in the US. Through a public campaign, the association raised the $200,000 necessary to buy the estate. The association has owned and operated Mount Vernon since 1858.

THE MANSION

The estate's main building is entered from the carriage side, not from the well-known river side, which has the broad, columned piazza that is Mount Vernon's hallmark. The Georgian farmhouse is set off by a rust-red roof and curved colonnades connecting two flanking wings. A weathervane bearing the dove of peace tops its distinctive cupola. The facade of the mansion is "rusticated board," a wood siding beveled and plastered with sand to resemble white stone.

First Floor – The large **dining room** or "new room" was the last addition to the house and is the most lavishly appointed. Here, as in the rest of the mansion, the decor is authentic to Washington's final years, and many of the furnishings belonged to him. The vertigris green that dominates the room was a color favored by Washington. It is set off by ornate white woodworking around the Palladian windows and in the ceiling trim. The 21 side chairs are part of an original set made for this room by John Aitken of Philadelphia, who also signed one of the mahogany sideboards. Washington characterized the ornate marble mantel, which was the gift of an Englishman, as "too elegant and costly...for my republican style of living."

The east-facing door in this room opens onto the piazza, which affords a pleasant **view** of the Potomac and the far Maryland shore. The center door in the piazza leads into the mansion's large central hall, whose pine paneling Washington had "grained" to resemble mahogany. Cross-ventilated from both the carriage and river sides, this hall was used for informal entertaining in the summer. On the south wall hangs a framed key to the Bastille prison in France, given to Washington by his French ally and friend, the Marquis de Lafayette.

Four rooms open off the hall. The small parlor used for informal family gatherings contains the harpsichord Washington ordered from England for his granddaughter Nelly, who became an accomplished musician. Formal entertaining was done in the west parlor, which is painted in Prussian blue, another favorite with Washington.

A fine example of colonial Virginia architecture, the room retains its original ceiling molding, door and mantel pediments, and wall paneling. A number of portraits of family members hang here. The small dining room is appointed with richly glazed vertigris green walls and mahogany furnishings. Over the mantle is an original **engraving** of the Washington family by Edward Savage. A bedroom opens off this room.

Second floor – A heavy "grained" staircase leads to five bedrooms off a central hall. The rooms have worn broad-planked floors and are furnished pleasantly but simply with four-poster beds. These chambers quartered so many guests that Washington once called his home "a well resorted tavern, as scarcely any strangers who are going from north to south, or from south to north, do not spend a day or two at it."

Mount Vernon

The **master bedchamber** occupies a more private space in the south section. Also simply furnished, this room contains the mahogany four-poster bed in which Washington died. The bed chamber also functioned as Martha Washington's office and contains the late 18C French desk from which she dispensed her duties as an "old-fashioned Virginia house-keeper," as she called herself.

A narrow back staircase in this wing leads to Washington's own first-floor study. This large room contains many pieces intimately associated with him, including his desk and his presidential desk chair, which he brought back to Mount Vernon with him, and a terrestrial globe commissioned from a London manufacturer.

The two wings attached to the mansion by curving colonnades housed a kitchen *(south)* and quarters for white servants *(north)*.

THE ESTATE

To locate the various outbuildings and points of interest throughout the estate, consult the map distributed at the ticket booth.

Outbuildings – Twelve small dependencies are scattered along the lanes leading from both sides of the house. These structures re-create the operations of a self-sufficient estate, from the curing, spinning, and laundry houses to the living quarters for overseers and slaves.

The stable at the south edge of the lower garden houses a fine example of an 18C coach. A small **museum**, built in 1928 to house Washington memorabilia, lies at the east edge of the upper garden. Along with jewelry, china, swords, and other personal items, it displays a **bust of General Washington** executed at Mount Vernon by the French sculptor, Jean Antoine Houdon.

In the museum annex *(located in the greenhouse)*, a **model** of the mansion depicts the various stages of its evolution. Other exhibits explain the archaeological digs ongoing at the estate.

Grounds – As an admiring 18C European visitor observed, Mount Vernon's grounds conform "to the best samples of the grand old homesteads of England." Today, the estate comprises 30 acres of landscaped gardens and forests. The carriage entrance to the house is fronted by a sweeping bowling green, bordered by stately trees. Several of the larger tulip poplars here were planted by Washington himself. On the river side of the house, a deer park slopes to the Potomac.

The upper garden on the north side of the bowling green is an ornamental flower garden, dominated by large boxwood hedges that date from Washington's day. The formal parterres are planted with annuals and perennials commonly found in 18C gardens. An imposing brick greenhouse, a reconstruction, forms the garden's north side. Opposite the upper garden, south of the bowling green, is the lower, or kitchen, garden where a variety of fruits, berries, and vegetables are grown.

Two different burial sites lie beyond the stables. George and Martha Washington were originally buried in the old family vault, a brick-fronted underground crypt. In the years following Washington's death, Congress proposed enshrining his remains in a crypt on the ground level of the CAPITOL. However, after years of complications and delays, his descendants decided against moving his remains. In 1831, they erected the present **tomb** of George and Martha Washington, building it of "Brick and upon a larger Scale," according to the wishes expressed in Washington's will. Beyond an iron grille, the couple's marble sarcophagi are visible within an open vault. Interred in the walls of the vault are 27 other family members. In front of the tomb are two marble obelisks in memory of Bushrod and John Augustine Washington, the 19C proprietors of Mount Vernon.

A path leads from the tomb to a shaded grove where a small monument memorializes the slaves buried in unmarked graves at Mount Vernon.

Located near the Wharf is the estate's most recent exhibit, a pioneer farm that features, among other activities, demonstrations of 18C animal husbandry, crop cultivation, brickmaking, and timber transformation.

★ WOODLAWN PLANTATION

Map p 145

time: 1 hour

Access – *Woodlawn is located 19 miles south of Washington.* **By car**: *Leave Washington by the 14th St. Bridge, take exit 11A (for National Airport) and continue south on the George Washington Memorial Parkway to Mount Vernon. Continue 3 miles west on Rte 235 and follow the signs to Woodlawn. Average round-trip driving time from Downtown: 1 1/4 hours.* **By public transportation**: *Take Metro to Huntington Station and transfer to a 9A (Fort Belvoir) bus to Woodlawn.*
Visit by guided tour (30min) only Feb–Dec daily 9:30am–4:30pm (4pm Sat and Sun only in Jan); closed Jan 1, Thanksgiving Day, Dec 25. Admission: $5, seniors and students $3.50, children under 5 free (discounted combination ticket for Woodlawn and Pope-Leighey House—p 156: $8, seniors and students $6). P ♿ ☎703-780-4000.

This gracious Georgian estate reflects the refinement of its original owners, Lawrence Lewis and Nelly Custis Lewis. Favored relatives of George Washington whose own MOUNT VERNON lies only three miles away, the Lewises brought to their home many of the furnishings and memorabilia of the original Washington estate.

A Wedding Gift – In 1797, Lawrence Lewis, Washington's nephew, came to Mount Vernon to serve as his uncle's personal secretary. There he met **Eleanor Parke** (Nelly) **Custis** *(see table p 117)*, the granddaughter George and Martha Washington had raised from early childhood. Well-educated, talented, and beautiful, Nelly had grown up in the influential society surrounding the Washingtons. Benjamin H. Latrobe, the prominent architect, said of her that she embodied more perfection "than I have ever seen before or conceived consistent with mortality." In 1799, after a quiet courtship, Nelly married Lawrence Lewis on February 22, Washington's birthday, at Mount Vernon.

Washington ceded a 2,000-acre tract west of Mount Vernon to the Lewises and urged them to begin building a home. He also deeded them a nearby mill and distillery, because, as he advised Lawrence, "a young man should have objects of employment. Idleness is disreputable." Washington died less than a year after the wedding, but the young couple, following his advice, began building. In 1802, Martha Washington died, and the Lewises moved into the completed north wing of the house.

Woodlawn Plantation was praised by visitors as a "lovely place," with "much to delight all who have a taste for the comforts and elegancies of life." Though the Lewises pursued a lifestyle they felt befitted their Washington heritage, they did so with some difficulty. The estate lands were never very productive, and the couple grappled with financial problems throughout their lives. In 1839, Lawrence, then in his early seventies, died, and Nelly went to live first with her son Lawrence at Audley Plantation in Clark County, and later with her daughter Parke in New Orleans.

An Era Ends – In 1846, the family offered Woodlawn at public sale. The land was purchased by a group of Quaker businessmen, who divided it into separate farms for a Quaker community. Four years later, the house itself was bought by John and Rachel Mason. It passed through a succession of private owners, including a playwright and a senator, all of whom modified and embellished the original structure. In 1949, a locally formed group, the Woodlawn Public Foundation, purchased the house, and in 1957, the estate became the property of the National Trust for Historic Preservation.

Mansion – The late Georgian style of Woodlawn may have been more the choice of Lawrence Lewis than that of prominent architect Dr William Thornton, who was involved in the construction of the house. Woodlawn bears a striking resemblance to Kenmore, Lewis's boyhood home located farther south in Fredericksburg, Virginia. Pleasingly proportioned, the structure has a 2-story central core with symmetrical 1-story wings that are connected to the main house by hyphens. From the simple portico over the entrance on the river side, the tops of several trees situated on the bowling green at Mount Vernon can be seen.

Woodlawn Plantation-west front

National Trust for Historic Preservation

Decorated as it might have been during the Lewises' lifetime, this house contains many of the furnishings that belonged to the family, including several that were brought from Mount Vernon. Opening off the center hall are a formal drawing room and family sitting room. Adept musicians, Nelly and her daughters often gave informal performances on the harp and piano that still dominate the drawing room. The firescreen, which Nelly worked, features a floral pattern popular in the first half of the 19C.

In the family sitting room, a lithograph depicts the French Marquis de Lafayette on a visit to Woodlawn in 1824. Off the sitting room, the master bedroom holds personal items of the Lewises. On a needlework frame by the fireplace is the unfinished piece Nelly was working on at the time of her death.

The 1-story hyphens connected to the center house were kitchen and work areas in the Lewises' day. They now hold a reception room *(south side)* and a dining room *(north side)*, which were added at the turn of the century. The two wings connected to the hyphens are used as administrative offices.

The second floor contains four bedrooms and a sewing room which open off a central hall.

The **grounds** are graced with large trees and boxwoods. The parterred garden is noted for its roses.

POPE-LEIGHEY HOUSE

On the grounds of Woodlawn, below the parking lot. Visit by guided tour (30min) only on the half hour. Open Mar–Dec daily 9:30am–4:30pm, the rest of the year Sat and Sun only 9:30am–4pm; closed Jan 1, Thanksgiving Day, Dec 25. Admission: $4, seniors and students $3, children under 5 free (discounted combination ticket for this house and Woodlawn available at Woodlawn mansion). ☎*703-780-4000.*

This small L-shaped house in a wooded setting is the only publically accessible example of what this century's most eminent American-born architect, **Frank Lloyd Wright** (1867-1959), called his "Usonian" architecture—functional, simply designed homes affordable to middle-class Americans. Built in 1941 for Loren Pope, a journalist in nearby Falls Church, Virginia, the 1,200sq ft, 5-room house cost roughly $7,000. The Leigheys bought the house from the Popes five years later. When it was threatened with demolition because of highway construction in 1964, Mrs Leighey donated it to the National Trust, who moved it to its current site.

The house contains the furniture that Wright designed for it and is built only of cypress, brick, glass, and concrete, following the Wright tenet to use as few materials as possible. Other Wright hallmarks—flowing space, strong horizontal lines, and organic unity—are also characteristic of the house.

★ GUNSTON HALL

Map p 145

time: 1 1/2 hours

Access – *Gunston Hall is located 22 miles south of Washington.* **By car:** *Leave Washington by the 14th St. Bridge and continue south on Rte 395 (I-95). Take exit 163, then follow the signs for roughly 8 miles to Gunston Hall. From* MOUNT VERNON *or* WOODLAWN, *continue south on US-1 and follow the signs. Average round-trip driving time from Downtown: 1 1/2 hours.*

Visit of the mansion by guided tour (30min) only daily 9:30am–5pm; closed Jan 1, Thanksgiving Day, Dec 25. Admission: $5, seniors $4, students $1.50, children under 6 free. ♿ *(limited)* ☎*703-550-9220.*

Brochures with map of the estate are available in the visitor center in the brick building housing the orientation center.

This fine colonial Georgian estate reflects the style and substance of plantation life favored by wealthy 18C Virginia planters. The gracious manor house and grounds were the home of **George Mason** (1725-1792), a respected thinker whose writings influenced the course of the Revolution and the development of the young Republic.

HISTORICAL NOTES

The Forgotten Sage – Now a rather obscure patriot, George Mason drafted many documents critical to the birth of the US. During the Revolutionary period, he wrote a number of pivotal statements delineating the colonists' rights, including the Fairfax Resolves (1774) and the Virginia **Declaration of Rights** (May 1776). The latter contained the statement "That all men are by nature equally free and independent and have certain inherent rights...namely, the enjoyment of life and liberty, with the means of acquiring and possessing property, and pursuing and obtaining happiness...." This wording was echoed by Jefferson, Mason's friend and protégé, in his writing of the Declaration of Independence (July 1776). It was also employed by other colonies in their own declarations, and, in 1789, by the French in their Declaration of the Rights of Man.

Mason strenuously opposed the original Constitution, because it had no Bill of Rights and did not call for the immediate abolition of the slave trade. His opposition was influential in the subsequent adoption in 1791 of the first ten amendments to the Constitution, commonly known as the Bill of Rights.

The Squire of Gunston Hall – Born in 1725 and descended from British gentry, George Mason was a fourth generation Virginian whose family possessed considerable land-holdings along the Potomac. When Mason was ten, his father died, and as eldest son, George inherited the family property. He received his education from tutors and the extensive law library of his uncle and guardian, John Mercer. In 1755, he began constructing his own home, Gunston Hall, naming it after other family estates in America and England. He situated it on the Virginia shoreline about a mile above the Potomac and not far from the Washington family estate of MOUNT VERNON. As young men, Mason and George Washington developed a friendship and mutual respect. Over the years, they frequently exchanged views on horticulture, politics, and the direction the new nation should take.

Mason was a prominent local figure, serving as a justice of Fairfax County, a member of the Alexandria Board of Trustees, and a founder of the Fairfax militia company. Though he also served as a member of the Virginia House of Burgesses and a delegate to the Constitutional Convention of 1787, he had a dislike of politics and preferred to exercise his influence quietly, through writing and private conversations. He also felt a great obligation to his nine children, who had been left motherless when Ann Mason died in 1773. Consequently, he did not often venture far from Gunston Hall.

Mason died at his home in 1792, just as the young Republic was being formulated. Gunston Hall remained in the family until 1866. After passing through a succession of owners, it was purchased in 1912 by Mr and Mrs Louis Hertle, who restored it and ultimately deeded it to the Commonwealth of Virginia to be administered by the National Society of the Colonial Dames of America *(see p 111)*.

VISIT

The brick building where tickets are purchased houses a small **museum** and **orientation center** with dioramas, exhibits, and a film explaining Mason's contributions and illustrating his life at Gunston Hall. Family and period memorabilia are also on display.

Mansion – Mason is presumed to have designed the exterior of his Georgian manor house, with its large symmetrical chimneys and dormer windows. The unembellished brick facade is offset with quoins, or corner stones, of the local buff-colored Aquia sandstone.

The carriage entrance features a pedimented portico with a fanlight above the door. The river entrance portico is a semi-octagonal porch with graceful ogee arches.

Bird's-eye view of Gunston Hall

Virginia Division of Tourism

The interior of the house contains some noteworthy mid-18C carved **woodwork★**. When George Mason was planning his house, he asked his brother Thomson, then studying law in England, to procure the services of an English craftsman for him. **William Buckland**, a carpenter-joiner, was engaged under an indenture and arrived in Virginia in 1755. Since Gunston Hall was Buckland's first commission, he took great pains to embellish it with a variety of woodworking styles. The present house contains a combination of original and re-created woodwork. The house is decorated with period furnishings, a few of which, such as the portraits, belonged to the Mason family.

In the central hall connecting the carriage and river entrances, Buckland used pilasters, chair railing and a double arch offset with a pinecone finial. The Masons' bedroom opens off the left of the hall, and directly across from it is the strikingly yellow **Chinese Dining Room**, the only surviving room in America featuring the scalloped Chinoiserie woodworking of the colonial period. Beyond the dining room, the formal parlor is embellished with intricate English Palladian style woodworking. Across the hall from this room is an informal room that was used as Mason's study and as a family dining room and sitting room. A wide wooden staircase in the center hall leads to seven bedrooms on the upper floor.

Grounds – The fenced courtyard adjacent to the north side of the house encloses several reconstructed dependencies. Beyond the house on the south side is a small frame schoolhouse, a reconstruction of the one in which the Mason children were tutored. A gravel path continues from the schoolhouse, connecting to an avenue of cedars that leads to the brick-walled family **graveyard**, where 16 family members are buried. The two raised sarcophagi contain the remains of George Mason and his wife, Ann.

A double row of magnolias and cedars lines Magnolia Avenue, the carriage approach to the house. On the river side, an impressive boxwood allée leads through **formal gardens** to an overlook above a garden terrace. In Mason's day, the now-forested fields sloping to the river were cleared for planting and the Potomac was visible from here. A mile-long walk through a wooded area leads to the river.

National Museum of American History – L. Minor/Smithsonian Institution

Practical Information

To help you locate addresses appearing in the Practical Information section, grid coordinates (e.g., H7, E2) referring to Michelin Street Map 48 of Central Washington DC are shown for many of the facilities, venues, public buldings, and memorials listed.

CALENDAR OF EVENTS

This calendar is subject to change. For up-to-date information, consult the quarterly published Calendar of Events brochures available from the Washington DC Convention and Visitors Association ☎789-7000. For events in Alexandria VA ☎703-838-4200 or 703-838-5005 (recorded). Unless otherwise specified, all telephone numbers shown are in the 202 calling area.

Date	Event/*Location*	☎
January		
1st Tue	**Congress convenes**, *Capitol*	
late	**Lee Birthdays Celebration**	
	Arlington House, Arlington National Cemetery (p 116)	703-557-0613
	Lee-Fendall House, Old Town Alexandria (p 150)	703-548-1789
	Robert E. Lee's Boyhood Home, Old Town Alexandria (p 149)	703-548-8454
	Chinese New Year Festival *Chinatown, H St. between 5th and 8th Sts.*	724-4091
Jan–Apr	**US Army Band Concert Series** *Bruckner Hall, Fort Myer, Arlington*	703-696-3399
February		
all month	**Black History Month** *(various locations throughout the city)*	
12	**Abraham Lincoln's Birthday**, *Lincoln Memorial*	619-7222
mid	**Revolutionary War Encampment** *Fort Ward Park, Alexandria*	703-838-4200
	Washington Boat Show, *Washington Convention Center*	789-1600
3rd Mon	**George Washington's Birthday Parade** *Old Town Alexandria*	703-838-4200
March		
early	**US Army Band Anniversary Concert**, *Kennedy Center*	703-696-3399
mid	**St Patrick's Day Parade**, *Downtown, Old Town Alexandria*	301-530-3917 703-838-4200
Mar–Apr	**Spring Flower Show**, *US Botanic Garden*	226-4082
	National Cherry Blossom Festival, *Tidal Basin*	737-2599
Easter Sun	**Easter Sunrise Service**, *Arlington National Cemetery*	475-0856
Easter Mon	**Easter Egg Roll**, *White House (p 77)*	456-2200
April		
all month	**Imagination Celebration**, *Kennedy Center*	416-8000
13	**Thomas Jefferson's Birthday**, *Jefferson Memorial*	619-7222
mid	**Spring Garden Tours**, *White House (p 77)*	456-2200
	Filmfest DC, *various theaters throughout the city*	727-2396
23	**Shakespeare's Birthday**, *Folger Shakespeare Library*	544-7077
late	**Georgetown House Tour**, *Georgetown*	338-1796
	Home and Garden Tour, *Old Town Alexandria*	703-838-4200
	George Washington Parkway Classic *George Washington Memorial Parkway*	703-549-4447
May		
early	**Georgetown Garden Tour**, *Georgetown*	333-4953
	Gross National Parade, *Georgetown*	686-3215
mid	**Goodwill Embassy Tour**, *Embassy Row (p 128)*	636-4225
late	**Kemper Open Pro-Ams Golf Tournament**, *area golf courses*	301-469-3737
30	**Memorial Day Weekend Concert**, *Capitol (west lawn)*	619-7222
31	**Memorial Day Jazz Festival**, *Oronoco Bay Park, Alexandria*	703-838-4844
all summer	**Ethnic festivals**, *Market Square, Old Town Alexandria*	703-838-4844

US Military Band Summer Concerts are held at 8pm from **Memorial Day to Labor Day**. For information contact: US Army Band ☎703-696-3399; US Marine Band ☎433-4011; US Navy Band ☎433-2525; US Air Force Band ☎767-5658.

Mon	Navy Band	Capitol (east side)
Tue	Army Band	Sylvan Theatre, Mall
	Air Force Band	Capitol (east side)
	Navy Band	Navy Memorial Plaza
	Marine Corps Sunset Parade	Marine Corps War Memorial
Wed	Marine Band	Capitol (east side)
Thur	Navy Band	Sylvan Theatre
Fri	Army Band	Capitol
	Air Force Band	Sylvan Theatre
Sat	Bands rotate	Navy Memorial Plaza
Sun	Marine Band	Sylvan Theatre

June		
early	**Red Cross Waterfront Festival**, *Old Town Alexandria*	703-549-8300
	Dupont-Kalorama Museum Walk *(p 125)* *Dupont-Kalorama neighborhood*	667-0441
Jun–Aug	**Summer Terrace Show**, *US Botanic Garden*	226-4082

July		
early	**Festival of American Folklife**, *Mall (p 42)*	357-2700
	DC Jazz Festival, *Freedom Plaza*	783-0360
	Custis-Fitzhugh Wedding *Robert E. Lee's Boyhood Home, Old Town Alexandria*	703-548-8454
4	**National Independence Day Celebrations** *Downtown, Capitol, Mall*	619-7222
14	**Bastille Day Waiters' Race**, *20th St. & Pennsylvania Ave.*	452-1132
	USA-Alexandria Birthday Celebration *Jones Point Park, Alexandria*	703-838-4844
late	**Latin-American Festival**, *Mall*	269-0101
	Virginia Scottish Games, *Alexandria*	703-838-5005
Jul–Aug	**Twilight Tattoo Services** (military band concerts) *Ellipse*	703-696-3570

August		
mid	**US Army Band's "1812 Overture"** *Sylvan Theatre, Mall*	703-696-3399
	Civil War Living History Day *Fort Ward Museum & Historic Site, Alexandria*	703-838-4848

September		
1st Sun	**Labor Day Weekend Concert**, *Capitol (west lawn)*	619-7222
early	**18C Fair**, *Market Square, Old Town Alexandria*	703-838-4242
mid	**Adams Morgan Day** *Adams Morgan (Columbia Rd. & 18th St. NW)*	322-3292
17	**Constitution Day Commemoration**, *National Archives*	501-5215
late	**Tour of Homes**, *Old Town Alexandria*	703-838-4200
	Rock Creek Park Day, *Rock Creek Park*	426-6832
	International Children's Festival *Wolf Trap Farm Park (p 171)*	703-642-0862
	Washington Cathedral Open House	537-6200

October		
mid	**Fall Garden Tours**, *White House (p 77)*	456-2200
	Columbus Day Ceremonies, *Columbus Memorial Plaza*	301-434-2332
end	**Washington International Horse Show** *USAir Arena, Landover MD*	301-840-0281
Oct–Dec	**US Army Band Fall Concert Series** *Bruckner Hall, Fort Myer, Arlington*	703-696-3399

November		
early	**Marine Corps Marathon** *Marine Corps War Memorial, Downtown and Northern VA*	703-690-3431
mid	**Veterans Day Ceremonies**, *Arlington National Cemetery, Vietnam Veterans Memorial*	475-0843 619-7222
	Historic Alexandria Antiques Show *Old Colony Inn, Old Town Alexandria*	703-838-4554

December		
1st Sat	**Scottish Christmas Walk**, *Old Town Alexandria*	703-838-4200
early	**Woodlawn Plantation Christmas** *(p 155)*	703-780-4000
	People's Christmas Tree Lighting, *Capitol*	224-3069
	National Christmas Tree Lighting, *Ellipse*	619-7222
	Carol Singing, *Wolf Trap Farm Park (p 171)*	433-4011
mid	**Christmas Candlelight Tours**, *Old Town Alexandria*	703-838-4200
end	**Christmas Candlelight Tours**, *White House (p 77)*	456-2200
Dec–Jan	**Christmas Poinsettia Show**, *US Botanic Garden*	226-4082

DC Committee to Promote Washington

Cherry Blossom Festival Parade

PLANNING YOUR TRIP

When to Visit – **Spring** is Washington's peak tourist season. The mild temperatures and the blossoming of the famous cherry trees *(late March or early April)* attract the greater part of the capital's 19-20 million annual visitors. Hotel reservations should be made well in advance and long lines are to be expected at the main sights.
The hot and humid **summer** weather can make touring uncomfortable and tiring, but the season's long days, extended operating hours for Smithsonian sights, and numerous outdoor events are a major draw.
Fall is a very pleasant season to visit Washington. Temperatures are moderate, the summer crowds have thinned out, and the often spectacular display of foliage and autumn blooms is an added attraction.
Winter months are unpredictable, with temperatures ranging from the high 40°s F to well below freezing. Severe snowstorms are infrequent in Washington.
As the mean monthly rainfall (approximately 3 inches) is uniform throughout the year, rainwear is recommended for all seasons. It is also advisable to carry a light-weight jacket in summer months since most buildings are chilly due to air-conditioning.

Mean Temperatures

	January	February	March	April	May	June
High	43°F/6°C	46°F/8°C	55°F/13°C	67°F/19°C	76°F/24°C	84°F/29°C
Low	28°F/-2°C	29°F/-2°C	37°F/3°C	46°F/8°C	56°F/13°C	65°F/18°C
	July	**August**	**September**	**October**	**November**	**December**
High	88°F/31°C	86°F/30°C	80°F/27°C	69°F/21°C	58°F/14°C	46°F/8°C
Low	70°F/21°C	69°F/21°C	62°F/17°C	50°F/10°C	40°F/4°C	31°F/-1°C

Public Holidays – Most banks, government offices, public buildings, and schools are closed on the following holidays:

New Year's Day	January 1
Martin Luther King's Birthday	3rd Monday in January
Presidents' Day	3rd Monday in February
Memorial Day	Last Monday in May
Independence Day	July 4
Labor Day	1st Monday in September
Columbus Day	Monday nearest October 12
Veterans Day	2nd Monday in November
Thanksgiving	4th Thursday in November
Christmas	December 25

Accommodations – The Washington area offers a wide range of accommodations from elegant Downtown hotels and modern hotel chains, to Bed & Breakfasts and campgrounds.
Hotel rates generally range from $55 to $200, rates being highest in spring and fall. Most hotels offer special rates for business travelers and families, and weekend rates are available throughout the year. Advance reservation is recommended throughout the year and especially in spring. Free reservation services are provided by Washington DC Accommodations, 1534 U St. NW, Washington DC 20009 ☎289-2220 or 800-554-2220 and by Capitol Reservations ☎800-VISIT-DC. The area has an increasing number of **Bed & Breakfast** accommodations with rates from $45 to $100. For information contact: Bed & Breakfast Accommodations Ltd., PO Box 12011, Washington DC 20005 ☎328-3510, or Bed & Breakfast League/Sweet Dreams and Toast, PO Box 9490, Washington DC 20016 ☎363-7767 (booking fee).
Low-cost accommodations are available at the **Washington International Youth Hostel**, 1009 11th St. NW ☎737-2333 (250 beds; open year-round) or at various campgrounds in the surrounding area with access to subway and trains, some of which offer free shuttle bus service to Washington. For information: **Capitol KOA Campground**, 768 Cecil Ave., Millersville MD 21108 ☎410-923-2771. AAA also has approved campground listings.

Advance Reservation for Sights – For guided tours of certain Washington sights (e.g., DIPLOMATIC RECEPTION ROOMS, HILLWOOD MUSEUM) advance reservation is highly recommended. Before leaving, consult the admission information preceding the sight descriptions in this guide for specific details on the attractions you intend to visit.
Tickets for **congressional visits** (special tours of some of the more popular sights, such as the WHITE HOUSE, CAPITOL, FBI, BUREAU OF ENGRAVING AND PRINTING) may be obtained by writing to your senators or representative *(see below)*. As each member of Congress is allotted a limited number of tickets, requests should be made several months in advance. These visits, which are generally scheduled early in the morning, are sometimes more extensive than the standard tours and, best of all, you avoid the long lines.
It is also wise to make reservations in advance for any of the special **annual tours** of the WHITE HOUSE, selected embassies *(see p 128)*, and Georgetown houses and gardens *(see p 106)*.

Visiting Your Senators or Representative – If you would like to meet the elected officials who represent you in Congress, you should write two to three months in advance to request an appointment. Call the Capitol ☎224-3121 or write:

Senator (name)	Representative (name)
Senate Office Building	House Office Building
Washington DC 20510	Washington DC 20515

GETTING THERE

A visa and valid passport are required for most **foreign visitors**. It is advisable to contact the US embassy or consulate in your country to inquire about entry formalities.

By Air – Washington is served by three major airports *(see map p 13)*.

Washington National Airport (DCA) – Domestic and commuter flights. Location: across the Potomac in Virginia 4 1/2 miles south of Downtown. ☎703-419-8000.

Access to DC from DCA:
- Metro subway system: Blue and Yellow lines.
- Washington Flyer shuttle: daily 6:25am–9:25pm every half hour between airport and the Downtown terminal, 1517 K St. NW (with stops at major hotels); one-way fare $8. ☎703-685-1400.
- Taxi: $10-15

Dulles International Airport (IAD) – Domestic commuter and international flights. Location: Loudoun County VA, 26 miles west of Downtown. ☎703-419-8000.

Access to DC from IAD:
- Airport–Metro shuttle between Dulles and West Falls Church Metro station (Orange line): 6am–10:30pm (7:30am Sat and Sun) every half hour; one-way fare $8. Time: 22 min. ☎703-685–1400.
- Washington Flyer shuttle: daily 5:20am–10:20pm every half hour between airport and the Downtown terminal, 1517 K St. NW (with stops at major hotels); one-way fare $16. Time: approx. 1 hour. ☎703-685-1400.
- Taxi: over $40.

Washington Flyer shuttle between National and Dulles Airports (and vice versa): daily 6am–11pm every hour; one-way fare $16. Time: 3/4 hour. ☎703-685-1400.

Baltimore-Washington International Airport (BWI) – Domestic, commuter, and some international flights. Location: 28 miles north of Washington and 8 miles south of Baltimore. ☎301-261-1000.

Access to DC from BWI:
- Amtrak to Union Station ☎800-USA-RAIL.
- Airport Connection shuttle: 7am–11pm every 1 1/2 hours (7:30am–8pm Sat and holidays every 2 1/2 hours) between airport and Capitol Hilton at 16th & K Sts. NW; one-way fare $14. ☎301-261-1091.

Airlines

Airline		Phone
Aeroflot		800-995-5555
Air France		800-237-2747
Air Jamaica		800-523-5585
All Nippon Airways		800-235-9262
American		800-433-7300
British Airways		800-247-9297
Continental	domestic	800-525-0280
	international	800-231-0856
Delta		800-221-1212
KLM		800-374-7747
Lufthansa		800-654-3880
Mexicana		800-531-7921
Midwest		800-621-5700
Midwest Express		800-452-2022
Northwest	domestic	800-225-2525
	international	800-447-4747
Saudi Arabian Air		800-472-8342
Swiss Air		800-221-4750
TWA	domestic	800-221-2000
	international	800-892-4141
USAir		800-428-4322
United		800-241-6522

By Train – Renovated UNION STATION is Washington's only railroad station. Located near Capitol Hill at Massachusetts and Delaware Aves. NE, the station is accessible by Metrorail (Red line). Amtrak provides direct daily service between the nation's capital and major destinations throughout the Northeast (from DC to Boston via Philadelphia and New York), Midwest, and South.

Washington, DC Convention & Visitors Assoc.

Union Station - interior

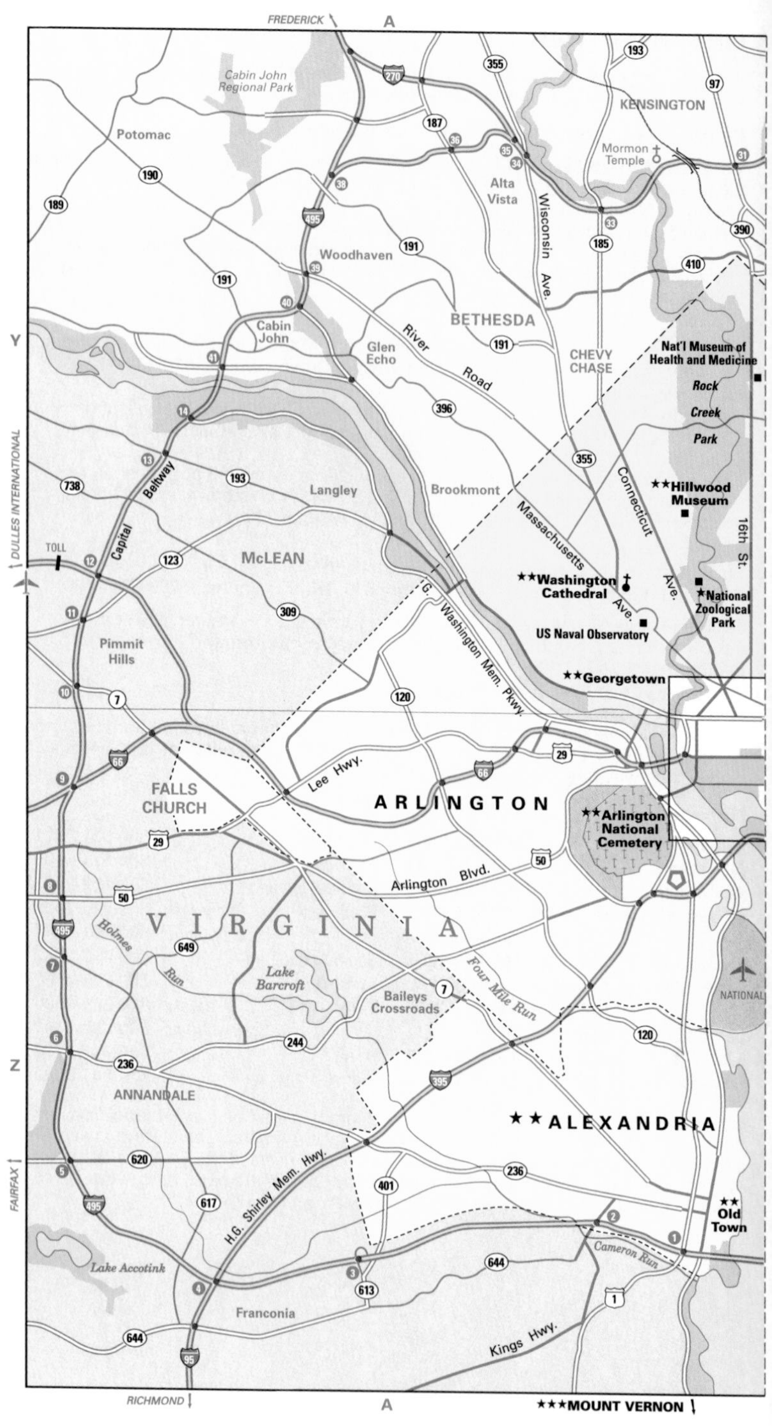

Some average rail travel times from DC:

Philadelphia .... 1 1/2 hours
New York .... 3 hours
Boston .... 8 hours

Overnight rail service from DC to:

Montreal .... 18 1/2 hours
Chicago .... 20 hours
Atlanta .... 13 1/2 hours
Miami .... 22 hours

For information and schedules ☎800-USA-RAIL; *for Metroliner service* ☎800-523-8720.

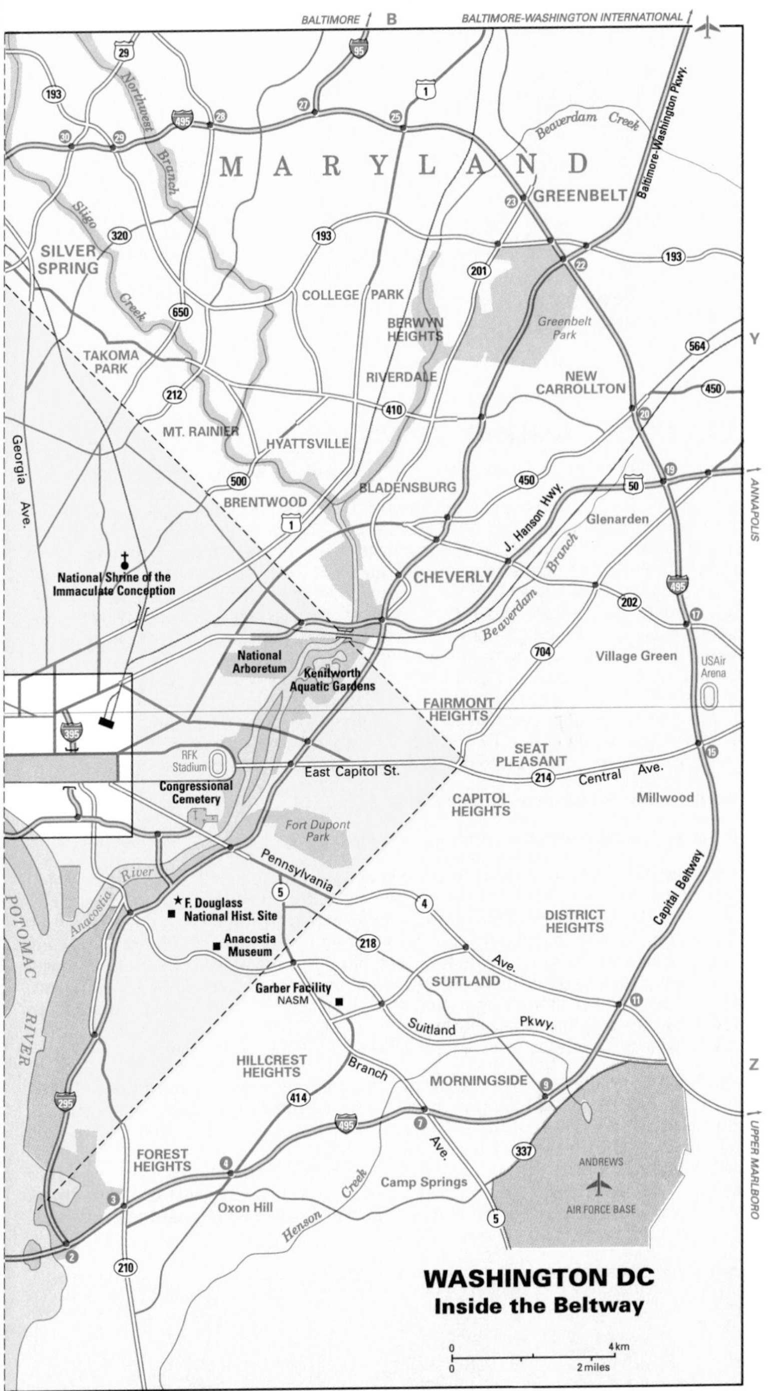

By Bus – Greyhound operates from the main bus terminal located at 1005 1st St. NE, a short walk from UNION STATION. Fares and schedules: ☎289-5155 or 800-231-2222.

By Car – *See map above.* Washington is situated at the crossroads of several major interstate routes: I-95 (north–south), I-66 (east), US-50 (west), I-270 (north–west). These and other roads leading to the capital connect with the Beltway (I-495) that encircles the city at a distance of about 12 miles from the center.

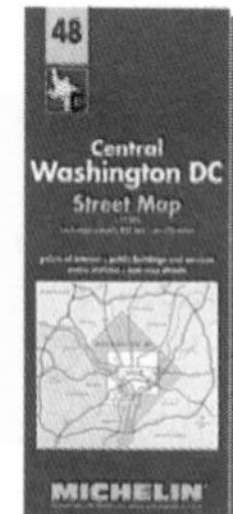

To help you locate addresses appearing in the Practical Information section, grid coordinates (e.g., H7, E2) referring to Michelin Street Map 48 of Central Washington DC are shown for many of the facilities, venues, public buildings, and memorials listed.

GETTING AROUND TOWN

For a description of the DC street system and a key to finding addresses see p 168.

On Foot – Washington is a city for walkers. The principal sights, government buildings, and entertainment and business centers are concentrated in the Northwest quadrant and on Capitol Hill. The logical street layout, the abundant greenery, and the well-manicured appearance of this quadrant make orientation easy and walking a pleasure. The city's most heavily visited areas, such as the Mall, Capitol Hill, and Georgetown, where parking is limited, are best visited on foot. However, most visitors will find walking uncomfortable and tiring during the summer months, when temperatures and humidity are high.
During rush hour (7–9:30am and 4–6:30pm) when no street parking is allowed, visitors should be aware of fast-moving vehicles in traffic lanes close to the sidewalks. Strict adherence to pedestrian walking signs is expected. Violators may be fined $10 for crossing in the middle of the block rather than at corners.
It is advisable to remain in the Northwest quadrant of the city after nightfall.

Tourmobile Sightseeing – *See p 169.*

Metro – *See Metro map and description pp 190-191.*

City Buses – The public bus system is known as **Metrobus**. Bus stops are indicated by red, white, and blue signs. The buses display the route number and final destination above the windshield. Fares are determined by the time of day and length of trip; fares are higher during rush hour. Exact fare is required. If more than one bus is required to reach a destination, transfers are free at time of ticket purchase. If a bus trip follows a ride on the Metro, transfers for the bus are free providing you collect the transfer at the originating station (machines distributing transfers are located at the escalators descending to rail level). There is no free transfer from the bus to Metro. To request a schedule ☎637-7000 (TDD ☎638-3780).

Taxis – Within the District of Columbia, you can hail a taxi on the street or at taxi stands at hotels and transportation terminals. Numerous taxi companies operate under the supervision of the DC Taxicab Commission (☎767-8380). When the "TAXI" sign is lit, the vehicle is available for hire.
DC taxis do not have meters; instead, the fare is calculated according to a **zone system**. The District is divided into five zones (each with subzones) that approximate concentric circles radiating from the Capitol with Zone 1 being closest to the Capitol.

Washington, DC Convention & Visitors Association

Bird's-eye view of central Washington

A ride within one zone or sub-zone is $3.20. (A reduced fare of $2.80 applies for travel only within a Zone 1 sub-zone, of which there are four.) The fare increases to $4.40 if crossing into a second zone or sub-zone, $5.50 if crossing into a third zone or sub-zone, etc. as described in the chart below:

Charge for Number of Zones/Sub-Zones Traveled

1 = $3.20	**3** = $5.50	**5** = $7.60	**7** = $9.80
2 = $4.40	**4** = $6.60	**6** = $8.70	**8** = $10.80

A ride from Zone 1 into another zone is the same as traveling from any other zone. A **zone map** with charges is displayed in the taxi, along with a list of passenger rights. It is not unusual for the driver to request payment before setting out or to pick up another passenger en route. However, each passenger pays full fare. If riding as a group, the first passenger pays full fare; all others pay $1.25 each.
If a rider enters the taxi during the evening rush hour (4–6:30pm), there is an additional $1 surcharge. A rider can expect **additional charges** for radio-dispatched telephone requests, multiple stops, waiting time, more than one piece of luggage, special assistance, or service during official snow emergencies.
If traveling to the suburbs from the District, fares are based on mileage ($2 for the first 1/2 mile and $0.70 for each additional 1/2 mile).

Private Vehicles – Given the efficiency of the public transportation system, the availability of taxis, and the ease with which the main sights can be reached on foot, a car is by no means indispensable to the visitor to Washington. When considering whether to drive in Washington, bear in mind that street parking is limited and rush-hour traffic jams are frequent. If you are staying outside the District, consider leaving your car at the parking facilities of one of the fringe Metro stations *(shown on Metro map p 191)* and riding the Metro into the city (it is advisable to arrive early on week-days, as these lots are often filled with commuters' vehicles). For excursions outside the city, a vehicle is recommended.

Car Rentals – Rental cars are available for persons 25 years of age and older (21 for a few rental car companies) with a major credit card and a valid driver's license. The average daily rate for a compact ranges from $38 to $46 with unlimited free miles; weekend rates are approximately 30–40% less. Weekly rates range from $158 to $231 with unlimited free mileage. Prices are higher during summer and special events.

Alamo	2780 Jefferson Davis Hwy., Arlington	800-327-9633
Avis	Union Station	800-331-1212
Budget	4727 Wisconsin Ave. NW	800-527-0700
Hertz	901 11th St. NW	800-654-3131
National	Union Station	800-227-7368

Most of the companies above have counters at the airports serving the metropolitan area.

24-Hour Service Stations

Most of the following stations are open 24 hours for fuel only. Vehicle maintenance service is available only during normal business hours.

Georgia Avenue Amoco	7605 Georgia Ave. NW	723-6868
Embassy Mobil E5	22nd & P Sts. NW	659-8560
KM Exxon	3535 Connecticut Ave. NW	364-6374
Morin & Captain Amoco B1	2450 Wisconsin Ave. NW	337-3697
Congressional Exxon H10	2nd & Massachusetts Ave. NW	543-9456
Ronnie's Amoco C13	400 Rhode Island Ave. NE	635-4545
Feet's Hillcrest Amoco	2801 Alabama Ave. SE	583-1100
Alabama Shell	4107 Alabama Ave. SE	584-0374
Kim's Texaco L14	1022 Pennsylvania Ave. SE	543-6725
P. A. Exxon M14	1201 Pennsylvania Ave. SE	546-6146

Parking – In the city, parking space on the street is very limited, and parking regulations are strictly enforced. Where available, metered parking is $0.25 for 15 minutes. For those streets indicated by red "Rush Hour Street" signs, parking is prohibited from 7–9:30am and 4–6:30pm. Residential parking areas are available for vehicles with residential stickers (contact: Bureau of Motor Vehicle Services ☎727-6680). Nonresidents are allowed to park in these areas for a maximum of two hours between 7am–8:30pm. Parking signs are color coded: green and white indicate hours when parking is allowed; red and white signs indicate hours when parking is not allowed. Parking spaces reserved for diplomats or government officials are reserved 24 hours per day for these individuals.
Private parking garages are easy to find throughout the central sections of the city. Rates range from $3 to $4 per hour with all-day rates from $5 to $10 depending on the location.

Unless otherwise indicated, all telephone numbers shown are in the 202 calling area. When telephoning Virginia or Maryland from within Washington DC proper, dial the appropriate area code (703 Virginia, 301 suburban Maryland or 410 eastern Maryland) before the seven-digit number.

DC STREET SYSTEM

DC Quadrants – The focal point of Washington's street system is the US Capitol building. From this prominent landmark emanate the four cardinal axes—North Capitol, East Capitol, and South Capitol Streets, and the Mall—that divide the city into four quadrants: Northwest, Northeast, Southeast, and Southwest.

Numbered streets running north–south are laid out in ascending order on either side of North and South Capitol Streets, while **lettered streets** running east–west begin on either side of the Mall–East Capitol axis. This arrangement gives rise to two sets of numbered streets and two sets of lettered streets. For example, the street one block east of the Capitol and the street one block west of the Capitol are both named 1st Street; similarly there is a C Street three blocks north and three blocks south of the Capitol. Since the same address may be found in each of the four quadrants, it is imperative that the appropriate designation (NE, SE, SW, NW) be attached to the address. **Avenues** bearing the names of the states of the Union run diagonally across the grid pattern and generally radiate from **circles** named after prominent Americans such as Washington, Sheridan, and Dupont.
Note the following particularities: in the NW and SW quadrants there are no A Streets owing to the location of the Mall; B Streets are replaced by Constitution Avenue (NE/NW) and Independence Avenue (SE/SW); there is no J Street and I Street is commonly spelled Eye Street. The lettered streets end at W Street beyond which a new alphabetical series begins with two-syllable names (Adams, Bryant, Channing, etc.).

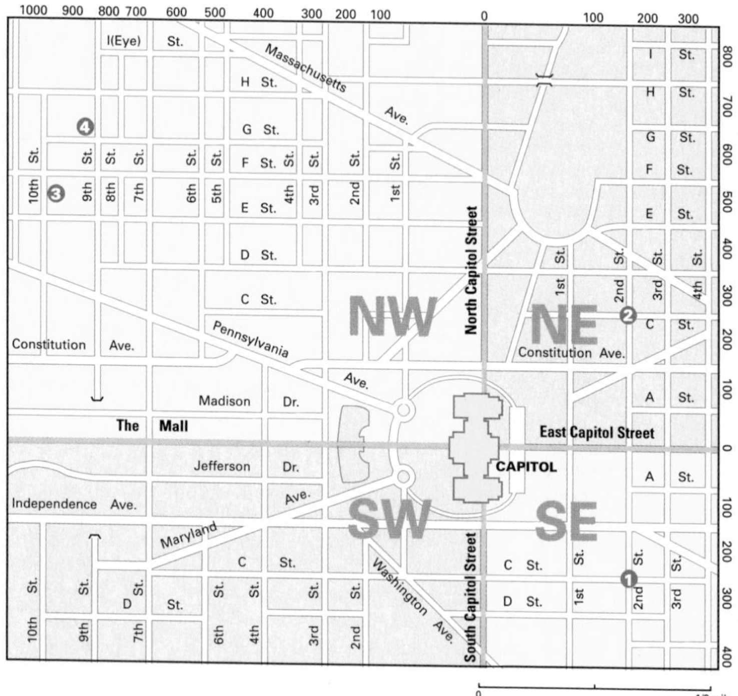

How to find an address – Once you have understood the city's rational street layout, you should be able to locate an address in the central parts of DC with ease. Bear in mind that the quadrant designation (NW, NE, SE, SW) indicates the location in relation to the Capitol and that building numbers run in series of 100 per block. The odd-even numbering of buildings in each of the four quadrants follows a distinct pattern according to the street's orientation in relation to the Capitol. As a general rule, in the **Northwest quadrant**, the north and east sides of streets and avenues are odd-numbered while the south and west sides are even-numbered.

1. The intersection of 2nd and C Streets SE is two streets east of the Capitol and (C being the 3rd letter) three streets south of East Capitol Street.

2. The Hart Senate Office Building, located at the intersection of 2nd and C Streets NE, is two streets east of the Capitol and three streets north of East Capitol Street.

3. Ford's Theatre at 511 10th Street NW is ten numbered streets west of the Capitol and five lettered streets north of the Mall between E (the 5th letter) and F Streets. The number 511 indicates that the theater is located on the east side of 10th Street.

4. The Martin Luther King Library at 901 G Street NW is located on G Street in the Northwest quadrant between 9th and 10th Streets. The odd-numbered street address (901) indicates that the library stands on the north side of G Street.

VISITOR INFORMATION

Washington Visitor Information Center H7 – *1455 Pennsylvania Ave. NW, Washington DC 20005; located in the Willard Collection shopping complex. Open Mon–Sat 9am–5pm* ☎ *789-7038.* Operated by the Washington, DC Convention and Visitors Association, this center provides free maps and literature to walk-in visitors and also responds to written and phone requests.

Smithsonian Information Center *(p 42)* K8 – *The Castle on the Mall at 1000 Jefferson Dr. SW. Open daily 9am–5:30pm* ☎ 357-2700. This state-of-the-art visitor center (interactive touch screens, video disks, electronic wall maps) is the place to plan your visit to Smithsonian attractions.

International Visitors Services – ☎ *939–5566.* A multilingual staff provides assistance and multilingual literature to visitors and international residents. A 24-hour language bank hot line ☎ 939-5566 provides assistance in over 45 languages.

Travelers Aid Society of Washington DC, Inc. – *Main office: 512 C St. NE, Open Mon–Fri 9am–5pm* ☎ *546-3120.* This organization offers assistance to travelers in emergency situations. It also provides relocation, job referral, orientation, counseling, and language/translation assistance to newcomers to the city.
Travelers Aid booths are also located at Union Station, Dulles International Airport ☎ 703-661-8636, and National Airport ☎ 703-419-3972.

American Express Travel Office – *(See* **Banks and Money Services** *p 170 for DC locations.)* Sightseeing information, travel services for cardholders.

Disabled Visitors – *Wheelchair access to the sights described in this guide is indicated on the floor plans and in the admission information accompanying the sight description by means of the ♿ symbol.*
The National Park Service, which administers many sights throughout the area, provides information on sights and events to the hearing impaired: TTY ☎ 619-7083.
The Smithsonian offers numerous services for disabled visitors. Write or call the Accessibilty Program, Arts and Industries Building, Room 1410, Smithsonian Institution, Washington DC 20560 ☎ 786-2942, TDD ☎ 786-2414 (open Mon–Fri 9am–5pm) to request a copy of *Smithsonian Access.*
The Washington Metropolitan Area Transit Authority has facilities and reduced fares for disabled riders on the Metro and public buses. A free publication, *Metro System Guide for Senior Citizens and People with Disabilities,* can be obtained by calling the Metro ☎ 637-7000, TDD ☎ 638-3780.
Handicapped stickers, permits, and license plates from all other jurisdictions are recognized in Washington DC. These should be displayed on the license plate or dashboard. Handicapped parking is free in any time zone and in metered areas for an unlimited length of time; however, parking is not allowed at meters 7–9:30am and 4–6:30pm. Disabled visitors must honor signs prohibiting parking at all times. Green and white traffic signs indicate when parking is allowed; red and white signs indicate when parking is not allowed. Handicapped parking is available at most of the National Park Service sights in the city.
For further information on facilities for disabled visitors, contact the **Information, Protection and Advocacy Center for Handicapped Individuals**, 4455 Connecticut Ave. NW, Suite B100, Washington DC 20008; ☎ 966-8081 (open Mon–Fri 8:30am–5pm) which publishes a series of practical booklets entitled *Access Washington.*

Tours – For visitors with little time at their disposal, we recommend following the two- or four-day itineraries *(see p 9)*. Addresses, opening hours, admission charges, and other useful information designed to help you organize your visit are included with each of the sight descriptions in this guide.
A variety of guided tours (sightseeing buses, walking tours, cruises, and specialty tours) are available to the visitor. Below is a selection of the principal tours:

Tourmobile Sightseeing – *Bus routes are indicated on the itinerary map pp 6-8.* Operating a concession authorized by the National Park Service, this company offers shuttle bus service to the principal Mall and Capitol Hill sights as well as to the WHITE HOUSE, KENNEDY CENTER, ARLINGTON CEMETERY, FREDERICK DOUGLASS NATIONAL HISTORIC SITE, and MOUNT VERNON. Daily tours *(except Christmas Day)* operate 9am–6:30pm, Jun 15–Labor Day, 9:30am– 4:30pm the rest of the year.
Tickets can be purchased from Tourmobile ticket booths located near many of the sights or from the driver of any of the blue and white buses, are valid all day, and entitle you to unlimited reboarding at any of the stops indicated with a blue and white Tourmobile sign. On-board commentary is provided by trained guides. Tickets: $8.50, children 3–11 $4. Combination tours to Mount Vernon/Arlington (daily April–October). Tickets: $25.50, children 3-11 $12.50; Frederick Douglass National Historic Site (daily June 15–Labor Day). Tickets: $16, children 3-11 $8. ☎ 554-7950.

Old Towne Trolley – Tours of Washington operate daily Memorial Day–Labor Day 9am–5pm (4pm the rest of the year) except Thanksgiving and Christmas Day. Every 30 minutes the visitor can board the orange and green trolleys at any of 16 locations including major hotels. The complete itinerary lasts about two hours and the same ticket allows free reboarding the entire day. Tickets $15, children 5–12 $7, under 5 free. ☎ 301-985-3020.

Gold Line-Gray Line – This company offers a large variety of year-round tours in and around Washington. Fares range from $20 for adults and $10 for children (ages 3-11) for a four-hour tour of interiors of public buildings to $60 for adults and $30 for children for a two-day "grand tour" of the principal sights. Excursions to Alexandria, Annapolis, Baltimore, Mount Vernon, Williamsburg, Civil War battlesites, and Atlantic City. ☎ 289-1995.

The following special **annual tours** allow you to visit sights that are usually closed to the public: the White House Spring Garden Tour and the White House Candlelight Tour *(p 77)*, Georgetown House and Garden Tours *(p 106)*, and Embassy Tour *(p 128)*. Advance reservation is strongly recommended for these popular tours.

Cruises on the Potomac River – Below are the principal boat cruises operating in the warm months:

Departing from DC – The *Spirit of Washington* offers dinner cruises down the Potomac to Alexandria daily Mar–Dec. The *Potomac Spirit* cruises to Mount Vernon late Mar–Oct (daily except Mon). Departure: Pier 4 at 6th and Water Sts. SW. N9. Reservations ☎554-8000.

Departing from Alexandria *(see map p 149)* – Dining cruises aboard *The Dandy*. Departure: Prince St. Reservations ☎703-683-6076. Narrated sight-seeing cruise (40min) along Old Town's waterfront aboard *The Admiral Tilp*. Operates Tue–Fri May–Labor Day; weekends April–October. Departure: Cameron St. ☎703-548-9000.

Banks and Money Services – Local banks are usually open Mon–Thu 9am–3pm (5pm Fri and noon Sat). Certain branches outside DC are open Sat 9am–noon. Some banks have drive-in window hours Mon–Fri from 9am–6pm (noon Sat). Weekend and extended hours are decreasing as more 24-hour automatic teller machines become available. Local banks usually do not cash checks from out-of-state banks. Most banks will cash brand-name travelers checks and give cash advances on major credit cards (American Express, Visa, Mastercard).

Foreign currency exchange, foreign travelers checks, foreign checks, and wire transfers are available through:

Thomas Cook Currency Services
1800 K St. NW 872-1233
3222 M St. NW 338-3325
50 Massachusetts Ave. NE (Union Station) 371-9219

Ruesch International Monetary Services
825 14th St. NW 408-1200

Riggs National Bank .... *(for nearest location)* 835-6000
503 Pennsylvania Ave. NW
17th & H Sts. NW
1913 Massachusetts Ave. NW (Dupont Circle)
2660 Virginia Ave. NW (Watergate complex)
201 Wisconsin Ave. NW (Georgetown)
5530 Connecticut Ave. NW (Chevy Chase Circle)

The Mutual of Omaha Business Service Center operates exchange booths at **Dulles International Airport** ☎703-661-8864 and at **National Airport** ☎703-419-8383.

American Express Travel Service offices sell domestic and foreign currency checks. Cardholders may receive local currency and cash personal checks. Offices (open Mon–Fri 9am–6pm) are situated in shopping malls throughout the city and at the following locations:

1150 Connecticut Ave. NW 457-1300
5300 Wisconsin Ave. NW 362-4000
1776 Pennsylvania Ave. NW 289-8800
1001 G St. NW (Metro Center) 393-0095

For cardholders enrolled in the Express Cash program (1-800-CASH-NOW), dispensers are available at all branches of First American Bank *(see Yellow Pages)* and at the following locations:

National Airport .... Upper Level, Trump Shuttle Ticketing
USAir, near Budget Car Rental
Dulles Airport .... Lower Level, Baggage Claim
Union Station .... Upper Level, opposite Gate G

The Press – The city's leading daily, *The Washington Post* (established 1877; daily circulation 855,000), known for its investigative reporting, is one of the country's most influential newspapers, providing national and international coverage. The "Weekend" section in the Friday edition lists entertainment, special events, and attractions for children. The Sunday edition (circulation 1.1 million) contains the "Guide to the Lively Arts," highlighting the performing arts. *The Post* also publishes the day's congressional and Supreme Court schedules. Another daily, *The Washington Times*, established in 1982, has a circulation of 94,000.

Community papers *(generally free of charge)*, such as the *InTowner, Uptown Citizen*, and the *Washington New Observer*, present local news and events. The Journal Newspapers *Alexandria Journal, Arlington Journal, Fairfax Journal, Montgomery Journal, Prince George's Journal* and *Prince William Journal* serve the Metropolitan area. The *City Paper*, an alternative weekly publication, covers local events and the cultural scene. *The Washingtonian*, a monthly magazine, features listings of restaurants, upcoming events, and stories about the city.

Several free publications (such as *This Week in the Nation's Capital*, and the monthly *Where Washington*) distributed at hotels throughout the metropolitan area publish feature articles on the city as well as practical information and listings of cultural events, restaurants, night spots, and shops.

Out-of-town and international newspapers and journals can be purchased at the following locations:

The Newsroom .... 1753 Connecticut Ave. at S St. NW 332-1489
Key Bridge News .... 3326 M St. NW, Georgetown 338-2626
The News World .... K St. between 17th St. & Connecticutt Ave. NW 872-0190
American Int'l News .... 1825 Eye St. NW 223-2526
B&B News .... 2621 Connecticut Ave. at Calvert St. NW 234-0494

Telephone – The four area codes within the metropolitan area are 202 (Washington DC), 703 (Virginia), 301 (suburban Maryland), and 410 (eastern Maryland). **Unless otherwise indicated, all telephone numbers given in this guide are in the 202 calling area.** When calling Virginia or Maryland from within Washington DC proper, the appropriate area code is required. Most calls within a distance of 12 miles from the Beltway are charged as local calls. Refer to the "Regional Calling Area" map in the local phone book. A local call costs $0.20 (DC) or $0.25 (outside DC) from a public phone booth.

PERFORMING ARTS

For complete listings of cultural events, consult the "Weekend" supplement in *The Washington Post* Friday edition, the monthly magazine *The Washingtonian,* or free publications such as *Where Washington* and *This Week in the Nation's Capital,* available at major hotels.

Tickets – Theaters and concert halls listed below generally sell tickets through their own box office; however, tickets for most performances and events throughout the metropolitan area are also available through the following agencies:

Ticketmaster – Phone orders ☎800-551-7328 or 432-7328. Tickets can also be purchased at Ticketmaster outlets at Hecht's and some retail music stores, as well as USAir Arena Box Office, 1 Harry S. Truman Dr., Landover MD (open daily 10am–9pm) ☎301-350-3400 (major credit cards accepted).

Ticketplace – Reduced-rate tickets on the day of the performance (cash only) available at Lisner Auditorium, George Washington University, 21st & H Sts. NW. ☎842-5387. Open Tue–Fri noon–4pm, Sat 11am–5pm.

John F. Kennedy Center for the Performing Arts H4 – *(See description p 100.)* *On the Potomac one block south of Virginia and New Hampshire Aves. NW.* Washington's premier showcase for the performing arts, the Kennedy Center hosts a year-round program of musical, theatrical, and film events featuring artists of national and international renown.

Concert Hall – (2759 seats) Home of the National Symphony Orchestra, which performs Sept–Jun and features world-famous guest conductors and orchestras. Annual Holiday Celebrations and Summer Pops series.

Opera House – (2318 seats) Home of the Washington Opera and host to visiting ballet companies, celebrated soloists, and Broadway musicals.

Theaters – **Eisenhower Theater** (1142 seats) features large-scale theatrical performances, both classic and contemporary. The intimate **Terrace Theater** (512 seats) is devoted to chamber music, recitals, dance, and theatrical productions. It also is the setting for the Center's national children's arts festival. The **Theater Lab** (350 seats) offers children's performances, workshops, and exhibits. The **American Film Institute** (AFI) theater (224 seats) is the city's finest repertory film theater (over 600 films shown annually).
For information, **ticket sales** and instant phone charge ☎467-4600. Toll free from outside the Washington area ☎800-444-1324. All major credit cards are accepted. For the hearing impaired TDD ☎416-8728. Infrared hearing devices are offered free of charge; pick up before the performance in the Hall of States.
Specially Priced Ticket (SPT) programs are offered for full-time students, senior citizens, military personnel, and the disabled (identification in person is required). Also there are other educational programs, as well as half-price tickets on the day of the performance.

Wolf Trap Farm Park for the Performing Arts – *Vienna VA. Access* **by car**: *From Foggy Bottom take Rte 66 west to Dulles Toll Rd. and take Wolf Trap exit (exit open two hours prior to performances); or take Rte 7 west from Beltway (exit 10) and follow the signs to Wolf Trap.* **By public transportation**: *Metro (Orange line) or Metrobus to West Falls Church Metro Station, then by Wolf Trap Metro Shuttle to the Filene Center (service begins 1 1/2 hours before the performance; charge approximately $3).*
Wolf Trap Farm Park is the country's only national park dedicated to the performing arts. It is situated on 100 acres of Virginia countryside just 20 minutes from Washington DC. The Filene Center, an outdoor amphitheater, open early Jun–mid-Sept, hosts concerts, dance, jazz, opera, operetta, and popular performances. Visitors can enjoy a relaxing dinner under the stars on the grounds or bring a picnic. The Barns, home of the Wolf Trap Opera Company during the summer months, is a year-round facility offering a variety of performances.
Tickets can be charged to major credit cards ☎703-218-6500. For more information ☎703-255-1900. Special arrangements for the disabled can be made by calling the National Park Service ☎703-255-1820 in advance.

Other Concert Halls – The following locations host various types of musical events:

DAR Constitution Hall J6	18th & D St. NW	638-2661
Lisner Auditorium (GWU) H5	21st & H St. NW	994-6800
USAir Arena (rock) *(map p 165)*	1 Harry S. Truman Dr. Landover MD 20785	301-350-3400
Robert F. Kennedy Stadium (rock) K17	East Capitol & 22nd Sts. SE	546-3337
Warner Theatre H8	513 13th St. NW	626-1050
Blues Alley (jazz)	Off Wisconsin Ave. & M St.	337-4141

Military Band Concerts – During the summer months, the bands of the US Army, Navy, Air Force, and Marines give free evening concerts on a rotating basis at three principal locations around the Mall: on the east terrace of the Capitol, at the Sylvan

Theatre (on the grounds of the Washington Monument) and at Navy Memorial Plaza. *See also* MARINE CORPS WAR MEMORIAL and THE NETHERLANDS CARILLON and *Calendar of Events p 160.* For further information:

Air Force ☎767-5658 **Navy** ☎433-2525 **Army** ☎703-696-3399 **Marines** ☎433-4011

Evening Parade – A popular Washington tradition, the **Marine Corps Evening Parade** takes place at the Marine Barracks at 8th & Eye Sts. SE. The one-hour performance of military favorites is given on Friday evenings at 8:45pm during the summer months. Advance reservation can be obtained by writing to the Marine Barracks (8th & Eye Sts. SE Washington DC 20390) or by calling ☎433-6060.

Free events – Several DC museums and sights (e.g., LIBRARY OF CONGRESS, NATIONAL GALLERY OF ART, THE PHILLIPS COLLECTION, FBI, OLD POST OFFICE, RENWICK GALLERY, and FOLGER SHAKESPEARE LIBRARY) sponsor free concerts and entertainment on a regular basis. For further information, refer to sight descriptions in this guide.

Dance – The **Washington Ballet** performs classical and contemporary ballet at the Kennedy Center during the spring, fall, and winter seasons. For information ☎362-3606.
See local listings for information on the city's diverse dance troupes.

Principal Theaters

Arena Stage N9	**Classic and contemporary drama** 3 theaters: Fichandler Stage, Kreeger Theatre, Old Vat Room 6th St. & Maine Ave. SW	488-3300
Eisenhower Theatre	**Classic and contemporary drama** KENNEDY CENTER H4	467-4600
Elizabethan Theatre	**Classic and contemporary drama** FOLGER SHAKESPEARE LIBRARY 201 E. Capitol St. SE	544-7077
Ford's Theatre *(p 94)* H8	**Touring companies, family theater** 511 10th St. NW	347-4833
The National Theatre H8	**Broadway shows** 1321 Pennsylvania Ave. NW	628-6161
Shakespeare Theatre K12	**Shakespearean and other classics** 450 7th St. NW	393-2700
Warner Theatre H8	**Broadway shows** 13th & E Sts. NW	783-4000

Small Theaters

d.c. space	**Alternative performing arts (theater, concerts)** 4250 Connecticut Ave. NW	282-2057
Gala Hispanic Theatre	**Works by Hispanic playwrights in Spanish and English** 1625 Park Rd. NW	234-7174
Horizons Theatre	**Works by women playwrights** 2700 S. Lang St., Arlington	703-519-9123
Source Theatre	**Off-Broadway style productions** 1835 14th St. NW	462-1073
Studio Theatre	**Off-Broadway style productions** 1333 P St. NW	332-3300
Sylvan Theatre	**Open-air theater, Armed Forces Bands, concerts, other free performances** Washington Monument grounds	619-7222
Woolly Mammoth Theatre	**Off-off-Broadway style productions** 1401 Church St. NW	393-3939

Movie Houses – The major shopping malls located outside the District *(see* **Shopping** *p 173)* contain multi-screen complexes showing popular first-run films. The movie houses in the Northwest quadrant listed below feature revivals and foreign films as well as a selection of first-run films. Consult local listings.

American Film Institute	**Film classics** KENNEDY CENTER H4	467-4600
The Biograph	2819 M St. NW	333-2696
Cineplex Odeon		
• Outer Circle (2 screens)	4849 Wisconsin Ave. NW	244-3116
• Dupont Circle (5 screens)	1350 19th St. NW	872-9555
• West End 1-4 (4 screens)	23rd & L St. NW	293-3152
• West End 5-7 (3 screens)	2301 M St. NW	452-9020
• Uptown (giant screen)	3426 Connecticut Ave. NW	966-5400
• Wisconsin Avenue (6 screens)	4000 Wisconsin Ave. NW	244-0880
Key Theatre (4 screens)	1222 Wisconsin Ave. NW	333-5100
K-B Janus Theatre (3 screens)	1660 Connecticut Ave. NW	232-8900
K-B Paris Theatre (3 screens)	5300 Wisconsin Ave. NW	686-7700

SHOPPING

The visitor to Washington can find everything from specialty shops and boutiques in **Georgetown** to established department stores situated in the heart of **Downtown**. Scattered throughout the city are several enclosed malls featuring multilevel arcades offering a wide selection of shops, restaurants, eateries, and movie theaters. Some of the more exclusive malls (Watergate, Willard Collection, Mazza Gallerie) house boutiques of internationally renowned designers.

Galleries, antique shops, and bookstores can be found in the neighborhoods of **Adams Morgan**, **Dupont Circle**, and around **Eastern Market** on Capitol Hill. Fashionable **Connecticut Avenue** from K Street to Dupont Circle presents fine shops and specialty stores. In **Old Town Alexandria**, visitors can find an array of gift and antique shops, and galleries.

Department Stores

Downtown:		
Hecht's Metro Center H8	12th & G Sts. NW	628-6661
Woodward & Lothrop H8	11th & F Sts. NW	347-5300
Friendship Heights NW/Chevy Chase:		
Lord & Taylor	5255 Western Ave. NW	362-9600
Saks Fifth Avenue	5555 Wisconsin Ave. NW	301-657-9000
Woodward & Lothrop	5400 Wisconsin Ave. NW	301-654-7600

Festival Markets

The Pavilion at the Old Post Office *(p 98)* J8	12th & Pennsylvania Ave. NW	289-4224
Union Station *(p 39)* H12	Massachusetts & Delaware Aves. NE	371-9441

DC Shopping Malls

Foxhall Square	3301 New Mexico Ave. NW	537-0787
Georgetown Park	3222 M St. NW	298-5577
International Square	1850 K St. NW	223-1850
L'Enfant Plaza Shopping Center	L'Enfant Plaza SW below L'Enfant Plaza Hotel across from Constitution Ave. SW	485-3300
Les Champs	Watergate complex 600 New Hampshire Ave. NW	338-0700
Mazza Gallerie	5300 Wisconsin Ave. NW Friendship Heights/Chevy Chase	966-6114
The Shops at National Place & National Press Bldg	1331 Pennsylvania Ave. NW	783-9090
Willard Collection	1455 Pennsylvania Ave. NW	783-1455

Outlying Shopping Malls

Virginia:		
Ballston Commons	4238 Wilson Blvd., Alexandria	703-243-8088
Fashion Centre at Pentagon City	I-395 at South Hayes St., Arlington	703-415-2400
The Galleria	2001 International Dr. & Rte 123 McLean VA	703-827-7700
Landmark Shopping Center	I-95 South, Alexandria	703-941-2582
Springfield Mall	I-95 South, Springfield VA	703-971-3000
Tysons Corner Center	1961 Chain Bridge Rd., McLean VA	703-893-9400
Maryland:		
Landover Mall	Landover & Brightseat Rds. Landover MD (off the Beltway)	301-341-3200
Montgomery Mall	Democracy Blvd., Bethesda MD	301-469-6000
White Flint Mall	11301 Rockville Pike, North Bethesda MD	301-468-5777

A selection of noteworthy **museum shops**
(for locations, see sight description in this guide):

Arthur M. Sackler Gallery	357-4880
Arts & Industries Building	357-1369
Corcoran Gallery of Art	638-3211
Decatur House	842-1856
Folger Shakespeare Library	544-4600
Freer Gallery of Art	357-4880
Hillwood Museum	686-8510
Hirshhorn Museum	357-1429
Library of Congress (James Madison Building)	707-0204
National Air & Space Museum	357-1387
National Building Museum	272-7706
National Gallery of Art	842-6466
National Museum of African Art	786-2147
National Museum of American Art	357-1545
National Museum of American History	357-1784
National Museum of Natural History	357-1535
National Portrait Gallery	357-1447
National Postal Museum	633-8180
Renwick Gallery	357-1445
Lyceum (Alexandria)	703-548-1812

SPECTATOR SPORTS

Professional Sports

Sport/Team	Season	Home Stadium	Information/Tickets
Baseball (AL) **Baltimore Orioles**	Apr–Sept	Memorial Stadium 33rd St., Baltimore MD	(info) 410-685-9800 (tickets) 410-481-7328
Football (NFL) **Washington Redskins**	Sept–Dec	RFK Stadium K17 22nd & E. Capitol Sts. SE	(info) 703-478-8900 (tickets) 546-2222
Hockey (NHL) **Washington Capitals**	Oct–Mar	USAir Arena *(map p 165)* 1 Harry S. Truman Dr. Landover MD	(info) 301-386-7000 (tickets) /432-7328
Basketball (NBA) **Washington Bullets**	Nov–Apr	USAir Arena *(map p 165)* 1 Harry S. Truman Dr. Landover MD	(info) 301-622-3865 (tickets) 432-7328

College Sports

University/Team	Sports	Home Games	Information/Tickets
Catholic University of America *Cardinals*		Campus: 7th St. & Michigan Ave. NE	319-5286
Gallaudet University *Bison*		Campus: 800 Florida Ave. NE	651-5603
Georgetown University *Georgetown Hoyas*		Campus: 37th & O Sts. NW and USAir Arena *(map p 165)*	687-2494
George Washington University *Colonials*		Various DC locations	994-7411
Howard University *Bison*		Various DC locations	806-7199
University of District of Columbia *Firebirds*		Campus: 4200 Connecticut Ave. NW	282-7748
University of Maryland *Terrapins*		College Park Campus College Park MD	301-314-7070

Horse Racing

Laurel Race Track – Laurel MD (20 miles northeast of Washington DC). Season: Oct–Mar and Jun–early July. ☎301-725-0400.

Pimlico – Baltimore MD (40 miles northeast of Washington DC). Season: Mar–May and Jul–Oct. The Preakness race (Triple Crown event) takes place on the third Sat in May. ☎410-542-9400.

Rosecroft Raceway – Oxon Hill/Fort Washington MD (7 miles southeast of Washington DC). Harness races only. Open year-round. ☎301-567-4000.

Charles Town Races – Charles Town WV (58 miles west of Washington DC). Open year-round. ☎304-725-7001.

Polo – Matches are held on Sunday afternoons mid-May–mid-Oct at Lincoln Memorial Polo Field, located between the Memorial and the Tidal Basin. The National Capital Park Polo Club sponsors local tournaments, US Polo Association tournaments, and matches between visiting teams. Consult local newspapers. In case of inclement weather, check with the National Park Service. ☎426-6841.

RECREATION

The District's two main recreational areas are the Mall and Rock Creek Park, both situated in the Northwest quadrant and administered by the National Park Service. Extending from the foot of the Capitol to the Lincoln Memorial and including the waterfront, Potomac Park, and the Tidal Basin to the south, the **Mall**, with its sprawling lawns and planted gardens, is well-suited to outdoor activities such as jogging, biking, picnicking, paddleboating, and a variety of sports (tennis, baseball, football, soccer, and polo).

Covering some 1,754 acres astride scenic Rock Creek in the heart of the Northwest quadrant, the rugged terrain of **Rock Creek Park** is crossed by an extensive network of paved roads, trails, bicycle and bridle paths. Facilities include picnic groves, playgrounds, tennis courts, golf course, and stables.

Biking – There are many bike routes in and around Washington. Parts of **Potomac Park** are designated for cyclists.

The picturesque **Chesapeake and Ohio Canal towpath**, which meanders 184 miles from Georgetown *(see p 107)* to Cumberland in Maryland, is very popular with cyclists and hikers.

Extending 17 miles from the Arlington Bridge to George Washington's estate in Virginia, the **Mount Vernon Trail** borders the western shore of the Potomac River alongside the George Washington Memorial Parkway.

Bike and boat rentals are available at the Washington Sailing Marina (Daingerfield Island) situated 1 1/2 miles south of National Airport.
Bikes can be rented throughout the Washington area; average fee is $5 per hour or $20-25 per day including road service.

For information concerning cycling events and bike routes contact:

National Park Service (bike-route maps)	619-7222
Potomac Pedalers Touring Club	363-8687
Washington Area Bicyclist Association	872-9830
Maryland National Capital Parks & Planning Commission	301-699-2407
Alexandria Department of Recreation & Parks	703-838-4343

Boating – *For sightseeing and dining cruises on the Potomac see p 170.* Because of its location on the Potomac River and its proximity to the Chesapeake Bay, Washington offers a range of activities for boating enthusiasts.
Renting a **paddleboat** on the Tidal Basin is a classic DC activity and a favorite with children. Boats can be rented from the Tidal Basin Boat House, 15th St. and Maine Ave. SW. L7 ☎484-0206.
Boating on the **Chesapeake and Ohio Canal** between Georgetown and Violettes Lock makes a delightful excursion. Mule-drawn barge trips (1 hour) depart from the towpath in Georgetown mid-Apr–mid-Oct *(see p 107)*. ☎472-4376.

Boat rentals – Fletcher's Boat House, 4940 Canal Rd. NW ☎244-0461; Swains Lock ☎301-299-9006.
Canoes and boats can also be rented from:

Thompson Boat Center H3 Rock Creek Parkway & Virginia Ave. NW ☎333-4861

Washington Sailing Marina George Washington Parkway, Alexandria (1 1/2 miles south of National Airport) ☎703-548-9027

Marinas (docking facilities only–no rentals)

Buzzard Point Boat Marina P12	Half & V Sts. SW	488-8400
Capitol Yacht Club M8	1000 Water St. SW	488-8110
Washington Marina L8	1300 Maine Ave. SW	554-0222

For information on sailing and boating events on Chesapeake Bay, apply to the Chesapeake Bay Yacht Racing Association, PO Box 1989, Annapolis MD 21404 ☎410-269-1194.

Equestrian Sports – There are numerous stables in and near the metropolitan area that provide mounts and riding instruction. Rock Creek Park has miles of designated bridle paths.

Rock Creek Park Horse Center, managed by the National Park Service, offers trail riding, lessons, and boarding year-round. ☎362-0117.

Meadowbrook Stables 8200 Meadowbrook Lane, Chevy Chase MD offers full riding and horse-care facilities. ☎301-589-9026.
The city's main equestrian event is the **International Horse Show** held annually at the end of October at the USAir Arena *(map p 165)*. ☎301-840-0281.

Golf – The following public golf courses are maintained by the **National Park Service**:

East Potomac Park N8 (par 65)	Hains Point SW	863-9007
Langston Park G18 (par 72)	25th St. & Benning Rd. NE	397-8638
Rock Creek Park (par 65)	16th & Rittenhouse Sts. NW	882-7332

In addition, there are numerous country club courses in the District where only members or guests of members can play.

Hiking – **Rock Creek Park** offers year-round hikes and nature walks guided by US park rangers. Favorite walks within the District include a 5-mile loop around Hains Point and the **Tidal Basin**, especially when the famous Japanese cherry trees are in bloom.

Theodore Roosevelt Island (H2), located off the banks of Foggy Bottom, has 2 1/2 miles of footpaths through woods, swamp, and marsh with a variety of native plants and animals.
The only access to the island is a footbridge on the Virginia side. Free parking is available. Information ☎703-285-2601.
For a hike outside the city limits, take the **Chesapeake and Ohio Canal towpath** to Old Anglers Inn (12.4 miles), Great Falls (14 miles), or Violettes Lock (22.2 miles). If you hike to Glen Echo Park (7 miles), you have the possibility of returning to Washington by Metro bus service. The trail system provides scenic but

J. Cohen/National Zoological Park

Giant Panda - National Zoo

sometimes rugged hiking conditions. Maps and books about the canal are sold at some information centers along the trail. For further information, call the C&O Canal National Historical Park ☎301-299-3613.
Mount Vernon Trail (see **Biking** *p 174*) is also designed for hikers.
For further information on hiking in the metropolitan area:

National Park Service	619-7222
Sierra Club	547-2326
Arlington County Department of Parks & Recreation	703-358-4747
Maryland National Capital Parks & Planning Commission	301-699-2407

Ice Skating – There are two major outdoor skating rinks in Washington (skate rentals available):

National Sculpture Garden & Ice Rink J9 On the Mall at Madison Dr. & 7th St. ☎371-5343.

Pershing Park Ice Rink H7 Pennsylvania Ave. & 14th St. NW ☎737-6938.

Squash and Racketball – The majority of squash and racketball facilities in the metropolitan area are open to members only. The following clubs allow visitors. Advance reservation is recommended; a credit card number is required for confirmation.

Capitol Hill Squash Club	214 D St. SE	547-2255
Skyline Club Crystal Gateway	Arlington VA	703-979-9660

Swimming – In general, hotel pools are reserved for guests only. Some private clubs with pools offer short-term memberships.
The DC Department of Recreation operates several outdoor pools in the summer (open mid-Jun–Labor Day). For locations and opening hours ☎576-6436.

Tennis – About 150 public court are available on a first-come, first-served basis at no charge. For more information and a list of court locations and schedules, contact the DC Department of Recreation ☎673-7672 (Mon–Fri 8:30am–4:30pm).
The National Park Service maintains the following courts:

East Potomac courts M8 (5 indoor, 9 outdoor courts), Hains Point SW. Reservations ☎554-5962.

Rock Creek Park courts (outdoor) 16th & Kennedy Sts. NW. Reservations ☎722-5949.

Montrose Park D3 R St. between 30th & 31st Sts. NW, Georgetown (first-come, first-served basis).

FEDERAL GOVERNMENT

Executive Branch

White House *(p 76)* H7	1600 Pennsylvania Ave. NW	456-1414
Office of The Vice President H6	Old Executive Office Building 17th St. & Pennsylvania Ave. NW	456-1414
Department of Agriculture K8	Independence Ave. between 12th & 14th Sts. SW	720-8732
Department of Commerce J7	4th St. between Constitution Ave. & E St. NW	482-2000
Department of Defense P3-4	The Pentagon, Arlington VA	703-545-6700
Department of Education K10	400 Maryland Ave. SW	708-5366
Department of Energy K8-9	1000 Independence Ave. SW	586-5000
Department of Health & Human Services K10	200 Independence Ave. SW	619-0257
Department of Housing & Urban Development L9	451 7th St. SW	708-1422
Department of the Interior J6	18th & C Sts. NW	208-3100
Department of Justice J9	Constitution Ave. between 9th & 10th Sts. NW	514-2000
Department of Labor J10	200 Constitution Ave. NW	219-6666
Department of State J5	2201 C St. NW	647-4000
Department of Transportation L9	400 7th St. SW	366-4000
Department of the Treasury *(p 87)* H7	Pennsylvania Ave. & 15th St. NW	622-2000
Department of Veterans Affairs G7	810 Vermont Ave. NW	233-4000
Environmental Protection Agency N10	401 M St. SW	260-2090

Legislative Branch

The Capitol *(p 30)* K11	941 North Capitol St. NE	224-3121
House of Representatives		224-3121
Senate		224-3121
Government Printing Office H11		783-3238

Judicial Branch

Federal Judicial Center	1 Columbus Circle NW (next to Union Station)	273-4000
Supreme Court K12	1 1st St. NE	479-3000
US Claims Court H7	717 Madison Pl. NW	219-9657

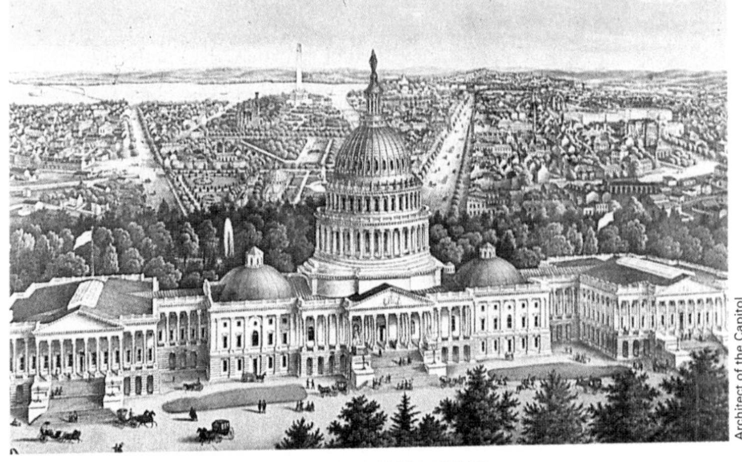

View from Capitol Hill (mid-19C)

Architect of the Capitol

LOCAL GOVERNMENT

General Information		727-1000
Office of the Mayor	441 4th St. NW, Suite 1100	727-3000
City Council (District Building) J8	1350 Pennsylvania Ave. NW	724-8000
DC Commission on the Arts G9	410 8th St. NW, Suite 500	724-5613
Consumer & Regulatory Affairs G9	614 H St. NW	727-7000
DC Court System G9	500 Indiana Ave. NW, Suite 1500	879-1700
Education Board J8	415 12th St. NW	724-4289
Fire Department D9	1923 Vermont Ave. NW	673-3331
Police Department J10	300 Indiana Ave. NW	727-4383
Public Health Commission G6	1660 L St. NW	673-7700
Public Library System H9	901 G St. NW	727-1101
Public Works D7	2000 14th St. NW	939-8000
Recreation Department A7	3149 16th St. NW	673-7665

INTERNATIONAL ORGANIZATIONS

American Red Cross J6	430 17th St. at D St. NW	737-8300
European Commission Delegation F5	2100 M St. NW	862-9500
International Bank for Reconstruction and Development (World Bank) H6	1818 H St. NW	477-1234
International Monetary Fund (IMF) H5	700 19th St. NW	623-7000
Organization for Economic Cooperation and Development (OECD) G5	2001 L St. NW	785-6323
Organization of American States *(p 86)* J6	17th St. & Constitution Ave. NW	458-3000
Pan American Health Organization H5	525 23rd St. NW	861-3200
United Nations H6	1889 F St. NW	289-8670
World Wildlife Fund F4	1250 24th St. NW	293-4800

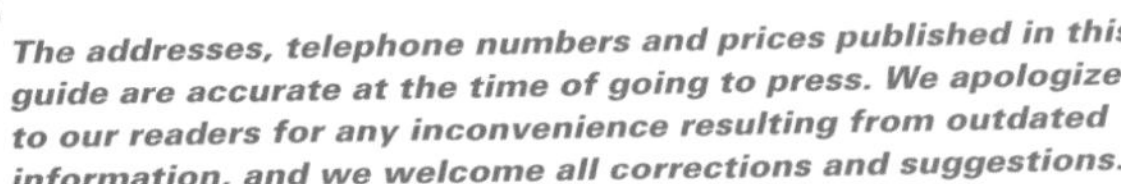

The addresses, telephone numbers and prices published in this guide are accurate at the time of going to press. We apologize to our readers for any inconvenience resulting from outdated information, and we welcome all corrections and suggestions.

MEMORIALS

The following list is a selection of the principal memorials and commemorative public sculpture in central Washington and nearby Arlington *(grid coordinates refer to Michelin Street Map 48)*:

Memorials described in this guide

Memorial	Location
Winston Churchill *(p 131)*	British Embassy—3100 Mass. Ave. NW
Justice William O. Douglas *(p 107)*	Chesapeake and Ohio Canal NW
Dupont Memorial Fountain *(p 120)*	Dupont Circle NW
Kahlil Gibran Memorial *(p 132)*	Opposite British Embassy
Jefferson Memorial *(p 71)* M7	Tidal Basin
Robert E. Lee Memorial *(p 116)*	Arlington National Cemetery
Lincoln Memorial *(p 72)* K4	Mall—West Potomac Park
Marine Corps War Memorial *(p 117)* K1	N. Meade St., Arlington VA.
Netherlands Carillon *(p 118)* K1	Jackson Ave., Arlington VA.
Gen Philip H. Sheridan *(p 128)*	Sheridan Circle NW
Vietnam Veterans Memorial *(p 73)* J5	Constitution Gardens, Mall NW
Vietnam Women's Memorial *(p 74)* J5	Constitution Gardens, Mall NW
Washington Monument *(p 70)* K7	Mall at 15th St.

Other Memorials

To locate a memorial listed below, use the grid coordinate to find the memorial's reference number on Michelin Street Map 48 (nos. 85-87 not shown on map).

Arlington *(main memorials and graves on the grounds of Arlington National Cemetery are shown on the site map p 115).*

	Memorial	Location
1	Seabees Memorial L2	Memorial Dr.
2	United Spanish War Veterans Memorial ("The Hiker") L2	Memorial Dr.
3	Adm Richard E. Byrd Memorial L2	Memorial Dr.
4	101st Army Airborne Division L2	Memorial Dr.
5	Lyndon B. Johnson Grove M4	Lady Bird Johnson Park, George Washington Memorial Pkwy.
6	Navy-Marine Memorial N5	Lady Bird Johnson Park, George Washington Memorial Pkwy.

Washington DC

	Memorial	Location
7	José Gervasio Artigas J6	18th St. & Constitution Ave. NW
8	Commodore John Barry G7	Franklin Park, 14th & K Sts. NW
9	Mary McLeod Bethune K14	Lincoln Park, E. Capitol & 11th Sts. NE
10	Sir William Blackstone J10	Constitution Ave. & 3rd St. NW
11	Simón Bolívar J6	18th St. at C St. & Virginia Aves. NW
12	Boy Scouts of America J7	Ellipse, west of 15th St. NW
13	President James Buchanan C7	Meridian Hill Park NW
14	Butt-Millet Memorial Fountain J6	Ellipse
15	Columbus Memorial H12	Columbus Plaza (Union Station) NE
16	Dante C7	Meridan Hill Park NW
17	DAR Founders J6	C St. between 17th & 18th Sts. NW
18	Jane A. Delano J6	American Red Cross, 17th & D Sts. NW
19	DC World War Memorial K6	Mall SE, West Potomac Park
20	Andrew Jackson Downing Urn K9	Mall SE, east of the Castle
21	Albert Einstein *(see p 99)* J5	22nd St. & Constitution Ave. NW
22	Emancipation Monument K14	Lincoln Park, E. Capitol & 11 Sts. NE
23	Robert Emmet D4	24th St. & Mass. Ave. NW
24	John Ericsson K4	Ohio Dr. & Independence Ave. SE
25	Adm David G. Farragut G6	Farragut Square, 17th & K Sts. NW
26	First Division Memorial H6	Between E St. & Executive Ave. NW
27	Benjamin Franklin J8	Old Post Office, 12th St. & Penn Ave. NW
28	Freedom Bell H12	Columbus Plaza (Union Station) NW
29	Albert Gallatin H7	North side of Treasury Bldg. NW
30	Bernardo de Gálvez J5	Virginia Ave. & E St. NW
31	Grand Army of the Republic Memorial J9	Indiana Ave. & 7th St. NW
32	President James A. Garfield K11	Capitol Reflecting Pool, Mall SE
33	Edward Gallaudet F13	Gallaudet University, Florida Ave. NE
34	Thomas Gallaudet F14	Gallaudet University, Florida Ave. NE
35	Samuel Gompers G8	Mass. Ave. & 10th St. NW
36	President Ulysses S. Grant K11	Capitol Reflecting Pool, Mall SE
37	Gen Nathanael Greene J13	Stanton Park, 5th & C Sts. NE
38	Alexander Hamilton H7	South side of Treasury Bldg. NW
39	Gen Winfield Scott Hancock J9	Pennsylvania Ave. & 7th St. NW
40	Joseph Henry K8	Mall SE, north of the Castle
41	President Andrew Jackson H7	Lafayette Park NW
42	Japanese Lantern K6	Tidal Basin
43	Japanese Pagoda L6	Tidal Basin
44	Joan of Arc C7	Meridan Hill Park NW
45	Commodore John Paul Jones K6	Mall SE at 17th St.
46	Benito Juárez H4	Virginia & New Hampshire Aves. NW
47	Gen Thaddeus Kosciuszko H7	Lafayette Park NW
48	General Lafayette H7	Lafayette Park NW
49	Abraham Lincoln J10	Judiciary Square, Indiana Ave. NW
50	Gen John A. Logan E8	Logan Circle, Vermont Ave. at 13th & P Sts. NW
51	Martin Luther F8	Vermont Ave. & 14th St. NW

52	Chief Justice John Marshall J10	John Marshall Park, C & 4th Sts. NW
53	Gen George M. McClellan D5	Connecticut & California Aves. NW
54	Maj Gen James B. McPherson G7	McPherson Square NW
55	Maj Gen George C. Meade J10	Penn. Ave. & 3rd St. NW
56	Andrew W. Mellon Memorial J9	Constitution Ave. at 6th St. NW
57	National Grange Marker K10	Mall at Madison Dr. & 4th St. NW
58	Nuns of the Battlefield F6	Rhode Island Ave. & M St. NW
59	Original Patentees of DC J7	Ellipse, west of 15th St. NW
60	Peace or Naval Monument K11	Penn. Ave. & 1st St. NW
61	Gen Albert Pike J10	3rd & D Sts. NW
62	Gen Casimir Pulaski H8	Freedom Plaza, Penn. Ave. at E & 13th Sts. NW
63	Gen John J. Pershing H7	Pershing Square at Penn. Ave. & 14th St. NW
64	Gen John A. Rawlings H6	Rawlings Park at 18th & E Sts. NW
65	Red Cross Memorial J6	American Red Cross, 17th St. between D & E Sts.
66	Sarah Rittenhouse E3	Montrose Park, R St. NW, Georgetown
67	Count Jean Baptiste Rochambeau H6	Lafayette Park NW
68	President Franklin D. Roosevelt J9	Penn. Ave. & 9th St. NW
69	President Theodore Roosevelt H2	Roosevelt Island NW
70	Gen José de San Martin J5	Virginia Ave. & 20th St. NW
71	Lt Gen Winfield Scott F7	Scott Circle, 16th St. & Mass. Ave. NW
72	Second Division Memorial J6	Ellipse, southwest corner
73	Serenity (William Henry Scheulze Memorial) C7	Meridian Hill Park NW
74	Gen William Tecumseh Sherman H7	Sherman Square, 15th & E Sts. NW
75	Taras Shevchenko E5	22nd, 23rd & P Sts. NW
76	Signers of the Declaration of Independence J6	Constitution Gardens, Mall NW
77	Gen Friedrich von Steuben H6	Lafayette Park NW
78	Taft Memorial J11	Constitution & Louisiana Aves. between 1st & 2nd Sts. NW
79	Maj Gen George H. Thomas F7	Thomas Circle,14th St. & Vermont Ave. NW
80	Titanic Memorial P10	Waterfront at P St. SW
81	US Navy Memorial J9	Market Square, 8th St. & Penn. Ave. NW
82	George Washington (statue) G4	Washington Circle NW
83	Daniel Webster F7	Mass. Ave., west of Scott Circle NW
84	John Witherspoon F6	Connecticut Ave. & N St. NW
85	National Law Enforcement Officers Memorial	Judiciary Square, E St. between 4th & 5th Sts. NW
86	Francis Scott Key Memorial	Francis Scott Key Memorial Bridge, Georgetown
87	Korean War Veterans Memorial	South of Lincoln Memorial

Washington, DC Convention & Visitors Assoc.

Washington Monument

LIBRARIES

Washington DC Public Libraries

Main Library:		
Martin Luther King Memorial Library H9	901 G St. NW	(Recording) 727-1111 (Librarian) 717-1211
Branches:		
Chevy Chase	5625 Connecticut Ave. NW	727-1341
Francis A. Gregory	3660 Alabama Ave. at 37th St. SE	727-1349
Georgetown E2	3260 R St. at Wisconsin Ave. NW	727-1353
Woodridge A16	Rhode Island Ave. & 18th St. NE	727-1401

University Libraries

American University/Bender Library and Resource Center	4400 Mass. Ave. NW	885-3200
Catholic University/John K. Mullen of Denver Memorial Library	6th & Michigan Ave. NE	635-5070
Gallaudet University Library	800 Florida Ave. NE	(Voice) 651-5217 (TDD) 651-5216
George Washington University/ Gelman Library	2130 H St. NW	994-6558
Georgetown University/ Lauinger Library	37th and N Sts. NW	687-7452
Howard University/Moorland-Spillgarn Research Center	6th & College Sts. NW	636-7239
Mt. Vernon College/Eckles Library	2100 Foxhall Rd. NW	331-3475
Southeastern University Library	501 Eye St. NW	488-8162
Strayer College/Wilkes Library	1100 16th St. NW	728-0048
Trinity College/Helen Sheehan Library	125 Michigan Ave. NE	939-5170
University of the District of Columbia	4200 Connecticut Ave. NW	282-3091

Research Facilities

Library of Congress K12	101 Independence Ave. at 1st St. SE	707-6500
Smithsonian Libraries	(16 branches, by appointment only)	357-2139
National Archives *(p 55)* J9	8th St. & Pennsylvania Ave. NW	501-5400
Folger Shakespeare Library K12	(scholars only) 201 E. Capitol St. SE	544-4600
Historical Society of Washington DC *(p 122)* F5	1307 New Hampshire Ave. NW	785-2068
National Geographic Society Library F7	16th & M Sts. NW	857-7783
Supreme Court K12	(only records & briefs available to general public) 1 1st St. NE	479-3177

POLICE

District of Columbia

Public Information Branch	300 Indiana Ave. NW	727-4383
First District L13	415 Fourth St. SW	727-4655
Second District	3320 Idaho Ave. NW	282-0070
Third District D6	1620 V St. NW	673-6930
Fourth District	6001 Georgia Ave. NW	576-6745
Fifth District D17	1805 Bladensburg Rd. NE	727-4510
Sixth District	100 42nd St. NE	727-4520
Seventh District	2501 Alabama Ave. SE	767-8020
US Parks Police		619-7300

POST OFFICES

Washington DC

National Capitol Station Post Office H12 – In City Post Office Building, Capitol St. & Massachusetts. Ave. NE (next to Union Station) ☎523-2628. Open Mon–Fri 7am–midnight, Sat & Sun 7am–8pm.

The main postal facility at 900 Brentwood Rd. NE houses the personnel offices and handles special mail requests ☎682-9595. Branch offices (hours vary, but in general open Mon–Fri 8am–6pm, Sat 9am–4pm) throughout the District are indicated on Michelin Street Map 48 by the symbol ✉.

Outlying Area (Main Post Offices only)

Maryland

Name	Address	Telephone
S. Maryland General Mail Facility	9201 Edgeworth Dr. Capitol Heights	301-499-7669
Bethesda	7400 Wisconsin Ave.	301-652-7401

Virginia

N. Virginia Sectional Center	8409 Lee Hwy., Merrifield	703-698-6300
Alexandria	1100 Wythe St.	703-549-4201
Arlington	318 N. Washington Blvd.	703-525-4838

Other Mail Services

DHL Worldwide Express	1776 Eye St. NW	296-6950
Federal Express		301-953-3333
UPS		301-595-9090

Washington, DC Convention & Visitors Assoc.

Fourth of July fireworks

INDEX

Points of interest described or mentioned in the guide appear in **bold** type. Practical information appears in *italics*. Names of persons, organizations, historic events and architectural styles appear in roman type.

Page numbers in **bold** type refer to the principal entry. Page numbers in *italics* refer to photographs or drawings.

Embassies, museums, and sports and outdoor activities are listed under **Embassies**, **Museums**, and **Sports and Recreation** respectively.

P. Wrenn

Smithsonian Institution: The Castle

T

U

V

W

Z

MICHELIN®

TRAVEL PUBLICATIONS

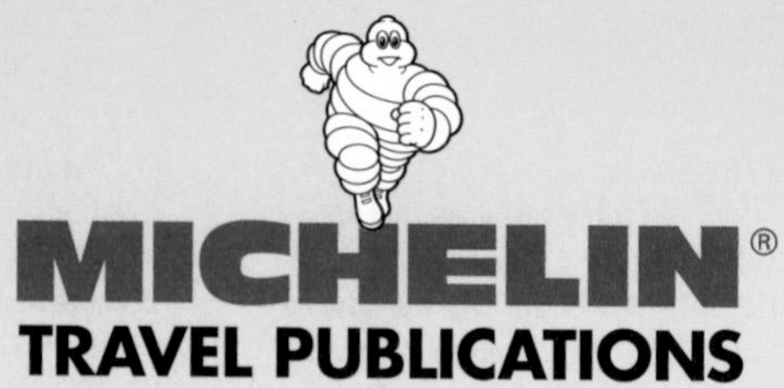

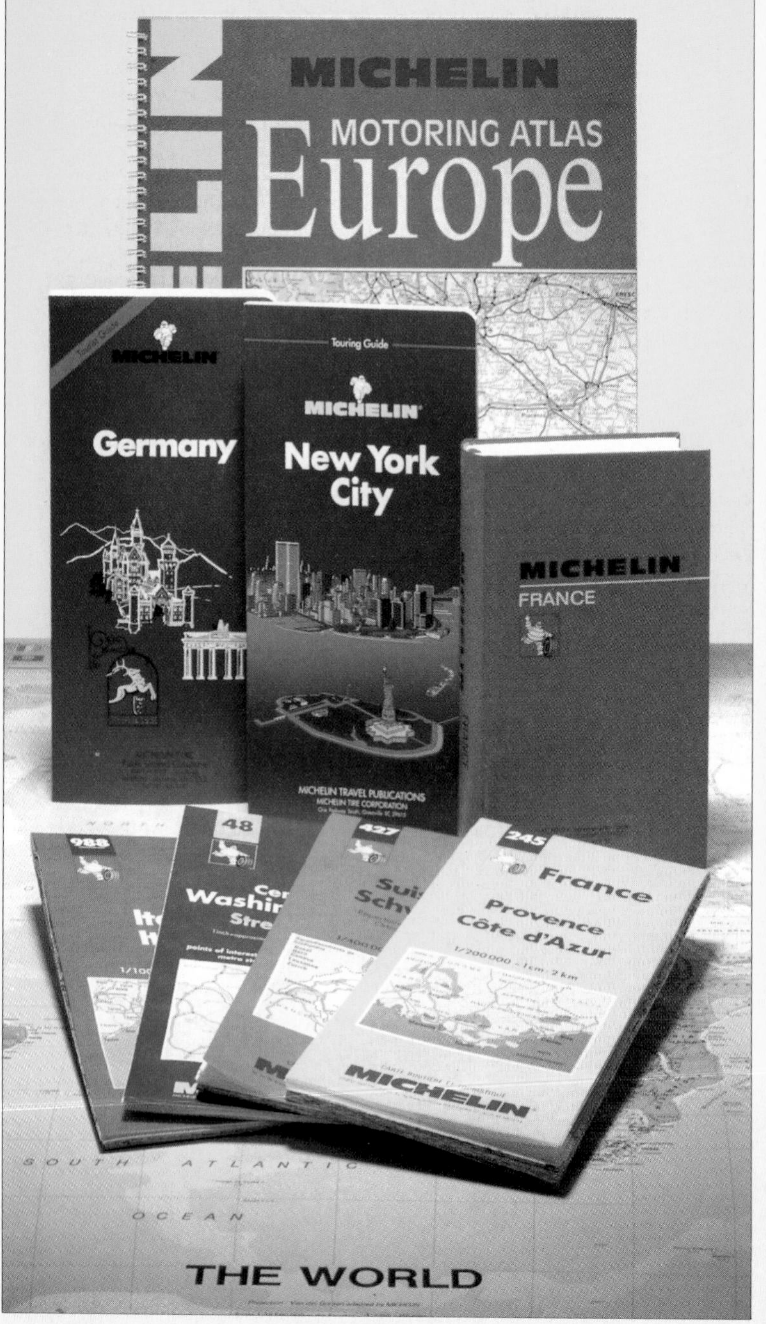
MICHELIN
MOTORING ATLAS
Europe
Touring Guide
MICHELIN
Germany
Touring Guide
MICHELIN
New York City
MICHELIN TRAVEL PUBLICATIONS
MICHELIN TIRE CORPORATION
MICHELIN
FRANCE
48
427
245
France
Provence
Côte d'Azur
1/200 000 - 1cm : 2 km
MICHELIN
SOUTH ATLANTIC
OCEAN
THE WORLD